Causal Inference and Di[illegible] Python – Machine Learning and Pearlian Perspective

Unlock the secrets of modern causal machine learning with DoWhy, EconML, PyTorch and more

Aleksander Molak

packt

BIRMINGHAM—MUMBAI

Causal Inference and Discovery in Python – Machine Learning and Pearlian Perspective

Group Product Manager: Ali Abidi

Publishing Product Manager: Dinesh Chaudhary

Senior Editor: Tazeen Shaikh

Technical Editor: Rahul Limbachiya

Copy Editor: Safis Editing

Project Coordinator: Farheen Fathima

Proofreader: Safis Editing

Indexer: Pratik Shirodkar

Production Designer: Shankar Kalbhor

Marketing Coordinators: Shifa Ansari and Vinishka Kalra

First published: June 2023

Production reference: 2120623

Published by Packt Publishing Ltd.
Livery Place
35 Livery Street
Birmingham
B3 2PB, UK.

ISBN 978-1-80461-298-9

`www.packtpub.com`

To my wife, Katia. You cause me to smile. I am grateful for every day we spend together.

Foreword

I have been following **Aleksander Molak**'s work on causality for a while.

I have been using libraries for causal inference, such as DoWhy, in my teaching at the University of Oxford, and causality is one of the key topics I teach in my course.

Based on the discussions with Aleksander, I have invited him to present a session at Oxford in our course in Fall 23.

Hence, I am pleased to write the foreword for Aleksander's new book, *Causal Inference and Discovery in Python*.

Despite causality becoming a key topic for AI and increasingly also for generative AI, most developers are not familiar with concepts such as causal graphs and counterfactual queries.

Aleksander's book makes the journey into the world of causality easier for developers. The book spans both technical concepts and code and provides recommendations for the choice of approaches and algorithms to address specific causal scenarios.

This book is comprehensive yet accessible. Machine learning engineers, data scientists, and machine learning researchers who want to extend their data science toolkit to include causal machine learning will find this book most useful.

Looking to the future of AI, I find the sections on causal machine learning and LLMs especially relevant to both readers and our work.

Ajit Jaokar

Visiting Fellow, Department of Engineering Science, University of Oxford, and Course Director, Artificial Intelligence: Cloud and Edge Implementations, University of Oxford

Contributors

About the author

Aleksander Molak is an independent machine learning researcher and consultant. Aleksander gained experience working with Fortune 100, Fortune 500, and Inc. 5000 companies across Europe, the USA, and Israel, helping them to build and design large-scale machine learning systems. On a mission to democratize causality for businesses and machine learning practitioners, Aleksander is a prolific writer, creator, and international speaker. As a co-founder of Lespire.io, an innovative provider of AI and machine learning training for corporate teams, Aleksander is committed to empowering businesses to harness the full potential of cutting-edge technologies that allow them to stay ahead of the curve.

This book has been co-authored by many people whose ideas, love, and support left a significant trace in my life. I am deeply grateful to each one of you.

About the reviewers

Nicole Königstein is an experienced data scientist and quantitative researcher, currently working as data science and technology lead at impactvise, an ESG analytics company, and as a technology lead and head quantitative researcher at Quantmate, an innovative FinTech start-up focused on alternative data in predictive modeling. As a guest lecturer, she shares her expertise in Python, machine learning, and deep learning at various universities. Nicole is a regular speaker at renowned conferences, where she conducts workshops and educational sessions. She also serves as a regular reviewer of books in her field, further contributing to the community. Nicole is the author of the well-received online course *Math for Machine Learning*, and the author of the book *Transformers in Action*.

Mike Hankin is a data scientist and statistician, with a B.S. from Columbia University and a Ph.D. from the University of Southern California (dissertation topic: sequential testing of multiple hypotheses). He spent 5 years at Google working on a wide variety of causal inference projects. In addition to causal inference, he works on Bayesian models, non-parametric statistics, and deep learning (including contributing to TensorFlow/Keras). In 2021, he took a principal data scientist role at VideoAmp, where he works as a high-level tech lead, overseeing all methodology development. On the side, he volunteers with a schizophrenia lab at the Veterans Administration, working on experiment design and multimodal data analysis.

Amit Sharma is a principal researcher at Microsoft Research India. His work bridges causal inference techniques with machine learning to enhance the generalization, explainability, and avoidance of hidden biases in machine learning models. To achieve these goals, Amit has co-led the development of the open-source DoWhy library for causal inference and the DiCE library for counterfactual explanations. The broader theme of his work revolves around leveraging machine learning for improved decision-making. Amit received his Ph.D. in computer science from Cornell University and his B.Tech. in computer science and engineering from the Indian Institute of Technology (IIT) Kharagpur.

Acknowledgments

There's only one name listed on the front cover of this book, but this book would not exist without many other people whose names you won't find on the cover.

I want to thank my wife, Katia, for the love, support, and understanding that she provided me with throughout the year-long process of working on this book.

I want to thank Shailesh Jain, who was the first person at Packt with whom I shared the idea about this book.

The wonderful team at Packt made writing this book a much less challenging experience than it would have been otherwise. I thank Dinesh Chaudhary for managing the process, being open to non-standard ideas, and making the entire journey so smooth.

I want to thank my editor, Tazeen Shaikh, and my project manager, Kirti Pisat. Your support, patience, amazing energy, and willingness to go the extra mile are hard to overstate. I am grateful that I had an opportunity to work with you!

Three technical reviewers provided me with invaluable feedback that made this book a better version of itself. I am immensely grateful to Amit Sharma (Microsoft Research), Nicole Königstein (impactvise), and Mike Hankin (VideoAmp) for their comments and questions that gave me valuable hints, sometimes challenged me, and – most importantly – gave me an opportunity to see this book through their eyes.

I want to thank all the people, who provided me with clarifications, and additional information, agreed to include their materials in the book, or provided valuable feedback regarding parts of this book outside of the formal review process: Kevin Hillstrom, Matheus Facure, Rob Donnelly, Mehmet Süzen, Ph.D., Piotr Migdał, Ph.D., Quentin Gallea, Ph.D., Uri Itai, Ph.D., prof. Judea Pearl, Alicia Curth.

I want to thank my friends, Uri Itai, Natan Katz, and Leah Bar, with whom we analyzed and discussed some of the papers mentioned in this book.

Additionally, I want to thank Prof. Frank Harrell and Prof. Stephen Senn for valuable exchanges on Twitter that gave me many insights into experimentation and causal modeling as seen through the lens of biostatistics and medical statistics.

I am grateful to the CausalPython.io community members who shared their feedback regarding the contents of this book: Marcio Minicz; Elie Kawerk, Ph.D.; Dr. Tony Diana; David Jensen; and Michael Wexler.

I received a significant amount of support from causalpython.io members and people on LinkedIn and Twitter who shared their ideas, questions, and excitement, or expressed their support for me writing this book by following me or liking and sharing the content related to this book. Thank you!

Finally, I want to thank Rahul Limbachiya, Vinishka Kalra, Farheen Fathima, Shankar Kalbhor, and the entire Packt team for their engagement and great work on this project, and the team at Safis Editing, for their helpful suggestions.

I did my best not to miss anyone from this list. Nonetheless, if I missed your name, the next line is for you.

Thank you!

I also want to thank you for buying this book.

Congratulations on starting your causal journey today!

Table of Contents

3

Regression, Observations, and Interventions 37

4

Graphical Models 55

7

The Four-Step Process of Causal Inference 125

8

Causal Models – Assumptions and Challenges 151

9

Causal Inference and Machine Learning – from Matching to Meta-Learners 173

10

Causal Inference and Machine Learning – Advanced Estimators, Experiments, Evaluations, and More 215

Part 3: Causal Discovery

12

Can I Have a Causal Graph, Please? 315

13

Causal Discovery and Machine Learning – from Assumptions to Applications 327

14

Causal Discovery and Machine Learning – Advanced Deep Learning and Beyond 371

15

Epilogue 399

Preface

I wrote this book with a purpose in mind.

My journey to practical causality was an exciting but also challenging road.

Going from great theoretical books to implementing models in practice, and from translating assumptions to verifying them in real-world scenarios, demanded significant work.

I could not find unified, comprehensive resources that could be my guide through this journey.

This book is intended to be that guide.

This book provides a map that allows you to break into the world of causality.

We start with basic motivations behind causal thinking and a comprehensive introduction to Pearlian causal concepts: structural causal model, interventions, counterfactuals, and more.

Each concept comes with a theoretical explanation and a set of practical exercises accompanied by Python code.

Next, we dive into the world of causal effect estimation. Starting simple, we consistently progress toward modern machine learning methods. Step by step, we introduce the Python causal ecosystem and harness the power of cutting-edge algorithms.

In the last part of the book, we sneak into the secret world of causal discovery. We explore the mechanics of how *causes leave traces* and compare the main families of causal discovery algorithms to unravel the potential of end-to-end causal discovery and human-in-the-loop learning.

We close the book with a broad outlook into the future of causal AI. We examine challenges and opportunities and provide you with a comprehensive list of resources to learn more.

Who this book is for

The main audience I wrote this book for consists of machine learning engineers, data scientists, and machine learning researchers with three or more years of experience, who want to extend their data science toolkit and explore the new unchartered territory of causal machine learning.

People familiar with causality who have worked with another technology (e.g., R) and want to switch to Python can also benefit from this book, as well as people who have worked with traditional causality and want to expand their knowledge and tap into the potential of causal machine learning.

Finally, this book can benefit tech-savvy entrepreneurs who want to build a competitive edge for their products and go beyond the limitations of traditional machine learning.

What this book covers

Chapter 1, Causality: Hey, We Have Machine Learning, So Why Even Bother?, briefly discusses the history of causality and a number of motivating examples. This chapter introduces the notion of spuriousness and demonstrates that some classic definitions of causality do not capture important aspects of causal learning (which human babies know about). This chapter provides the basic distinction between statistical and causal learning, which is a cornerstone for the rest of the book.

Chapter 2, Judea Pearl and the Ladder of Causation, provides us with a definition of the **Ladder of Causation** – a crucial concept introduced by Judea Pearl that emphasizes the differences between observational, interventional, and counterfactual queries and distributions. We build on top of these ideas and translate them into concrete code examples. Finally, we briefly discuss how different families of machine learning (supervised, reinforcement, semi-, and unsupervised) relate to causal modeling.

Chapter 3, Regression, Observations, and Interventions, prepares us to take a look at linear regression from a causal perspective. We analyze important properties of observational data and discuss the significance of these properties for causal reasoning. We re-evaluate the problem of statistical control through the causal lens and introduce **structural causal models** (**SCMs**). These topics help us build a strong foundation for the rest of the book.

Chapter 4, Graphical Models, starts with a refresher on graphs and basic graph theory. After refreshing the fundamental concepts, we use them to define **directed acyclic graphs** (**DAGs**) – one of the most crucial concepts in Pearlian causality. We briefly introduce the sources of causal graphs in the real world and touch upon causal models that are not easily describable using DAGs. This prepares us for *Chapter 5*.

Chapter 5, Forks, Chains, and Immoralities, focuses on three basic graphical structures: forks, chains, and immoralities (also known as colliders). We learn about the crucial properties of these structures and demonstrate how these graphical concepts manifest themselves in the statistical properties of the data. The knowledge we gain in this chapter will be one of the fundamental building blocks of the concepts and techniques that we introduced in *Part 2* and *Part 3* of this book.

Chapter 6, Nodes, Edges, and Statistical (In)Dependence, builds on top of the concepts introduced in *Chapter 5* and takes them a step further. We introduce the concept of **d-separation**, which will allow us to systematically evaluate conditional independence queries in DAGs, and define the notion of **estimand**. Finally, we discuss three popular estimands and the conditions under which they can be applied.

Chapter 7, The Four-Step Process of Causal Inference, takes us to the practical side of causality. We introduce DoWhy – an open source causal inference library created by researchers from Microsoft – and show how to carry out a full causal inference process using its intuitive APIs. We demonstrate how to define a causal model, find a relevant estimand, estimate causal effects, and perform **refutation tests**.

Chapter 8, Causal Models – Assumptions and Challenges, brings our attention back to the topic of assumptions. Assumptions are a crucial and indispensable part of any causal project or analysis. In this chapter, we take a broader view and discuss the most important assumptions from the point of view of two causal formalisms: the **Pearlian** (graph-based) framework and the **potential outcomes** framework.

Chapter 9, Causal Inference and Machine Learning – from Matching to Meta-learners, opens the door to causal estimation beyond simple linear models. We start by introducing the ideas behind **matching** and **propensity scores** and discussing why propensity scores should not be used for matching. We introduce meta-learners – a class of models that can be used for the estimation of **conditional average treatment effects** (**CATEs**) and implement them using DoWhy and EconML packages.

Chapter 10, Causal Inference and Machine Learning – Advanced Estimators, Experiments, Evaluations, and More, introduces more advanced estimators: **DR-Learner**, **double machine learning** (**DML**), and **causal forest**. We show how to use CATE estimators with experimental data and introduce a number of useful evaluation metrics that can be applied in real-world scenarios. We conclude the chapter with a brief discussion of counterfactual explanations.

Chapter 11, Causal Inference and Machine Learning – Deep Learning, NLP, and Beyond, introduces deep learning models for CATE estimation and a PyTorch-based CATENets library. In the second part of the chapter, we take a look at the intersection of causal inference and NLP and introduce **CausalBert** – a Transformer-based model that can be used to remove spurious relationships present in textual data. We close the chapter with an introduction to the **synthetic control estimator**, which we use to estimate causal effects in real-world data.

Chapter 12, Can I Have a Causal Graph, Please?, provides us with a deeper look at the real-world sources of causal knowledge and introduces us to the concept of automated **causal discovery**. We discuss the idea of expert knowledge and its value in the process of causal analysis.

Chapter 13, Causal Discovery and Machine Learning – from Assumptions to Applications, starts with a review of assumptions required by some of the popular causal discovery algorithms. We introduce four main families of causal discovery methods and implement key algorithms using the gCastle library, addressing some of the important challenges on the way. Finally, we demonstrate how to encode expert knowledge when working with selected methods.

Chapter 14, Causal Discovery and Machine Learning – Advanced Deep Learning and Beyond, introduces an advanced causal discovery algorithm – **DECI**. We implement it using the modules coming from an open source Microsoft library, Causica, and train it using PyTorch. We present methods that allow us to work with datasets with hidden confounding and implement one of them – **fast causal inference** (**FCI**) – using the `causal-learn` library. Finally, we briefly discuss two frameworks that allow us to combine observational and interventional data in order to make causal discovery more efficient and less error-prone.

Chapter 15, Epilogue, closes *Part 3* of the book with a summary of what we've learned, a discussion of causality in business, a sneak peek into the (potential) future of the field, and pointers to more resources on causal inference and discovery for those who are ready to continue their causal journey.

To get the most out of this book

The code for this book is provided in the form of Jupyter notebooks. To run the notebooks, you'll need to install the required packages.

The easiest way to install them is using Conda. Conda is a great package manager for Python. If you don't have Conda installed on your system, the installation instructions can be found here: `https://bit.ly/InstallConda`.

Note that Conda's license might have some restrictions for commercial use. After installing Conda, follow the environment installation instructions in the book's repository `README.md` file (`https://bit.ly/InstallEnvironments`).

If you want to recreate some of the plots from the book, you might need to additionally install Graphviz. For GPU acceleration, CUDA drivers might be needed. Instructions and requirements for Graphviz and CUDA are available in the same `README.md` file in the repository (`https://bit.ly/InstallEnvironments`).

The code for this book has been *only tested on Windows 11* (64-bit).

Software/hardware covered in the book	**Operating system requirements**
Python 3.9	Windows, macOS, or Linux
DoWhy 0.8	Windows, macOS, or Linux
EconML 0.12.0	Windows, macOS, or Linux
CATENets 0.2.3	Windows, macOS, or Linux
gCastle 1.0.3	Windows, macOS, or Linux
Causica 0.2.0	Windows, macOS, or Linux
Causal-learn 0.1.3.3	Windows, macOS, or Linux
Transformers 4.24.0	Windows, macOS, or Linux

Download the example code files

You can download the example code files for this book from GitHub at `https://github.com/PacktPublishing/Causal-Inference-and-Discovery-in-Python`. If there's an update to the code, it will be updated in the GitHub repository.

We also have other code bundles from our rich catalog of books and videos available at `https://github.com/PacktPublishing/`. Check them out!

Conventions used

There are a number of text conventions used throughout this book.

`Code in text`: Indicates code words in text, database table names, folder names, filenames, file extensions, pathnames, dummy URLs, user input, and Twitter handles. Here is an example: "We'll model the adjacency matrix using the `ENCOAdjacencyDistributionModule` object."

A block of code is set as follows:

```
preds = causal_bert.inference(
    texts=df['text'],
    confounds=df['has_photo'],
)[0]
```

Any command-line input or output is written as follows:

```
$ mkdir css
$ cd css
```

Bold: Indicates a new term, an important word, or words that you see onscreen. For instance, words in menus or dialog boxes appear in **bold**. Here is an example: "Select **System info** from the **Administration** panel."

> **Tips or important notes**
> Appear like this.

Get in touch

Feedback from our readers is always welcome.

General feedback: If you have questions about any aspect of this book, email us at `customercare@packtpub.com` and mention the book title in the subject of your message.

Errata: Although we have taken every care to ensure the accuracy of our content, mistakes do happen. If you have found a mistake in this book, we would be grateful if you would report this to us. Please visit `www.packtpub.com/support/errata` and fill in the form.

Piracy: If you come across any illegal copies of our works in any form on the internet, we would be grateful if you would provide us with the location address or website name. Please contact us at `copyright@packt.com` with a link to the material.

If you are interested in becoming an author: If there is a topic that you have expertise in and you are interested in either writing or contributing to a book, please visit `authors.packtpub.com`.

Share Your Thoughts

Once you've read *Causal Inference and Discovery in Python*, we'd love to hear your thoughts! Scan the QR code below to go straight to the Amazon review page for this book and share your feedback.

`https://packt.link/r/1-804-61298-7`

Your review is important to us and the tech community and will help us make sure we're delivering excellent quality content.

Download a free PDF copy of this book

Thanks for purchasing this book!

Do you like to read on the go but are unable to carry your print books everywhere? Is your eBook purchase not compatible with the device of your choice?

Don't worry, now with every Packt book you get a DRM-free PDF version of that book at no cost.

Read anywhere, any place, on any device. Search, copy, and paste code from your favorite technical books directly into your application.

The perks don't stop there, you can get exclusive access to discounts, newsletters, and great free content in your inbox daily

Follow these simple steps to get the benefits:

1. Scan the QR code or visit the link below

`https://packt.link/free-ebook/9781804612989`

2. Submit your proof of purchase
3. That's it! We'll send your free PDF and other benefits to your email directly

Part 1: Causality – an Introduction

Part 1 of this book will equip us with a set of tools necessary to understand and tackle the challenges of causal inference and causal discovery.

We'll learn about the differences between observational, interventional, and counterfactual queries and distributions. We'll demonstrate connections between linear regression, graphs, and causal models.

Finally, we'll learn about the important properties of graphical structures that play an essential role in almost any causal endeavor.

This part comprises the following chapters:

- *Chapter 1, Causality – Hey, We Have Machine Learning, So Why Even Bother?*
- *Chapter 2, Judea Pearl and the Ladder of Causation*
- *Chapter 3, Regression, Observations, and Interventions*
- *Chapter 4, Graphical Models*
- *Chapter 5, Forks, Chains, and Immoralities*

1

Causality – Hey, We Have Machine Learning, So Why Even Bother?

Our journey starts here.

In this chapter, we'll ask a couple of questions about causality.

What is it? Is causal inference different from statistical inference? If so – how?

Do we need causality at all if machine learning seems good enough?

If you have been following the fast-changing machine learning landscape over the last 5 to 10 years, you have likely noticed many examples of – as we like to call it in the machine learning community – the *unreasonable effectiveness* of modern machine learning algorithms in computer vision, natural language processing, and other areas.

Algorithms such as DALL-E 2 or GPT-3/4 made it not only to the consciousness of the research community but also the general public.

You might ask yourself – if all this stuff works so well, why would we bother and look into something else?

We'll start this chapter with a brief discussion of the history of causality. Next, we'll consider a couple of motivations for using a causal rather than purely statistical approach to modeling and we'll introduce the concept of confounding.

Finally, we'll see examples of how a causal approach can help us solve challenges in marketing and medicine. By the end of this chapter, you will have a good idea of why and when causal inference can be useful. You'll be able to explain what confounding is and why it's important.

In this chapter, we will cover the following:

- A brief history of causality
- Motivations to use a causal approach to modeling
- How not to lose money… and human lives

A brief history of causality

Causality has a long history and has been addressed by most, if not all, advanced cultures that we know about. Aristotle – one of the most prolific philosophers of ancient Greece – claimed that understanding the causal structure of a process is a necessary ingredient of knowledge about this process. Moreover, he argued that being able to answer *why*-type questions is the essence of scientific explanation (Falcon, 2006; 2022). Aristotle distinguishes four types of causes (material, formal, efficient, and final), an idea that might capture some interesting aspects of reality as much as it might sound counterintuitive to a contemporary reader.

David Hume, a famous 18th-century Scottish philosopher, proposed a more unified framework for cause-effect relationships. Hume starts with an observation that we never observe cause-effect relationships in the world. The only thing we experience is that some events are conjoined:

"*We only find, that the one does actually, in fact, follow the other. The impulse of one billiard-ball is attended with motion in the second. This is the whole that appears to the outward senses. The mind feels no sentiment or inward impression from this succession of objects: consequently, there is not, in any single, particular instance of cause and effect, any thing which can suggest the idea of power or necessary connexion*" (original spelling; Hume & Millican, 2007; originally published in 1739).

One interpretation of Hume's theory of causality (here simplified for clarity) is the following:

- We only observe how the movement or appearance of object A precedes the movement or appearance of object B
- If we experience such a succession a sufficient number of times, we'll develop a feeling of expectation
- This feeling of expectation is the essence of our concept of causality (it's not about the world; it's about a feeling we develop)

Hume's theory of causality

The interpretation of Hume's theory of causality that we give here is not the only one. First, Hume presented another definition of causality in his later work *An Enquiry Concerning the Human Understanding* (1758). Second, not all scholars would necessarily agree with our interpretation (for example, Archie (2005)).

This theory is very interesting from at least two points of view.

First, elements of this theory have a high resemblance to a very powerful idea in psychology called conditioning. **Conditioning** is a form of learning. There are multiple types of conditioning, but they all rely on a common foundation – namely, **association** (hence the name for this type of learning – **associative learning**). In any type of conditioning, we take some event or object (usually called stimulus) and associate it with some behavior or reaction. Associative learning works across species. You can find it in humans, apes, dogs, and cats, but also in much simpler organisms such as snails (Alexander, Audesirk & Audesirk, 1985).

> **Conditioning**
>
> If you want to learn more about different types of conditioning, check this `https://bit.ly/MoreOnConditioning` or search for phrases such as `classical conditioning` versus `operant conditioning` and names such as `Ivan Pavlov` and `Burrhus Skinner`, respectively.

Second, most classic machine learning algorithms also work on the basis of association. When we're training a neural network in a supervised fashion, we're trying to find a function that maps input to the output. To do it efficiently, we need to figure out which elements of the input are useful for predicting the output. And, in most cases, association is just good enough for this purpose.

Why causality? Ask babies!

Is there anything missing from Hume's theory of causation? Although many other philosophers tried to answer this question, we'll focus on one particularly interesting answer that comes from… human babies.

Interacting with the world

Alison Gopnik is an American child psychologist who studies how babies develop their world models. She also works with computer scientists, helping them understand how human babies build common-sense concepts about the external world. Children – to an even greater extent than adults – make use of associative learning, but they are also insatiable experimenters.

Have you ever seen a parent trying to convince their child to stop throwing around a toy? Some parents tend to interpret this type of behavior as *rude*, *destructive*, or *aggressive*, but babies often have a different set of motivations. They are running systematic experiments that allow them to learn the laws of physics and the rules of social interactions (Gopnik, 2009). Infants as young as 11 months prefer to perform experiments with objects that display unpredictable properties (for example, can pass through a wall) than with objects that behave predictably (Stahl & Feigenson, 2015). This preference allows them to efficiently build models of the world.

What we can learn from babies is that we're not limited to observing the world, as Hume suggested. We can also interact with it. In the context of causal inference, these interactions are called **interventions**, and we'll learn more about them in *Chapter 2*. Interventions are at the core of what many consider the Holy Grail of the scientific method: **randomized controlled trial**, or **RCT** for short.

Confounding – relationships that are not real

The fact that we can run experiments enhances our palette of possibilities beyond what Hume thought about. This is very powerful! Although experiments cannot solve all of the philosophical problems related to gaining new knowledge, they can solve some of them. A very important aspect of a properly designed randomized experiment is that it allows us to avoid **confounding**. Why is it important?

A **confounding variable** influences two or more other variables and produces a *spurious* association between them. From a purely statistical point of view, such associations are indistinguishable from the ones produced by a causal mechanism. Why is that problematic? Let's see an example.

Imagine you work at a research institute and you're trying to understand the causes of people drowning. Your organization provides you with a huge database of socioeconomic variables. You decide to run a regression model over a large set of these variables to predict the number of drownings per day in your area of interest. When you check the results, it turns out that the biggest coefficient you obtained is for daily regional ice cream sales. Interesting! Ice cream usually contains large amounts of sugar, so maybe sugar affects people's attention or physical performance while they are in the water.

This hypothesis might make sense, but before we move forward, let's ask some questions. How about other variables that we did not include in the model? Did we add enough predictors to the model to describe all relevant aspects of the problem? What if we added too many of them? Could adding just one variable to the model completely change the outcome?

> **Adding too many predictors**
>
> Adding *too many* predictors to the model might be harmful from both statistical and causal points of view. We will learn more on this topic in *Chapter 3*.

It turns out that this is possible.

Let me introduce you to *daily average temperature* – our confounder. Higher daily temperature makes people more likely to buy ice cream and more likely to go swimming. When there are more people swimming, there are also more accidents. Let's try to visualize this relationship:

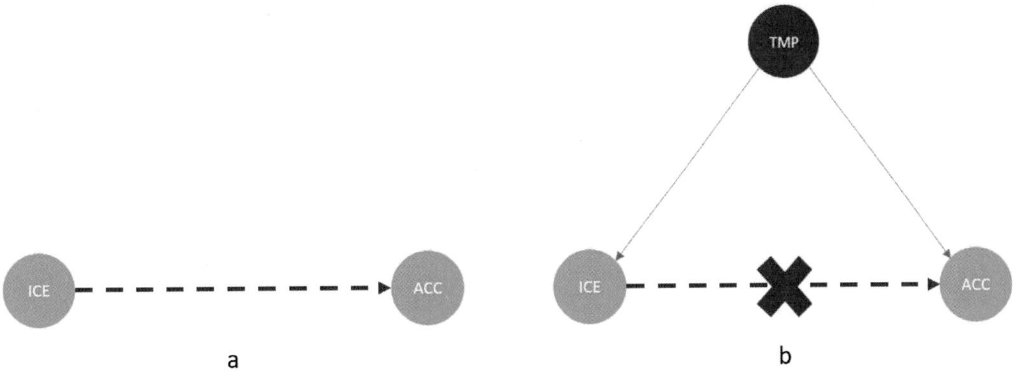

Figure 1.1 – Graphical representation of models with two (a) and three variables (b). Dashed lines represent the association, solid lines represent causation. ICE = ice cream sales, ACC = the number of accidents, and TMP = temperature.

In *Figure 1.1*, we can see that adding the average daily temperature to the model removes the relationship between regional ice cream sales and daily drownings. Depending on your background, this might or might not be surprising to you. We'll learn more about the mechanism behind this effect in *Chapter 3*.

Before we move further, we need to state one important thing explicitly: confounding is a *strictly causal concept*. What does it mean? It means that we're not able to say much about confounding using purely statistical language (note that this means that Hume's definition as we presented it here *cannot capture it*). To see this clearly, let's look at *Figure 1.2*:

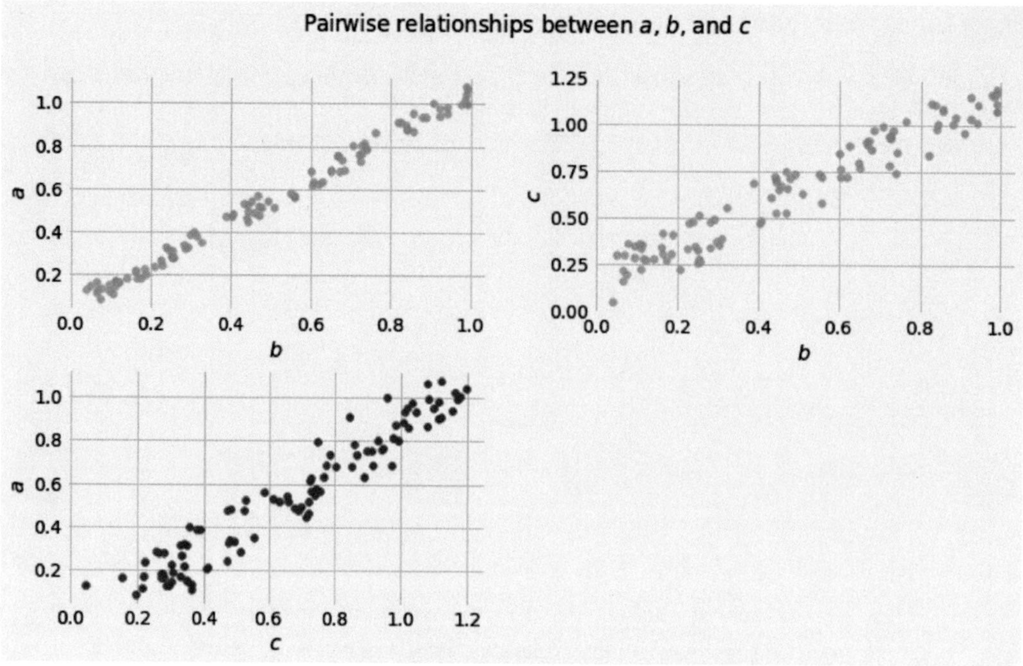

Figure 1.2 – Pairwise scatterplots of relations between a, b, and c.
The code to recreate the preceding plot can be found in the Chapter_01.ipynb notebook (`https://github.com/PacktPublishing/Causal-Inference-and-Discovery-in-Python/blob/main/Chapter_01.ipynb`).

In *Figure 1.2*, blue points signify a *causal* relationship while red points signify a *spurious* relationship, and variables *a*, *b*, and *c* are related in the following way:

- *b* causes *a* and *c*
- *a* and *c* are causally independent

Figure 1.3 presents a graphical representation of these relationships:

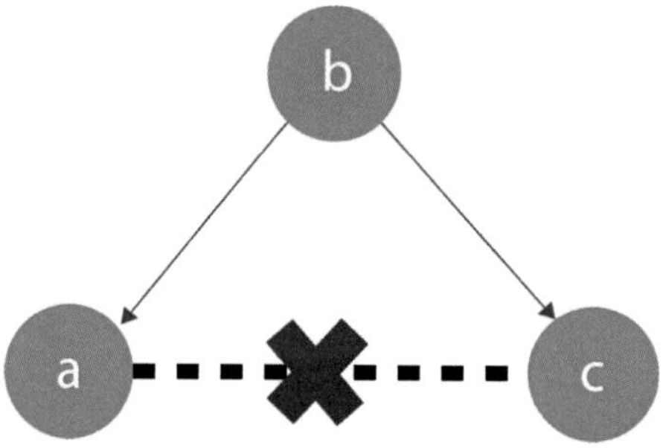

Figure 1.3 – Relationships between a, b, and c

The black dashed line with the red cross denotes that there is no causal relationship between a and c in any direction.

Hey, but in *Figure 1.2* we see some relationship! Let's unpack it!

In *Figure 1.2*, *non-spurious* (blue) and *spurious* (red) relationships look pretty similar to each other and their correlation coefficients will be similarly large. In practice, most of the time, they just cannot be distinguished based on solely statistical criteria and we need causal knowledge to distinguish between them.

> **Asymmetries and causal discovery**
>
> If fact, in some cases, we can use noise distribution or functional asymmetries to find out which direction is causal. This information can be leveraged to recover causal structure from observational data, but it also requires some assumptions about the data-generating process. We'll learn more about this in *Part 3, Causal Discovery* (*Chapter 13*).

Okay, we said that there are some spurious relationships in our data; we added another variable to the model and it changed the model's outcome. That said, I was still able to make useful predictions without this variable. If that's true, why would I care whether the relationship is spurious or non-spurious? Why would I care whether the relationship is causal or not?

How not to lose money... and human lives

We learned that randomized experiments can help us avoid confounding. Unfortunately, they are not always available. Sometimes, experiments can be too costly to perform, unethical, or virtually impossible (for example, running an experiment where the treatment is a migration of a large group of some population). In this section, we'll look at a couple of scenarios where we're limited to observational data but we still want to draw causal conclusions. These examples will provide us with a solid foundation for the next chapters.

A marketer's dilemma

Imagine you are a tech-savvy marketer and you want to effectively allocate your direct marketing budget. How would you approach this task? When allocating the budget for a direct marketing campaign, we'd like to understand what return we can expect if we spend a certain amount of money on a given person. In other words, we're interested in estimating the effect of our actions on some customer outcomes (Gutierrez, Gérardy, 2017). Perhaps we could use supervised learning to solve this problem? To answer this question, let's take a closer look at what exactly we want to predict.

We're interested in understanding how a given person would react to our content. Let's encode it in a formula:

$$\tau_i = Y_i(1) - Y_i(0)$$

In the preceding formula, the following applies:

- τ_i is the treatment effect for person i
- $Y_i(1)$ is the outcome for person i when they received the treatment T (in our example, they received marketing content from us)
- $Y_i(0)$ is the outcome for the same person i given they did not receive the treatment T

What the formula says is that we want to take the person *i*'s outcome Y_i when this person does not receive treatment T and subtract it from the same person's outcome when they receive treatment T.

An interesting thing here is that to solve this equation, we need to know what person *i*'s response is under treatment and under no treatment. In reality, we can never observe the same person under two mutually exclusive conditions at the same time. To solve the equation in the preceding formula, we need counterfactuals.

Counterfactuals are estimates of how the world would look if we changed the value of one or more variables, holding everything else constant. Because counterfactuals cannot be observed, the true causal effect τ is unknown. This is one of the reasons why classic machine learning cannot solve this problem for us. A family of causal techniques usually applied to problems like this is called **uplift modeling**, and we'll learn more about it in *Chapter 9* and *10*.

Let's play doctor!

Let's take another example. Imagine you're a doctor. One of your patients, Jennifer, has a rare disease, *D*. Additionally, she was diagnosed with a high risk of developing a blood clot. You study the information on the two most popular drugs for *D*. Both drugs have virtually identical effectiveness on *D*, but you're not sure which drug will be safer for Jennifer, given her diagnosis. You look into the research data presented in *Table 1.1*:

Drug	**A**		**B**	
Blood clot	Yes	No	Yes	No
Total	27	95	23	99
Percentage	22%	78%	19%	81%

Table 1.1 – Data for drug A and drug B

The numbers in *Table 1.1* represent the number of patients diagnosed with disease *D* who were administered drug *A* or drug *B*. Row 2 (**Blood clot**) gives us information on whether a blood clot was found in patients or not. Note that the percentage scores are rounded. Based on this data, which drug would you choose? The answer seems pretty obvious. 81% of patients who received drug *B* did not develop blood clots. The same was true for only 78% of patients who received drug *A*. The risk of developing a blood clot is around 3% lower for patients receiving drug *B* compared to patients receiving drug *A*.

This looks like a fair answer, but you feel skeptical. You know that blood clots can be very risky and you want to dig deeper. You find more fine-grained data that takes the patient's gender into account. Let's look at *Table 1.2*:

Drug	**A**		**B**	
Blood clot	Yes	No	Yes	No
Female	24	56	17	25
Male	3	39	6	74
Total	27	95	23	99
Percentage	22%	78%	18%	82%
Percentage (F)	30%	70%	40%	60%
Percentage (M)	7%	93%	7.5%	92.5%

Table 1.2 – Data for drug A and drug B with gender-specific results added. F = female, M = male. Color-coding added for ease of interpretation, with better results marked in green and worse results marked in orange.

Something strange has happened here. We have the same numbers as before and drug *B* is still preferable for all patients, but it seems that drug *A* works better for females and for males! Have we just found a medical Schrödinger's cat (`https://en.wikipedia.org/wiki/Schr%C3%B6dinger%27s_cat`) that flips the effect of a drug when a patient's gender is observed?

If you think that we might have messed up the numbers – don't believe me, just check the data for yourself. The data can be found in `data/ch_01_drug_data.csv` (`https://github.com/PacktPublishing/Causal-Inference-and-Discovery-in-Python/blob/main/data/ch_01_drug_data.csv`).

What we've just experienced is called **Simpson's paradox** (also known as the **Yule-Simpson effect**). Simpson's paradox appears when data partitioning (which we can achieve by controlling for the additional variable(s) in the regression setting) significantly changes the outcome of the analysis. In the real world, there are usually many ways to partition your data. You might ask: okay, so how do I know which partitioning is the *correct* one?

We could try to answer this question from a pure machine learning point of view: perform cross-validated feature selection and pick the variables that contribute significantly to the outcome. This solution is good enough in some settings. For instance, it will work well when we only care about making predictions (rather than decisions) and we know that our production data will be independent and identically distributed; in other words, our production data needs to have a distribution that is virtually identical (or at least similar enough) to our training and validation data. If we want more than this, we'll need some sort of a (causal) world model.

Associations in the wild

Some people tend to think that purely associational relationships happen rarely in the real world or tend to be weak, so they cannot bias our results too much. To see how surprisingly strong and consistent spurious relationships can be in the real world, visit Tyler Vigen's page: `https://www.tylervigen.com/spurious-correlations`. Notice that relationships between many variables are sometimes very strong and they last for long periods of time! I personally like the one with space launches and sociology doctorates and I often use it in my lectures and presentations. Which one is your favorite? Share and tag me on LinkedIn, Twitter (See the Let's stay in touch section in *Chapter 15* to connect!) so we can have a discussion!

Wrapping it up

"Let the data speak" is a catchy and powerful slogan, but as we've seen earlier, data itself is not always enough. It's worth remembering that in many cases *"data cannot speak for themselves"* (Hernán, Robins, 2020) and we might need more information than just observations to address some of our questions.

In this chapter, we learned that when thinking about causality, we're not limited to observations, as David Hume thought. We can also experiment – just like babies.

Unfortunately, experiments are not always available. When this is the case, we can try to use observational data to draw a causal conclusion, but the data itself is usually not enough for this purpose. We also need a causal model. In the next chapter, we'll introduce the *Ladder of Causation* – a neat metaphor for understanding three levels of causation proposed by Judea Pearl.

References

Alexander, J. E., Audesirk, T. E., & Audesirk, G. J. (1985). *Classical Conditioning in the Pond Snail Lymnaea stagnalis.* The American Biology Teacher, 47(5), 295–298. `https://doi.org/10.2307/4448054`

Archie, L. (2005). *Hume's Considered View on Causality.* [Preprint] Retrieved from: `http://philsci-archive.pitt.edu/id/eprint/2247` (accessed 2022-04-23)

Falcon, A. "Aristotle on Causality", *The Stanford Encyclopedia of Philosophy* (Spring 2022 Edition), Edward N. Zalta (ed.). `https://plato.stanford.edu/archives/spr2022/entries/aristotle-causality/`. Retrieved 2022-04-23

Gopnik, A. (2009). *The philosophical baby: What children's minds tell us about truth, love, and the meaning of life.* New York: Farrar, Straus and Giroux

Gutierrez, P., & Gérardy, J. (2017). *Causal Inference and Uplift Modelling: A Review of the Literature.* Proceedings of The 3rd International Conference on Predictive Applications and APIs in Proceedings of Machine Learning Research, 67, 1-13

Hernán M. A., & Robins J. M. (2020). *Causal Inference: What If.* Boca Raton: Chapman & Hall/CRC

Hume, D., & Millican, P. F. (2007). *An enquiry concerning human understanding. Oxford: Oxford University Press*

Kahneman, D. (2011). *Thinking, Fast and Slow.* Farrar, Straus and Giroux

Lorkowski, C. M. `https://iep.utm.edu/hume-causation/`. Retrieved 2022-04-23

Stahl, A. E., & Feigenson, L. (2015). Cognitive development. *Observing the unexpected enhances infants' learning and exploration.* Science, 348(6230), 91–94. `https://doi.org/10.1126/science.aaa3799`

2

Judea Pearl and the Ladder of Causation

In the last chapter, we discussed why association is not sufficient to draw causal conclusions. We talked about **interventions** and **counterfactuals** as tools that allow us to perform causal inference based on observational data. Now, it's time to give it a bit more structure.

In this chapter, we're going to introduce the concept of **the Ladder of Causation**. We'll discuss associations, interventions, and counterfactuals from theoretical and mathematical standpoints. Finally, we'll implement a couple of **structural causal models** in Python to solidify our understanding of the three aforementioned concepts. By the end of this chapter, you should have a firm grasp of the differences between associations, interventions, and counterfactuals. This knowledge will be a foundation of many of the ideas that we'll discuss further in the book and allow us to understand the mechanics of more sophisticated methods that we'll introduce in *Part 2, Causal Inference*, and *Part 3, Causal Discovery*.

In this chapter, we will cover the following topics:

- The concept of the Ladder of Causation
- Conceptual, mathematical, and practical differences between associations, interventions, and counterfactuals

From associations to logic and imagination – the Ladder of Causation

In this section, we'll introduce the concept of *the Ladder of Causation* and summarize its building blocks. *Figure 2.1* presents a symbolic representation of the Ladder of Causation. The higher the rung, the more sophisticated our capabilities become, but let's start from the beginning:

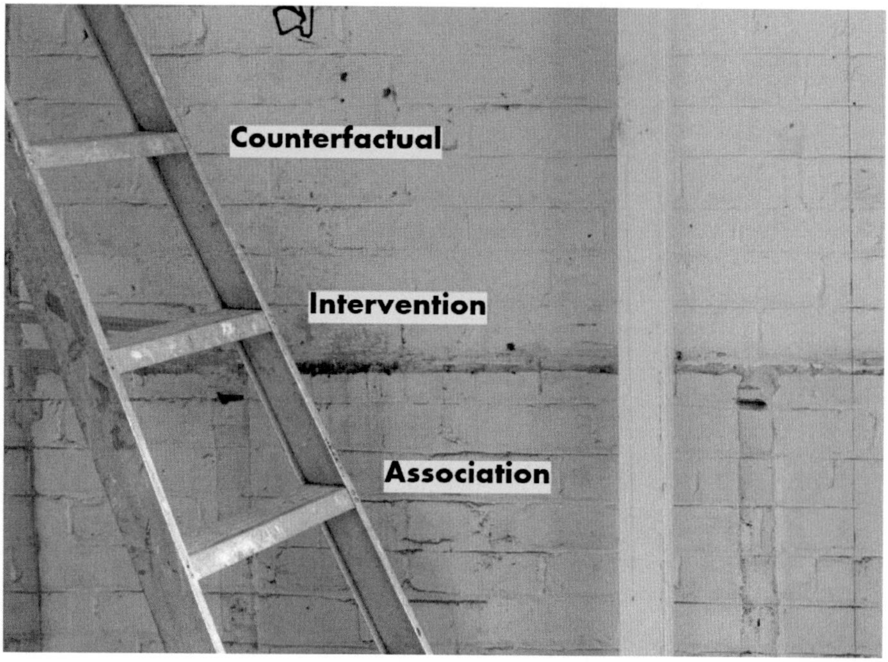

Figure 2.1 – The Ladder of Causation. Image by the author, based on a picture by Laurie Shaw (`https://www.pexels.com/photo/brown-wooden-door-frame-804394/`)

The Ladder of Causation, introduced by Judea Pearl (Pearl, Mackenzie, 2019), is a helpful metaphor for understanding distinct levels of relationships between variables – from simple associations to counterfactual reasoning. Pearl's ladder has three rungs. Each rung is related to different activity and offers answers to different types of causal questions. Each rung comes with a distinct set of mathematical tools.

> **Judea Pearl**
>
> Judea Pearl is an Israeli-American researcher and computer scientist, who devoted a large part of his career to researching causality. His original and insightful work has been recognized by **Association for Computing Machinery** (**ACM**), who awarded him with the Turing Award – considered by many the equivalent of the Nobel Prize in computer science. *The Ladder of Causation* was introduced in Pearl's popular book on causality, *The Book of Why* (Pearl, Mackenzie, 2019).

Rung one of the ladder represents **association**. The activity that is related to this level is *observing*. Using association, we can answer questions about how seeing one thing changes our beliefs about another thing – for instance, how observing a successful space launch by SpaceX changes our belief that SpaceX stock price will go up.

Rung two represents **intervention**. Remember the babies from the previous chapter? The action related to rung two is *doing* or *intervening*. Just like babies throwing their toys around to learn about the laws of physics, we can intervene on one variable to check how it influences some other variable. Interventions can help us answer questions about what will happen to one thing if we change another thing – for instance, if I go to bed earlier, will I have more energy the following morning?

Rung three represents **counterfactual reasoning**. Activities associated with rung three are *imagining* and *understanding*. Counterfactuals are useful to answer questions about what would have happened if we had done something differently. For instance, would I have made it to the office on time if I took the train rather than the car?

Table 2.1 summarizes the three rungs of *the Ladder of Causation*:

Rung	Action	Question
Association (1)	*Observing*	How does observing X change my belief in Y?
Intervention (2)	*Doing*	What will happen to Y if I do X?
Counterfactual (3)	*Imagining*	If I had done X, what would Y be?

Table 2.1 – A summary of the three rungs of the Ladder of Causation

To cement our intuitions, let's see an example of each of the rungs.

Imagine that you're a doctor and you consider prescribing drug *D* to one of your patients. First, you might recall hearing other doctors saying that *D* helped their patients. It seems that in the sample of doctors you heard talking about *D*, there is an association between their patients taking the drug and getting better. That's rung one. We are skeptical about the rung one evidence because it might just be the case that these doctors only treated patients with certain characteristics (maybe just mild cases or only patients of a certain age). To overcome the limitation of rung one, you decide to read articles based on randomized clinical trials.

Randomized controlled trials

Randomized controlled trials (**RCTs**), sometimes referred to as *randomized experiments*, are often considered the gold standard for causal inference. The key idea behind RCTs is **randomization**. We randomly assign subjects in an experiment to treatment and control groups, which helps us achieve *deconfounding*. There are many possible RCT designs. For an introduction and discussion, check out Matthews (2006). We also briefly discuss RCTs in *Chapter 12*.

These trials were based on interventions (rung two) and – assuming that they were properly designed – they can be used to determine the relative efficacy of the treatment. Unfortunately, they cannot tell us whether a patient would be better off if they had taken the treatment earlier, or which of two available treatments with similar relative efficacy would have worked better for this particular patient. To answer this type of question, we need rung three.

Now, let's take a closer look at each of the rungs and their respective mathematical apparatus.

Associations

In this section, we'll demonstrate how to quantify **associational relationships** using **conditional probability**. Then, we'll briefly introduce structural causal models. Finally, we'll implement conditional probability queries using Python.

We already learned a lot about associations. We know that associations are related to *observing* and that they allow us to generate predictions. Let's take a look at mathematical tools that will allow us to talk about associations in a more formal way.

We can view the mathematics of rung one from a couple of angles. In this section, we'll focus on the perspective of **conditional probability**.

> **Conditional probability**
>
> Conditional probability is the probability of one event, given that another event has occurred. A mathematical symbol that we use to express conditional probability is | (known as a *pipe* or *vertical bar*). We read $P(X|Y)$ as a *probability of X given Y*. This notation is a bit simplified (or abused if you will). What we usually mean by $P(X|Y)$ is $P(X = x|Y = y)$, the probability that the variable X takes the value x, given that the variable Y takes the value y. This notation can also be extended to continuous cases, where we want to work with probability densities – for example, $P(0 < X < 0.25|Y > 0.5)$.

Imagine that you run an internet bookstore. What is the probability that a person will buy book A, given that they bought book B? This question can be answered using the following conditional probability query:

$P(book\ A|book\ B)$

Note that the preceding formula does not give us any information on the causal relationship between both events. We don't know whether buying book A *caused* the customer to buy book B, buying book B caused them to buy book A, or there is another (unobserved) event that caused both. We only get information about *non-causal association* between these events. To see this clearly, we will implement our bookstore example in Python, but before we start, we'll briefly introduce one more important concept.

Structural causal models (SCMs) are a simple yet powerful tool to encode causal relationships between variables. You might be surprised that we are discussing a causal model in the section on association. Didn't we just say that association is usually not enough to address causal questions? That's true. The reason why we're introducing an SCM now is that we will use it as our *data-generating process*. After generating the data, we will pretend to forget what the SCM was. This way, we'll mimic a frequent real-world scenario where the true data-generating process is unknown, and the only thing we have is observational data.

Let's take a small detour from our bookstore example and take a look at *Figure 2.2*:

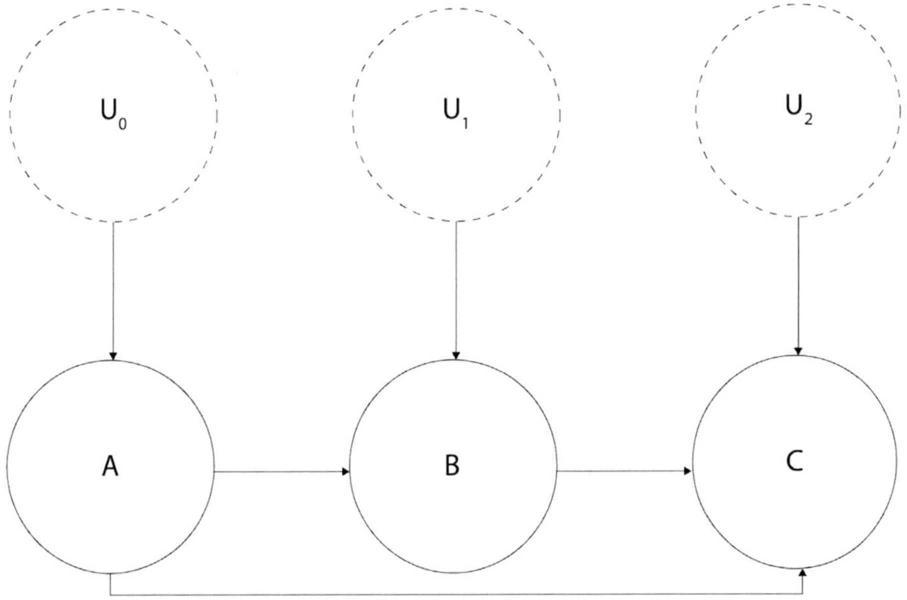

Figure 2.2 – A graphical representation of a structural causal model

Circles or *nodes* in the preceding figure represent variables. Lines with arrows or *edges* represent relationships between variables.

As you can see, there are two types of variables (marked with dashed versus regular lines). Arrows at the end of the lines represent the *direction* of the relationship.

Nodes **A**, **B**, and **C** are marked with solid lines. They represent the observed variables in our model. We call this type of variable **endogenous**. Endogenous variables are always children of at least one other variable in a model.

The other type of nodes (U_X nodes) are marked with dashed lines. We call these variables **exogenous**, and they are represented by *root* nodes in the graph (they are not descendants of any other variable; Pearl, Glymour, and Jewell, 2016). Exogenous variables are also called **noise variables**.

Noise variables

Note that most causal inference and causal discovery methods require that noise variables are uncorrelated with each other (otherwise, they become unobserved confounders). This is one of the major difficulties in real-world causal inference, as sometimes, it's very hard to be sure that we have met this assumption.

An SCM can be represented graphically (as in *Figure 2.2*) or as a series of equations. These two representations have different properties and might require different assumptions (we'll leave this complexity out for now), but they refer to the same object – a **data-generating process**.

Let's return to the SCM from *Figure 2.2*. We'll define the functional relationships in this model in the following way:

$$A := f_A(U_0)$$

$$B := f_B(A, U_1)$$

$$C := f_C(A, B, U_2)$$

A, B, C, and U_X represent the nodes in *Figure 2.1*, and := is an **assignment operator**, also known as a **walrus operator**. We use it here to emphasize that the relationship that we're describing is *directional* (or asymmetric), as opposed to the regular equal sign that suggests a symmetric relation. Finally, f_A, f_B, f_C represent arbitrary functions (they can be as simple as a summation or as complex as you want). This is all we need to know about SCMs at this stage. We will learn more about them in *Chapter 3*.

Equipped with a basic understanding of SCMs, we are now ready to jump to our coding exercise in the next section.

Let's practice!

For this exercise, let's recall our bookstore example from the beginning of the section.

First, let's define an SCM that can generate data with a non-zero probability of buying book A, given we bought book B. There are many possible SCMs that could generate such data. *Figure 2.3* presents the model we have chosen for this section:

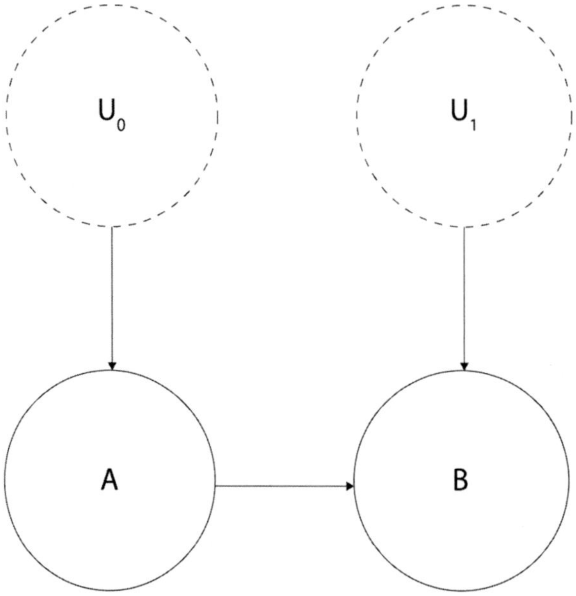

Figure 2.3 – A graphical model representing the bookstore example

To precisely define causal relations that drive our SCM, let's write a set of equations:

$$U_0 \sim U(0, 1)$$

$$U_1 \sim N(0, 1)$$

$$A := 1_{\{U_0 > .61\}}$$

$$B := 1_{\{(A + .5 * U_1) > .2\}}$$

In the preceding formulas, U_0 is a continuous random variable uniformly distributed between 0 and 1. U_1 is a normally distributed random variable, with a mean value of 0 and a standard deviation of 1. A and B are binary variables, and $1_{\{f\}}$ is an indicator function.

> **The indicator function**
>
> The notation for the indicator function might look complicated, but the idea behind it is very simple. The indicator function returns 1 when the condition in the curly braces is met and returns 0 otherwise. For instance, let's take the following function:
>
> $$X = 1_{\{Z>0\}}$$
>
> If $Z > 0$ then $X = 1$, otherwise $X = 0$.

Now, let's recreate this SCM in code. You can find the code for this exercise in the notebook for this chapter `https://bit.ly/causal-ntbk-02`:

1. First, let's import the necessary libraries:

```
import numpy as np
from scipy import stats
```

2. Next, let's define the SCM. We will use the object-oriented approach for this purpose, although you might want to choose other ways for yourself, which is perfectly fine:

```
class BookSCM:

    def __init__(self, random_seed=None):
        self.random_seed = random_seed
        self.u_0 = stats.uniform()
        self.u_1 = stats.norm()

    def sample(self, sample_size=100):
        """Samples from the SCM"""
        if self.random_seed:
            np.random.seed(self.random_seed)

        u_0 = self.u_0.rvs(sample_size)
```

```
        u_1 = self.u_1.rvs(sample_size)
        a = u_0 > .61
        b = (a + .5 * u_1) > .2

        return a, b
```

Let's unpack this code. In the `__init__()` method of our `BookSCM`, we define the distributions for U_0 and U_1 and set a random seed for reproducibility; the `.sample()` method samples from U_0 and U_1, computes values for A and B (according to the formulas specified previously), and returns them.

Great! We're now ready to generate some data and quantify an association between the variables using *conditional probability*:

1. First, let's instantiate our SCM and set the random seed to `45`:

```
scm = BookSCM(random_seed=45)
```

2. Next, let's sample `100` samples from it:

```
buy_book_a, buy_book_b = scm.sample(100)
```

Let's check whether the shapes are as expected:

```
buy_book_a.shape, buy_book_b.shape
```

The output is as follows:

```
((100,), (100,))
```

The shapes are correct. We generated the data, and we're now ready to answer the question that we posed at the beginning of this section – what is the probability that a person will buy book *A*, given that they bought book *B*?

3. Let's compute the $P(book\ A|book\ B)$ conditional probability to answer our question:

```
proba_book_a_given_book_b = buy_book_a[buy_book_b].sum() / buy_
book_a[buy_book_b].shape[0]
print(f'Probability of buying book A given B: {proba_book_a_
given_book_b:0.3f}')
```

This returns the following result:

```
Probability of buying book A given B: 0.638
```

As we can see, the probability of buying book *A*, given we bought book *B*, is 63.8%. This indicates a positive relationship between both variables (if there was no association between them, we would expect the result to be 50%). These results inform us that we can make meaningful predictions using observational data alone. This ability is the essence of most contemporary (supervised) machine learning models.

Let's summarize. Associations are useful. They allow us to generate meaningful predictions of potentially high practical significance in the absence of knowledge of the data-generating process. We used an SCM to generate hypothetical data for our bookstore example and estimated the strength of association between book A and book B sales, using a conditional probability query. Conditional probability allowed us to draw conclusions in the absence of knowledge of the true data-generating process, based on the observational data alone (note that although we knew the true SCM, we did not use any knowledge about it when computing the conditional probability query; we virtually *forgot* anything about the SCM before generating the predictions). That said, associations only allow us to answer rung one questions.

Let's climb to the second rung of *the Ladder of Causation* to see how to go beyond some of these limitations.

What are interventions?

In this section, we'll summarize what we've learned about interventions so far and introduce mathematical tools to describe them. Finally, we'll use our newly acquired knowledge to implement an intervention example in Python.

The idea of intervention is very simple. We change one thing in the world and observe whether and how this change affects another thing in the world. This is the essence of scientific experiments. To describe interventions mathematically, we use a special *do*-operator. We usually express it in mathematical notation in the following way:

$$P(Y = 1 | do(X = 0))$$

The preceding formula states that the probability of $Y = 1$, given that we set X to 0. The fact that we need to change X's value is critical here, and it highlights the inherent difference between *intervening* and *conditioning* (conditioning is the operation that we used to obtain conditional probabilities in the previous section). Conditioning only modifies our *view* of the data, while intervening affects the distribution by *actively* setting one (or more) variable(s) to a *fixed value* (or a distribution). This is very important – intervention *changes* the system, but conditioning *does not*. You might ask, what does it mean that *intervention changes the system*? Great question!

The graph saga – parents, children, and more

When we talk about graphs, we often use terms such as *parents*, *children*, *descendants*, and *ancestors*. To make sure that you can understand the next subsection clearly, we'll give you a brief overview of these terms here.

We say that the node X is a *parent* of the node Y and that Y is a *child* of X when there's a direct arrow from X to Y. If there's also an arrow from Y to Z, we say that Z is a grandchild of X and that X is a grandparent of Z. Every child of X, all its children and their children, their children's children, and so on are descendants of X, which is their *ancestor*. For a more formal explanation, check out *Chapter 4*.

Changing the world

When we intervene in a system and fix a value or alter the distribution of some variable – let's call it X – one of three things can happen:

- The change in X will influence the values of its descendants (assuming X has descendants and excluding special cases where X's influence is canceled – for example, $f(x) = x - x$)
- X will become independent of its ancestors (assuming that X has ancestors)
- Both situations will take place (assuming that X has descendants and ascendants, excluding special cases)

Note that none of these would happen if we *conditioned* on X, because conditioning *does not change* the value of any of the variables – it *does not* change the system.

Let's translate interventions into code. We will use the following SCM for this purpose:

$U_0 \sim N(0, 1)$

$U_1 \sim N(0, 1)$

$A := U_0$

$B := 5A + U_1$

The graphical representation of this model is identical to the one in *Figure 2.3*. Its functional assignments are different though, and – importantly – we set A and B to be continuous variables (as opposed to the model in the previous section, where A and B were binary; note that this is a new example, and the only thing it shares with the bookstore example is the structure of the graph):

1. First, we'll define the sample size for our experiment and set a random seed for reproducibility:

```
SAMPLE_SIZE = 100
np.random.seed(45)
```

2. Next, let's build our SCM. We will also compute the correlation coefficient between A and B and print out a couple of statistics:

```
u_0 = np.random.randn(SAMPLE_SIZE)
u_1 = np.random.randn(SAMPLE_SIZE)
a = u_0
b = 5 * a + u_1

r, p = stats.pearsonr(a, b)
print(f'Mean of B before any intervention: {b.mean():.3f}')
print(f'Variance of B before any intervention: {b.var():.3f}')
print(f'Correlation between A and B:\nr = {r:.3f}; p =
{p:.3f}\n')
```

We obtain the following result:

```
Mean of B before any intervention: -0.620
Variance of B before any intervention: 22.667
Correlation between A and B:
r = 0.978; p = 0.000
```

As we can see, the correlation between values of A and B is very high ($r = .978; p < .001$). It's not surprising, given that B is a simple linear function of A. The mean of B is slightly below zero, and the variance is around `22`.

3. Now, let's intervene on A by fixing its value at `1.5`:

```
a = np.array([1.5] * SAMPLE_SIZE)
b = 5 * a + u_1
```

We said that an intervention *changes the system*. If that's true, the statistics for B should change as a result of our intervention. Let's check it out:

```
print(f'Mean of B after the intervention on A: {b.mean():.3f}')
print(f'Variance of B after the intervention on A:
{b.var():.3f}\n')
```

The result is as follows:

```
Mean of B after the intervention on A: 7.686
Variance of B after the intervention on A: 0.995
```

Both the mean and variance have changed. The new mean of B is significantly greater than the previous one. This is because the value of our intervention on A (1.5) is much bigger than what we'd expect from the original distribution of A (centered at 0). At the same time, the variance has shrunk. This is because A became constant, and the only remaining variability in B comes from its stochastic parent, U_1.

What would happen if we intervened on B instead? Let's see and print out a couple of statistics:

```
a = u_0
b = np.random.randn(SAMPLE_SIZE)

r, p = stats.pearsonr(a, b)

print(f'Mean of B after the intervention on B: {b.mean():.3f}')
print(f'Variance of B after the intervention on B: {b.var():.3f}')
print(f'Correlation between A and B after intervening on B:\nr =
{r:.3f}; p = {p:.3f}\n')
```

This results in the following output:

```
Mean of B after the intervention on B: 0.186
Variance of B after the intervention on B: 0.995
Correlation between A and B after intervening on B:
r = -0.023; p = 0.821
```

Note that the correlation between A and B dropped to almost zero ($r = -.023$), and the corresponding p-value indicates a lack of significance ($p = .821$). This indicates that after the intervention, A and B became (linearly) independent. This result suggests that there is no causal link from B to A. At the same time, previous results demonstrated that intervening on A changes B, indicating that there is a causal link from A to B (we'll address what a *causal link* means more systematically in *Chapter 4*).

Before we conclude this section, we need to mention one more thing.

Correlation and causation

You might have heard the phrase that *correlation is not causation*. That's approximately true.

How about the opposite statement? Is *causation correlation*?

Let's see.

Figure 2.4 presents the data generated according to the following set of structural equations:

$X := \mathcal{U}(-2, 2)$

$Y := X^2 + 0.2 \times \mathcal{N}(0, 1)$

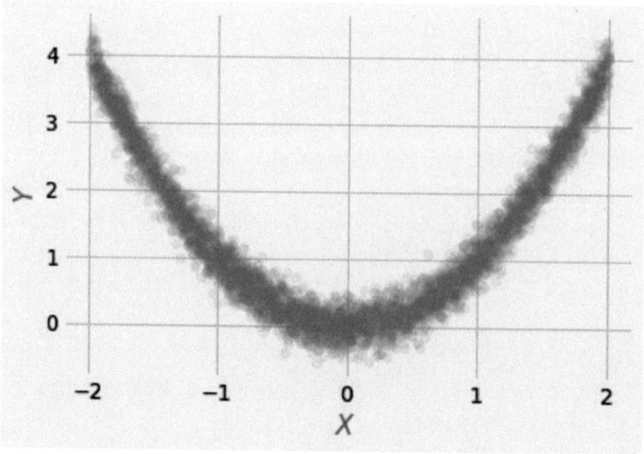

Figure 2.4 – A scatter plot of the data from a causal data-generating process

Although from the structural point of view, there's a clear causal link between X and Y, the correlation coefficient for this dataset is essentially equal to 0 (you can experiment with this data in the notebook: `https://bit.ly/causal-ntbk-02`). The reason for this is that the relationship between X and Y is not *monotonic*, and popular correlation metrics such as Pearson's r or Spearman's *rho* cannot capture non-monotonic relationships. This leads us to an important realization that a lack of traditional correlation does not imply independence between variables.

A number of tools for more general independence testing exist. For instance, information-theoretic metrics such as the **maximal information coefficient** (**MIC**) (Reshef et al., 2011; Reshef et al., 2015; Murphy, 2022, pp. 217–219) work for non-linear, non-monotonic data out of the box. The same goes for the **Hilbert-Schmidt independence criterion** (**HSIC**) (Gretton et al., 2007) and a number of other metrics.

Another scenario where you might see no correlation although causation is *present* is when your sampling does not cover the entire support of relevant variables. Take a look at *Figure 2.5*.

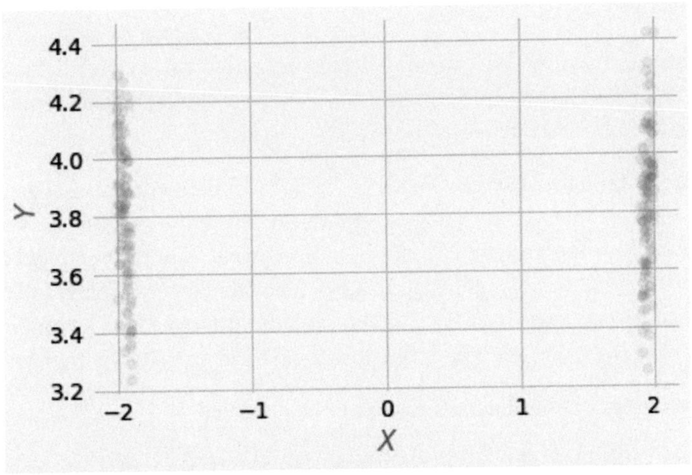

Figure 2.5 – A scatterplot of data with selective sampling.

This data is a result of exactly the same process as the data presented in *Figure 2.4*. The only difference is that we sampled according to the following condition:

$$X_{sample} = 1.9 < X < -1.9$$

It's virtually impossible to estimate the true relationship between *X* and *Y* from this data, even with sophisticated tools.

Situations such as these can happen in real life. Everything from faulty sensors to selection bias in medical studies can remove a substantial amount of information from observational data and push us toward wrong conclusions.

In this section, we looked into interventions in greater detail. We introduced the *do*-operator and discussed how it differs from conditioning. Finally, we implemented a simple SCM in Python and demonstrated how interventions on one variable affect the distribution of other variables.

If all of this makes you a little dizzy, don't worry. For the vast majority of people coming from a statistical background, conversion to causal thinking takes time. This is because causal thinking requires breaking certain habits we all pick up when we learn statistical thinking. One such habit is thinking in terms of variables as basic entities rather than in terms of the process that generated these variables.

Ready for more? Let's step up to rung three – the world of counterfactuals!

What are counterfactuals?

Have you ever wondered where you would be today if you had chosen something different in your life? Moved to another city 10 years ago? Studied art? Dated another person? Taken a motorcycle trip in Hawaii? Answering these types of questions requires us to create alternative worlds, worlds that we have never observed. If you've ever tried doing this for yourself, you already know intuitively what counterfactuals are.

Let's try to structure this intuition. We can think about counterfactuals as a minimal modification to a system (Pearl, Glymour, and Jewell, 2016). In this sense, they are similar to interventions. Nonetheless, there is a fundamental difference between the two.

Counterfactuals can be thought of as *hypothetical* or *simulated* interventions that assume a *particular state of the world* (note that interventions do not require any assumptions about the state of the world). For instance, answering a counterfactual question such as "*Would John have bought the chocolate last Friday had he seen the ad last week?*" requires us to know many things about John (and his environment) in the past. On the other hand, we don't need to know anything about John's life or environment from last week in order to perform an intervention (show John an ad and see whether he buys).

Contrary to interventions, counterfactuals can never be observed.

We can also view the difference between counterfactuals and interventions from another angle – two different counterfactual causal models can lead to the same interventional distribution.

For instance, Pearl (2009) describes a two-model scenario where the average (interventional) causal effect for a drug is equal to 0. This is true for both models.

The difference is that in one model, no patient is affected by the drug, while in the second model, all patients are affected by the drug – a pretty striking difference. As you can expect, counterfactual outcomes for both models differ (for more details, check out Pearl (2009, pp. 33–38)).

One idea that emphasizes the fundamental difference between counterfactuals and interventions is that interventional queries can be computed as the expected value of counterfactual queries over the population (Huszár, 2019). This fact further underlines the asymmetry between the two and, at the same time, reveals the deep, beautiful structure of Pearlian causal formalism.

Let's get weird (but formal)!

Now, it's time to express counterfactuals mathematically. Before we do so, let's set up an example so that we can refer to something familiar, while exploring the inherent weirdness of *the Counterfactual Wonderland*. Imagine you had a coffee this morning and now you feel bad in your stomach. Would you feel the same or better if you hadn't had your coffee?

Note that we cannot answer this question with interventions. A randomized experiment would only allow us to answer questions such as "*What is the probability that people similar to you react to coffee the way you reacted, given similar circumstances?*" or "*What is the probability that you'll feel bad after drinking a coffee in the morning on a day similar to today, given similar circumstances?*"

Counterfactuals are trying to answer a different question: "*Given an alternative world that is identical to ours and only differs in the fact that you did not drink coffee this morning (plus the necessary consequences of not drinking it), what is the probability that you'd feel bad in your stomach?*"

Let's try to formalize it. We'll denote the fact that you drank coffee this morning by $X = 1$ and the fact that you now feel bad as $Y_{X=1} = 1$. The $\cdot_{X=1}$ subscript informs us that the outcome, Y, happened in the world where you had your coffee in the morning ($X = 1$). The quantity we want to estimate, therefore, is the following:

$$P(Y_{X=0} = 1|X = 1, Y_{X=1} = 1)$$

We read this as the probability that you'd feel bad if you hadn't had your coffee, given you had your coffee and you feel bad.

Let's unpack it:

- $P(Y_{X=0} = 1)$ stands for the probability that you'd feel bad (in the alternative world) if you hadn't had your coffee
- $X = 1$ denotes that you had your coffee in the real world
- $Y_{X=1} = 1$ says that you had your coffee and you felt bad (in the real world)

Note that everything on the right side of the conditioning bar comes from the actual observation. The expression on the left side of the conditional bar refers to the alternative, hypothetical world.

Many people feel uncomfortable seeing this notation for the first time. The fact that we're conditioning on $X = 1$ to estimate the quantity in the world where $X = 0$ seems pretty counterintuitive. On a deeper level, this makes sense though. This notation makes it virtually impossible to reduce counterfactuals to *do* expressions (Pearl, Glymour, and Jewell, 2016). This reflects the inherent relationship between interventions and counterfactuals that we discussed earlier in this section.

Counterfactual notation

In this book, we follow the notation used by Pearl, Glymour, and Jewell (2016). There are also other options available in the literature. For instance, Peters, Janzing, and Schölkopf propose (2017) using different style of notation. Another popular choice is notation related to Donald Rubin's *potential outcomes* framework. It is worth making sure you understand the notation well. Otherwise, it can be a major source of confusion.

The fundamental problem of causal inference

Counterfactuals make it very clear that there's an inherent and fundamental problem with causal inference. Namely, we can never observe the same object (or subject) receiving two mutually exclusive treatments at the same time in the same circumstances.

You may wonder, given the fundamental problem of causal inference (Holland, 1986), whether there is any way to compute counterfactuals. It turns out that there is.

Computing counterfactuals

The basic idea behind computing counterfactuals is simple in theory, but the goal is not always easily achievable in practice. This is because computing counterfactuals requires an SCM that is *fully specified* at least for all the relevant variables. What does it mean? It means that we need to have full knowledge about functions that relate to relevant variables in the SCM and full knowledge about the values of *all* relevant exogenous variables in a system. Fortunately, if we know structural equations, we can compute noise variables describing the subject in the **abduction** step (see the following *Computing counterfactuals step by step* callout).

Computing counterfactuals step by step

Judea Pearl and colleagues (Pearl, Glymour and Jewell, 2016) proposed a three-step framework for computing counterfactuals:

- **Abduction**: Using evidence to calculate values of exogenous variables
- **Modification (originally called an action)**: Replacing the structural equation for the treatment with a counterfactual value
- **Prediction**: Using the modified SCM to compute the new value of the outcome under the counterfactual

We will apply this framework soon.

Let's take our coffee example. Let T denote our treatment – drinking coffee, while U will characterize you fully as an individual in our simplified world. $U = 1$ stands for coffee sensitivity, while $U = 0$ stands for a lack thereof. Additionally, let's assume that we know the causal mechanism for reaction to coffee. The mechanism is defined by the following SCM:

$$T := t$$

$$Y := TU + (T - 1)(U - 1)$$

Great! We know the outcome under the actual treatment, $Y_{T=1} = 1$ (you drank the coffee and you felt bad), but we don't know your characteristics (U). Can we do something about it?

It turns out that our model allows us to unambiguously deduct the value of U (that we'll denote as u), given we know the values of Y and T. Let's solve for u by transforming our structural equation for Y:

$$u = \frac{T + Y - 1}{2T - 1}$$

Now, let's assign the values for T and Y:

$$u = \frac{1 + 1 - 1}{2 * 1 - 1} = \frac{2 - 1}{2 - 1} = 1$$

The value we obtained for U reveals that you're a coffee-sensitive person.

This step (solving for the values of exogenous variables U) is called **abduction**.

Now, we have all the elements necessary to compute counterfactual outcomes at our disposal – a causal model and knowledge about your personal characteristics.

We're ready for the next step, **modification**. We will fix the value of our treatment at the counterfactual of interest, ($T = 0$):

$$T := 0$$

$$Y := 0U + (0 - 1)(U - 1)$$

Finally, we're ready for the last step, **prediction**. To make a prediction, we need to substitute U with the value(s) of your personal characteristic(s) that we computed before:

$$Y := 0 * 1 + (0 - 1)(1 - 1) = 0$$

And here is the answer – you wouldn't feel bad if you hadn't had your coffee!

Neat, isn't it?

Deterministic and probabilistic counterfactuals

You might have noticed that when we introduced our coffee example, we were speaking in terms of probability, although we solved it deterministically. That's a great observation!

In the real world, we are not always able to compute counterfactuals deterministically. Fortunately, the three-step framework that we introduced earlier generalizes well for probabilistic settings. To learn more on how to compute probabilistic counterfactuals, please refer to *Chapter 4* of *Causal inference in statistics: A primer* (Pearl, Glymour, and Jewell, 2016) or an excellent YouTube video by Brady Neal (Neal, 2020).

Time to code!

The last thing we'll do before concluding this section is to implement our counterfactual computation in Python:

1. First, we'll create a `CounterfactualSCM` class with three methods corresponding to the three steps of counterfactual computation – *abduction*, *modification*, and *prediction*:

```
class CounterfactualSCM:

    def abduct(self, t, y):
        return (t + y - 1)/(2*t - 1)

    def modify(self, t):
        return lambda u: t * u + (t - 1) * (u - 1)

    def predict(self, u, t):
        return self.modify(t)(u)
```

   Note that each method implements the steps that we performed in the preceding code:

   - `.abduct()` computes the value of *U*, given the values for treatment and the actual outcome
   - `.modify()` modifies the SCM by assigning *t* to *T*
   - `.predict()` takes the modified SCM and generates the counterfactual prediction by assigning the actual value of *U* to the modified SCM

2. Let's instantiate the SCM and assign the known treatment and outcome values to the `t` and `y` variables respectively:

```
coffee = CounterfactualSCM()
t = 1
y = 1
```

3. Next, let's obtain the value of *U* by performing *abduction* and print out the result:

```
u = coffee.abduct(t=t, y=y)
u
```

   The result is congruent with our computations:

```
1.0
```

4. Finally, let's compute the counterfactual prediction:

```
coffee.predict(u=u, t=0)
```

   Et voila! Here's our answer:

```
0.0
```

If you hadn't had your coffee in the morning, you'd feel better now.

This concludes our section on counterfactuals. We learned that counterfactuals are different than interventions. At the same time, there's a deeper link between rung two and rung three of *the Ladder of Causation*. We learned about the fundamental problem of causal inference, and we've seen that even though it's hard, we can compute counterfactuals when we meet certain assumptions. Finally, we practiced computing counterfactuals using mathematical tools and Python code.

Counterfactuals will briefly return in *Part 2, Causal Inference*, where we'll see them in the context of counterfactual explanations.

Extra – is all machine learning causally the same?

So far, when we have spoken about machine learning, we mainly mean supervised methods. You might wonder what the relationship is between other types of machine learning and causality.

Causality and reinforcement learning

For many people, the first family of machine learning methods that come to mind when thinking about causality is **reinforcement learning** (**RL**).

In the classic formulation of RL, an agent interacts with the environment. This suggests that an RL agent can make interventions in the environment. Intuitively, this possibility moves RL from an *associative* rung one to an *interventional* rung two. Bottou et al. (2013) amplify this intuition by proposing that causal models can be reduced to multiarmed bandit problems – in other words, that RL bandit algorithms are special cases of rung two causal models.

Although the idea that all RL is causal might seem intuitive at first, the reality is more nuanced. It turns out that even for certain bandit problems, the results might not be optimal if we do not model causality explicitly (Lee and Bareinboim, 2018).

Moreover, *model-based RL algorithms* can suffer from confounding. This includes models such as the famous DeepMind's MuZero (Schrittwieser et al., 2019), which was able to master games such as Chess, Go, and many others without explicitly knowing the rules.

Rezende and colleagues (2020) proposed to deconfound these models by using **back-door criterion** (we will learn more about back-door criterion in *Chapter 6*. Wang et al. (2022) proposed adding a causal model to the RL algorithm and using a ratio between causal and non-causal terms in a reward function, in order to encourage an agent to explore the space where the non-causal term is larger, which suggests that the causal model might be causally biased.

For a comprehensive overview of the literature on the relationships between causality and RL, check Kaddour et al. (2022), pp. 70–98.

Causality and semi-supervised and unsupervised learning

Peters et al. (2017, pp. 72–74) proposed that semi-supervised methods can be used for causal discovery, leveraging the information-theoretic asymmetry between conditional and unconditional probabilities. Based on a similar idea, Sgouritsa et al. (2015) proposed *unsupervised inverse regression* as a method to discover which causal direction between two variables is the correct one. Wu et al. (2022) explored the links between causality and semi-supervised learning in the context of *domain adaptation*, while Vowels et al. (2021) used unsupervised neural embeddings for the causal discovery of video representations of *dynamical systems*.

Furthermore, data augmentation in semi-supervised learning can be seen as a form of representation disentanglement, making the learned representations *less* confounded. As deconfounding is only partial in this case, these models cannot be considered fully causal, but perhaps we could consider putting these partially deconfounded representations somewhere between rungs one and two of *the Ladder of Causation* (Berrevoets, 2023).

In summary, the relationship between different branches of contemporary machine learning and causality is nuanced. That said, most broadly adopted machine learning models operate on rung one, not having a causal world model. This also applies to large language models such as GPT-3, GPT-4, LlaMA, or LaMDA, and other popular generative models such as DALL-E 2. Models such as GPT-4 can sometimes correctly answer causal or counterfactual queries, yet their general performance suggests that these abilities do not always generalize well (for a brief discussion and references check *Chapter 11*).

Wrapping it up

In this chapter, we introduced the concept of *the Ladder of Causation*. We discussed each of the three rungs of the ladder: associations, interventions, and counterfactuals. We presented mathematical apparatus to describe each of the rungs and translated the ideas behind them into code. These ideas are foundational for causal thinking and will allow us to understand more complex topics further on in the book.

Additionally, we broadened our perspective on causality by discussing the relationships between causality and various families of machine learning algorithms.

In the next chapter, we'll take a look at the link between observations, interventions, and linear regression to see the differences between rung one and rung two from yet another perspective. Ready?

References

Berrevoets, J., Kacprzyk, K., Qian, Z., & van der Schaar, M. (2023). *Causal Deep Learning*. arXiv preprint arXiv:2303.02186.

Bottou, L., Peters, J., Quiñonero-Candela, J., Charles, D. X., Chickering, D. M., Portugaly, E., Ray, D., Simard, P., & Snelson, E. (2013). *Counterfactual Reasoning and Learning Systems: The Example of Computational Advertising*. J. Mach. Learn. Res., 14 (1), 3207–3260.

Gretton, A., Fukumizu, K., Teo, C. H., Song, L., Schölkopf, B., & Smola, A. (2007). *A Kernel Statistical Test of Independence*. NIPS.

Holland, P. (1986). *Statistics and Causal Inference. Journal of the American Statistical Association*, 81, 945–960.

Huszár, F. (2019, January 24). *Causal Inference 3: Counterfactuals*. `https://www.inference.vc/causal-inference-3-counterfactuals/`.

Kaddour, J., Lynch, A., Liu, Q., Kusner, M. J., & Silva, R. (2022). *Causal Machine Learning: A Survey and Open Problems. arXiv, abs/2206.15475*

Lee, S., & Bareinboim, E. (2018). *Structural Causal Bandits: Where to Intervene? Proceedings of the 32nd International Conference on Neural Information Processing Systems*, 2573–2583.

Matthews, J. N. S. (2006). *Introduction to Randomized Controlled Clinical Trials (2nd ed.)*. Chapman and Hall/CRC.

Murphy, K. (2022). *Probabilistic Machine Learning*. MIT Press.

Neal, B. (2020, December 9). *14.2 - Computing Counterfactuals* [Video]. YouTube. `https://www.youtube.com/watch?v=wuYda40rqgo`.

Pearl, J. (2009). *Causality: Models, Reasoning and Inference (2nd. Ed.)*. Cambridge University Press.

Pearl, J., Glymour, M., & Jewell, N. P. (2016). *Causal inference in statistics: A primer*. Wiley.

Pearl, J., & Mackenzie, D. (2019). *The book of why*. Penguin Books.

Peters, J., Janzing, D., & Schölkopf, B. (2017). *Elements of Causal Inference: Foundations and Learning Algorithms*. MIT Press.

Reshef, D. N., Reshef, Y. A., Finucane, H. K., Grossman, S. R., McVean, G., Turnbaugh, P. J., Lander, E. S., Mitzenmacher, M., & Sabeti, P. C. (2011). *Detecting novel associations in large data sets. Science, 334* (6062), 1518–1524. `https://doi.org/10.1126/science.1205438`.

Reshef, D.N., Reshef, Y.A., Sabeti, P.C., & Mitzenmacher, M. (2015). *An Empirical Study of Leading Measures of Dependence*. arXiv, abs/1505.02214.

Jimenez Rezende, D., Danihelka, I., Papamakarios, G., Ke, N.R., Jiang, R., Weber, T., Gregor, K., Merzic, H., Viola, F., Wang, J.X., Mitrovic, J., Besse, F., Antonoglou, I., & Buesing, L. (2020). *Causally Correct Partial Models for Reinforcement Learning*. arXiv, abs/2002.02836.

Schrittwieser, J., Antonoglou, I., Hubert, T., Simonyan, K., Sifre, L., Schmitt, S., Guez, A., Lockhart, E., Hassabis, D., Graepel, T., Lillicrap, T. & Silver, D. (2019). *Mastering Atari, Go, Chess and Shogi by Planning with a Learned Model.* Nature.

Sgouritsa, E., Janzing, D., Hennig, P., & Schölkopf, B. (2015). *Inference of Cause and Effect with Unsupervised Inverse Regression.* AISTATS.

Vowels, M. J., Camgoz, N. C., & Bowden, R. (2021). *Shadow-Mapping for Unsupervised Neural Causal Discovery*. arXiv, 2104.08183

Wang, Z., Xiao, X., Xu, Z., Zhu, Y. ; Stone, P.. (2022). Causal Dynamics Learning for Task-Independent State Abstraction. *Proceedings of the 39th International Conference on Machine Learning*, in *Proceedings of Machine Learning Research, 162*, 23151–23180.

Wu, X., Gong, M., Manton, J. H., Aickelin, U., & Zhu, J. (2022). *On Causality in Domain Adaptation and Semi-Supervised Learning: an Information-Theoretic Analysis*. arXiv. 2205.04641

3

Regression, Observations, and Interventions

In this chapter, we're going to build a link between **associations**, **interventions**, and **regression** models. We'll look into the logic of **statistical control** – a tool used by scientists in the hopes of making their models more robust. Finally, we'll look into the connection between regression and structural models.

By the end of this chapter, you should have a solid understanding of statistical control and how it can help in estimating causal effects from observational data. This knowledge will allow us to build the more complex non-linear models introduced in *Part 2, Causal Inference*.

In this chapter, we'll cover the following topics:

- Associations in observational data versus linear regression
- Causal perspective on statistical control
- Regression and structural models

Starting simple – observational data and linear regression

In previous chapters, we discussed the concept of association. In this section, we'll quantify associations between variables using a regression model. We'll see the geometrical interpretation of this model and demonstrate that regression can be performed in an arbitrary direction. For the sake of simplicity, we'll focus our attention on linear cases. Let's start!

Linear regression

Linear regression is a basic data-fitting algorithm that can be used to predict the expected value of a dependent (target) variable, Y, given values of some predictor(s), X. Formally, this is written as $\hat{Y}_{X=x} = E[Y|X = x]$.

In the preceding formula, $\hat{Y}_{X=x}$ is the predicted value of Y given that X takes the value(s) x. $E[.]$ is the **expected value** operator. Note that X can be multidimensional. In such cases, X is usually represented as a matrix, $\mathbf{X}$, with shape $N \times D$, where N is the number of observations and D is the dimensionality of X (the number of predictor variables). We call the regression model with multidimensional X a **multiple regression**.

An important feature of linear regression is that it allows us to easily quantify the strength of the relationship between predictors and the target variable by computing regression **coefficients**. Intuitively, regression coefficients can be thought of as the amount of change in the *predicted* output variable relative to a unit change in the input variable.

> **Coefficients and multiple regression**
>
> In multiple regression with k predictors $X_1, \ldots, X_k$, each predictor, X_j, has its respective coefficient, β_j. Each coefficient, β_j, represents the *relative* contribution of X_j to the change in the predicted target, $\hat{Y}$, holding everything else *constant*.

Let's take a model with just one predictor, X. Such a model can be described by the following formula:

$$\hat{y}_i = \alpha + \beta x_i$$

In the preceding formula, $\hat{y}_i$ is a predicted value for observation i, α is a learned **intercept** term, x_i is the observed value of X, and β is the regression coefficient for X. We call α and β model parameters.

Let's build a simple example:

1. First, we'll define our data-generating process. We'll make the process follow the (preceding) linear regression formula and assign arbitrary values to the (true) parameters α^* and β^*. We'll choose *1.12* as the value of α^* and *0.93* as the value of β^* (you can use other values if you want). We will also add noise to the model and mark it as ϵ. We choose ϵ to be normally distributed with zero mean and a standard deviation of one. Additionally, we'll scale ϵ by *0.5*. With these values, our data-generating formula becomes the following:

$$y_i = 1.12 + 0.93x_i + 0.5\,\epsilon_i$$

> **Non-linear associations and interactions**
>
> Non-linear associations are also quantifiable. Even linear regression can be used to model some non-linear relationships. This is possible because linear regression has to be *linear in parameters*, not necessarily in the data. More complex relationships can be quantified using entropy-based metrics such as mutual information (Murphy, 2022; pp. 213-218). Linear models can also handle **interaction** terms. We talk about interaction when the model's output depends on a multiplicative relationship between two or more variables. In linear regression, we model the interaction between two predictors by adding an additional multiplicative term to the equation. For instance, if we want to model an interaction between two features, X_1 and X_2, we add the multiplication of X_1 and X_2 to the equation: $Y = X_1 + X_2 + X_1X_2$.

2. Next, we'll translate our data-generating formula into code in order to generate the data. The code for this chapter is in the `Chapter_03.ipynb` notebook (`https://bit.ly/causal-ntbk-03`).

Let's put it to work!

1. We'll start by importing the libraries that we're going to use in this chapter. We're going to use `statsmodels` to fit our linear regression model:

```
import numpy as np
import statsmodels.api as sm
import matplotlib.pyplot as plt
plt.style.use('fivethirtyeight')
```

statsmodels

`statsmodels` is a popular statistical library in Python that offers support for `R`-like syntax and `R`-like model summaries (in case you haven't heard of `R`, it is a popular open source statistical programming language). `statsmodels` is a great choice if you want to work with traditional statistical models. The package offers convenient model summaries that contain *p* -values and other useful statistics. If you come from a Scikit-learn background, you might find the `statsmodels` API a bit confusing. There are several key differences between the two libraries. One of them is the `.fit()` method, which in `statsmodels` returns an instance of a wrapper object that can be further used to generate predictions. For more details on `statsmodels`, refer to the documentation: `https://bit.ly/StatsmodelsDocs`.

2. Next, we'll set a random seed for reproducibility and define the number of samples that we're going to generate:

```
np.random.seed(45)
N_SAMPLES = 5000
```

3. Then, we'll define our model parameters, $\alpha^{\wedge *}$ and $\beta^{\wedge *}$:

```
alpha = 1.12
beta = 0.93
epsilon = np.random.randn(N_SAMPLES)
```

4. Finally, we'll use our model formula to generate the data:

```
X = np.random.randn(N_SAMPLES)
y = alpha + beta * X + 0.5 * epsilon
```

5. There's one more step that we need to take before fitting the model. `statsmodels` requires us to add a constant feature to the data. This is needed to perform the intercept computations. Many libraries perform this step implicitly; nonetheless, `statsmodels` wants us to do it

explicitly. To make our lives easier, the authors have provided us with a convenient method, `.add_constant()`. Let's apply it!

```
X = sm.add_constant(X)
```

Now, our `X` has got an extra column of ones at column index `0`. Let's print the first five rows of `X` to see it:

```
print(X[:5, :])
```

The result is as follows:

```
[[ 1.          0.11530002]
 [ 1.         -0.43617719]
 [ 1.         -0.54138887]
 [ 1.         -1.64773122]
 [ 1.         -0.32616934]]
```

Now, we're ready to fit the regression model using `statsmodels` and print the summary:

```
model = sm.OLS(y, X)
fitted_model = model.fit()
print(fitted_model.summary())
```

The output of the model summary is presented in *Figure 3.1*. We marked the estimated coefficients with a red ellipse:

```
                            OLS Regression Results
==============================================================================
Dep. Variable:                      y   R-squared:                       0.771
Model:                            OLS   Adj. R-squared:                  0.771
Method:                 Least Squares   F-statistic:                 1.681e+04
Date:                Sun, 05 Jun 2022   Prob (F-statistic):               0.00
Time:                        10:51:22   Log-Likelihood:                -3615.0
No. Observations:                5000   AIC:                             7234.
Df Residuals:                    4998   BIC:                             7247.
Df Model:                           1
Covariance Type:            nonrobust
==============================================================================
                 coef    std err          t      P>|t|      [0.025      0.975]
------------------------------------------------------------------------------
const          1.1243      0.007    159.391      0.000       1.110       1.138
x1             0.9212      0.007    129.669      0.000       0.907       0.935
==============================================================================
Omnibus:                        0.129   Durbin-Watson:                   1.986
Prob(Omnibus):                  0.938   Jarque-Bera (JB):                0.163
Skew:                           0.002   Prob(JB):                        0.922
Kurtosis:                       2.972   Cond. No.                         1.02
==============================================================================
```

Figure 3.1 – A summary of the results of a simple linear regression model

The coefficient marked `const` is α, the estimate of the true α^* parameter, while the coefficient marked `x1` is β, the estimate of β^*. They are slightly different from their true counterparts ($\alpha^* = 1.12$, $\beta^* = 0.93$). This is because we made our model noisy by adding the ϵ term. You can see that both coefficients are associated with p-values below *0.001* (check the column named `P>|t|`), which indicates that they are **statistically significant** at the customary $p < .05$ level.

p-values and statistical significance

Broadly speaking, the p-value is a statistical device meant to help distinguish between the signal and the noise in statistical comparisons or summaries. More precisely, the p-value is the probability of observing data at least as extreme as we observed, given that the *null hypothesis* is true.

The **null hypothesis** usually states that there is *no effect* or *no difference* between two or more objects that we compare. In the context of linear regression, we test two types of null hypotheses:

- Null hypotheses for coefficients (including the intercept)
- A null hypothesis for the entire model

The null hypothesis for a given coefficient states that this coefficient is not significantly different from zero. The null hypothesis for the model states that the entire model is not significantly different from the **null model** (in the context of simple regression analysis, the null model is usually represented as an intercept-only model).

If you want to learn more about null hypotheses and hypothesis testing, check out this video series from Khan Academy: `https://bit.ly/KhanHypothesisTesting`.

Given a null hypothesis, p-values are used as a convenient quantitative summary that helps us understand whether we can safely reject this null hypothesis for some threshold value (a good practice is to pick the threshold value before starting the analysis or – preferably – before starting the data collection process).

Because p-values are the probability of observing data *at least as extreme* as ours under the null hypothesis, the lower the p-value, the *less likely* the null hypothesis is. In other words, the lower the p-value, the *less* comfortable we are in holding that the null hypothesis is true, and the *more likely* we are to agree that it should be *rejected*. If the p-value is lower than the threshold that we picked, we say that we *reject the null hypothesis* (note that we don't say that we've proven an alternative to the null hypothesis).

Although p-values have been widely adopted in modern statistics and science, they have also been widely abused. This has led to multiple severe critiques of p-values and statistical significance, highlighting that they are frequently misused and misinterpreted, which can lead to detrimental real-world consequences. For a critical overview, check out Wasserstein and Lazar (2016).

Geometric interpretation of linear regression

Linear regression can also be viewed from a geometric point of view. Let's plot the data we generated alongside the fitted regression line:

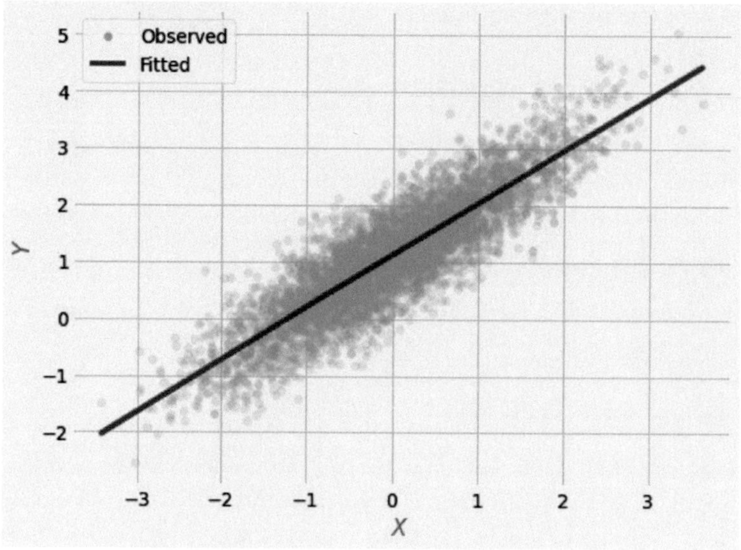

Figure 3.2 – Generated data and fitted regression line

Each blue dot in *Figure 3.2* represents a single observation, while the red line represents the best-fit line found by the linear regression algorithm. In the case of multiple regression, the line becomes a *hyperplane*.

> **Regression and correlation**
>
> If we imagine the plot in *Figure 3.2* without the red line, we are still able to recognize a strong linear relationship between X and Y. This might remind some of you of the concept of correlation. In fact, there are a number of similarities between Pearson's correlation coefficient and linear regression. For instance, if we standardize a coefficient of X in the regression model $Y \sim X$, it will have the same value as Pearson's r between X and Y. There are also some differences. For instance, Pearson's r between X and Y will be the same as Pearson's r between Y and X, yet unstandardized coefficients in regression models $Y \sim X$ and $X \sim Y$ will typically differ.

Reversing the order

Regression is a purely statistical *rung 1* model and we can use it to quantify the association between X and Y as well as between Y and X. In other words, regression does not say anything about the data's causal structure. In particular, there might be no causal link between two variables at all but we can still find a relationship between them using a regression model.

In the first chapter, we discussed the example of an association between ice cream sales and drownings. We showed that this association was *spurious*, but the regression model would still quantify it as existing (assuming that the association would be strong enough and possible to express using the model of choice, in our case *linear* regression). This is the nature of the first rung of *The Ladder of Causation* and – as we mentioned in *Chapter 2* – it can be very useful in certain cases.

> **More on regression vocabulary**
>
> When we use X as a predictor and Y as a target variable (also called the **dependent variable**), we say that we regress Y on X. If we use Y as a predictor of X, we say that we regress X on Y. Regressing Y on X can be also expressed in `R`-style notation as $Y \sim X$, and regressing X on Y as $X \sim Y$. We will use this notation across the book to describe various models. We decided to use `R`-style notation because of its neatness and simplicity. In some cases, though, it might be clearer to just say that we *regress Y on X* rather than using a formula. We'll use this descriptive style where clarity demands it.

To make it more hands-on, let's see what the reversed regression model looks like. We will now regress X on Y. The code to build the reversed model is very similar to the code to build the original model, so we won't discuss it here. If you want to examine the code for yourself, you can find it in the `Chapter_03.ipynb` notebook (`https://bit.ly/causal-ntbk-03`).

Let's take a look at the results summary in *Figure 3.3*:

```
                            OLS Regression Results
==============================================================================
Dep. Variable:                      y   R-squared:                       0.771
Model:                            OLS   Adj. R-squared:                  0.771
Method:                 Least Squares   F-statistic:                 1.681e+04
Date:                Sun, 05 Jun 2022   Prob (F-statistic):               0.00
Time:                        19:16:00   Log-Likelihood:                -3375.0
No. Observations:                5000   AIC:                             6754.
Df Residuals:                    4998   BIC:                             6767.
Df Model:                           1
Covariance Type:            nonrobust
==============================================================================
                 coef    std err          t      P>|t|      [0.025      0.975]
------------------------------------------------------------------------------
const         -0.9441      0.010    -96.048      0.000      -0.963      -0.925
x1             0.8368      0.006    129.669      0.000       0.824       0.849
==============================================================================
Omnibus:                        0.590   Durbin-Watson:                   1.994
Prob(Omnibus):                  0.745   Jarque-Bera (JB):                0.582
Skew:                          -0.026   Prob(JB):                        0.748
Kurtosis:                       3.003   Cond. No.                         2.83
==============================================================================
```

Figure 3.3 – Results summary for the reversed model

As we can see, the coefficients have changed. In particular, the *intercept* is now negative. As we're now regressing *X* on *Y*, the intercept became the point where the fitted line crosses the *X* axis (rather than the *Y* axis as in the original model). You can verify that the fitted line crosses the *X* axis below 0 by looking at *Figure 3.4* (the reversed model) and *Figure 3.2* (the original model):

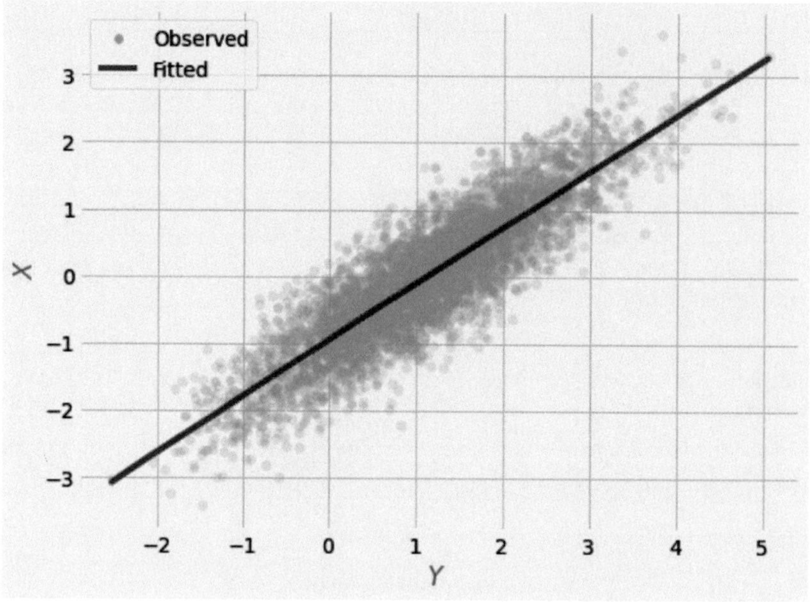

Figure 3.4 – Visualization of the reversed model

The regression model itself cannot help us understand which variable is the cause and which is the effect. To determine this, we need some sort of external knowledge.

Causal attributions become even more complicated in *multiple regression*, where each additional predictor can influence the relationship between the variables in the model. For instance, the learned coefficient for variable *X* might be 0.63, but when we add variable *Z* to the model, the coefficient for *X* changes to -2.34. A natural question in such cases is: if the coefficient has changed, what is the true effect here?

Let's take a look at this issue from the point of view of statistical control.

Should we always control for all available covariates?

Multiple regression provides scientists and analysts with a tool to perform **statistical control** – a procedure to remove *unwanted* influence from certain variables in the model. In this section, we'll discuss different perspectives on statistical control and build an intuition as to why statistical control can easily lead us astray.

Let's start with an example. When studying predictors of dyslexia, you might be interested in understanding whether parents smoking influences the risk of dyslexia in their children. In your model, you might want to control for parental education. Parental education might affect how much attention parents devote to their children's reading and writing, and this in turn can impact children's skills and other characteristics. At the same time, education level might decrease the probability of smoking, potentially leading to confounding. But how do we actually know whether it *does* lead to confounding?

In some cases, we can refer to previous research to find an answer or at least a hint. In other cases, we can rely on our intuition or knowledge about the world (for example, we know that a child's current skills cannot cause the parent's past education). However, in many cases, we will be left without a clear answer. This inevitable uncertainty led to the development of various heuristics guiding the choice of variables that should be included as statistical controls.

Navigating the maze

One of the existing heuristics is to control for as many variables as possible. This idea is based on *"the (…) assumption that adding CVs [control variables] necessarily produces more conservative tests of hypotheses"* (in: Becker et al., 2016). Unfortunately, this is not true. Moreover, controlling for wrong variables can lead to severely distorted results, including spurious effects and reversed effect signs.

Some authors offer more fine-grained heuristics. For example, Becker and colleagues (Becker et al., 2016; `https://bit.ly/BeckersPaper`) shared a set of 10 recommendations on how to approach statistical control. Some of their recommendations are as follows (the original ordering is given in parentheses):

- If you are not sure about a variable, don't use it as a control (1)
- Use conceptually meaningful control variables (3)
- Conduct comparative tests of relationships between the independent variables and control variables (7)
- Run results with and without the control variables and contrast the findings (8)

We'll see a couple of examples of scenarios leading to confounding in a while, but first, let's take a look at some of the author's recommendations.

If you don't know where you're going, you might end up somewhere else

Recommendations (1) and (3) discourage adding variables to the model. This might sound reasonable – if you're not sure, don't add, because you might break something by accident. It seems rational, perhaps because most of us have seen or participated in situations like this in real life – someone does not understand how something works, they do something that seems sensible to them, but they are not aware of their own blind spots and the thing is now broken.

An important aspect of this story is that the thing is *now* broken. This suggests that it *worked properly before*. This is not necessarily a valid assumption to make from a causal point of view. *Not including* a variable in the model might also lead to *confounding* and *spuriousness*. This is because there are various patterns of **independence structure** possible between any three variables. Let's consider the **structural causal model** (**SCM**) presented in *Figure 3.5*:

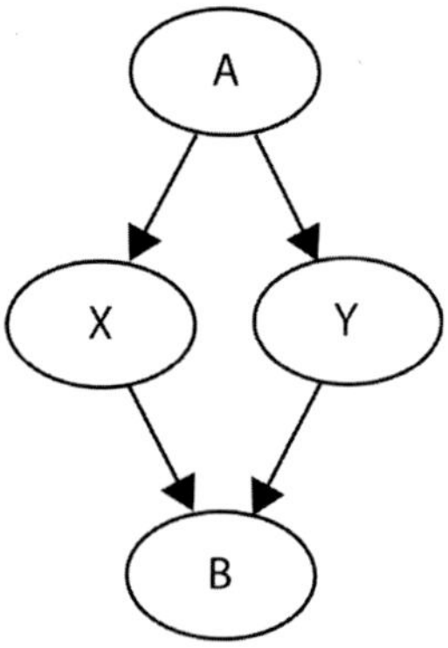

Figure 3.5 – An example SCM with various patterns leading to spurious associations

> **More on SCM graphical representations**
>
> The representation of the SCM in *Figure 3.5* differs slightly from the representations we used in the previous chapter. First, it does not contain noise variables. You can think of this representation as a simplified version with *implicit* noise variables – clearer and more focused. Second, nodes are represented as ellipses rather than circles. This is because we used the default mode of the `graphviz` library to generate them. The difference in the shapes does not have any particular meaning *in our case*. However, this is a great opportunity to introduce `graphviz` – a software package and a Python library for graph visualization. It's a useful tool when you work with causal models and smaller graphs or networks. To learn the basic `graphviz` syntax, you can refer to the notebooks accompanying this book. For a more comprehensive introduction, check out `https://bit.ly/GraphvizDocs`.

From the model structure, we can clearly see that X and Y are *causally* independent. There's no arrow between them, nor is there a directed path that would connect them indirectly. Let's fit four models and analyze which variables, when controlled for, lead to spurious relationships between X and Y:

1. First, we'll start simple with a model that regresses Y on X.
2. Then, we'll add A to this model.
3. Next, we'll fit a model without A, but with B.
4. Finally, we'll build a model with all four variables.

What is your best guess – out of the four models, which ones will correctly capture causal independence between *X* and *Y*? I encourage you to write your hypotheses down on a piece of paper before we reveal the answer. Ready? Let's find out!

The code for this experiment is in the `Chapter_03.ipynb` notebook (`https://bit.ly/causal-ntbk-03`). Follow these steps:

1. First, let's define the SCM:

```
a = np.random.randn(N_SAMPLES)
x = 2 * a + 0.5 * np.random.randn(N_SAMPLES)
y = 2 * a + 0.5 * np.random.randn(N_SAMPLES)
b = 1.5 * x + 0.75 * y
```

   Note that all the coefficients that we use to scale the variables are arbitrarily chosen.

2. Next, let's define four model variants and fit the models iteratively:

```
# Define four model variants
variants = [
    [x],
    [x, a],
    [x, b],
    [x, a, b]
]

# Fit models iteratively and store the results
for variant in variants:
    X = sm.add_constant(np.stack(variant).T)
    model = sm.OLS(y, X)
    fitted_model = model.fit()
```

3. Finally, let's examine the results in *Table 3.1*:

Model	X		A		B	
	p-value	Coefficient	p-value	Coefficient	p-value	Coefficient
$Y \sim X$	< .001	0.947	-	-	-	-
$Y \sim X + A$	.6565	0.014	<.001	1.967	-	-
$Y \sim X + B$	< .001	-2.000	-	-	< .001	1.333
$Y \sim X + A + B$	< .001	-2.000	<.001	0.000	< .001	1.333

Table 3.1 – Summary of the results of four regression models

What we see in *Table 3.1* is that the only model that recognized the causal independence of X and Y correctly (large p-value for X, suggesting the lack of significance) is the second model ($Y \sim X + A$). This clearly shows us that all other statistical control schemes led to invalid results, including the model that does not control for *any* additional variables.

Why did controlling for A work while all other schemes did not? There are three elements to the answer:

- First, A is a confounder between X and Y and we need to control for it in order to remove confounding. This situation is structurally identical to the one in the ice cream example in the first chapter.
- Second, X, Y, and B form a pattern that we call a **collider** or **immorality**. This pattern has a very interesting behavior – it enables the flow of information between the parent variables (X and Y in our case) when we control for the child variable (B in our example). This is exactly the opposite of what happened when we controlled for A!
- Third, not controlling for *any* variable leads to the same result in terms of the *significance* of X as controlling for A and B (note that the results are different in terms of *coefficients*, yet as we're now interested in the structural properties of the system, this is of secondary importance). This is precisely because the effects of controlling for A and controlling for B are exactly the opposite from a *structural point of view* and they cancel each other out!

We'll devote the whole of *Chapter 5*, to a detailed discussion on the *collider* and two other graphical patterns (you already know their names, don't you?).

Get involved!

Now, let's get back to the recommendations given by Becker and colleagues. Recommendations (7) and (8) are interesting. Running comparative tests between variables can be immensely helpful in discovering causal relationships between them. Although Becker proposes to run these tests only between independent and control variables, we do not have to (and should not) restrict ourselves to this. In fact, comparative independence tests are an essential ingredient of some of the causal discovery methods that we'll discuss in *Part 3, Causal Discovery*.

To control or not to control?

The fact that smart people all over the world create heuristics to decide whether a given variable should be included in the model highlights how difficult it is to understand causal relationships between variables in complex and noisy real-world scenarios.

If we have full knowledge about the causal graph, the task of deciding which variables we should control for becomes relatively easy (and after reading the next couple of chapters, you might even find it almost trivial). If the true causal structure is unknown, the decision is fundamentally difficult.

There's no one-size-fits-all solution to the control-or-not-to-control question, but understanding causality will help you make much better decisions in this regard.

Causality does not give you a new angle on statistical control; it gives you new eyes that allow you to see what's *invisible* from the perspective of *rung 1* of *The Ladder of Causation*. For a summary of what constitutes good and bad controls, check out the excellent paper by Cinelli et al. (2022; `https://bit.ly/GoodBadControls`).

Regression and structural models

Before we conclude this chapter, let's take a look at the connection between regression and SCMs. You might already have an intuitive understanding that they are somehow related. In this section, we'll discuss the nature of this relationship.

SCMs

In the previous chapter, we learned that SCMs are a useful tool for encoding causal models. They consist of a set of variables (exogenous and endogenous) and a set of functions defining the relationships between these variables. We saw that SCMs can be represented as graphs, with nodes representing variables and directed edges representing functions. Finally, we learned that SCMs can produce interventional and counterfactual distributions.

> **SCM and structural equations**
>
> In causal literature, the names **structural equation model** (**SEM**) and **structural causal model** (**SCM**) are sometimes used interchangeably (e.g., Peters et al., 2017). Others refer to SEMs as a family of specific multivariate modeling techniques with latent variables (e.g., Bollen and Noble, 2011). SEM as a modeling technique is a vast and rich topic. For a good introduction, check out the book by Kline (2015); for Judea Pearl's account on SEM and causality, check out Pearl (2012).

Linear regression versus SCMs

Linear regression is a model that allows us to quantify the (relative) strength of a (linear in parameters) relationship between two or more variables. There is no notion of causal directionality in linear regression, and in this sense, we don't know which direction (if any) is the *causally correct* one. This condition is known as *observational equivalence* (Peters et al., 2017).

Finding the link

In the previous section, we used linear regression to estimate coefficients that we interpreted as *causal* estimates of the strength of a relationship between variables.

When fitting the four models describing the SCM from *Figure 3.5*, we saw that in the correct model ($Y \sim X + A$), the estimate of the coefficient for A was equal to 1.967. That's very close to the true coefficient, which was equal to 2. This result shows the direction of our conclusion.

Linear regression can be used to estimate causal effects, given that we know the underlying causal structure (which allows us to choose which variables we should control for) and that the underlying system is linear in terms of parameters.

Linear models can be a *useful microscope* for causal analysis (Pearl, 2013).

To cement our intuition regarding the link between linear regression and SCMs, let's build one more SCM that will be linear in terms of parameters but non-linear in terms of data and estimate its coefficients with linear regression:

1. As usual, let's first start by defining the causal structure. *Figure 3.6* presents a graphical representation of our model.

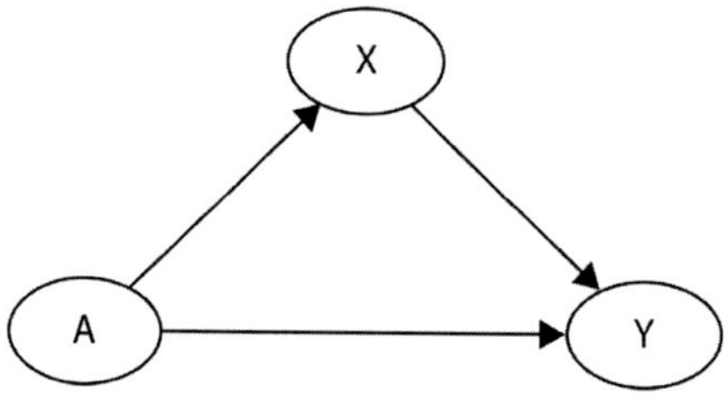

Figure 3.6 – Graphical representation of an example SCM

2. Next, let's define the functional assignments (we'll use the same settings for sample size and random seed as previously):

```
a = np.random.randn(N_SAMPLES)
x = 2 * a + .7 * np.random.randn(N_SAMPLES)
y = 2 * a + 3 * x + .75 * x**2
```

3. Let's add a constant and then initialize and fit the model:

```
X = sm.add_constant(np.stack([x, x**2, a]).T)
model = sm.OLS(y, X)
fitted_model = model.fit()
print(fitted_model.summary(xname=['const', 'x',
     'x^2', 'a']))
```

Note that our functional assignment contained not only X but also X^2. We want to make sure that we add the square term to the model as well. This is the simplest way to introduce non-linearity into a linear regression model. Also, note that the model is still linear in parameters (we only use addition and multiplication).

Another important thing to notice is that we included A in the model. The reason for this is that A is a confounder in our dataset and – as we learned before – we need to control for a confounder in order to get unbiased estimates.

Great, let's see the results!

```
                            OLS Regression Results
==============================================================================
Dep. Variable:                      y   R-squared:                       1.000
Model:                            OLS   Adj. R-squared:                  1.000
Method:                 Least Squares   F-statistic:                 3.294e+32
Date:                Sun, 05 Mar 2023   Prob (F-statistic):               0.00
Time:                        12:51:10   Log-Likelihood:                 30899.
No. Observations:                1000   AIC:                        -6.179e+04
Df Residuals:                     996   BIC:                        -6.177e+04
Df Model:                           3
Covariance Type:            nonrobust
==============================================================================
                 coef    std err          t      P>|t|      [0.025      0.975]
------------------------------------------------------------------------------
const       -2.22e-16   3.57e-16     -0.622      0.534   -9.23e-16    4.79e-16
x              3.0000   4.14e-16   7.25e+15      0.000       3.000       3.000
x^2            0.7500   4.78e-17   1.57e+16      0.000       0.750       0.750
a              2.0000   8.67e-16   2.31e+15      0.000       2.000       2.000
==============================================================================
Omnibus:                        0.858   Durbin-Watson:                   1.912
Prob(Omnibus):                  0.651   Jarque-Bera (JB):                0.763
Skew:                          -0.062   Prob(JB):                        0.683
Kurtosis:                       3.054   Cond. No.                         24.4
==============================================================================
```

Figure 3.7 – The results of the model with a non-linear term

Figure 3.7 presents the results of our regression analysis. The coefficient for X is marked as `x`, the coefficient for X^2 as `x^2`, and the coefficient for A as `a`. If we compare the coefficient values to the true coefficients in our SCM, we can notice that they are *exactly* the same! This is because we modeled Y as a deterministic function of X and A, not adding any noise.

We can also see that the model correctly decoded the coefficient for the non-linear term (X^2). Although the relationship between X^2 and Y is non-linear, they are related by a linear functional assignment.

Regression and causal effects

We've seen an example of linear regression with a single predictor and an example with an additional quadratic term. In the purely linear case, the *causal* interpretation of the regression result is straightforward: the coefficient of X represents the magnitude of the causal impact of X on Y.

To solidify our intuition, let's see an example.

If the coefficient of X is equal to 6.7, we expect that by increasing the value of X by 1, we will see an increase of 6.7 in Y.

This also generalizes to multiple regression. If we had three predictors, X_1, X_2, and X_3, each of their respective coefficients would have an analogous interpretation. The coefficient of X_1 would quantify the causal effect of X_1 on Y (holding everything else constant) and so on.

When we add a *transformed* version of a variable to the model (as we did by adding X^2), the interpretation becomes slightly less intuitive.

To understand how to interpret the coefficients in such a model, let's get back to the simple univariate case first.

Let's represent the univariate case with the following simplified formula (we omit the intercept and noise):

$$Y = \beta_1 X_1$$

We said before that the coefficient quantifies the magnitude of X_1's impact on Y. This can be understood as a derivative of Y with respect to X_1.

If you know a thing or two about calculus, you will quickly notice that this derivative is equal to β_1 – our coefficient. If you don't, don't worry.

Now, let's add the quadratic term to our equation:

$$Y = \beta_1 X_1 + \beta_2 X_1^2$$

Taking the derivative of this expression with respect to X_1 will give us the following:

$$\frac{dY}{dX_1} = \beta_1 + 2\beta_2 X_1$$

Note that we can get this result by applying a technique called the **power rule** (`https://bit.ly/MathPowerRule`) to our equation.

An interesting thing is that now the magnitude of X_1's impact on Y depends on the value of X_1. It's no longer quantified solely by its coefficient. When the effect of a variable on the outcome depends on this variable's value, we say that the effect is **heterogeneous**. We'll discuss heterogeneous effects in *Part 2, Causal Inference*.

Note that another perspective on the quadratic term is that this is a special case of interaction between X_1 and itself. This is congruent with the multiplicative definition of interaction that we presented earlier in this chapter. In this light, the quadratic term can be seen as $X_1 \cdot X_1$.

To summarize, adding non-linear terms to linear regression models makes the interpretation of these models more difficult (although not impossible). This is true in both – associational and causal – approaches.

The causal interpretation of linear regression *only holds* when there are *no spurious relationships* in your data. This is the case in two scenarios: when you control for a set of all necessary variables (sometimes this set can be empty) or when your data comes from a properly designed randomized experiment.

Any time you run regression analysis on arbitrary real-world observational data, there's a significant risk that there's hidden confounding in your dataset and so causal conclusions from such analysis are likely to be (causally) biased.

Additionally, remember that in order to obtain a valid regression model, a set of core regression assumptions should be met (linearity in parameters, homoscedasticity of variance, independence of observations, and normality of Y for any fixed value of X). To learn more about these assumptions, check out Westfall & Arias (2022, pp. 17-19).

Wrapping it up

That was a lot of material! Congrats on reaching the end of *Chapter 3*!

In this chapter, we learned about the links between regression, observational data, and causal models. We started with a review of linear regression. After that, we discussed the concept of statistical control and demonstrated how it can lead us astray. We analyzed selected recommendations regarding statistical control and reviewed them from a causal perspective. Finally, we examined the links between linear regression and SCMs.

A solid understanding of the links between observational data, regression, and statistical control will help us move freely in the world of much more complex models, which we'll start introducing in *Part 2, Causal Inference.*

We're now ready to take a more detailed look at the graphical aspect of causal models. See you in the next chapter!

References

Becker, T. E., Atinc, G., Breaugh, J. A., Carlson, K. D., Edwards, J. R., & Spector, P. E. (2016). *Statistical control in correlational studies: 10 essential recommendations for organizational researchers. Journal of Organizational Behavior*, 37(2), 157–167.

Bollen, K. A. & Noble, M. D. (2011). *Structural equation models and the quantification of behavior.* PNAS Proceedings of the National Academy of Sciences of the United States of America, 108(Suppl 3), 15639–15646.

Cinelli, C., Forney, A., & Pearl, J. (2022). *A Crash Course in Good and Bad Controls. Sociological Methods & Research*, 0 (0), 1-34.

Kline, R. B. (2015). *Principles and Practice of Structural Equation Modeling.* Guilford Press.

Murphy, K. P. (2022). *Probabilistic Machine Learning: An Introduction.* MIT Press.

Pearl, J. (2012). *The causal foundations of structural equation modeling.* In Hoyle, R. H. (Ed.), *Handbook of structural equation modeling* (pp. 68–91). Guilford Press.

Pearl, J. (2013). *Linear Models: A Useful "Microscope" for Causal Analysis. Journal of Causal Inference*, 1(1), 155-170.

Peters, J., Janzing, D., & Schölkopf, B. (2017). *Elements of Causal Inference: Foundations and Learning Algorithms*. MIT Press.

Wasserstein, R. L. & Lazar, N. A. (2016) *The ASA Statement on p-Values: Context, Process, and Purpose. The American Statistician*, 70(2), 129-133

Westfall, P. H. & Arias, A. L. (2022). *Understanding Regression Analysis: A Conditional Distribution Approach*. CRC Press LLC.

4
Graphical Models

Welcome to *Chapter 4*!

So far, we have used graphs mainly to visualize our models. In this chapter, we'll see that from the causal point of view, graphs are much more than just a visualization tool. We'll start with a general refresher on graphs and basic graph theory. Next, we'll discuss the idea of **graphical models** and the role of **directed acyclic graphs** (**DAGs**) in causality. Finally, we'll look at how to talk about causality beyond DAGs. By the end of this chapter, you should have a solid understanding of what graphs are and how they relate to causal inference and discovery.

This knowledge will give us the foundations to understand *Chapter 5*. This and the next chapter are critical to understanding the very essence of causal inference as understood in this book.

In this chapter, we'll cover the following:

- A refresher on graphs
- Graphical models in causality
- Causal directed acyclic graphs (DAGs)
- Causality beyond DAGs

Graphs, graphs, graphs

This section will be a quick refresher on graphs and basic graph theory. If you're not familiar with graphs – don't worry – you can treat this section as a crash course on the topic.

Let's start!

Graphs can be defined in multiple ways. You can think of them as discrete mathematical structures, abstract representations of real-world entities and relations between them, or computational data structures. What all of these perspectives have in common are the basic building blocks of graphs: **nodes** (also called vertices) and **edges** (links) that connect the nodes.

Types of graphs

We can divide graphs into types based on several attributes. Let's discuss the ones that are the most relevant from the causal point of view.

Undirected versus directed

Directed graphs are graphs with directed edges, while **undirected graphs** have undirected edges. *Figure 4.1* presents an example of a directed and undirected graph:

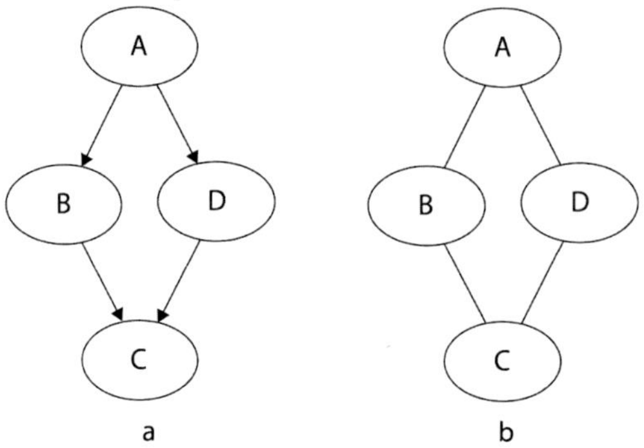

Figure 4.1 – Directed (a) and undirected (b) graphs

As we saw in the previous chapter, we mark the edge direction with an arrow. Lines without arrows denote undirected edges. In the literature, we sometimes also see a line with two arrows (in both directions) to denote an undirected edge or to denote correlation rather than causation (for example, in *structural equation models*).

In certain cases, we might not have full knowledge of the orientation of all the edges in a graph of interest.

When we know all the edges in the graph, but we are unsure about the direction of some of them, we can use **complete partially directed acyclic graphs** (**CPDAGs**) to represent such cases.

CPDAGs are a special case of a broader class of *partially directed* graphs.

We'll see in *Part 3, Causal Discovery,* that some causal discovery methods can in certain cases only recover partial causal structures from the data. Such structures can be encoded as *partially directed* graphs.

In general, you can also see graphs with different types of edges, denoting different types of relations between nodes. This is often the case in knowledge graphs, network science, and in some applications of graph neural networks. In this book, we'll focus almost exclusively on graphs with one edge type.

Cyclic versus acyclic

Cyclic graphs are graphs that allow for loops. In general, loops are paths that lead from a given node to itself. Loops can be direct (from a node to itself; so-called **self-loops**) or indirect (going through other nodes).

Figure 4.2 presents an example of an **acyclic graph** and a cyclic one:

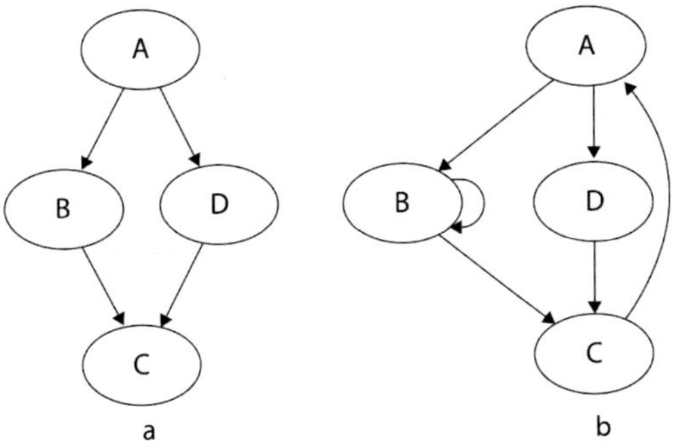

Figure 4.2 – Acyclic (a) and cyclic (b) graphs

The graph on the right side of *Figure 4.2 (b)* contains two types of loops. There's a self-loop between node *B* and itself and there are two other larger loops. Can you find them?

Let's start from *A*. There are two paths we can take. If we move to *B*, we can either stay at *B* (via its self-loop) or move to *C*. From *C*, we can only get back to *A*.

If we move from *A* to *D* instead, this will also lead us to *C* and back to *A* from there.

Most methods that we'll present in this book will assume that the underlying system can be accurately represented by an acyclic graph. That said, there also exist causal methods that support cyclic relationships. We'll discuss them briefly in the last section of this chapter.

Connected versus disconnected

In **connected graphs**, every node has an edge with at least one other node (for example, *Figure 4.3 (a)*). A **fully-connected graph** contains edges between all possible pairs of variables. **Disconnected graphs** contain no edges:

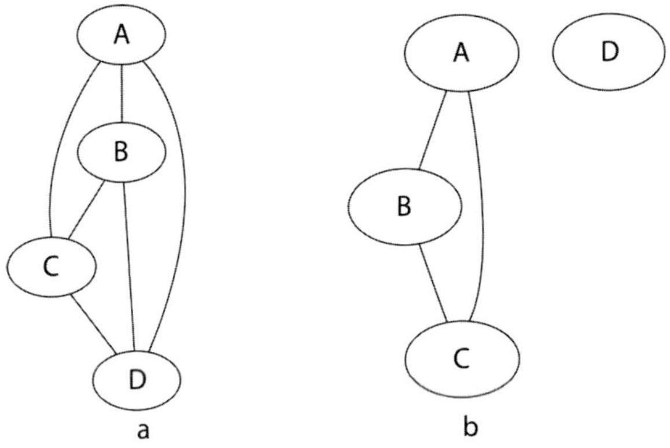

Figure 4.3 – Connected (a) and partially connected (b) graphs

In *Figure 4.3*, we can see a fully-connected graph on the left (*a*) and a partially connected one on the right (*b*). Note that real-world causal graphs are rarely fully connected (that would mean that everything is *directly* causally related to everything else either as a cause or as an effect).

Weighted versus unweighted

Weighted graphs contain additional information on the edges. Each edge is associated with a number (called a **weight**), which may represent the strength of connection between two nodes, distance, or any other metric that is useful in a particular case. In certain cases, weights might be restricted to be positive (for example, when modeling distance). *Unweighted graphs* have no weights on the edges; alternatively, we can see them as a special case of a weighted graph with all edge weights set to 1. In the context of causality, edge weights can encode the strength of the causal effect (note that it will only make sense in the linear case with all the structural equations being linear with no interactions).

Graph representations

Now we're ready to talk about various ways we can represent a graph.

We've seen enough graphs so far to understand how to present them visually. This representation is very intuitive and easy to work with for humans (at least for small graphs), but not very efficient for computers.

People figured out a couple of ways to represent graphs in a computer-readable form. One pretty intuitive way is to represent a graph as a list of nodes and a list of edges. One of the advantages of this method is that it can be easily expanded to add extra information about nodes or edges. It's also relatively human-readable for small graphs. At the same time, it's not very efficient computationally speaking.

To optimize certain types of computations, we can represent a graph as an **adjacency matrix**. This representation preserves the information about the graph structure and – possibly – the strength of connections between the nodes. A limitation of adjacency matrices is that they cannot contain any metadata about nodes or edges, but this can be easily overcome.

Adjacency matrices

An unweighted **adjacency matrix** is a matrix that only contains zeros and ones. One represents an edge, and zero represents a lack of an edge. Nodes are encoded as row and column indices. We usually use zero-indexing, which means that we start counting from zero (we'll refer to the first row of the matrix as the 0th row).

Adjacency matrices are square $M \times M$ matrices where M is the number of nodes. Each positive entry in the matrix encodes an edge between a pair of nodes.

Let's see a couple of examples to make it clearer. We'll start with something very simple:

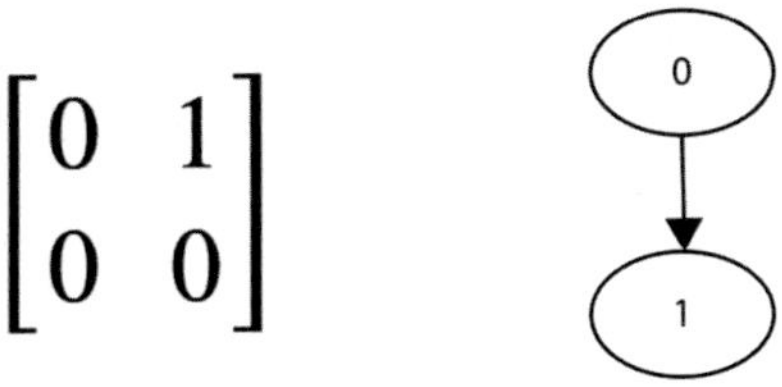

Figure 4.4 – A 2 × 2 adjacency matrix and the corresponding graph

Figure 4.4 presents a 2 × 2 adjacency matrix and its corresponding graph. The only non-zero element (*1*) in the matrix is located in the upper-right corner. Its index is (0, 1) because the element is in the 0th row and the first column. It means that there's only one edge in the graph that goes from node 0 (the row index) to node 1 (the column index). You can verify this in the graph on the right.

Let's see another example:

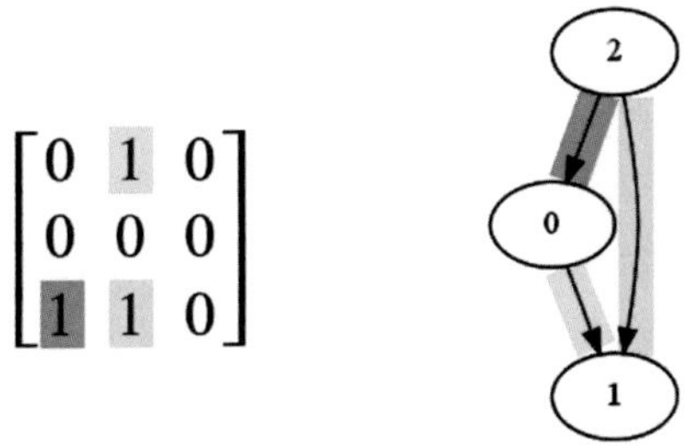

Figure 4.5 – A 3 × 3 adjacency matrix and the corresponding graph

In *Figure 4.5*, we see a 3 × 3 adjacency matrix with three non-zero entries. Their respective indices are (0, 1), (2, 0), and (2, 1). This translates to three edges: from node 0 to node 1, from node 2 to node 0, and from node 2 to node 1.

You can see the respective edges in the corresponding graph. We added color-coding to make the correspondence between the matrix and the graph easier to identify.

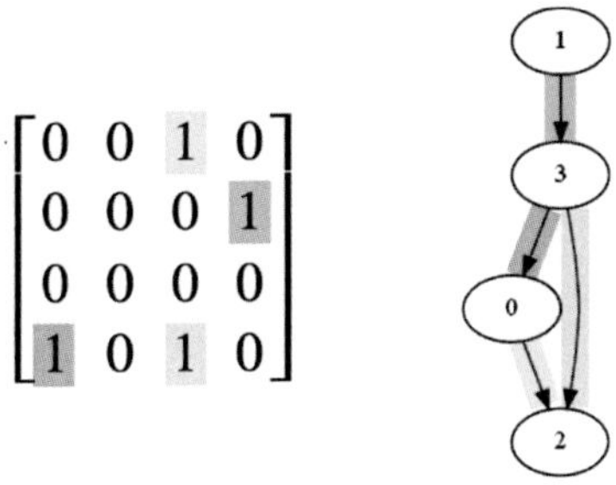

Figure 4.6 – A 4 × 4 adjacency matrix and the corresponding graph

Figure 4.6 presents a larger 4 × 4 matrix and the corresponding 4-node graph:

There are four 1-entries that translate to four edges in the graph: from 0 to 2, from 1 to 3, from 3 to 0, and from 3 to 2. The non-zero entries in the matrix and the respective edges are color-coded for your convenience.

Directed and acyclic

Have you noticed that all the matrices in our examples had *zeros on the diagonal*?

This is not by accident. All the preceding matrices represent valid *DAGs* – a type of graph with no cycles and with directed edges only.

How is it related to the values on the diagonal?

Any diagonal entry in a matrix will have an index in the (i, i) form, denoting an edge from node i to itself.

In other words, any 1-entry on the diagonal would denote a self-loop.

This means that a valid *DAG* should always have *zeros on the diagonal*. Self-loops, represented by ones in the diagonal would lead to cyclicity and DAGs are acyclic by definition.

If you're familiar with matrix linear algebra, you might have thought that the fact that a matrix has only zeros in the diagonal provides us with important information about its trace and eigenvalues.

That's great intuition!

This idea is leveraged by some of the **causal discovery** methods to make sure that a graph that we're trying to find is a valid DAG. We'll learn more about these methods in *Part 3, Causal Discovery*.

Graphs in Python

Now we're ready for some practice.

There are many options to define graphs in Python and we're going to practice two of them: using **graph modeling language** (**GML**) and using adjacency matrices. *Figure 4.7* presents a GML definition of a three-node graph with two edges and the resulting graph. The code from *Figure 4.7* and the remaining part of this section is available in the notebook for *Chapter 4* in the *Graphs in Python* section (`https://bit.ly/causal-ntbk-04`):

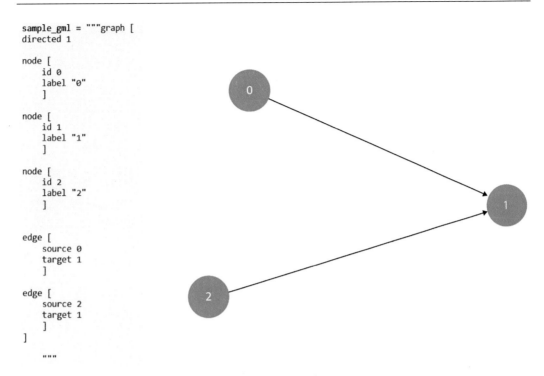

```
sample_gml = """graph [
directed 1

node [
    id 0
    label "0"
    ]

node [
    id 1
    label "1"
    ]

node [
    id 2
    label "2"
    ]


edge [
    source 0
    target 1
    ]

edge [
    source 2
    target 1
    ]
]
    """
```

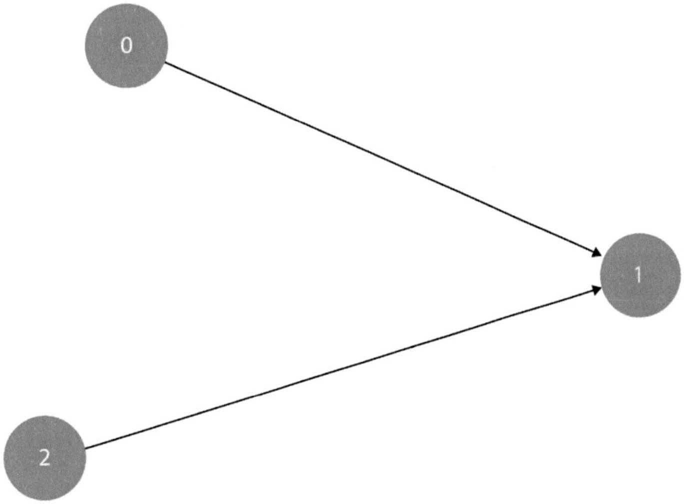

Figure 4.7 – GML definition of a graph and the resulting graph

> **Graph languages in Python**
>
> The GML language is supported by the NetworkX and DoWhy Python libraries. More details on GML and its syntax can be found here: `https://bit.ly/GMLDocs`.
>
> Another popular graph language is DOT. A dedicated Python library called `pydot` (`https://bit.ly/PyDOTDocs`) allows you to easily read, write, and manipulate DOT graphs in pure Python. DOT is used by `graphviz` and can be used with NetworkX and DoWhy.

GML syntax can be parsed using the NetworkX `parse_gml()` function, which returns a `networkx.classes.digraph.DiGraph` instance (*digraph* is shorthand for *directed graph*). The usage is very simple:

```
graph = nx.parse_gml(sample_gml)
```

GML is pretty flexible, but also pretty verbose. Let's define the same graph using an adjacency matrix:

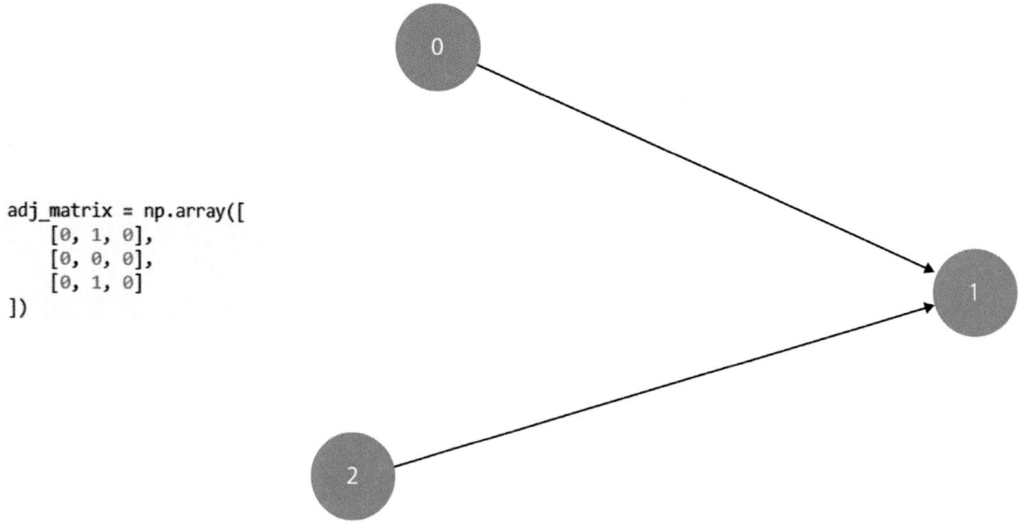
adj_matrix = np.array([
[0, 1, 0],
[0, 0, 0],
[0, 1, 0]
])
0
1
2

Figure 4.8 – Adjacency matrix of a graph and the resulting graph

Figure 4.8 presents an adjacency matrix created using NumPy and the resulting graph. As you can see, this definition is much more compact. It's also directly usable (without additional parsing) by many algorithms. To build a NetworkX graph from an adjacency matrix, we need just one line of code:

```
graph = nx.DiGraph(adj_matrix)
```

By using `nx.DiGraph`, we tell NetworkX that we want to get a directed graph. To create an undirected one, use the `nx.Graph` object.

To get some practice, create the following graph using GML and an adjacency matrix yourself and visualize it using NetworkX:

- Directed acyclic graph
- Six nodes
- Six edges: (0, 1), (0, 3), (0, 5), (3, 2), (2, 4), (4, 5)

You should get a result similar to the one presented in *Figure 4.9*:

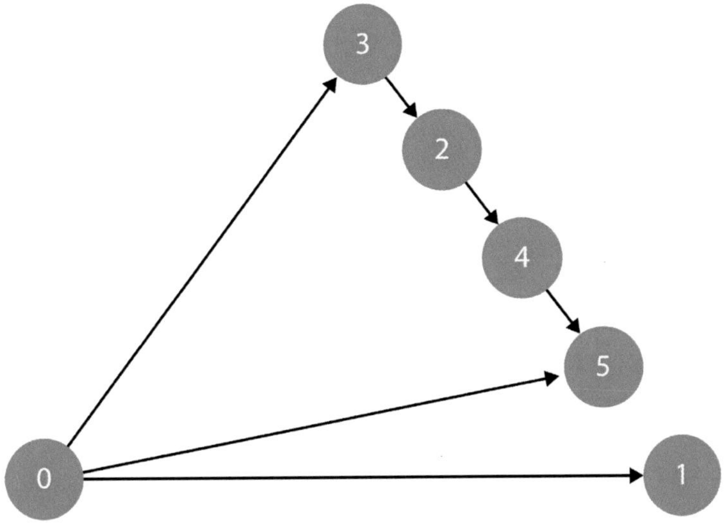

Figure 4.9 – The resulting graph

In this section, we discussed various types of graphs. We learned what a DAG is and how to construct it in Python. We've seen that graphs can be represented in many different ways and used two of these ways (*GML* and *adjacency matrices*) to build our own graphs. We're now ready to discuss graphical models.

What is a graphical model?

In this section, we're going to discuss what **graphical causal models** (**GCMs**) are and how they can help in causal inference and discovery.

GCMs can be seen as a useful framework that integrates probabilistic, structural, and graphical aspects of causal inference.

Formally speaking, we can define a graphical causal model as a set consisting of a graph and a set of functions that induce a joint distribution over the variables in the model (Peters et al., 2017).

The basic building blocks of GCM graphs are the same as the basic elements of any directed graph: nodes and directed edges. In a GCM, each node is associated with a variable.

Importantly, in GCMs, edges have a strictly causal interpretation, so that $A \rightarrow B$ means that A causes B (this is one of the differentiating factors between causal models and Bayesian networks; Pearl & Mackenzie, 2019, pp. 111-113). GCMs are very powerful because certain combinations of nodes and edges can reveal important information about the data. In other words, the sheer graph structure is in some cases enough to decode information about statistical relationships between variables.

This also works in the other direction – in certain cases, we can infer the true causal graph structure by looking at the statistical relationships alone. The latter is possible when a special assumption called the **faithfulness assumption** and some other conditions are met. Although *faithfulness* seems a relatively light assumption on face value, a deeper examination reveals underlying challenges (Uhler et al., 2013). We'll learn more about faithfulness in *Chapter 5*.

These properties of GCMs are the basis of many causal inference and discovery methods and can also be leveraged for *domain adaptation* even in the presence of unobserved confounders (Magliacane et al., 2018) – a flexible and very practical extension of the causal discovery toolbox.

To summarize, GCMs can be seen as a useful and powerful framework that unifies probabilistic, structural, and graphical perspectives on causal inference. GCMs are powerful because they offer the possibility to translate between the graphical properties of a model and the statistical properties of the data.

All that said, definitions of GCMs are not entirely consistent in the literature. In most places in this book, we'll talk about SCMs as consisting of a graph and a set of functional assignments. This will allow us to avoid the confusion related to the inconsistencies in the literature, while preserving the most important elements of the graphical and functional representations.

Now, let's solidify our knowledge of DAGs.

DAG your pardon? Directed acyclic graphs in the causal wonderland

We'll start this section by reviewing definitions of causality. Then, we'll discuss the motivations behind DAGs and their limitations. Finally, we'll formalize the concept of a DAG.

Definitions of causality

In the first chapter, we discussed a couple of historical definitions of causality. We started with Aristotle, then we briefly covered the ideas proposed by David Hume. We've seen that Hume's definition (as we presented it) was focused on associations. This led us to look into how babies learn about the world using experimentation. We've seen how experimentation allows us to go beyond the realm of observations by interacting with the environment. The possibility of interacting with the environment is at the heart of another definition of causality that comes from Judea Pearl.

Pearl proposed something very simple yet powerful. His definition is short, ignores ontological complexities of causality, and is pretty actionable. It goes as follows: *A* causes *B* if *B listens* to *A* (Pearl & Mackenzie, 2019).

What does it mean that one variable *listens* to another? In Pearlian terms, it means that if we change *A*, we also observe a change in *B*.

The concept of a change in one variable leading to a change in another one is inherently related to the logic of interventions. Let's see what happens when we combine this definition with the idea of a DAG.

DAGs and causality

Visualize a simple DAG: $A \rightarrow B \rightarrow C$. Now imagine that we perform an intervention on node B and now the value of B entirely depends on our decision.

In such a case, we expect that C will change its value accordingly, as *C listens to B*.

On the other hand, under the intervention, A will no longer influence B, because our intervention fully controls the value of B. To reflect this in the graph, we remove the edge from A to B.

The operation of removing the incoming edges from a node that we intervene upon is sometimes referred to as graph mutilation.

Graph mutilation is an intuitive way of presenting the impact of intervention and it reveals a deep insight – that an intervention changes the structure of information flow between variables.

The good news is that we don't always need interventions to alter the information flow in the data. If we know which paths in the graph should remain open and which should be closed, we can leverage the power of **d-separation** and statistical control to close and open the paths in the graph, which will allow us to describe causal quantities in purely statistical terms under certain conditions. Moreover, in some scenarios, it will allow us to learn the structure of the data-generating process from the data generated by this process. We'll learn more about d-separation in *Chapter 6*, and more about learning the structure of the data-generating process in *Part 3, Causal Discovery*.

Before we continue, let's formally define DAGs.

Let's get formal!

DAG G consists of a set of vertices V and a set of directed edges E. Each node V_i is associated with a random variable X_i. Let's denote an edge from a vertex i to another vertex j as $i \rightarrow j$. We call V_i a **parent** of V_j and we call V_j a **child** of V_i. For any directed path $i \rightarrow \ldots \rightarrow j$, with $k \in \mathbb{Z}_0^+$ (non-negative) vertices between i and j, we call V_i an **ancestor** of V_j and we call V_j a **descendant** of V_i. Note that because $k \geq 0$, parents are a special case of ancestors and children are a special case of descendants.

By definition, in a DAG, there are no paths that start at vertex i that lead back to vertex i (either directly or indirectly).

Limitations of DAGs

DAGs seem to capture certain intuitions about causality really well. My best guess is that most people would agree that talking about the direction of causal influence makes sense (can you think of *undirected causality*?). At the same time, I believe that fewer people would agree that causal influence cannot be cyclic. Let's see an example.

Imagine an interaction between two partners. One partner says something at time t_0, the other partner responds at time t_1. We could build a simple model of a conversation between the partners in the following way:

$$P_{X=1}(t_j) := f(P_{X=2}(t_{j-1}), I_{X=1}(t_{j-1}))$$

$$P_{X=2}(t_{j+1}) := f(P_{X=1}(t_j), I_{X=2}(t_j))$$

In the preceding formula, $P_X(t_j)$ is partner *X*'s utterance at time t_j, I_X is partner *X*'s internal state at time t_j, and $f(.)$ is some function (for the sake of this example, we don't care what function exactly).

To be precise, we should also model changes in I_X (internal states of partners), but we'll leave it out for simplicity.

If we run these equations sequentially for a number of steps, we'll see that what partner 1 said at time t_j will become dependent on what they said at time t_{j-2}.

The same is true for partner 2. This constitutes an (indirect) cycle.

Another example – perhaps more intuitive for some readers – comes from the field of economics. When demand for product *P* grows, the producer might increase the supply in the hope of collecting potential profits from the market. Increased supply might cause a price drop, which in turn can increase demand further.

Theoretically, we could try to model both examples as an *unrolled* sequence of variables, but there are potential problems with this approach. The main one is that we need to produce a new variable for each timestep, creating a very inefficient representation.

Taking a more general perspective, causal DAGs in particular, and SCMs in general, have limitations. As expressed by Peters and colleagues: SCMs are an "abstraction of underlying physical processes – abstraction whose domain of validity as causal models is limited" (Peters et al., 2017). That said, SCMs (but not DAGs) can be adapted to work with cycles (e.g. Mooji & Classen, 2020).

Sources of causal graphs in the real world

We have discussed graphs from several perspectives now, yet we haven't tackled an important practical question: what is the source of causal graphs in the real world?

In this section, we'll provide a brief overview of such sources and we'll leave a more detailed discussion for *Part 3* of the book.

On a high level, we can group the ways of obtaining causal graphs into three classes:

- Causal discovery
- Expert knowledge
- A combination of both

Let's discuss them briefly.

Causal discovery

Causal discovery and **causal structure learning** are umbrella terms for various kinds of methods used to uncover causal structure from observational or interventional data. We devote the entirety of *Part 3* of this book to this topic.

Expert knowledge

Expert knowledge is a term covering various types of knowledge that can help define or disambiguate causal relations between two or more variables. Depending on the context, expert knowledge might refer to knowledge from randomized controlled trials, laws of physics, a broad scope of experiences in a given area, and more.

Combining causal discovery and expert knowledge

Some causal discovery algorithms allow us to easily incorporate expert knowledge as a priority. This means that we can either *freeze* certain edges in the graph or *suggest* the existence or direction of these edges. We will discuss some such approaches in *Part 3* of the book.

Extra – is there causality beyond DAGs?

In this extra section, we'll give a brief overview of some non-DAG-based approaches to causality. This is definitely an incomplete and somehow subjective guide.

Dynamical systems

The scenario with two interacting partners that we discussed in the previous section describes a dynamical system. This particular example is inspired by the research by an American ex-rabbi turned psychologist called John Gottman, who studies human romantic relationships from a dynamical systems point of view (for an overview: Gottman & Notarius, 2000; Gottman et al., 1999).

Dynamical systems are often described using differential equations and cannot be solved analytically (for a toy example of differential equations applied to romantic relationships, check Strogatz, 1988).

Dynamical systems have been extensively studied in physics (Strogatz, 2018), biology (Cosentino & Bates, 2011), and psychology (Nowak & Vallacher, 1998), among other fields.

The dynamical approach is closely related to non-linear dynamics, simulation, chaos theory, and complexity science. Research in these fields is often focused on system-level effects rather than interactions between single variables. An important concept in complexity science is **emergence** – a phenomenon in which we can observe certain properties at the system level that cannot be observed at its constituent parts' level. This property is sometimes described as a *system being more than the sum of its parts.*

Cyclic SCMs

Because SCMs constitute a very useful framework for causal inference, there are many attempts to generalize it to cyclic cases. For instance, Forré, & Mooij (2017) proposed σ-separation – a generalization of d-separation for cyclical systems. Moreover, the same authors presented a causal discovery algorithm that not only works with cycles, but can also handle latent confounders (Forré, & Mooij, 2018). Interestingly, Mooij & Classen (2020) showed that **FCI** (which stands for **fast causal inference**) – a popular causal discovery algorithm – also gives correct results for data generated with cyclical systemsunder certain circumstances.

Wrapping it up

We started this chapter by refreshing our knowledge of graphs and learned how to build simple graphs using Python and the NetworkX library. We introduced GCMs and DAGs and discussed some common limitations and challenges that we might face when using them.

Finally, we examined selected approaches to model causal systems with cycles.

Now you have the ability to translate between the visual representation of a graph and an adjacency matrix. The basic DAG toolkit that we've discussed in this chapter will allow you to work smoothly with many causal inference and causal discovery tools and will help you represent your own problems as graphs, which can bring a lot of clarity – even in your work with traditional (non-causal) machine learning.

The knowledge you gained in this chapter will be critical to understanding the next chapter and the next two parts of this book. Feel free to review this chapter anytime you need.

In the next chapter, we'll learn how to use basic graphical structures to understand the fundamental mechanics of causal inference and causal discovery.

References

Cosentino, C., & Bates, D. (2011). *Feedback control in systems biology*. CRC Press.

Forré, P., & Mooij, J. M. (2017). *Markov properties for graphical models with cycles and latent variables*. arXiv preprint arXiv:1710.08775.

Forré, P., & Mooij, J. M. (2018). *Constraint-based causal discovery for non-linear structural causal models with cycles and latent confounders*. arXiv preprint arXiv:1807.03024.

Gottman, J. M., & Notarius, C. I. (2000). *Decade review: Observing marital interaction*. Journal of marriage and family, 62(4), 927-947.

Gottman, J., Swanson, C., & Murray, J. (1999). *The mathematics of marital conflict: Dynamic mathematical nonlinear modeling of newlywed marital interaction*. Journal of Family Psychology, 13(1), 3.

Magliacane, S., Van Ommen, T., Claassen, T., Bongers, S., Versteeg, P., & Mooij, J. M. (2018). *Domain adaptation by using causal inference to predict invariant conditional distributions*. Advances in neural information processing systems, 31.

Mooij, J. M., & Claassen, T. (2020). *Constraint-based causal discovery using partial ancestral graphs in the presence of cycles*. In Conference on Uncertainty in Artificial Intelligence (pp. 1159-1168). PMLR.

Nowak, A., & Vallacher, R. R. (1998). *Dynamical social psychology* (Vol. 647). Guilford Press.

Pearl, J., & Mackenzie, D. (2019). *The book of why*. Penguin Books.

Peters, J., Janzing, D., & Schölkopf, B. (2017). *Elements of Causal Inference: Foundations and Learning Algorithms*. MIT Press.

Strogatz, S. H. (1988). Love affairs and differential equations. *Mathematics Magazine, 61*(1), 35-35.

Strogatz, S. H. (2018). *Nonlinear dynamics and chaos: with applications to physics, biology, chemistry, and engineering*. CRC Press.

Uhler, C., Raskutti, G., Bühlmann, P., & Yu, B. (2013). Geometry of the faithfulness assumption in causal inference. *The Annals of Statistics*, 436-463.

5

Forks, Chains, and Immoralities

Welcome to Chapter 5!

In the previous chapter, we discussed the basic characteristics of graphs and showed how to use graphs to build graphical models. In this chapter, we will dive deeper into graphical models and discover their powerful features.

We'll start with a brief introduction to the mapping between distributions and graphs. Next, we'll learn about three basic graphical structures – forks, chains, and colliders – and their properties.

Finally, we'll use a simple linear example to show in practice how the graphical properties of a system can translate to its statistical properties.

The material discussed in this chapter will provide us with a solid foundation for understanding classic causal inference and *constraint-based* discovery methods and will prepare us for understanding other families of algorithms that we'll introduce in *Parts 2* and *3* of this book.

In this chapter, we cover the following key topics:

- Graphs and distributions and how to map between them
- Forks, chains, and colliders or…immoralities
- Forks, chains, colliders, and regression

Graphs and distributions and how to map between them

In this section, we will focus on the mappings between the statistical and graphical properties of a system.

To be more precise, we'll be interested in understanding how to translate between graphical and statistical independencies. In a perfect world, we'd like to be able to do it in both directions: from graph independence to statistical independence and the other way around.

It turns out that this is possible under certain assumptions.

The key concept in this chapter is one of *independence*. Let's start by reviewing what it means.

How to talk about independence

Generally speaking, we say that two variables, X and Y, are independent when our knowledge about X does not change our knowledge about Y (and vice versa). In terms of probability distributions, we can express it in the following way:

$$P(Y) = P(Y|X)$$

$$P(X) = P(X|Y)$$

In other words: the marginal probability of Y is the same as the conditional probability of Y given X and – respectively – the marginal probability of X is the same as the conditional probability of X given Y.

In plain English: learning something new about X will not change our beliefs about Y (and the other way around).

Probabilities and beliefs

You might have noticed that we talk about "knowledge" and "beliefs" in the context of probability here. This vocabulary is usually associated with the Bayesian approach to probability (as opposed to the frequentist approach). We use the Bayesian approach here because we believe it brings a more intuitive perspective on independence. At the same time, we use both frequentist and Bayesian concepts in this book (and discuss them where we believe it's important). Bayesian and frequentist are two different approaches to statistics. They converge to virtually identical results in large sample sizes but put accents slightly differently (e.g., we can sensibly talk about *beliefs* in the Bayesian framework but not really in the frequentist framework).

For an introduction to some of the fundamental differences between the two approaches, check out Jake VanderPlas' talk (`https://bit.ly/BayesianVsFrequentsist`). For slightly more formal treatment, check out the **Massachusetts Institute of Technology** (**MIT**) course notes PDF (`https://bit.ly/BayesVsFreqMIT`).

One interesting consequence of the independence between two variables is that their joint distribution factorizes into the product of the marginals (Bishop, 2006):

$$P(X, Y) = P(X)P(Y)$$

More general notation for independence involves the symbol, $\perp\!\!\!\perp$ (usually called *double up tack*), whose form visually encodes the notion of orthogonality (`https://bit.ly/OrthogonalityMath`). Using $\perp\!\!\!\perp$, we can express the fact that X and Y are independent in the following way:

$$X \perp\!\!\!\perp Y$$

The concept of independence plays a vital role in statistics and causality. As we will learn soon, its generalization – **conditional independence** – is even more important. We say that X and Y are conditionally independent given Z, when X does not give us any new information about Y assuming that we observed Z.

Let's see how to encode *conditional independence* using the notation we just introduced.

We can express the fact that X is independent of Y given Z in the following way:

$$X \perp\!\!\!\perp Y|Z$$

Equivalently, in terms of probabilities:

$$P(X, Y|Z) = P(X|Z)P(Y|Z)$$

Note that we factorized the joint distribution of X and Y (given Z) into a product of two simple conditionals ($X|Z$ and $Y|Z$) using the property introduced earlier ($P(X, Y) = P(X)P(Y)$).

Now, let's introduce a simple yet useful distinction. We will use the symbol, $\perp\!\!\!\perp_P$, to denote *independence in the distribution* and $\perp\!\!\!\perp_G$ to denote *independence in the graph*. To say that X and Y are independent in their distributions, we'll use the following:

$$X \perp\!\!\!\perp_P Y$$

On the other hand, to say that X and Y are independent in the graph, we'll say:

$$X \perp\!\!\!\perp_G Y$$

Equipped with this new shiny notation, let's discuss why mapping between graphical and distributional independence might be important to us.

Choosing the right direction

The basic goal of *causal inference* is to estimate the causal effect of one set of variables on another. In most cases, to do it accurately, we need to know which variables we should control for. We've seen in previous chapters that to accurately control for confounders, we need to go beyond the realm of pure statistics and use the information about the data-generating process, which can be encoded as a (causal) graph. In this sense, the ability to translate between graphical and statistical properties is central to causal inference.

Having the translation ability in the other direction – from statistical to graphical properties – is essential for *causal discovery*, a process that aims at recreating the causal graph from observational and/or interventional data.

To enable the mappings in both directions, we need to meet certain criteria. Let's revise them.

Independence in a graph – a working definition

We say that two nodes are *unconditionally* (or marginally) *independent* in the graph when there's *no open path* that connects them *directly* or *indirectly*.

We say that two nodes, X and Y, are *conditionally independent* given (a set of) node(s) Z when Z blocks *all open paths* that connect X and Y.

In other words, (in)dependence in the graph is a function of open paths between nodes in this graph. We'll use and enrich this intuition in the current chapter and build a more formal perspective on top of it in *Chapter 6*.

Conditions and assumptions

We'll start the discussion with assumptions that are important from the causal *inference* point of view. After this, we'll move to assumptions related to causal *discovery*, and we'll finish with a brief overview of a more general concept of causal sufficiency.

Conditions for causal inference

From the *causal inference* point of view, we need to make sure that we can map the graphical (conditional) independencies into statistical (conditional) independencies.

In order to achieve this we need to satisfy the **causal Markov condition** (also known as the *causal Markov assumption* or *(local) Markov property*).

The *causal Markov condition* states that the node, V_i, is independent of all its non-descendants (excluding its parents) given its parents. Therefore, formally, it can be presented as follows:

$$V_i \perp\!\!\!\perp_G V_j \,\middle|\, PA(V_i) \;\forall_{j \neq i \in G(V,E) \setminus \{DE(V_i),\, PA(V_i)\}}$$

This formula might look discouraging, but in fact, it says something relatively simple. Let's dissect and analyze it step by step:

- We start with $V_i \perp\!\!\!\perp_G V_j$. The symbol, $\perp\!\!\!\perp_G$, denotes independence in the graph. Therefore, the statement says that nodes, V_i and V_j, are independent in the graph or – in other words – that there are no open paths between them.

Next, we have the conditioning bar, $|$, and $PA(V_i)$. The latter stands for *parents of node* V_i. These are all the nodes that have edges *directed at* V_i. This conditioning part of the formula informs us that the independence between V_i and V_j only holds when we control for (the set of) parents of the node, V_i.

Next, we have $\forall_{j \neq i \in G(V,E)}$. The $\forall$ symbol means "*for all*". What we say here is that the node, V_i, is independent of all other nodes ($j \neq i$) in the graph $G(V, E)$, where G represents our graph (**directed acyclic graph** (**DAG**)) of interest, V is a set of all vertices (nodes) in this graph, and E is a set of all edges in this graph.

Finally, we have the cryptic $\setminus\{DE(V_i), PA(V_i)\}$. Let's start with the \ symbol. We read it as "*excluding*". Curly brackets denote a set, and we have two elements in this set:

- $DE(V_i)$, which represents a set of all *descendants* of the node, V_i
- $PA(V_i)$, which represents a set of *parents* of V_i

Putting it all together: the node, V_i, is independent of all other nodes in the graph, G, excluding the *descendants* and *parents* of this node, given its *parents*. If this is not entirely clear to you at this stage, that's perfectly fine. We'll reiterate this concept while discussing **d-separation** in the next chapter.

In the meantime, feel free to take a look at *Figure 5.1* and *Figure 5.2*, which depict two examples of graphs in which the causal Markov condition holds. In both cases controlling for $PA(V_i)$ – the parent node of the node, V_i, removes the association between nodes V_i and V_j. Note that the relationships between V_i and V_j are different in both figures. In *Figure 5.1*, the nodes, V_i and V_j, have a common cause ($PA(V_i)$), in *Figure 5.2*, the node, V_j is a grandparent of V_i. If the causal Markov condition holds, the association between the nodes V_i and V_j should be removed in both cases. Note that if there was an unobserved common cause of both nodes (V_i and V_j) in any of the scenarios, controlling for $PA(V_i)$ would not render the nodes independent, and the condition would be violated:

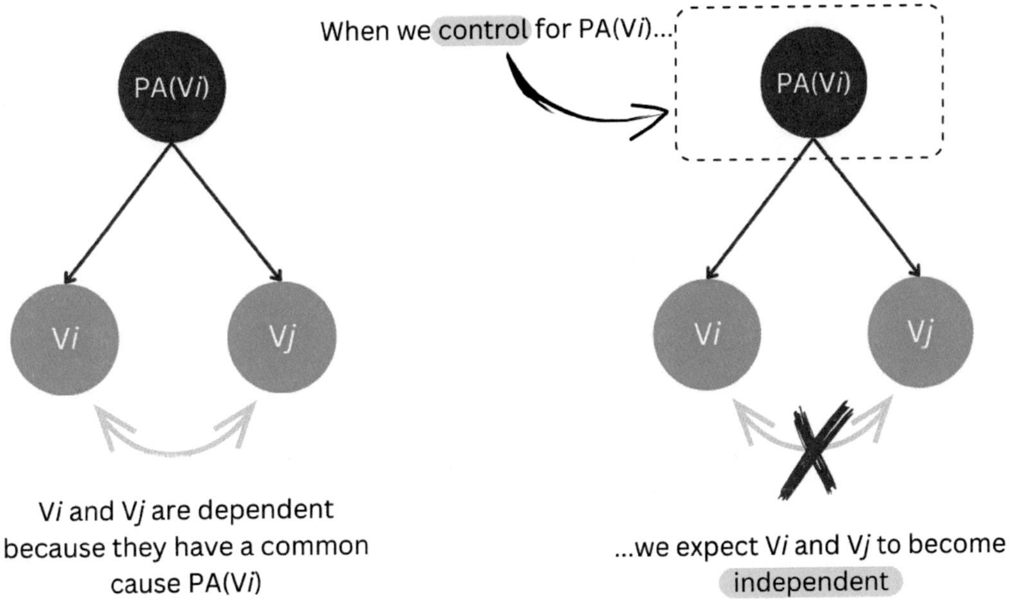

Figure 5.1 – Causal Markov condition – example one

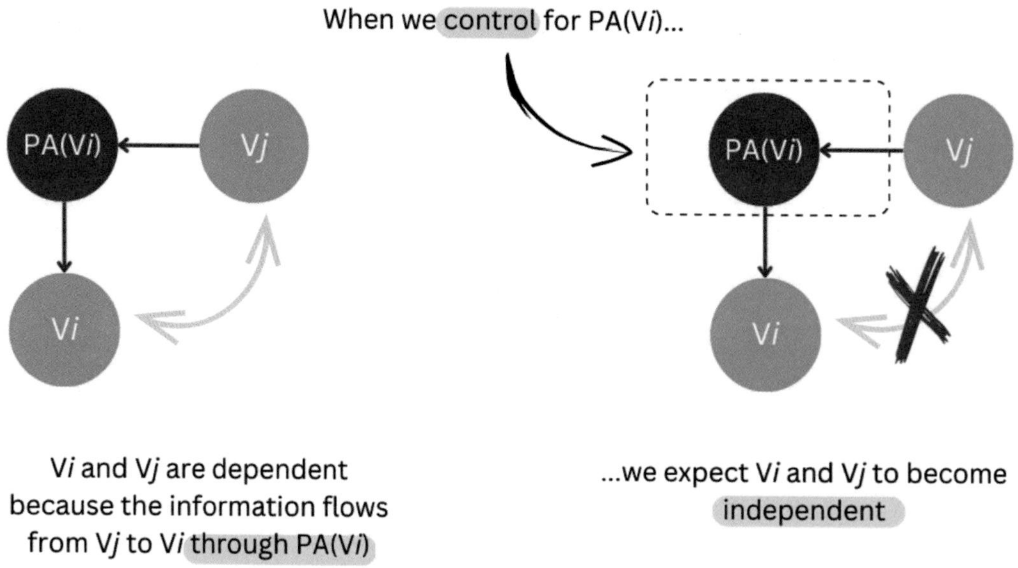

Figure 5.2 – Causal Markov condition – example two

The important statement is that when the causal Markov condition holds, the following is true:

$$X \perp\!\!\!\perp_G Y|Z \Rightarrow X \perp\!\!\!\perp_P Y|Z$$

We read it as: X and Y are independent in the graph given Z, then they are also statistically independent given Z. This is known as the **global Markov property**. In fact, we could show that the *global Markov property*, the *local Markov property*, and another property called the *Markov factorization property* are equivalent (Lauritzen 1996, pp. 51-52 for a formal proof; Peters et al., 2017, pp. 101 for an overview).

Assumptions for causal discovery

So far, we have discussed the importance of mapping between graphical and distributional independence structures. Now, let's reverse the direction. Causal discovery aims at discovering (or learning) the true causal graph from observational and/or (partially) interventional data. In general, this task is difficult. Nonetheless, it's possible when certain conditions are met.

Causal discovery has a couple of different flavors. In this section, we'll focus on a family of methods called **constrain-based causal discovery** (sometimes also called **independence-based causal discovery**). These methods are designed to find statistical independencies in the observational data and try to recreate the true causal graph from these independencies. One of the main assumptions behind this family of methods is called the **faithfulness assumption**. Its simplest formulation is the following:

$$X \perp\!\!\!\perp_P Y|Z \Rightarrow X \perp\!\!\!\perp_G Y|Z$$

This might look familiar. Note that it's the exact reverse of the global Markov property that we discussed in the previous section. The formula says that if X and Y are independent in the distribution given Z, they will also be independent in the graph given Z.

As we mentioned in the previous chapter, the faithfulness assumption might be difficult to fulfill sometimes. The most critical reason for this is the estimation error when testing for conditional independence in the finite sample size regime (Uhler et al., 2013). Moreover, it's not very difficult to find situations where the assumption is violated. Intuitively, any situation where one variable influences another through two different paths and these paths cancel each other out completely would lead to the violation of *faithfulness*. That said, although it's relatively easy to come up with such examples (for example, Neal, 2020, pp. 100-101; Peters et al., 2017, pp. 107-108), the probability of encountering them in the real world is very small (Sprites et al., 2000, pp. 68-69). Therefore, the first problem is much more serious and more difficult to tackle in practice than the second one.

The last assumption that we will discuss in this section is called the **causal minimality condition** (also known as the **causal minimality assumption**).

Although the *global Markov property* that we discussed earlier is pretty powerful, it leaves us with some uncertainty regarding the true structure of a graph we're trying to retrieve.

It turns out that there might be more than one graph that entails the same distribution! That's problematic when we want to recover causal structure (represented as a causal graph) because the mapping between the graph and the distribution is ambiguous. To address this issue, we use the causal minimality condition.

The causal minimality assumption states that DAG G is minimal to distribution, P, if and only if G induces P, but no proper sub-graph of G induces P. In other words, if graph G induces P, removing *any* edge from G should result in a distribution that is different than P.

Causal minimality can be seen from various perspectives (Neal, 2020, pp. 21-22; Pearl, 2009, p. 46; Peters & Schölkopf, 2017, pp. 107-108). Although the assumption is usually perceived as a form of *Ockham's razor*, its implications have practical significance for constraint-based causal discovery methods and their ability to recover correct causal structures.

Other assumptions

Before we conclude this section, let's discuss one more important assumption that is very commonly used in causal discovery and causal inference. It's an assumption of **no hidden confounding** (sometimes also referred to as **causal sufficiency**). Although meeting this assumption is not necessary for *all* causal methods, it's pretty common.

Note that causal sufficiency and the causal Markov condition are related (and have some practical overlap), but they are not identical. For further details, check out Scheines (1996).

In many real-world scenarios, we might find it challenging to verify whether hidden confounding exists in a system of interest.

In this section, we reviewed the concept of statistical and graphical independence, discussed the motivations for mapping between graphical and statistical independencies, and examined conditions that allow us to perform such mappings.

Now, let's discuss three basic graphical structures that are immensely helpful in determining sets of conditional independencies.

Ready?

Chains, forks, and colliders or...immoralities

On a sunny morning of June 1, 2020, Mr. Huang was driving his gleaming white Tesla on one of Taiwan's main highways. The day was clear, and the trip was going smoothly. Mr. Huang engaged the autopilot and set the speed to 110 km/h. While approaching the road's 268-kilometer mark, he was completely unaware that only 300 meters ahead, something unexpected was awaiting him. Nine minutes earlier, another driver, Mr. Yeh, had lost control of his vehicle. His white truck was now overturned, almost fully blocking two lanes of the highway right at the 268.3-kilometer mark.

Around 11 seconds later, to Mr. Huang's dismay, his Tesla crashed into the overturned truck's rooftop. Fortunately, the driver, Mr. Huang, survived the crash and came out of the accident without any serious injuries (Everington, 2020).

A chain of events

Many modern cars are equipped with some sort of collision warning or collision prevention system. At a high level, a system like this consists of a detector (or detector module) and an alerting system (sometimes also an automatic driving assistance system). When there's an obstacle on the collision course detected by the detector, it sends a signal that activates the alerting system. Let's say that the detector is in state 1 when it detects an obstacle and it's in state 0 when it detects no obstacles.

Figure 5.3 presents a DAG representing our collision warning system:

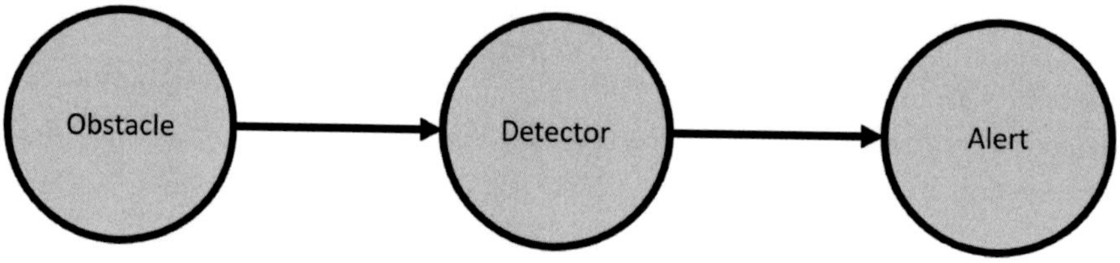

Figure 5.3 – A DAG representing a collision warning system

An important fact about a system such as the one presented in *Figure 5.3* is that the existence of the obstacle does not give us any new information about the alert when we know the detector state. The obstacle and the alert are *independent, given the detector state.*

In other words, when the detector *thinks* there is a pedestrian in front of the car, the alarm will set off even if there's no pedestrian in front of the car. Similarly, if there's an obstacle on the road and the detector does not recognize it as an obstacle, the alert will remain silent.

In particular, if a detector is based on a computer vision system and the model *hallucinates* a pedestrian on the car's course, the alert will set off. On the other hand, when there's a real pedestrian in front of the car and the model fails to recognize them, the alert will remain silent.

An example of an unexpected detector system behavior went viral in August 2022. A TikToker, RealRusty, shared a video showing how his car's object detection system reacted to a horse-drawn carriage (`https://bit.ly/HorseVsTesla`).

Another great example of a chain of causally-linked events comes from Judea Pearl's and Dana Mackenzie's *The Book of Why* (Pearl & Mackenzie, 2019, pp. 113-114). The authors discuss the mechanics of a fire alarm. The chain is *fire → smoke → alarm* because the alarm is actually controlled by a smoke particle detector rather than any other indicator of fire such as temperature.

Let's abstract the structure that these two examples share.

Chains

First, let's replace the variables in the graph from *Figure 5.3* with *A*, *B*, and *C*. This general structure is called a **chain**, and you can see it in *Figure 5.4*:

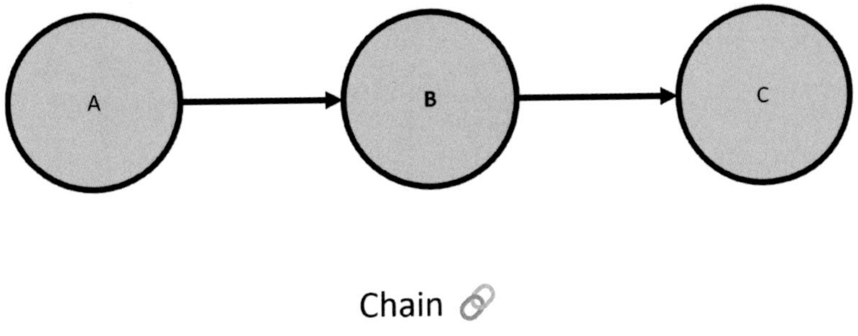

Figure 5.4 – A chain structure

We can generalize the independence property from our collision warning example to *all* chain structures. It means that in every structure that can be encoded as $A \rightarrow B \rightarrow C$, *A* and *C* are independent in the graph given *B*. Therefore, formally, it can be presented as follows:

$$A \perp\!\!\!\perp_G C \mid B$$

Intuitively, controlling for *B* closes the only open path that exists between *A* and *C*. Note that *A* and *C* become *dependent* when we *do not* control for *B*.

Translating this back to our object detection system: if we do not observe the detector state, the presence of the obstacle within the system's range becomes correlated with the safety response (alarm and emergency breaking).

You might already see where it's going. If we're able to fulfill the assumptions that we discussed in the previous section (causal Markov condition, no hidden confounding), we can now predict conditional independence structure in the data from the graph structure itself (and if that's true we can also figure out which variables we should control for in our model to obtain valid causal effect estimates(!) – we'll learn more on this in the next chapter). Moreover, predicting the graph structure from the observational data alone also becomes an option. That's an exciting possibility, but let's take it slowly.

Now, let's see what happens if we change the direction of one of the edges in our *chain* structure.

Forks

Figure 5.5 represents a **fork**. A fork is a structure where the edge between nodes *A* and *B* is reversed compared to the *chain* structure:

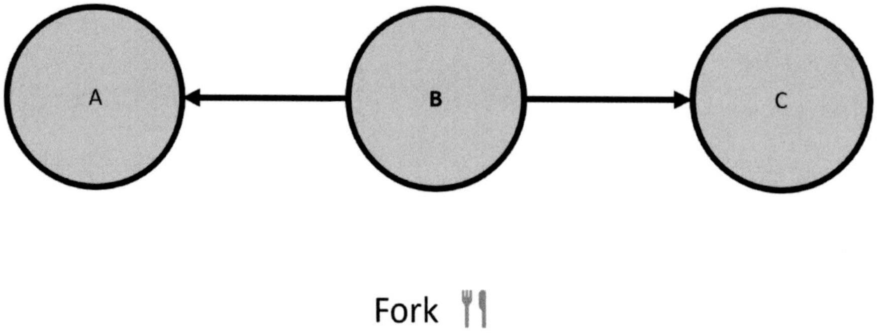

Figure 5.5 – A fork structure

In the fork, node *B* becomes what we usually call **a common cause** of nodes *A* and *C*.

Imagine you're driving your car, and you suddenly see a llama in the middle of the road.

The detector recognizes the llama as an obstacle. The emergency brake kicks in before you even realize it. At the same time, a small subcortical part of your brain called the *amygdala* sends a signal to another structure, the *hypothalamus*, which in turn activates your *adrenal glands*. This results in an *adrenaline* injection into your bloodstream. Before you even notice, your body has entered a state that is popularly referred to as a *fight-or-flight* mode.

The presence of a llama on the road caused the detector to activate the emergency brake and caused *you* to develop a rapid response to this potentially threatening situation.

This makes the llama on the road a common cause of your stress response and the detector's response.

However, when we control for the llama on the road, your threat response and the detector's response become independent. You might feel stressed because you're running late for an important meeting or because you had a tough conversation with your friend, and this has zero connection to the detector state.

Note that in the real world, you would also likely react with a *fight-or-flight* response to the mere fact that the emergency brakes were activated. The path, *llama → detector → brakes → fight-or-flight*, will introduce a spurious connection between *llama* and *flight-or-fight* that can be removed by controlling for the *brakes* variable.

Let's build a more formal example to clear any confusion that can come from this connection.

Let's take a look at *Figure 5.5* once again and think about conditional independencies. Are A and C *unconditionally dependent*?

In other words: are A and C dependent when we *do not* control for B? The answer is *yes*.

Why are they dependent? They are dependent because they both *inherit* some information from B. At the same time, the information *inherited* from B is all they have in common.

Let's take a look at a simple structural model that describes a fork structure to see how independence manifests itself in the distribution:

$$U_A \sim \mathcal{N}(0, 1)$$

$$U_B \sim \mathcal{N}(0, 1)$$

$$U_C \sim \mathcal{N}(0, 1)$$

$$B := U_B$$

$$A := B + U_A$$

$$C := B + U_C$$

In the preceding formula, $U_{X \in \{A, B, C\}}$ represents independently distributed noise variables (here, they follow a normal distribution, but they don't have to in general) and $:=$ is the assignment operator that you might remember from previous chapters.

Now imagine that we only look at observations where $B = 0$.

What would happen?

When $B = 0$, then A and C will only be influenced by their respective noise terms that are independent by definition.

We can therefore conclude that in forks, A and C are conditionally independent given B. Formally, it can be presented as follows:

$$A \perp\!\!\!\perp C | B$$

In case we do not control for *B*, *A* and *C* are *dependent*. This independence pattern is identical to the one that we've obtained from the *chain* structure.

This is not great news.

It seems that chains and forks lead to the same pattern of conditional independence, and if we want to recreate a true graph from the data, we end up not knowing how to orient the edges in the graph!

This might sound disappointing, but before we let the disappointment take over, let's examine the last structure in this section.

Colliders, immoralities, or v-structures

As you can see, the **collider** has many names. Is that the only thing that makes this structure special? Let's check!

Let's take a look at *Figure 5.6*. In the *collider*, causal influence flows from two different parents into a single child node:

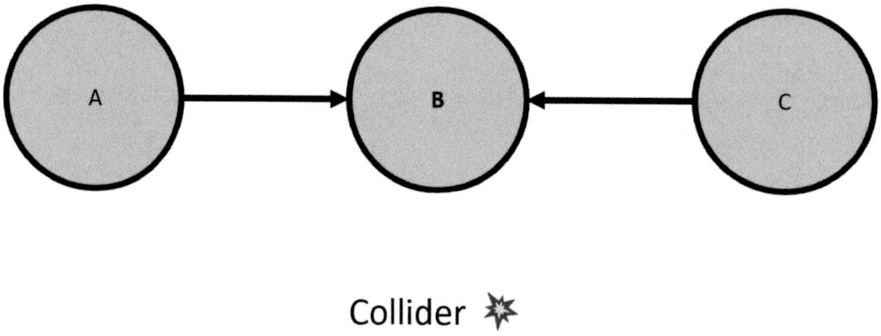

Figure 5.6 – A collider structure

The most important characteristic of a collider is that its independence pattern is *reversed* compared to chains and forks. So, what does it mean?

In colliders, *A* and *C* are *unconditionally independent*. Formally speaking, this can be represented as follows:

$A \perp\!\!\!\perp C$

When we control for *B*, they become *dependent*! Formally represented as follows:

$A \not\perp\!\!\!\perp C|B$

In the preceding formula, the slashed $\not\perp\!\!\!\perp$ symbol reads *is dependent*. As you can see, this pattern is exactly the reverse of the one that we've seen for chains and forks!

And this time that's great news!

We can leverage the collider structure to unambiguously orient edges in a graph every time we see it (there might be some challenges to this, but we skip them for now). Moreover, if we're lucky, colliders can help us orient ambiguous edges coming from chains and forks. We'll see an example of such behavior in *Part 3, Causal Discovery*.

To extend our series of driving examples, let's think about llamas on the road and driving against the sun. I think that most people would agree it's reasonable to say that whether you drive against the sun is independent of whether there's a llama on the road.

Now, let's assume that your detector reacts with some probability to the sun reflexes as if there was an obstacle on the road.

In this case, whether there's a llama on the road becomes (negatively) correlated with whether you drive against the sun if you only control for the detector reaction.

Figure 5.7 symbolically demonstrates the loss of independence between the two when we control for the detector state:

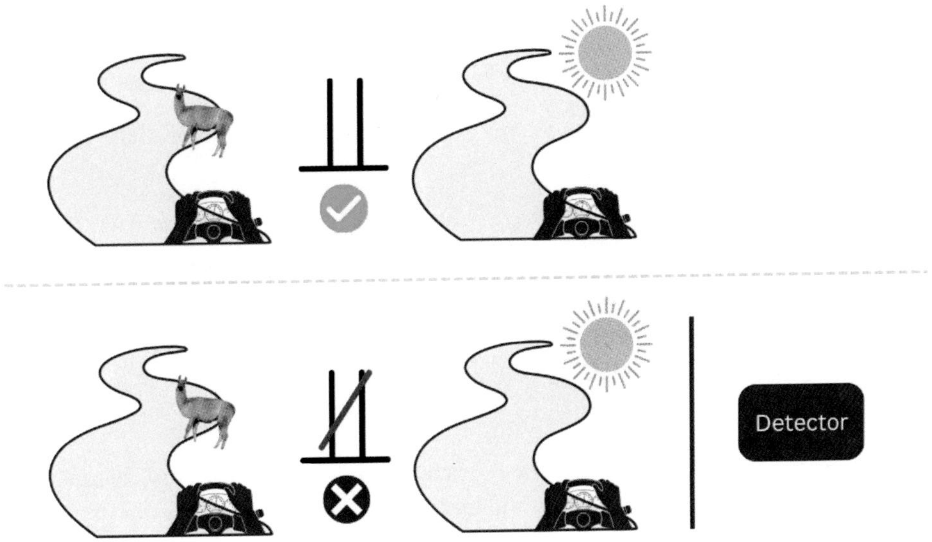

Figure 5.7 – A visual representation of independence structures in the collider example

The loss of independence between two variables, when we control for the collider, sounds surprising to many people at first. It was also my experience.

I found that for many people, examples involving real-world objects (even if these objects are llamas) bring more confusion than clarity when it comes to colliders.

Let's build a slightly more abstract yet very simple example to make sure that we clarify any confusion you might still have.

Take a look at *Figure 5.6* once again to refresh the graphical representation of the problem.

Now, let's imagine that both *A* and *C* randomly generate integers between *1* and *3*. Let's also say that *B* is a sum of *A* and *C*. Now, let's take a look at values of *A* and *C* when the value of $B = 4$. The following are the combinations of *A* and *C* that lead to $B = 4$:

- $A = 1, C = 3$
- $A = 2, C = 2$
- $A = 3, C = 1$

Can you see the pattern? Although *A* and *C* are unconditionally independent (there's no correlation between them as they randomly and independently generate integers), they become correlated when we observe *B*! The reason for this is that when we hold *B* constant and the value of *A* increases, the value of *C* has to decrease if we want to keep the value of *B* constant.

If you want to make it more visual, you can think about two identical glasses of water. If you randomly pour some water from one glass to the other, the total amount of water in both glasses will remain the same (assuming that we don't spill anything). If you repeat this *n* times and measure the amount of water in both glasses at each stage, the amount of water between the glasses will become negatively correlated.

I hope that this example will help you cement your intuition about colliders' conditional independence properties.

Thanks to the unique properties of colliders, they can be immensely helpful when we're trying to recover graph structures from observational data. Moreover, we can sometimes use colliders to disambiguate neighboring structures (we'll see an example of this in *Part 3, Causal Discovery*).

Unfortunately, this is not always the case. Let's discuss these scenarios now.

Ambiguous cases

As we've seen earlier, various graphical configurations might lead to the same statistical independence structure. In some cases, we might get lucky and have enough colliders in the graph to make up for it. In reality, though, we might often not be that fortunate.

Does this mean that the discussion we have had so far leads us to the conclusion that, in many cases, we simply cannot recover the graph from the data?

That's not entirely true. Even in cases where some edges cannot be oriented using constraint-based methods, we can still obtain some useful information!

Let's introduce the concept of the **Markov equivalence class** (**MEC**). A set of DAGs, $\mathcal{D} = \{ G_0(V, E_0), \ldots, G_n(V, E_n) \}$, is *Markov equivalent* if and only if all DAGs in $\mathcal{D}$ have the same skeleton and the same set of colliders (Verma & Pearl, 1991).

A **skeleton** is basically an undirected version of a DAG – all the edges are in place, but we have no information on the arrows. If we add the edges for all the collider structures that we've found, we will obtain a **complete partially-directed acyclic graph** (**CPDAG**).

If we take the CPDAG and generate a set of all possible DAGs from it, we'll obtain a *MEC*. MECs can be pretty useful. Even if we cannot recover a full DAG, a MEC can significantly reduce our uncertainty about the causal structure for a given dataset.

Before we conclude this section, let's take a look at *Figure 5.8*, which presents a simple MEC:

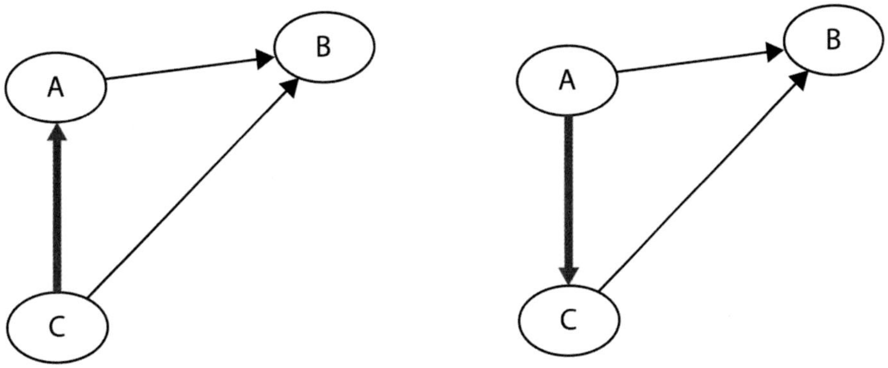

Figure 5.8 – An example of a MEC

The graphs in *Figure 5.8* have the same set of edges. If we removed the arrows and left the edges undirected, we would obtain two *identical* graphs, which is an indicator that both graphs have the same *skeleton*.

The collider ($A \rightarrow B \leftarrow C$) is present in both graphs. The only difference between the two graphs is the direction of the edge between nodes A and C. We can conclude that – consistently with our definition – the graphs in *Figure 5.8* meet the criteria for constituting a MEC.

Great!

Now, having a solid understanding of the three basic conditional independence structures – *chains*, *forks*, and *colliders* – we're ready to put this knowledge into action!

Forks, chains, colliders, and regression

In this section, we will see how the properties of chains, forks, and colliders manifest themselves in regression analysis. The very type of analysis that we'll conduct in this section is actually at the heart of some of the most classic methods of causal inference and causal discovery that we'll be working with in the next two parts of this book.

What we're going to do now is to generate three datasets, each with three variables, *A*, *B*, and *C*. Each dataset will be based on a graph representing one of the three structures: a chain, a fork, or a collider. Next, we'll fit one regression model per dataset, regressing *C* on the remaining two variables, and analyze the results. On the way, we'll plot pairwise scatterplots for each dataset to strengthen our intuitive understanding of a link between graphical structures, statistical models, and visual data representations.

Let's start with graphs. *Figure 5.9* presents chain, fork, and collider structures:

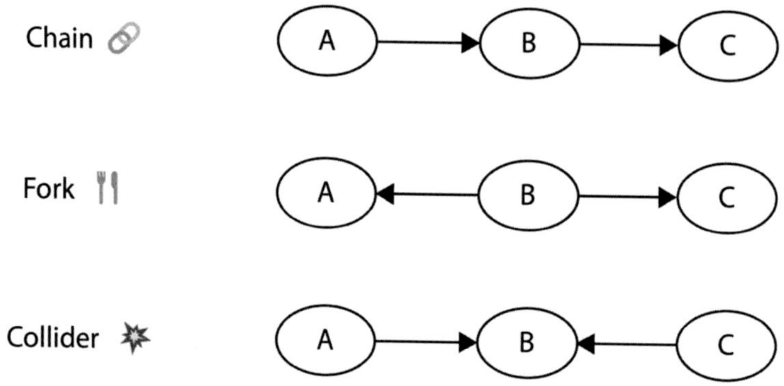

Figure 5.9 – Graphical representations of chain, fork, and collider structures

We will use the graphs from *Figure 5.9* to guide our data-generating process. Note that we omitted the *noise variables* for clarity of presentation.

The code for this section can be found in the `Chapter_05.ipynb` notebook (`https://bit.ly/causal-ntbk-05`).

First, let's define the general parameters:

```
NOISE_LEVEL = .2
N_SAMPLES = 1000
```

`NOISE_LEVEL` will determine the standard deviation of noise variables in our datasets. `N_SAMPLES` simply determines the sample size.

Generating the chain dataset

Now, we're ready to generate the data for the chain structure:

```
a = np.random.randn(N_SAMPLES)
b = a + NOISE_LEVEL*np.random.randn(N_SAMPLES)
c = b + NOISE_LEVEL*np.random.randn(N_SAMPLES)
```

Our code follows the logic of a chain-structured graph – *A* directly influences *B* (but not *C*) and *B* influences *C* (but not *A*). *C* does not have any further influence.

Let's plot pairwise scatterplots for this dataset. We present them in *Figure 5.10*:

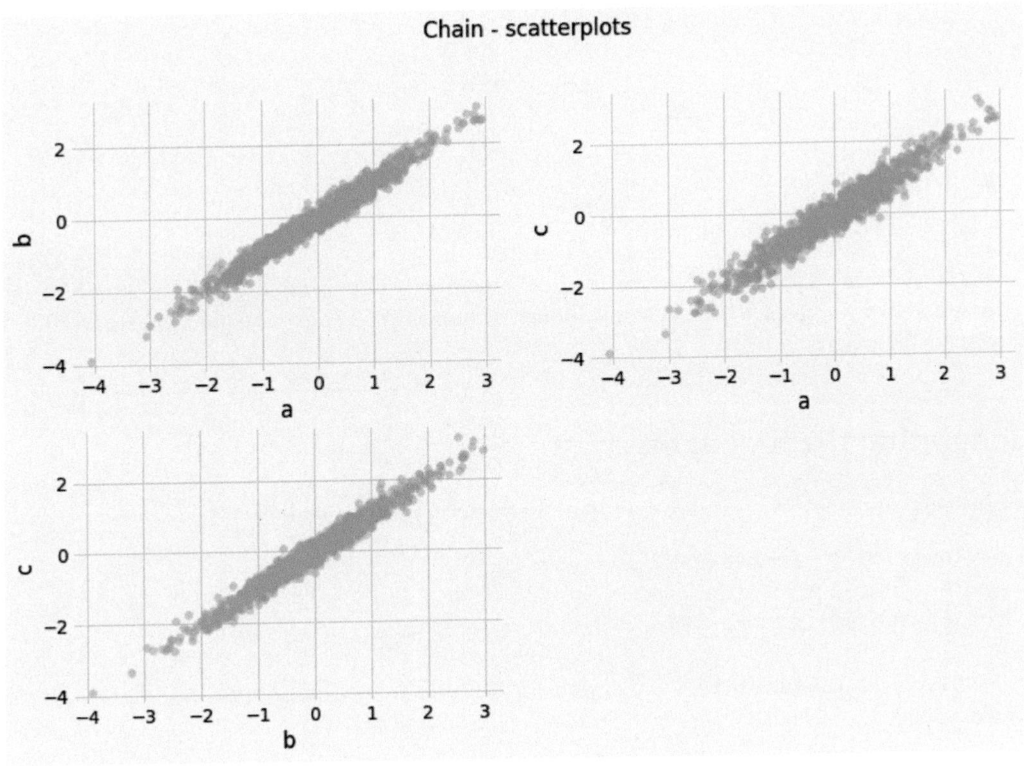

Figure 5.10 – Pairwise scatterplots for the dataset generated according to a chain-structured graph

We can see that all the scatterplots in *Figure 5.10* are very similar. The pattern is virtually identical for each pair of variables, and the correlation is consistently pretty strong. This reflects the characteristics of our data-generating process, which is linear and only slightly noisy.

How to read scatterplots

Scatterplots are a popular way to visualize bivariate data. Visual examination can help us quickly assess what kind of relationship (if any) exists between variables. A plot in this box shows us five different scatterplots with varying strengths of relationships between variables. In the leftmost panel, we see an almost perfect positive correlation (**Pearson's r = 0.99**), in the middle panel, there's virtually no relation between the variables. In the rightmost panel, there is an almost perfect *negative* correlation (**Pearson's r = -0.99**)

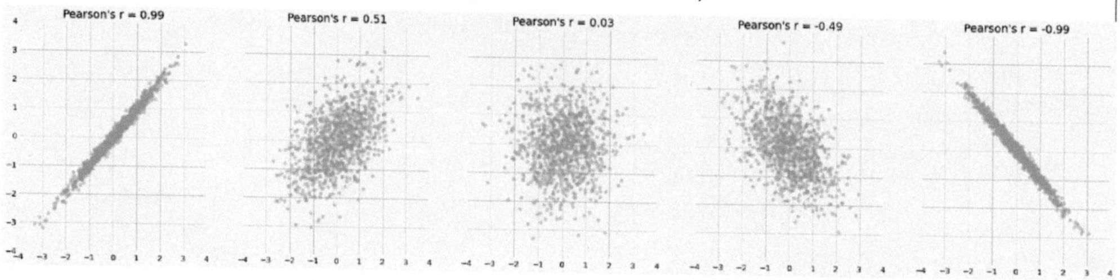

Note that the correlation metric that we used – **Pearson's r** – can only capture linear relationships between two variables. Metrics for non-linear relationships are also available, but we won't discuss them here.

Generating the fork dataset

Now, let's do the same for the fork structure. We'll start with generating the data:

```
b = np.random.randn(N_SAMPLES)
a = b + NOISE_LEVEL*np.random.randn(N_SAMPLES)
c = b + NOISE_LEVEL*np.random.randn(N_SAMPLES)
```

In *Figure 5.11*, we can see pairwise scatterplots for the fork. What's your impression? Do they look similar to the ones in *Figure 5.10*?

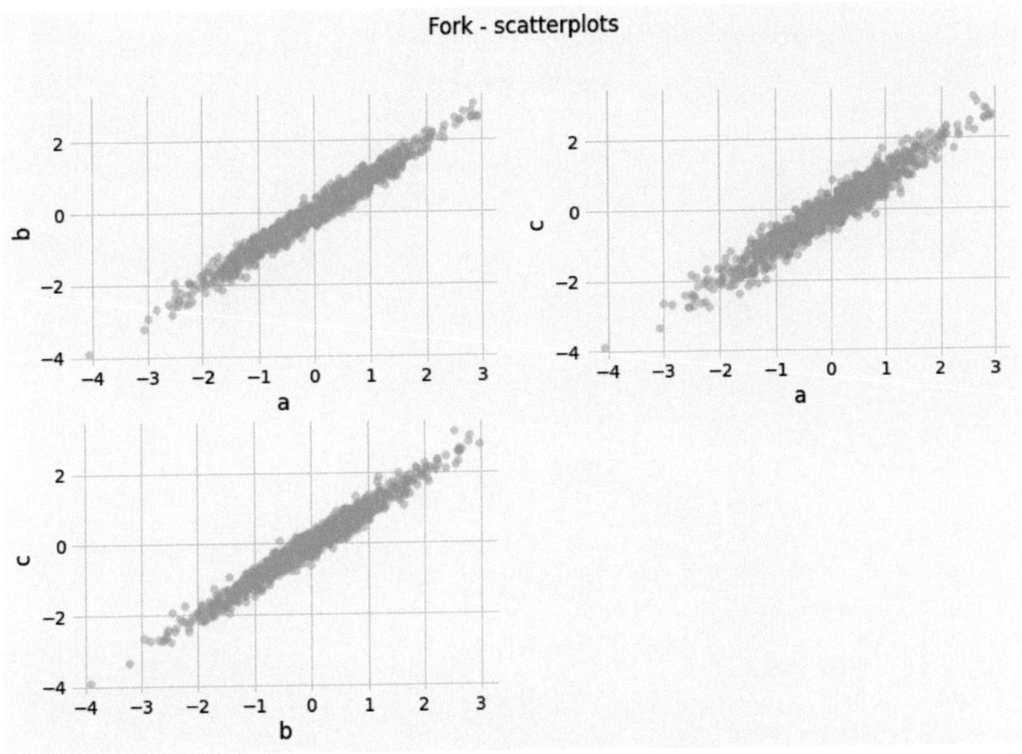

Figure 5.11 – Pairwise scatterplots for the dataset generated according to a fork-structured graph

Both figures (*Figure 5.10* and *Figure 5.11*) might differ in detail (note that we generate independent noise variables for each dataset), but the overall pattern seems very similar between the chain and fork datasets.

That's an interesting observation! What do you expect to see for colliders?

Let's see!

Generating the collider dataset

Let's start with the data:

```
a = np.random.randn(N_SAMPLES)
c = np.random.randn(N_SAMPLES)
b = a + c + NOISE_LEVEL*np.random.randn(N_SAMPLES)
```

Figure 5.12 presents pairwise scatterplots for the collider dataset:

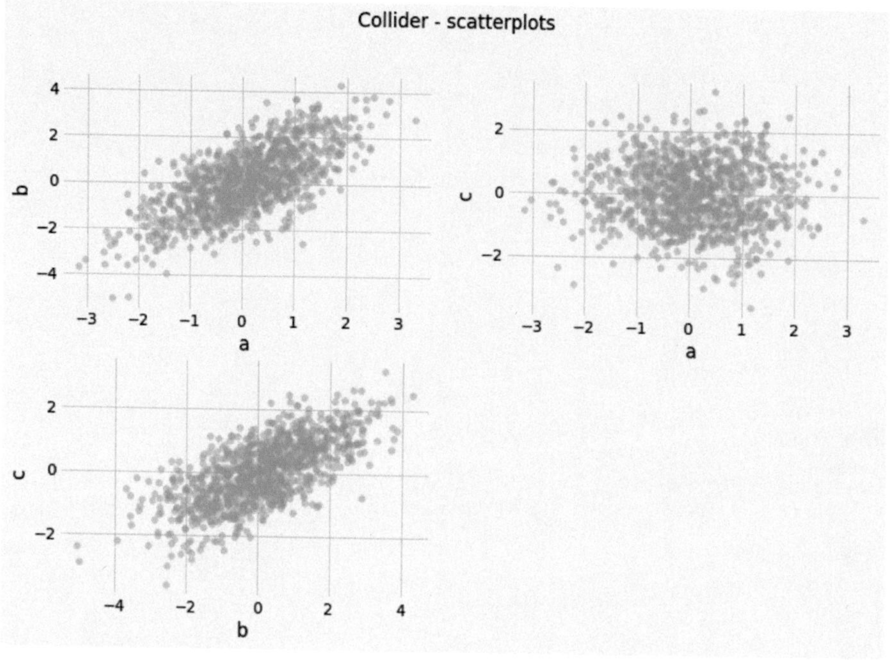

Figure 5.12 – Pairwise scatterplots for the dataset generated according to a collider-structured graph

This time the pattern is pretty different! Relationships between *a* and *b* (top left) and *b* and *c* (bottom left) seem to be noisier. Moreover, it seems there's no correlation between *A* and *C* (top right). Note that this result is congruent with what we said about the nature of colliders earlier in this chapter. Additionally, when we take a look at the data-generating process, this shouldn't be very surprising because the data generating process renders *A* and *C* entirely independent, evidence for, which you can also see in the code.

Fitting the regression models

Now, let's take all three datasets we generated and model them using multiple linear regression.

In each case, we'll regress *C* on *A* and *B*. We'll use `statsmodels` to fit the regression models. The code for each of the three models is identical:

```
X = pd.DataFrame(np.vstack([a, b]).T, columns=['A', 'B'])
X = sm.add_constant(X, prepend=True)
model = sm.OLS(c, X)
results = model.fit()
```

In the first line, we create a pandas dataframe using NumPy arrays containing our predictors (*A* and *B*). This will make `statsmodels` automatically assign the correct variable names in the model summary.

After fitting the models (for the full flow, check out the code in the notebook (`https://bit.ly/causal-ntbk-05`)), we're ready to print the model summaries and compare the results.

Figure 5.13 provides us with a compact summary of all three models. We used yellow and red ellipses to mark the *p*-values for each of the models:

Chain

	coef	std err	t	P>|t|	[0.025	0.975]
const	-0.0086	0.007	-1.320	0.187	-0.021	0.004
A	-0.0238	0.033	-0.729	0.466	-0.088	0.040
B	1.0217	0.032	31.645	0.000	0.958	1.085

Fork

	coef	std err	t	P>|t|	[0.025	0.975]
const	0.0077	0.006	1.241	0.215	-0.004	0.020
A	0.0090	0.031	0.292	0.770	-0.052	0.070
B	0.9938	0.032	31.372	0.000	0.932	1.056

Collider

	coef	std err	t	P>|t|	[0.025	0.975]
const	2.082e-17	1.35e-17	1.536	0.125	-5.77e-18	4.74e-17
A	-1.0000	2.01e-17	-4.97e+16	0.000	-1.000	-1.000
B	1.0000	1.39e-17	7.19e+16	0.000	1.000	1.000

Figure 5.13 – The results of regression analysis of three basic conditional independence structures

In *Figure 5.13*, there are three rows printed out for each model. The top row is marked as `const`, and we'll ignore it. The remaining two rows are marked with `A` and `B`, which denote our variables, *A* and *B*, respectively.

For the sake of our analysis, we'll use the customary threshold of 0.05 for *p*-values. We'll say that *p*-values greater than 0.05 indicate a non-significant result (no influence above the noise level), and *p*-values lower than or equal to 0.05 indicate a significant result.

We can see that for the chain model, only one predictor (*B*) is significant.

Why is that?

We've seen a clear linear relationship between *A* and *C* in *Figure 5.10*. It turns out that these two observations are consistent. Multiple linear regression computes the effects of predictors on the expected value of the dependent variable, *given* all other variables.

It means that we no longer look at pairwise relationships (such as in the scatterplots earlier in this section) but rather at conditional pairwise relationships. The result of the regression analysis is also congruent with the intuition that we've built in the example at the beginning of this chapter.

When we look at the results for the fork, we see the same pattern.

Again, only one predictor is significant, and again it turns out to be *B*. The logic behind the difference between the pairwise scatterplot and regression result is virtually identical to the one that we just discussed for the chain.

The model for the collider gives us a different pattern. For this model, both *A* and *B* are significant predictors of *C*. If you now take a look at *Figure 5.12* again, you can clearly see that there's no relationship between *A* and *C*.

This non-existing relationship between *A* and *C* is the essence of **spurious relationships**! They are an artifact, but – interestingly – this artifact is not only a side-effect of the method we used, and you can observe them in real life!

Spurious relationships in real life

Many companies might hire people based on their skills and their personality traits. Imagine that company *X* quantifies a person's coding skills on a scale from one to five. They do the same for the candidate's ability to cooperate and hire everyone who gets a total score of at least seven. Assuming that coding skills and ability to cooperate are independent in the population (which doesn't have to be true in reality), you'll observe that in company *X*, people who are better coders are less likely to cooperate on average, and those who are more likely to cooperate have fewer coding skills. You could conclude that being non-cooperative is related to being a better coder, yet this conclusion would be incorrect in the general population. To see why this happens, recall the water glasses example from the *Colliders, immoralities, or v-structures* section and think of coding skills and cooperativeness as water. Controlling for the *hiring status* is like keeping the total amount of *water* (coding skills + cooperation skills) constant. Pouring some water from one glass (e.g., coding skills glass) into another (cooperativeness glass) makes them negatively correlated when controlling for the hiring status (the total amount of water).

Before we conclude this section, I want to ask you to recall our discussion on **statistical control** from *Chapter 3*, and think again about the question that we asked in one of the sections – should we always control for all the available variables? – knowing what we've learned in this chapter.

We will see how to methodologically address the *to-control-or-not-to-control* question in the next chapter.

In this section, we saw how the properties of chains, forks, and colliders manifest themselves in the realm of statistical analysis. We examined pairwise relationships between variables and compared them to conditional relationships that we observed as a result of multiple regression analysis. Finally, we deepened our understanding of confounding.

Wrapping it up

This chapter introduced us to the three basic conditional independence structures – chains, forks, and colliders (the latter also known as immoralities or *v*-structures). We studied the properties of these structures and demonstrated that colliders have unique properties that make constraint-based causal discovery possible. We discussed how to deal with cases when it's impossible to orient all the edges in a graph and introduced the concept of MECs. Finally, we got our hands dirty with coding the examples of all the structures and analyzed their statistical properties using multiple linear regression.

This chapter concludes the first, introductory part of this book. The next chapter starts on the other side, in the fascinating land of causal inference. We'll go beyond simple linear cases and see a whole new zoo of models.

Ready?

References

Bishop, C. M. (2006). *Pattern Recognition and Machine Learning*. Springer.

Everington, K. (2020, Jun 2). *Video shows Tesla on autopilot slam into truck on Taiwan highway*. Taiwan News. `https://www.taiwannews.com.tw/en/news/3943199`.

Lauritzen, S. L. (1996). *Graphical Models*. Oxford University Press.

Neal, B. (2020, December, 17). *Introduction to Causal Inference from a Machine Learning Perspective* [Lecture notes]. `https://www.bradyneal.com/Introduction_to_Causal_Inference-Dec17_2020-Neal.pdf`.

Pearl, J. (2009). *Causality*. Cambridge, UK: Cambridge University Press.

Peters, J., Janzing, D. & Schölkopf, B. (2017). *Elements of Causal Inference: Foundations and Learning Algorithms*. MIT Press.

Pearl, J., & Mackenzie, D. (2019). *The Book of Why*. Penguin Books.

Scheines, R. (1996). *An introduction to causal inference*. [Manuscript]

Spirtes, P., Glymour, C., & Scheines, R. (2000). *Causation, Prediction, and Search*. MIT Press.

Uhler, C., Raskutti, G., & Bühlmann, P., & Yu, B. (2013). *Geometry of the faithfulness assumption in causal inference*. The Annals of Statistics, 436-463.

Verma, T., & Pearl, J. (1991). *Equivalence and synthesis of causal models*. UCLA.

Part 2: Causal Inference

In the first chapter of *Part 2*, we will deepen and strengthen our understanding of the important properties of graphical models and their connections to statistical quantities.

In *Chapter 7*, we'll introduce the four-step process of causal inference that will help us translate what we've learned so far into code in a structured manner.

In *Chapter 8*, we'll take a deeper look at important causal inference assumptions, which are critical to run unbiased causal analysis.

In the last two chapters, we'll introduce a number of causal estimators that will allow us to estimate average and individualized causal effects.

This part comprises the following chapters:

6

Nodes, Edges, and Statistical (In)dependence

Welcome to *Part 2* of our book! Congratulations on getting this far!

In this part, we'll dive into the world of causal inference. We'll combine all the knowledge that we've gained so far and start building on top of it. This chapter will introduce us to two powerful concepts – **d-separation** and estimands.

Combining these two concepts with what we've learned so far will equip us with a flexible toolkit to compute causal effects.

Further down the road, we'll discuss **back-door** and **front-door** criteria – two powerful methods to identify causal effects – and introduce a more general notion of Judea Pearl's **do-calculus**. Finally, we'll present **instrumental variables** – a family of techniques broadly applied in econometrics, epidemiology, and social sciences.

After reading this chapter and working through the exercises, you will be able to take a simple dataset and – assuming that the data meets necessary assumptions – compute causal effect estimates yourself.

In this chapter, we will cover the following topics:

- The notion of d-separation
- The notion of an estimand
- Back-door and front-door criteria
- Do-calculus
- Instrumental variables

Ready? Let's go!

You're gonna keep 'em d-separated

In the previous chapter, we learned that colliders have a **unique conditional independence pattern** that sets them apart from chains and forks. The idea of d-separation builds on these properties. In general, we say that two nodes in a **directed acyclic graph** (**DAG**) G are d-separated when *all paths* between them are *blocked*. When is a path between two nodes blocked?

A simple answer is when there's a *collider* on a path between them or if there's a *fork* or a *chain* that contains another variable that we control for (or a descendant of such a variable).

Let's formalize this definition and make it a little bit more general at the same time. Instead of talking about blocking a path between two nodes with another node, we will talk about paths between *sets of nodes* blocked by another *set of nodes*. We will denote sets of nodes with capital cursive script letters, $\mathcal{X}$, $\mathcal{Y}$, and $\mathcal{Z}$.

Thinking in terms of sets of nodes rather than single nodes is useful when we work with scenarios with multiple predictors and/or multiple confounders. If you prefer thinking in terms of single nodes X, Y, and Z, imagine these nodes as a single-element set, and the same definition will work for you!

Let's go!

For any three disjoint sets of nodes $\mathcal{X}$, $\mathcal{Y}$, and $\mathcal{Z}$, a path between $\mathcal{X}$ and $\mathcal{Y}$ is blocked by $\mathcal{Z}$ in the following scenarios:

- If there's a fork, $i \leftarrow j \rightarrow k$, or a chain, $i \rightarrow j \rightarrow k$, in this path such that the middle node is $j \in \mathcal{Z}$
- If there's a collider, $i \rightarrow j \leftarrow k$, on this path such that neither j nor any of its descendants belong to $\mathcal{Z}$ (Pearl, 2009)

In other words, if there's a chain or fork between $\mathcal{X}$ and $\mathcal{Y}$, we need to control for the middle node to close the path between $\mathcal{X}$ and $\mathcal{Y}$. If there's a collider between $\mathcal{X}$ and $\mathcal{Y}$, we should leave it uncontrolled altogether with all its descendants. That's it!

Information flow in a graph

Note, that sometimes, when talking about d-separation, we might refer to *information flow in a graph*. An important thing to remember is that this information flow is *non-directional*. This lack of directionality is closely related to the notions of correlation and confounding. D-separation allows us to control the information flow in the graph. We'll learn more about this topic in the next section.

Now, let's do some practice!

Practice makes perfect – d-separation

When learning a new concept, a good intellectual understanding is often necessary, but it's practicing that makes us retain knowledge in the long term. To strengthen our understanding of *d*-separation, let's play a game. We'll call it *Keep 'em d-separated.*

I'll generate five graphs of increasing complexity for you and ask you to indicate which nodes we need to observe (or control for) to *d*-separate X and Y. In other words, your task is to decide which nodes should become the members of the set $\mathcal{Z}$ in order for X and Y to be *d*-separated. You will find the correct answers at the end of this section.

Figure 6.1 presents our two first examples:

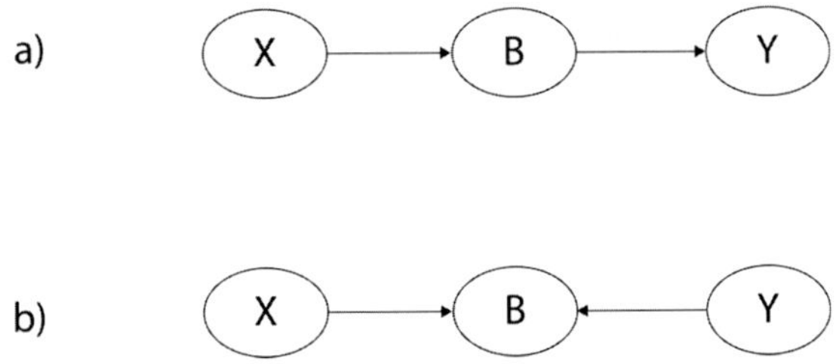

Figure 6.1 – The first two DAGs in the Keep 'em d-separated game

Which nodes of DAGs **a** and **b** from *Figure 6.1* should be observed in order to make the X and Y nodes *d*-separated? I encourage you to write your answers down on a piece of paper and then compare them with the answers at the end of the chapter.

OK, let's add some more complexity! *Figure 6.2* presents the third DAG in our game:

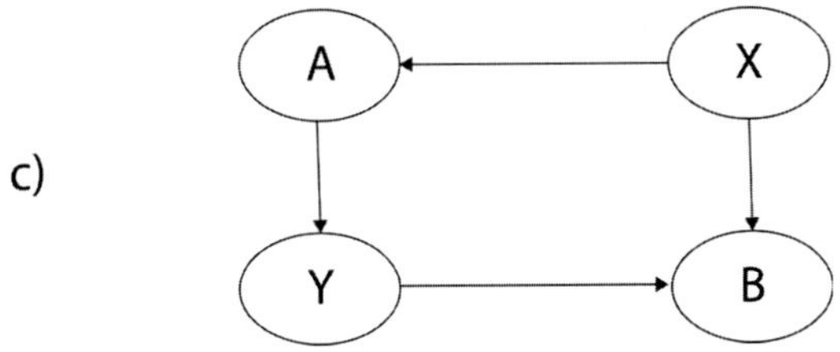

Figure 6.2 – DAG number 3 in our Keep 'em d-separated game

Got your answers?

Great, let's make it more fun! *Figure 6.3* presents the fourth example in *Keep 'em d-separated*:

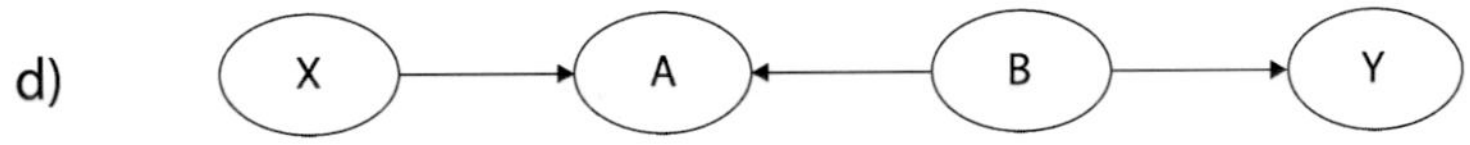

Figure 6.3 – DAG number 4 in our Keep 'em d-separated game

DAGs similar to DAG **d** in *Figure 6.3* are often more challenging, but I am sure you'll find the right answer!

OK, now, it's time for something more advanced! *Figure 6.4* presents the last example in our game:

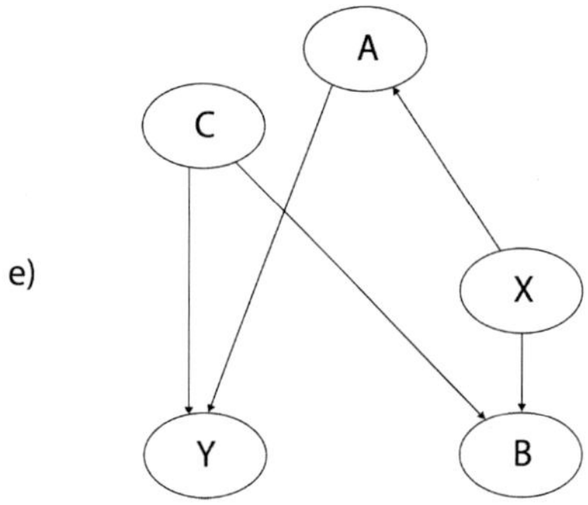

Figure 6.4 – The final DAG in the Keep 'em d-separated game

Do you have your answers ready?

If you found some of the DAGs challenging, that's completely natural.

I am sure that, with practice, you'll feel more confident about them! You can find more similar DAG games on the pgmpy web page (`https://bit.ly/CausalGames`).

It's time to reveal the answers now!

Figure 6.5 contains all five DAGs for your reference.

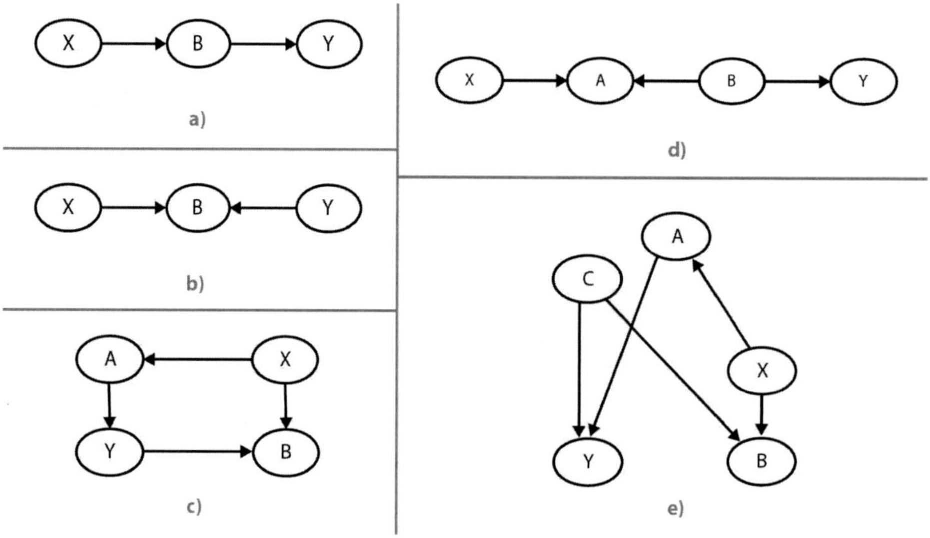

Figure 6.5 – All DAGs from the Keep 'em d-separated game

Let's start with DAG **a**.

DAG **a** is a chain. To block the path between X and Y, we need to control for B.

DAG **b** is a collider. This means that the path is already blocked by the middle node, and we don't need to do anything.

In DAG **c**, we can find two paths connecting X and Y:

- $X \rightarrow A \rightarrow Y$
- $X \rightarrow B \leftarrow Y$

The first path is a chain. In order to block it, we need to control for A. The second path is a collider, and we don't need to do anything to block it, as it's already blocked.

Note that you can view DAG **c** as a combination of DAGs **a** and **b**.

Let's get another one. We can see that in DAG **d**, there are two overlapping structures:

- A collider, $X \rightarrow A \leftarrow B$
- A fork, $A \leftarrow B \rightarrow Y$

There are several options for how to approach DAG **d**:

- The simplest one is to do nothing (the collider blocks the path).
- We can also control for B – there's no benefit to this, but it also does not harm us (except that it increases model complexity).
- Finally, we can control for A (which will open the path) and for B, which will close the path.

If we're only interested in estimating the effect of X on Y, most of the time, we would likely choose the first answer as the simplest one.

Okay, let's jump to our last friend, DAG **e**.

Let's unpack it. There are essentially two paths from X to Y:

- $X \rightarrow A \rightarrow Y$
- $X \rightarrow B \leftarrow C \rightarrow Y$

We can see right away that the first path represents a chain. Controlling for A closes this path. The second path contains a collider, so not controlling for anything keeps the path closed. Another solution is to block for A, B, and C (note how controlling for C closes the path that we opened by controlling for B).

With this exercise, we conclude the first section of *Chapter 6*. Let's review what we've learned.

We introduced the notion of *d*-separation. We saw that d-separation is all about blocking paths between (sets of) nodes in a DAG. Paths in a graph can be blocked by using the fundamental logic of the tools that we already have in our toolbox, the three basic conditional independence structures – chains, forks, and colliders (or immoralities).

The knowledge of d-separation effectively enables us to build *estimands* – an essential step in the *four-step causal inference process*. Let's learn more!

Estimand first!

In this section, we're going to introduce the notion of an *estimand* – an essential building block in the causal inference process.

We live in a world of estimators

In statistical inference and machine learning, we often talk about *estimates* and *estimators*. Estimates are basically our best guesses regarding some quantities of interest given (finite) data. Estimators are computational devices or procedures that allow us to map between a given (finite) data sample and an estimate of interest.

Let's imagine you just got a new job. You're interested in estimating how much time you'll need to get from your home to your new office. You decide to record your commute times over 5 days. The data you obtain looks like this:

[22.1, 23.7, 25.2, 20.0, 21.8]

One thing you can do is to take the arithmetic average of these numbers, which will give you the so-called sample mean - your estimate of the true average commute time. You might feel that this is not enough for you and you'd prefer to fit a distribution to this data rather than compute a point-wise estimate (this approach is commonly used in Bayesian statistics).

The arithmetic mean of our data, as well as the parameters of the distribution that we might have decided to fit to this data, are *estimates*. A computational device that we use to obtain estimates is an *estimator*.

Estimators might be as simple as computing the arithmetic mean and as complex as a 550 billion-parameter language model. Linear regression is an estimator, and so is a neural network or a random forest model.

So, what is an estimand?

The basic answer is that an *estimand* is a quantity that we're interested in estimating. If an estimator is the *how*, an estimand is the *what*.

Let's get some context to understand the significance of estimands in causal inference.

In *Chapter 1*, we said that confounding is a causal concept, and to discuss it, we need to go beyond the realm of sheer data. In *Chapter 4*, we learned that *graphical causal models* can encode the causal structure of a system that we're modeling. In the first section of this chapter, we learned that an important property of d-separation is that it allows us to control the flow of information in a graph.

Let's try to stretch our thinking about confounding a bit for a minute. What does it mean that a relationship between two variables is confounded?

Can you recall the example from the first chapter (ice cream, drownings, and temperature, presented in *Figure 1.1*)? You can use *Figure 6.6* as a quick refresher:

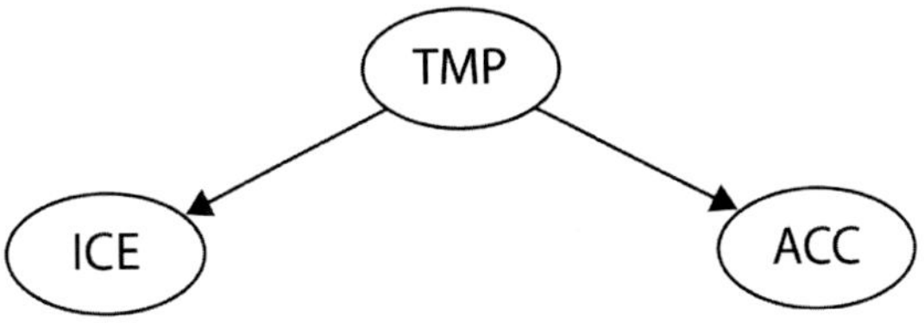

Figure 6.6 – A graphical representation of the problem from Chapter 1 (Figure 1.1)

In this example, we perceived ice cream sales (*ICE*) and the number of accidents with drownings (*ACC*) as related although, actually, they were not (causally) related. We said that this relationship was *spurious*.

We can think of this type of relationship as a result of the unconstrained (undirected) flow of information in the graph. This is great news because now we have a d-separation that can help us constrain this flow and – as a consequence – *deconfound* the relationship between the variables that we're interested in.

Getting back to our example from the first chapter, we could naively choose to define our model as the following:

$ACC \sim ICE$

Let's translate this model syntax to mathematical notation.

What we want to estimate is the *causal effect* of *ICE* on *ACC*. In other words, we want to understand what the change would be in *ACC* if we *intervened* on *ICE*. Therefore, the quantity we're interested in is the following (for the sake of simplicity, we will assume that all our variables are discrete):

$$P(ACC = acc|do(ICE = ice))$$

If we used our naïve model, our estimand would look like this:

$$P(ACC = acc|do(ICE = ice)) = P(ACC = acc|ICE = ice)$$

We already know that this is incorrect in our case. We know that the relationship between *ACC* and *ICE* is spurious! To get the correct *estimate* of the causal effect of *ICE* on *ACC*, we need to control for temperature (*TMP*). The correct way to model our problem is, therefore, the following:

$ACC \sim ICE + TMP$

This translates to the following:

$$P(ACC = acc|do(ICE = ice)) = \sum_{tmp} P(ACC = acc|ICE = ice, TMP = tmp)P(TMP = tmp)$$

To make it a bit more readable, we can simplify the notation:

$$P(ACC|do(ICE)) = \sum_{tmp} P(ACC|ICE, TMP)P(TMP)$$

This formula is an example of the so-called **causal effect rule**, which states that given a graph, *G*, and a set of variables, *Pa*, that are (causal) parents of *X*, the causal effect of *X* on *Y* is given by the following (Pearl, Glymour, and Jewell, 2016):

$$P(Y = y|do(X = x)\big) = \sum_{z} P(Y = y|X = x, Pa = z)P(Pa = z)$$

Note that what we're doing in our example is congruent with point 1 in our definition of *d*-separation – if there's a fork between the two variables, *X* and *Y*, we need to control for the middle node in this fork in to order block a path between *X* and *Y*.

In our example, *TMP* is the middle node in the fork between *ICE* and *ACC*, and so controlling for it blocks the non-causal path between *ICE* and *ACC*. This is how we obtain a correct *estimand* for our model (sometimes, there might be more than one correct estimand per model).

All that we've done so far in this section has *one essential goal* – to find an estimand that allows us to compute unbiased causal effects from observational data. Although it won't be always possible, it will be *possible* sometimes. And sometimes, it can bring us tremendous benefits.

Let's summarize this section.

In this section, we learned what *estimands* are and how they are different from estimators and *estimates*. We built a correct estimand for our ice cream example from the first chapter and showed how this estimand is related to a more general *causal effect rule*. Finally, we discussed the links between estimands, *d*-separation, and confounding.

In the following sections, we'll focus on techniques that allow us to obtain causal estimands, given complete or partially complete graphs.

The back-door criterion

The back-door criterion is most likely the best-known technique to find causal estimands given a graph. And the best part is that you already know it!

In this section, we're going to learn how the back-door criterion works. We'll study its logic and learn about its limitations. This knowledge will allow us to find good causal estimands in a broad class of cases. Let's start!

What is the back-door criterion?

The back-door criterion aims at blocking spurious paths between our treatment and outcome nodes. At the same time, we want to make sure that we leave all directed paths unaltered and are careful not to create new spurious paths.

Formally speaking, a set of variables, $\mathcal{Z}$, satisfies the back-door criterion, given a graph G, and a pair of variables, if no node in $\mathcal{Z}$ is a descendant of X, and $\mathcal{Z}$ blocks all the paths between X and Y that contain an arrow into X (Pearl, Glymour, and Jewell, 2016).

In the preceding definition, $X \rightarrow \ldots \rightarrow Y$ means that there is a *directed* path from X to Y. This path might be direct or pass through other nodes.

You can see that when we looked for the estimand in our ice cream example, we did precisely this – we blocked all the paths between *ICE* and *ACC* that contained an arrow into *ICE*. *TMP* is not a descendant of *ICE*, so we also met the second condition. Finally, we haven't opened any new spurious paths (in our very simple graph, there was not even the opportunity to do so).

Back-door and equivalent estimands

Let's consider the graph in *Figure 6.7*:

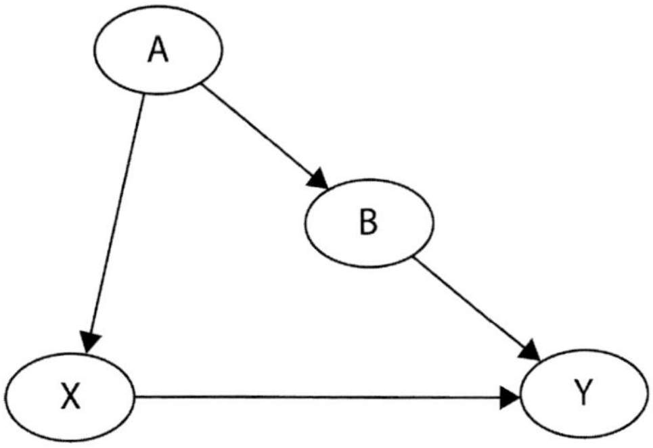

Figure 6.7 – A graph with a confounding pattern

Given the model presented in *Figure 6.7*, which nodes should we control for in order to estimate the causal effect of X on Y?

According to our definition of the back-door criterion, we need to block all the paths that have an arrow *into* X. We should not control for any descendants of X nor open any new paths. We can fulfill these conditions in three different ways:

- Controlling for A
- Controlling for B
- Controlling for both – A and B

They will all provide us with different but *equivalent* estimands. In particular, the following equality is true for our model (again, assuming discrete variables for simplicity):

$$P(Y = y|do(X = x)) = \sum_a P(Y = y|X = x, A = a)P(A = a) = \sum_b P(Y = y|X = x, B = b)P(B = b)$$

This equality opens a very interesting possibility to us (note that we omitted the third case (controlling for A and B) in the equality for the sake of readability).

If it is sufficient to only control for one of the variables (A or B) to obtain a correct estimand for $X \rightarrow Y$, we can essentially estimate the causal effect of X on Y even if one of the variables remains unobserved!

Equivalent estimands versus equal estimates

Although for certain models we might find two or more equivalent estimands, estimates computed based on these (equivalent) estimands might differ slightly. This is natural in a finite sample size regime. Nonetheless, if your sample size is big enough, the differences should be negligible. Big differences might suggest an erroneous estimand, a lack of model convergence, or errors in the model code.

Let's consider a modified model from *Figure 6.7*, where one of the variables is unobserved. *Figure 6.8* presents this model:

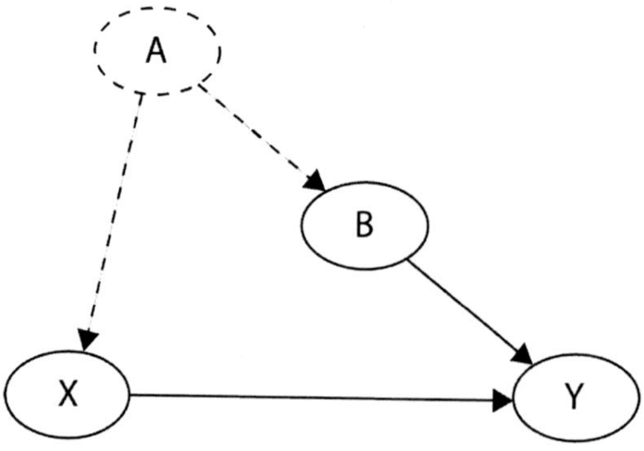

Figure 6.8 – A graph with a confounding pattern and one unobserved variable

The node A and two edges ($A \rightarrow B$ and $A \rightarrow X$) marked with dashed lines are all unobserved, yet we assume that the overall causal structure is known (including the two unobserved edges).

In other words, we don't know anything about A or what the functional form of A's influence on X or B is. At the same time, we assume that A exists and has no other edges than the one presented in *Figure 6.8*.

A refresher on the do-operator

The *do*-operator informs us that we're working with interventional rather than observational distribution. In certain cases, interventional and observational distributions might be the same. For instance, if your true causal graph has a form of $X \rightarrow Y$, then $P(Y = y|do(X = x)) = P(Y = y|X = x)$, yet whenever confounding appears, we need to adjust for the confounders' effects by controlling for additional variables in the right-hand side of the equation.

Our estimand for the model presented in *Figure 6.8* would be identical to the second estimand for the fully observed model:

$$P(Y = y|do(X = x)) = \sum_{b} P(Y = y|X = x, B = b)P(B = b)$$

That's powerful! Imagine that recording A is the most expensive part of your data collection process. Now, understanding the back-door criterion, you can essentially just skip recording this variable! How cool is that?

One thing we need to remember is that to keep this estimand valid, we need to be sure that the overall causal structure holds. If we changed the structure a bit by adding a direct edge from A to Y, the preceding estimand would lose its validity.

That said, if we completely removed A and all its edges from the model, our estimand would still hold. Can you explain why? (Check the *Answers* section at the end of the chapter for the correct answer.)

Let's summarize.

In this section, we learned about the back-door criterion and how it can help us build valid causal estimands. We saw that, in some cases, we might be able to build more than one valid estimand for a single model. We also demonstrated that the back-door criterion can be helpful in certain cases of unobserved confounding.

Although the back-door criterion is powerful, it has its limitations.

The front-door criterion

In this section, we're going to discuss the **front-door criterion** – a device that allows us to obtain valid causal estimands in (some) cases where the back-door criterion fails.

Can GPS lead us astray?

In their 2020 study, Louisa Dahmani and Véronique Bohbot from McGill University showed that there's a link between GPS usage and spatial memory decline (Dahmani and Bohbot, 2020). Moreover, the effect is *dose-dependent*, which means that the more you use GPS, the more spatial memory decline you experience.

The authors argue that their results suggest a causal link between GPS usage and spatial memory decline. We already know that something that *looks* connected does not necessarily *have to* be connected in reality.

The authors also know this, so they decided to add a longitudinal component to their design. This means that they observed people over a period of time, and they noticed that those participants who used more GPS had a greater decline in their memory.

Imagine that you decide to discuss this study with your colleague Susan. The time component seems promising to you, but Susan is somehow critical about the results and interpretation and proposes another hypothesis – the link between GPS usage and spatial memory decline is *purely spurious.*

They seem related – argues Susan – because there's a common cause for using GPS and memory decline – **low global motivation** (Pelletier et al., 2007). Susan argues that people with low global motivation are reluctant to learn new things (so they are not interested in remembering new information, including spatial information) and they try to avoid effort (hence, they prefer to use GPS more often, as it allows them to avoid the effortful process of decision-making while driving).

She also claims that low global motivation tends to *expand* – unmotivated people look for solutions that can take the burden of doing stuff from them, and if these solutions work, they use them more often. They are also less and less interested in learning new things with age.

Inspired by Susan's proposition, you search through studies on the effects of GPS on spatial memory, but you cannot find one that would control for global motivation. The situation seems hopeless – if global motivation is a confounder, it's an unobserved one, and so, we cannot use the back-door criterion to deconfound the relationship between GPS usage and spatial memory decline.

Let's encode Susan's model graphically alongside the model containing both hypotheses (motivation and GPS usage). *Figure 6.9* presents both models:

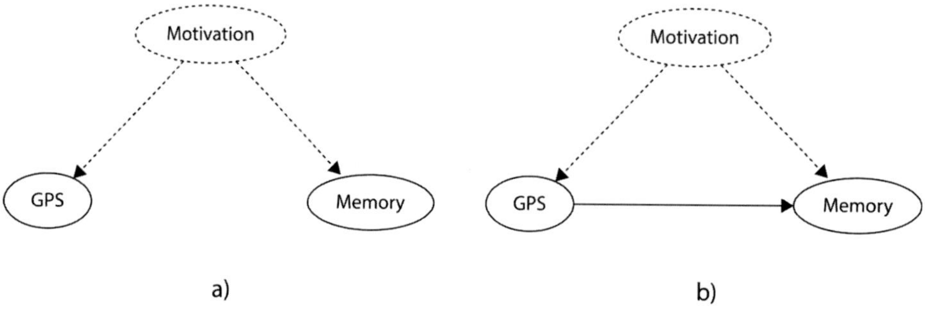

Figure 6.9 – A model presenting Susan's hypothesis (a) and the "full" hypothesis (b)

As we can see, none of the two models can be deconfounded because the confounder is unobserved (dashed lines).

In such a case, the back-door criterion cannot help us, but there's another criterion we could possibly use that relies on the concept of *mediation*. This would require us to find a variable that *mediates* the relationship between GPS usage and memory decline.

Let's look for one!

Mediators and mediation

We can say that the influence of one variable (X) on another (Y) is *mediated* by a third variable, Z (or a set of variables, $\mathcal{Z}$), when at least one path from X to Y goes through Z. We can say that Z *fully mediates* the relationship between X and Y when the only path from X to Y goes through Z. If there are paths from X to Y that do not pass through Z, the mediation is *partial*.

London cabbies and the magic pebble

In their famous 2000 study of London cab drivers, Eleanor A. Maguire and her colleagues from University College London demonstrated that experience as a taxi driver is related to hippocampus's volume (Maguire et al., 2000). The **hippocampus** is a pebble-sized (40-55 mm) brain structure, responsible for creating new memories – in particular, spatial memories (O'Keefe and Nadel, 1978).

London cab drivers need to pass a very restrictive exam checking their spatial knowledge and are not allowed to use any external aids in the process.

The exam is preceded by an extensive training period, which typically takes between 3 and 4 years. The drivers are required to memorize and be able to navigate over *"26,000 streets and thousands of points of interest in London"* (Griesbauer et al., 2021).

One study (Woollett and Maguire, 2011) showed that drivers who failed this exam did not show an increase in hippocampal volume. At the same time, in those who passed the exam, a systematic increase in hippocampal volume was observed. During the continuing training over a 4-year period, hippocampal volume was associated with an improvement in spatial memory (only in those who were in continuous training).

Let's try to incorporate these results into our model. We'll hypothesize that GPS usage negatively impacts the relative volume of the hippocampus, which in turn impacts spatial memory. *Figure 6.10* presents the updated model:

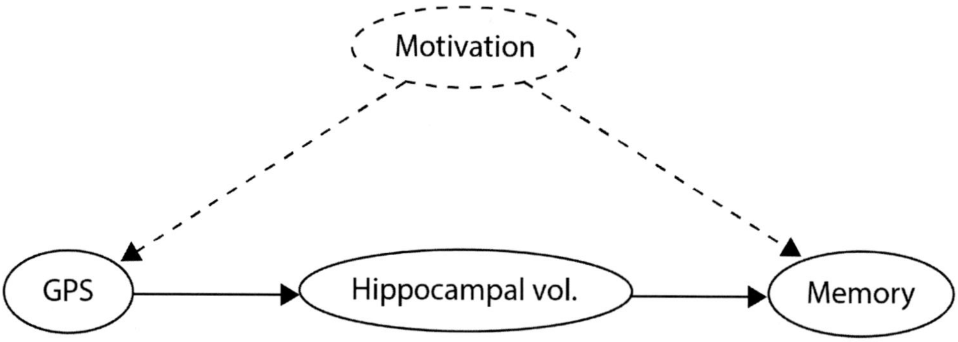

Figure 6.10 – An updated model, including hippocampal volume as a mediator

In our new hypothetical model, we assume that hippocampal volume fully mediates the effects of GPS usage on a decline in spatial memory.

The second important assumption we make is that motivation can only affect *hippocampal volume indirectly through GPS usage*. This assumption is critical in order to make the criterion that we're going to introduce next – the front-door criterion – useful to us.

If motivation would be able to influence hippocampal volume *directly*, front-door would be of no help. Luckily enough, the assumption that motivation cannot directly change the volume of the hippocampus seems reasonable (though perhaps you could argue against it!).

Opening the front door

The front-door criterion is an example of a divide-and-conquer strategy. It divides a graph into two parts, uses relatively simple rules to determine the causal effects in these sub-parts, and combines them together again.

Let's see it step by step.

To make the notation more readable, we'll replace variable names with symbols. *Figure 6.11* presents the graph with updated variable names:

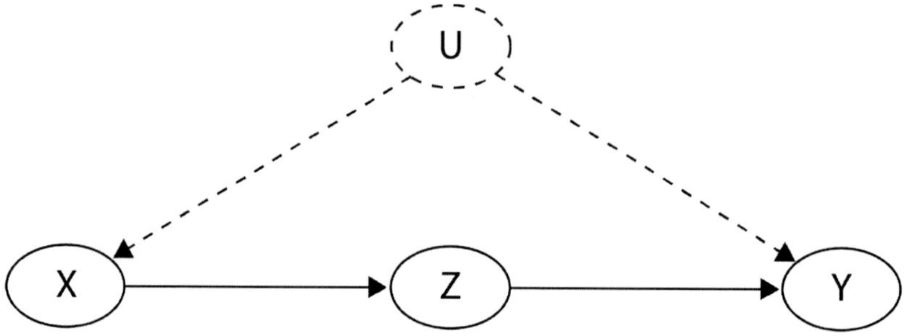

Figure 6.11 – A model with updated variable names

First, let's take a look at the relationship between X and Z. There's one back-door path between them, $X \leftarrow U \rightarrow Y \leftarrow Z$, but it's already blocked. Can you see how?

There's a collider, $U \rightarrow Y \leftarrow Z$, that blocks the flow of the information. Therefore, we can identify the causal effect of X on Z in the following way:

$$P(Z = z|do(X = x)) = P(Z = z|X = x)$$

That's great!

How about the effect of Z on Y?

There's one open back-door path, $Z \leftarrow X \leftarrow U \rightarrow Y$. There's no collider on this path and U is unobserved, so we cannot control for it. Fortunately, we can control for the other variable, X. A valid estimand of the causal effect of Z on Y is, therefore, the following:

$$P(Y = y|do(Z = z)) = \sum_{x} P(Y = y|Z = z, X = x)P(X = x)$$

That's pretty awesome! We just blocked the back-door path from Z to Y by simply controlling for X. Now, we're ready to combine both estimands back together:

$$P(Y = y|do(X = x)) = \sum_{z} P(Y = y|do(Z = z))P(Z = z|do(X = x))$$

Now, let's drop *do*-operators from the right-hand side by substituting them according to the preceding equalities. This leads us to the following:

$$P(Y = y|do(X = x)) = \sum_{z} P(Z = z|X = x) \sum_{x'} P(Y = y|X = x', Z = z)P(X = x')$$

This formula is called the **front-door formula** (Pearl et al., 2016) or **front-door adjustment**.

It might look a little discouraging, perhaps because of the cryptic x' in the index of the second sum. We need this unfriendly x' because we're combining two different formulas, and we want to hold X from one formula constant when we're iterating over (the same) X from the other formula.

You can think about it as seeing X from two different angles or – perhaps – as X being in two different places at the same time (I guess in sci-fi movies they usually call it *bilocation*).

Three simple steps toward the front door

In general, we can say that a set of variables, $\mathcal{Z}$, satisfies the front-door criterion, given the graph, G, and a pair of variables, $X \rightarrow \ldots \rightarrow Y$, if the following applies (Pearl et al., 2016):

- $\mathcal{Z}$ intercepts all directed paths from X to Y
- There are no open back-door paths from X to $\mathcal{Z}$
- All back-door paths from $\mathcal{Z}$ to Y are blocked by X

Front-door in practice

Let's implement a hypothetical model of our GPS example. You can find the code for this chapter in the following notebook: `https://bit.ly/causal-ntbk-06`.

First, let's define a **structural causal model (SCM)** that will generate hypothetical data for us. We're going to implement it as a Python class, similar to what we did in *Chapter 2*. Let's start with the imports:

```
import numpy as np
import pandas as pd
from scipy import stats
from sklearn.linear_model import LinearRegression
import matplotlib.pyplot as plt
plt.style.use('fivethirtyeight')
```

We import basic scientific packages. Note that this time we did not import Statsmodels' (Seabold and Perktold, 2010) linear regression module but, rather, the implementation from Scikit-learn (Pedregosa et al., 2011).

We did this on purpose to leverage the simple and intuitive interface that Scikit-learn offers. At the same time, we'll be less interested in the well-formatted output of the model results – a great feature of Statsmodels.

Perfect! Let's define our SCM!

```
class GPSMemorySCM:

    def __init__(self, random_seed=None):
        self.random_seed = random_seed
        self.u_x = stats.truncnorm(0, np.infty, scale=5)
        self.u_y = stats.norm(scale=2)
        self.u_z = stats.norm(scale=2)
        self.u = stats.truncnorm(0, np.infty, scale=4)
```

In the `.init()` method, we define the distributions for all the exogenous variables in the model (we omitted them for readability in the preceding figures). We use a truncated normal distribution for `u_x` and `u` to restrict them to positive values and normal distribution for `u_y` and `u_z`

For clarity, you might want to take a look at *Figure 6.12*, which shows our full graphical model with exogenous variables:

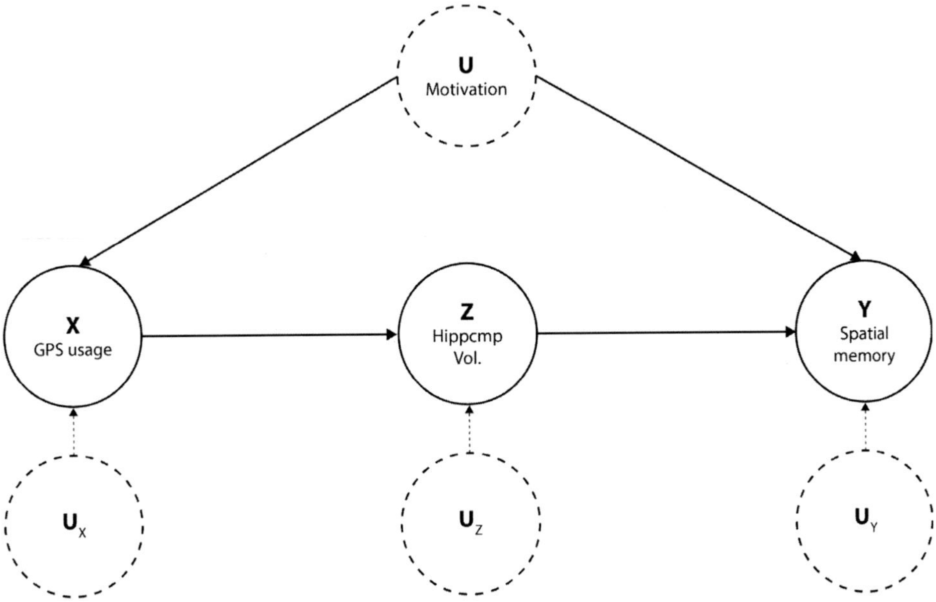

Figure 6.12 – A full model with exogenous variables

Next, we define the `.sample()` method.

Calling this method will return an *observational* distribution from our system. Note that all the coefficients are hypothetical and not based on actual research:

```
def sample(self, sample_size=100, treatment_value=None):
    """Samples from the SCM"""
    if self.random_seed:
        np.random.seed(self.random_seed)

    u_x = self.u_x.rvs(sample_size)
    u_y = self.u_y.rvs(sample_size)
    u_z = self.u_z.rvs(sample_size)
    u = self.u.rvs(sample_size)

    if treatment_value:
        gps = np.array([treatment_value]*sample_size)
    else:
        gps = u_x + 0.7*u

    hippocampus = -0.6*gps + 0.25*u_z
    memory = 0.7*hippocampus + 0.25*u

    return gps, hippocampus, memory
```

First, we fix the random seed if a user provided a value for it.

Next, we sample exogenous variables.

Finally, we compute the values of the three observed variables in our model, `gps`, `hippocampus`, and `memory`, which represent GPS usage, hippocampal volume, and spatial memory change respectively.

You might have noticed that there's an additional `if` statement that checks for `treatment_value`. It allows us to generate *interventional* distribution from the model if a value for `treatment_value` is provided.

The last method in our SCM implementation is `.intervene()`. It's a syntactic sugar wrapper around `.sample()`. The `.intervene()` method returns an interventional distribution from our model:

```
    def intervene(self, treatment_value, sample_size=100):
        """Intervenes on the SCM"""
        return self.sample(treatment_value=treatment_value, sample_
size=sample_size)
```

Its purpose is to make the code cleaner and our process more explicit.

Note that passing either `None` or `0` as a treatment value will result in a special case of *null* intervention, and the outcome will be identical to the observational sample.

Great! Let's instantiate the model and generate some observational data:

```
scm = GPSMemorySCM()
gps_obs, hippocampus_obs, memory_obs = scm.sample(600)
```

Generating observational data is as simple as calling the `.sample()` method.

Next, let's run an experiment. We will use a range of treatments from 1 to 20 units of GPS usage:

```
treatments = []
experiment_results = []

# Sample over a range of treatments
for treatment in np.arange(1, 21):
    gps_hours, hippocampus, memory = scm.intervene(treatment_
value=treatment, sample_size=30)
    experiment_results.append(memory)
    treatments.append(gps_hours)
```

For each treatment value, we sample 30 observations. We store treatment values and outcome values in the `treatments` and `experiment_results` lists respectively.

Figure 6.13 presents the relationship between GPS usage and spatial memory change in observational and interventional samples:

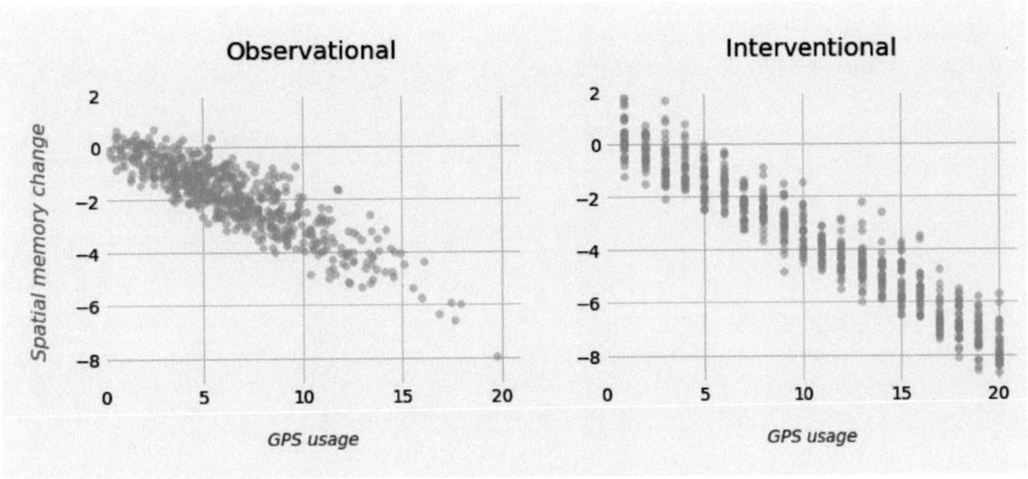

Figure 6.13 – Scatterplots of GPS usage versus spatial memory change

As you can see, the distributions in the scatterplots differ.

Let's fit two linear regression models – one on the observational data and one on the interventional data – and compare the results. What results do you expect?

Let's check your guess!

First, let's instantiate two regression models and train them:

```
lr_naive = LinearRegression()
lr_naive.fit(
    X=gps_obs.reshape(-1, 1),
    y=memory_obs
)
```

We train the first model, `lr_naive`, on the observational data. We regress spatial memory change on GPS usage.

You might have noticed that when we pass `gps_obs` to the `.fit()` method, we change the array's shape. This is because `sklearn` models require 2D arrays of shape (n, d), where n is the number of observations and d is the dimensionality of the design matrix (or a number of features if you will), and our original array was 1D with shape $(n,)$ as we only have one feature.

The second model will use the same variables but generated in our experiment, rather than recorded from observations.

Before we train it, we need to unpack our treatment (GPS usage) and outcome (spatial memory change). This is because we generated 30 samples for each of the 20 intervention levels, and we stored them as a nested list of lists.

For ease of comparison with the observational models, we want to reshape the model to have 600 observations rather than 20*30 observations:

```
treatments_unpack = np.array(treatments).flatten()
results_unpack = np.array(experiment_results).flatten()

lr_experiment = LinearRegression()
lr_experiment.fit(
    X=treatments_unpack.reshape(-1, 1),
    y=results_unpack
)
```

Perfect. Now, let's generate predictions from both models on test data:

```
X_test = np.arange(1, 21).reshape(-1, 1)

preds_naive = lr_naive.predict(X_test)
preds_experiment = lr_experiment.predict(X_test)
```

We start by generating test data. It's as simple as generating a sequence between 1 and 20. These numbers quantify the number of units of GPS usage.

Next, we query both models to generate predictions on test data. *Figure 6.14* presents a scatterplot of the interventional distribution and predictions from both models:

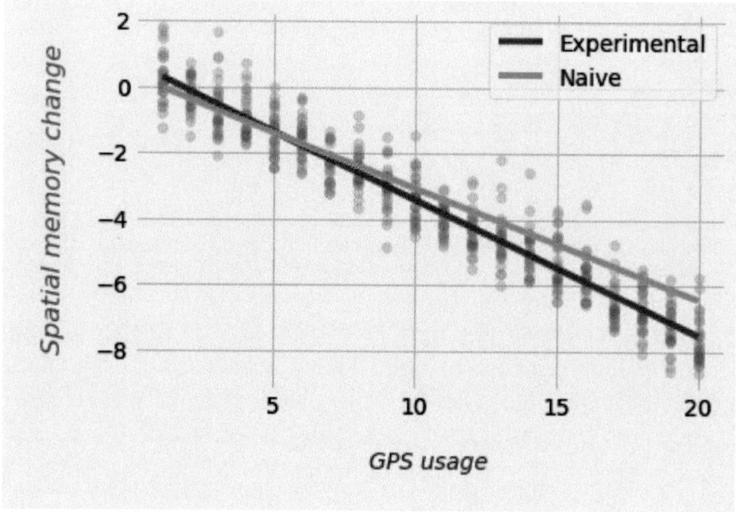

Figure 6.14 – A scatterplot of the interventional distribution and two fitted regression lines

We can see pretty clearly that the naive model does not fit the experimental data very well.

Let's compare the values for the regression coefficients for both models:

```
print(f'Naive model:\n{lr_naive.coef_}\n')
print(f'Experimental model:\n{lr_experiment.coef_}')
```

This results in the following output:

```
Naive model:
-0.3246130171160016

Experimental model:
-0.4207238110947806
```

As expected, the coefficient values for both models differ.

Let's figure out how to get a valid causal coefficient from observational data using the front-door criterion in three simple steps.

The linear bridge to the causal promised land

It turns out that when we're lucky enough that our model of interest is linear and the front-door criterion can be applied, we can compute the valid estimate of the causal effect of X on Y in three simple steps:

- Fit a model, $Z \sim X$
- Fit a model, $Y \sim Z + X$
- Multiply the coefficients from model 1 and model 2

Let's code it:

1. First, we train the model to regress Z on X ($Z \sim X$). Note that we only use observational data to fit this (and the following) model:

    ```
    lr_zx = LinearRegression()
    lr_zx.fit(
        X=gps_obs.reshape(-1, 1),
        y=hippocampus_obs
    )
    ```

2. Next, let's train the model to regress Y on X and Z. Note that in both cases, we follow the same logic that we followed in the continuous case described previously:

    ```
    lr_yxz = LinearRegression()
    lr_yxz.fit(
        X=np.array([gps_obs, hippocampus_obs]).T,
        y=memory_obs
    )
    ```

3. Finally, let's multiply the coefficients for both models:

```
lr_zx.coef_[0] * lr_yxz.coef_[1]
```

We take the 0th coefficient from the first model (there's just one coefficient, for GPS usage) and the 1st coefficient for the second model (because we're interested in the effect of hippocampal volume on spatial memory *given* GPU usage), and we multiply them together.

This gives us the following estimate of the causal effect:

```
-0.43713599902679
```

Good job! This is pretty close to the experimental model!

Values estimated from experiments and values estimated from observational data may differ in finite sample regimes, and that's utterly natural. The larger the sample size, the smaller the discrepancy between them we should expect *on average*.

Great!

We saw that the front-door-adjusted estimate was pretty close to the estimate obtained from the experimental data, but what actually is the true effect that we're trying to estimate, and how close are we?

We can answer this question pretty easily if we have a full linear SCM. The true effect in a model such as ours is equal to the product of coefficients on causal paths from $X \rightarrow Z$ and $Z \rightarrow Y$. The idea of multiplying the coefficients on a directed causal path can be traced back to Sewall Wright's *path analysis*, introduced as early as 1920 (Wright, 1920).

In our case, the true causal effect of GPS usage on spatial memory will be -0.6 * 0.7 = -0.42. The coefficients (-0.6 and 0.7) can be read from the definition of our SCM.

It turns out that our front-door-adjusted and experimental estimates were pretty close (~4% and <1% errors respectively), while the naïve estimate was more than 22% off. Imagine that you can improve the conversion rate of a marketing campaign by 20% for your client – an actual result that one of the causal machine learning companies where a colleague of mine used to work demonstrated.

It's time to conclude this section. We learned what the front-door criterion is. We discussed three conditions (and one additional assumption) necessary to make the criterion work and showed how to derive an *adjustment formula* from the basic principles. Finally, we built an SCM and generated observational and interventional distributions to show how the front-door criterion can be used to accurately approximate experimental results from observational data.

Are there other criteria out there? Let's do-calculus!

In the real world, not all causal graphs will have a structure that allows the use of the back-door or front-door criteria. Does this mean that we cannot do anything about them?

Fortunately, no. Back-door and front-door criteria are special cases of a more general framework called *do*-calculus (Pearl, 2009). Moreover, *do*-calculus has been proven to be complete (Shpitser and Pearl, 2006), meaning that if there is an identifiable causal effect in a given DAG, G, it can be found using the rules of *do*-calculus.

What are these rules?

The three rules of do-calculus

Before we can answer the question, we need to define some new helpful notation.

Given a DAG G, we can say that $G_{\overline{X}}$ is a modification of G, where we removed all the *incoming* edges to the node *X*. We will call $G_{\underline{X}}$ a modification of G, where we removed all the *outgoing* edges from the node *X*.

For example, $G_{\overline{X}\underline{Z}}$ will denote a DAG, G, where we removed all the incoming edges to the node *X* and all the outgoing edges from the node *Z*.

Perfect. Now, let's see the rules (Pearl, 2009, and Malina, 2020):

- *Rule 1*: When an observation can be ignored:

$$P(Y = y|do(X = x), Z = z, W = w) = P(Y = y|do(X = x), W = w) \ if (Y \perp\!\!\!\perp Z|X, W)_{G_{\overline{X}}}$$

- *Rule 2*: When intervention can be treated as an observation:

$$P(Y = y|do(X = x), do(Z = z), W = w) = P(Y = y|do(X = x), Z = z, W = w) \ if (Y \perp\!\!\!\perp Z|X, W)_{G_{\overline{X}\underline{Z}}}$$

- *Rule 3*: When intervention can be ignored:

$$P(Y = y|do(X = x), do(Z = z), W = w) = P(Y = y|do(X = x), W = w) \ if (Y \perp\!\!\!\perp Z|X, W)_{G_{\overline{X}\overline{Z(W)}}}$$

In *rule 3*, *Z*(*W*) is the set of *Z*-nodes that are not ancestors of any *W*-nodes in the altered DAG, $G_{\overline{X}}$.

These rules might look pretty overwhelming! Let's try to decode their meaning.

Rule 1 tells us that we can *ignore* any observational (set of) variable(s), *Z*, when *Z* and the outcome, *Y*, are independent, given *X* and *W* in a modified DAG, $G_{\overline{X}}$.

Rule 2 tells us that any intervention over a (set of) variable(s), *Z*, can be *treated as an observation* when *Z* and the outcome *Y* are independent given *X* and *W* in a modified DAG $G_{\overline{X}\underline{Z}}$.

Finally, *rule 3* tells us that any intervention over a (set of) variable(s), *Z*, can be *ignored* when *Z* and the outcome, *Y*, are independent, given *X* and *W* in a modified DAG, $G_{\overline{X}, \overline{Z(W)}}$.

All this might sound complicated at first, until you realize that what it requires in practice is to take your DAG, find the (set of) confounders (denoted as *Z* in our rules), and check whether any of the rules apply. Plus, you can stack the transformations into arbitrary long sequences if this helps! The good part is that this work can also be automated.

It might take some time to fully digest the rules of *do*-calculus, and that's OK. Once you get familiar with them, you'll have a very powerful tool in your toolbox.

If you want to learn more about *do*-calculus, check out Pearl (2009) for formal definitions and step-by-step examples, Spitser and Pearl (2006) for the proof of completeness, and Stephen Malina's blog for intuitive understanding (Malina, 2020 – `https://stephenmalina.com/post/2020-03-09-front-door-do-calc-derivation/`).

Before we conclude this section, let's see one more popular method that can be used to identify causal effects.

Instrumental variables

Instrumental variables (**IVs**) are a family of deconfounding techniques that are hugely popular in econometrics. Let's take a look at the DAG in *Figure 6.15*:

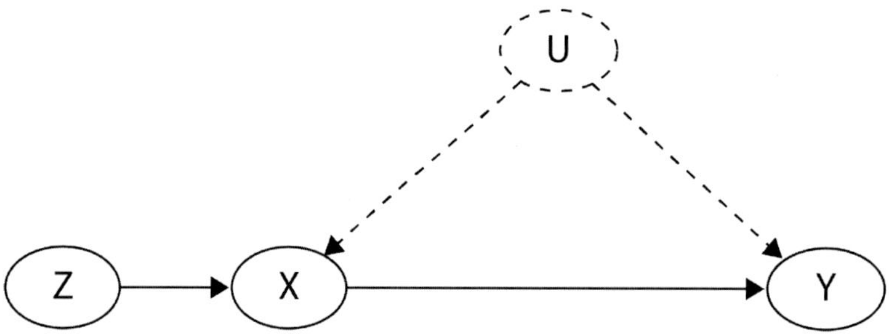

Figure 6.15 – An example DAG for the IV technique

We're interested in estimating the causal effect of X on Y. You can see that we cannot use the back-door criterion here because U is unobserved. We cannot use the front-door criterion either because there's no mediator between X and Y.

Not all is lost though! It turns out that we can use the IV technique to estimate our causal effect of interest. Let's see how to do it.

The three conditions of IVs

Instrumental variable methods require a special variable called an *instrument* to be present in a graph. We will use Z to denote the instrument. Our effect of interest is the causal effect of X on Y.

An *instrument* needs to meet the following three conditions (Hernán and Robins, 2020):

- The instrument, Z, is associated with X
- The instrument, Z, doesn't affect Y in any way except through X
- There are no common causes of Z and Y

The first condition talks about *association* rather than *causation*. The nature of the relationship between Z and X determines how much information we'll be able to extract from our instrument. Theoretically speaking, we can even use instruments that are only weakly (non-directly) associated with X (in such a case, they are called **proxy instruments**), yet there's a cost to this.

In certain cases, the only thing we'll be able to obtain will be the lower and upper bounds of the effect, and in some cases, these bounds might be very broad and, therefore, not very useful (Hernán and Robins, 2020).

We're lucky though!

Calculating causal effects with IVs

Let's take a look at *Figure 6.15* once again. The variable Z is associated with X, it does not affect Y other than through X, and there are no common causes of Z and Y; therefore, Z meets all of the criteria of being an *instrument*. Moreover, in our DAG, the relationship between Z and X is causal and direct, which allows us to approximate the exact causal effect (as opposed to just bounds)!

To calculate the causal effect of X on Y in a linear case, all we need to do is fit two linear regression models and compute the ratio of their coefficients!

The two models are as follows:

- $Y \sim Z$
- $Y \sim X$

We compute the ratio by dividing the coefficient for the first model by the coefficient from the second model.

Et voilà!

To see a step-by-step example of computing the IV estimation in a linear model, check the notebook accompanying this chapter (`https://bit.ly/causal-ntbk-06`).

Estimation using IVs can be extended to non-linear and non-parametric cases (for example, Li et al., 2022, and Carroll et al., 2004).

All this makes IVs pretty flexible and broadly adopted, yet in practice, it might be difficult to find good instruments or verify that the necessary assumptions (for instance, a lack of influence of Z on Y other than through X) are met.

There are a couple of resources if you want to dive deeper into IVs. For a great technical and formal overview, check out *Chapter 16* of the excellent book *Causal Inference: What If?* by Miguel Hernán and James Robbins from the Harvard School of Public Health (Hernán and Robins, 2020).

For practical advice on how to find good instruments, intuitions, and great real-world examples, check out *Chapter 7* of Scott Cunningham's *Causal Inference: The Mixtape* (Cunningham, 2021). I am sure you'll love the latter, in particular if you're a hip-hop aficionado.

In this section, we learned about *do*-calculus, a flexible framework to identify causal effects that generalizes back-door and front-door criteria. We discussed the three rules of *do*-calculus that allow us to find causal effects in any DAG that is identifiable (hence, the completeness of *do*-calculus).

In the second part of this section, we introduced the IV technique – a popular method of causal effect identification and estimation that has been widely adopted in econometrics, epidemiology, and social sciences.

Finally, we learned how to use IVs in a linear case and linked to the resources demonstrating how the method can be extended to non-linear and non-parametric cases.

Wrapping it up

We learned a lot in this chapter, and you deserve some serious applause for coming this far!

In this chapter, we learned a lot. We started with the notion of *d*-separation. Then, we showed how *d*-separation is linked to the idea of an *estimand*. We discussed what causal estimands are and what their role is in the causal inference process.

Next, we discussed two powerful methods of causal effect identification, the back-door and front-door criteria, and applied them to our ice cream and GPS usage examples.

Finally, we presented a generalization of front-door and back-door criteria, the powerful framework of *do*-calculus, and introduced a family of methods called instrumental variables, which can help us identify causal effects where other methods fail.

The set of methods we learned in this chapter gives us a powerful causal toolbox that we can apply to real-world problems.

In the next chapter, we'll demonstrate how to properly structure an end-to-end causal inference process using the DoWhy library (Sharma and Kiciman, 2020), and we will get ready to set sail for the journey into the stormy waters of causal machine learning.

Answer

Controlling for B (*Figure 6.7*) essentially removes A's influence on X and Y. If we remove A from the graph, it will not change anything (up to noise) in our estimate of the relationship strength between X and Y. Note that in a graph with a removed node A, controlling for B becomes irrelevant (it does not hurt us to do so, but there's no benefit to it either).

References

Carroll, R. J., Ruppert, D., Crainiceanu, C. M., Tosteson, T. D., and Karagas, M. R. (2004). *Nonlinear and Nonparametric Regression and Instrumental Variables. Journal of the American Statistical Association,* 99(467), 736-750.

Cunningham, S. (2021). *Causal Inference: The Mixtape*. Yale University Press.

Dahmani, L., and Bohbot, V. D. (2020). *Habitual use of GPS negatively impacts spatial memory during self-guided navigation*. Scientific reports, 10(1), 6310.

Griesbauer, E. M., Manley, E., Wiener, J. M., and Spiers, H. J. (2022). *London taxi drivers: A review of neurocognitive studies and an exploration of how they build their cognitive map of London. Hippocampus,* 32(1), 3-20.

Hernán M. A., Robins J. M. (2020). *Causal Inference: What If*. Boca Raton: Chapman and Hall/CRC.

Hejtmánek, L., Oravcová, I., Motýl, J., Horáček, J., and Fajnerová, I. (2018). *Spatial knowledge impairment after GPS guided navigation: Eye-tracking study in a virtual town. International Journal of Human-Computer Studies*, 116, 15-24.

Koller, D., and Friedman, N. (2009). *Probabilistic Graphical Models: Principles and Techniques*. MIT Press.

Li, C., Rudin, C., and McCormick, T. H. (2022). *Rethinking Nonlinear Instrumental Variable Models through Prediction Validity. Journal of Machine Learning Research*, 23(96), 1-55.

Maguire, E. A., Gadian, D. G., Johnsrude, I. S., Good, C. D., Ashburner, J., Frackowiak, R. S., and Frith, C. D. (2000). *Navigation-related structural change in the hippocampi of taxi drivers*. Proceedings of the National Academy of Sciences of the United States of America, 97(8), 4398-4403.

Malina, S. (2020, March 9). *Deriving the front-door criterion with the do-calculus*. `https://stephenmalina.com/post/2020-03-09-front-door-do-calc-derivation/`.

Murphy, K. P. (2022). *Probabilistic Machine Learning: An introduction*. MIT Press.

O'Keefe, J., Nadel, L. (1978). *The hippocampus as a cognitive map*. Clarendon Press.

Pearl, J. (2009). *Causality: Models, reasoning, and inference*. Cambridge University Press.

Pearl, J., Glymour, M., and Jewell, N. P. (2016*). Causal inference in statistics: A primer*. Wiley.

Pearl, J., and Mackenzie, D. (2019). *The Book of Why*. Penguin.

Pelletier, L. G., Sharp, E., Blanchard, C., Lévesque, C. Vallerand, R. J., and Guay, F. (2007). *The general motivation scale (GMS): Its validity and usefulness in predicting success and failure at self-regulation*. Manuscript in preparation. University of Ottawa.

Pedregosa, F., Varoquaux, G., Gramfort, A., Michel, V., Thirion, B., Grisel, O., Blondel, M., Prettenhofer, P., Weiss, R., Dubourg, V., Vanderplas, J., Passos, A., Cournapeau, D., Brucher, M., Perrot, M., and Duchesnay, E. (2011). *Scikit-learn: Machine Learning in Python. Journal of Machine Learning Research*, 12, 2825-2830.

Seabold, S., and Perktold, J. (2010). *statsmodels: Econometric and statistical modeling with Python*. 9th Python in Science Conference.

Sharma, A., and Kiciman, E. (2020). *DoWhy: An End-to-End Library for Causal Inference*. arXiv Preprint arXiv:2011.04216.

Shpitser, I., and Pearl, J. (2006). *Identification of conditional interventional distributions*. In Proceedings of the 22nd Conference on Uncertainty in Artificial Intelligence, UAI 2006 (pp. 437-444).

Shpitser, I., VanderWeele, T., and Robins, J. M. (2010). *On the validity of covariate adjustment for estimating causal effects*. In Proceedings of the 26th Conference on Uncertainty in Artificial Intelligence, UAI 2010, 527-536. AUAI Press.

Woollett, K., and Maguire, E. A. (2011). *Acquiring "the Knowledge" of London's layout drives structural brain changes. Current Biology*, 21(24), 2109-2114.

Wright, S. (1920). *The Relative Importance of Heredity and Environment in Determining the Piebald Pattern of Guinea-Pigs*. Proceedings of the National Academy of Sciences, 6(6), 320–332.

7

The Four-Step Process of Causal Inference

Welcome to *Chapter 7*!

This is a true milestone in our journey. In this chapter, we'll learn how to neatly structure the entire causal inference process using the DoWhy library (Sharma & Kiciman, 2020). By the end of this chapter, you'll be able to write production-ready causal inference pipelines using linear and non-linear estimators.

We'll start with an introduction to DoWhy and its sister library, EconML (Battochi et al., 2019). After that, we'll see how to use the **graph modeling language** (**GML**), which we introduced briefly in *Chapter 4* to translate our assumptions regarding the data-generating process into graphs. Then, we'll see how to compute causal **estimands** and causal **estimates** using DoWhy. Finally, we'll introduce **refutation tests** and see how to apply them to our models. We'll conclude the chapter with an example of a complete causal inference process. By the end of this chapter, you'll have a solid understanding of the mechanics of the causal inference process and be able to carry it out for your own problems.

In this chapter, we'll cover the following topics:

- Introduction to DoWhy and EconML
- Practical GML and graphs
- Causal estimands and estimates in DoWhy
- Refutation tests
- A full causal process example using DoWhy and EconML

Introduction to DoWhy and EconML

In this section, we'll introduce the DoWhy and EconML packages.

We'll start with an overview of the Python causal ecosystem and then discuss what DoWhy and EconML are.

Then, we'll share why they are the packages of choice for this book.

Finally, we'll dive deeper into DoWhy's APIs and look into the integration between DoWhy and EconML.

Yalla!

Python causal ecosystem

The Python causal ecosystem is dynamically expanding. It is becoming increasingly rich and powerful. At the same time, it can also be confusing, especially when you're just starting your causal journey.

The following list presents a selection of actively developed Python causal packages that I am aware of at the time of writing this book:

- `CATENets`: A package implementing a number of neural network-based conditional average treatment effect estimators in JAX and PyTorch. We introduce `CATENets` in *Chapter 11*: `https://github.com/AliciaCurth/CATENets`.
- `causal-learn`: A causal discovery package from Carnegie-Mellon University. It is a Python translation and extension of the famous Java library Tetrad. It includes implementations of a number of conditional independence tests: `https://github.com/cmu-phil/causal-learn`.
- `causalimpact`: This package is a port to its R counterpart. It uses structural Bayesian models to estimate causal effects in quasi-experimental time series data: `https://github.com/jamalsenouci/causalimpact`.
- `causalinference`: A causal inference package implementing a number of basic causal estimators: `https://causalinferenceinpython.org/`.
- `causallib`: This package provides a suite of causal methods, encapsulated in an sklearn-style API. It includes meta-algorithms and an evaluation suite. It is an intuitive and flexible API that is supported by IBM: `https://github.com/IBM/causallib`.
- `CausalPy`: Four popular quasi-experimental methods implemented on top of the PyMC Python Bayesian framework. The package offers synthetic control, interrupted time series, difference-in-differences, and regression discontinuity methods: `https://github.com/pymc-labs/CausalPy`.

- `CausalML`: A library for uplift modeling and causal inference backed by Uber. The authors declare that it's stable and incubated for long-term support. Algorithms can be integrated into DoWhy's flow: `https://github.com/uber/causalml`.
- `Causica`: A package implementing an end-to-end causal algorithm, DECI. We discuss DECI in *Part 3*, *Causal Discovery*: `https://github.com/microsoft/causica`.
- `CDT`: A library with a broad selection of causal discovery methods. Some methods are ported from R packages. At the time of writing (September 2022), it does not include methods created later than 2019: `https://fentechsolutions.github.io/CausalDiscoveryToolbox/html/index.html`.
- `Differences`: A package that implements a number of quasi-experimental techniques based on the difference-in-differences technique: `https://github.com/bernardodionisi/differences`.
- `DoubleML`: A Python and R package implementing a set of methods based on **double machine learning** (**DML**): `https://docs.doubleml.org/stable/index.html`.
- `DoWhy`: A complete framework for DAG-based causal inference. Causal discovery is on the roadmap: `https://py-why.github.io/dowhy`.
- `EconML`: A library focused on modeling heterogeneous treatment effects using machine learning. It is similar in scope to `CausalML`. It is supported by Microsoft and deeply integrated with DoWhy: `https://github.com/microsoft/EconML`.
- `gCastle`: A comprehensive library for causal discovery. It contains implementations of many classic causal discovery algorithms as well as some of the most recent ones. It was developed by Huawei's Noah's Ark Lab. We'll use it in *Part 3*, *Causal Discovery*: `https://github.com/huawei-noah/trustworthyAI/tree/master/gcastle`.
- `GRAPL` (`grapl-causal`): A computational library for working with causal graphs. It includes advanced identification algorithms, such as **directed acyclic graphs** (**DAGs**): `https://github.com/max-little/GRAPL`.
- `LiNGAM`: A causal discovery package implementing a number of `LiNGAM`-family algorithms: `https://lingam.readthedocs.io/en/latest/index.html`.
- `PySensemakr`: A Python implementation of the R `sensemakr` library. It implements a number of causal sensitivity analysis tools for regression models: `https://github.com/nlapier2/PySensemakr`.
- `Semopy`: A package for structural equation modeling in Python: `https://semopy.com/`.
- `scikit-uplift`: A library focused on uplift modeling using an sklearn-style API: `https://www.uplift-modeling.com/en/latest/user_guide/index.html`.

- `tfcausalimpact`: A native Python implementation of R's `causalimpact` built on top of TensorFlow Probability. It provides a flexible framework for estimating causal effects in quasi-experimental time series data using structural Bayesian models: `https://github.com/WillianFuks/tfcausalimpact`.
- `YLearn`: A package containing a mixture of causal methods, such as a number causal effect estimators, one causal discovery algorithm (at the time of writing), and other utilities: `https://ylearn.readthedocs.io/en/latest/`.

As you can see, we have many options to choose from. You might be wondering – what's so special about DoWhy and EconML that we've chosen to use these particular packages in the book?

Why DoWhy?

There are at least six reasons why I think choosing DoWhy as the foundation of your causal ecosystem is a great idea. Let me share them with you:

- DoWhy offers a well-designed, consistent, and practical API
- DoWhy is designed in a way that enables you to run the entire causal inference process in *four clearly defined* and *easily reproducible steps*
- DoWhy integrates smoothly with many other libraries (such as EconML, scikit-learn, and CausalML)
- DoWhy is actively maintained by a team of seasoned researchers and developers
- DoWhy is supported by organizations such as Microsoft and AWS, which increases the chances for long-term stable development
- DoWhy looks into the future with a frequently updated roadmap

Oui, mon ami, but what is DoWhy?

The official documentation (`https://bit.ly/DoWhyDocs`) describes DoWhy as an *end-to-end causal inference library*. I like to think of it as a framework. DoWhy offers a comprehensive toolkit for causal inference. In most cases, you won't need to go for another package to address your causal inference problem.

With the new experimental GCM API (Blobaum et al., 2022; for more details, see `https://bit.ly/DoWhyGCM`), DoWhy becomes even more powerful! Another great thing about DoWhy is that it translates a complex process of causal inference into a set of simple and easily reproducible steps.

DoWhy's API zoo

The version of DoWhy that we use across the book (0.8) offers three ways to work with causal models: the main API based on the `CausalModel` class; the high-level pandas API, which allows you to perform interventions directly on pandas DataFrames; and an experimental GCM API that allows us to easily estimate causal effects and compute interventions, counterfactuals, and attribute distributional changes between datasets in just a couple lines of code.

How about EconML?

EconML is a Python package built as a part of Microsoft Research's *ALICE* project (`https://bit.ly/MsftAlice`). Its main goal is to estimate causal effects from observational data via machine learning (Battochi et al., 2019). The package provides us with a scikit-learn-like API for fitting causal machine learning estimators. On top of this, we get a series of very useful methods for obtaining causal effects, confidence intervals, and integrated interpretability tools such as tree interpreters or Shapley values.

One of the great things about EconML is that it's deeply integrated with DoWhy. This integration allows us to call EconML estimators from within DoWhy code without even explicitly importing EconML. This is a great advantage, especially when you're in the early experimental stage of your project and your code does not have a strong structure. The integration allows you to keep your code clean and compact and helps to avoid excessive clutter.

Great, now that we've had a short introduction, let's jump in and see how to work with DoWhy and EconML. We'll learn more about both libraries on the way.

In the next four sections, we'll see how to use the main DoWhy API to perform the following four steps of causal inference:

1. Modeling the problem
2. Finding the estimand(s)
3. Computing the estimates
4. Validating the model

Before we start, let's generate some data.

We're going to use the `GPSMemorySCM` class from *Chapter 6* for this purpose. The code for this chapter is in the `Chapter_07.ipynb` notebook (`https://bit.ly/causal-ntbk-07`).

Let's initialize our SCM, generate 1,000 observations, and store them in a data frame:

```
scm = GPSMemorySCM()
gps_obs, hippocampus_obs, memory_obs = scm.sample(1000)

df = pd.DataFrame(np.vstack([gps_obs, hippocampus_obs,
    memory_obs]).T, columns=['X', 'Z', 'Y'])
```

Note that we denoted the columns for GPS with *X*, hippocampal volume with *Z*, and spatial memory with *Y*.

Naturally, in most real-world scenarios, we'll work with real-world data rather than generated data. Nonetheless, in both cases, it's important to keep your naming conventions clean and consistent between your data frame, your graph, and your `CausalModel` object. Any inconsistencies might result in distorted or unexpected results.

Great, we're now ready to take the first step!

Step 1 – modeling the problem

In this section, we'll discuss and practice step 1 of the four-step causal inference process: *modeling the problem*.

We'll split this step into two substeps:

1. Creating a graph representing our problem
2. Instantiating DoWhy's `CausalModel` object using this graph

Creating the graph

In *Chapter 3*, we introduced a graph language called GML. We'll use GML to define our data-generating process in this section.

Figure 7.1 presents the GPS example from the previous chapter, which we'll model next. Note that we have omitted variable-specific noise for clarity:

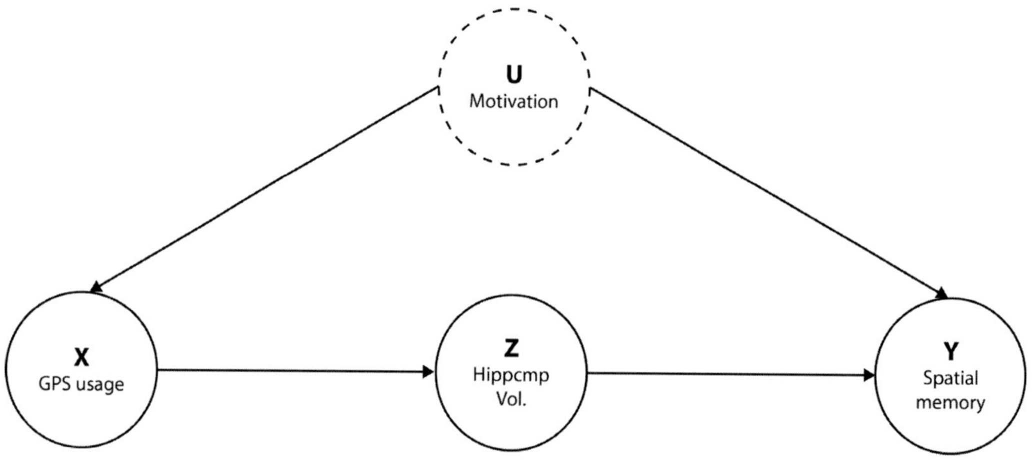

Figure 7.1 – The graphical model from Chapter 6

Note that the graph in *Figure 7.1* contains an unobserved variable, *U*. We did not include this variable in our dataset (it's unobserved!), but we'll include it in our graph. This will allow DoWhy to recognize that there's an unobserved confounder in the graph and find a relevant estimand for us automatically.

Great! Let's translate the model from *Figure 7.1* into a GML graph:

```
gml_graph = """
graph [
    directed 1

    node [
        id "X"
        label "X"
    ]
    node [
        id „Z"
        label „Z"
    ]
    node [
        id "Y"
        label "Y"
    ]
    node [
        id „U"
        label „U"
    ]

    edge [
        source "X"
        target "Z"
    ]
    edge [
        source "Z"
        target "Y"
    ]
    edge [
        source "U"
        target "X"
    ]
    edge [
        source "U"
        target "Y"
    ]
]
"""
```

Our definition starts with the `directed` keyword. It tells the parser that all edges in the graph should be directed. To obtain an undirected graph, you can use `undirected` instead.

Next, we define the nodes. Each node has a unique ID and a label. Finally, we define the edges. Each edge has a source and a target. The entire definition is encapsulated in a Python multiline string.

Let's put our graph into action!

Building a CausalModel object

To instantiate a `CausalModel` object for our problem, we need to provide the constructor with four things: data as a pandas data frame, a GML graph, the name of the treatment variable in the data frame, and the name of the outcome variable in the data frame.

We denoted GPS – our treatment – with *X*. Our outcome – memory change – was denoted by *Y*. Our data is represented by a pandas data frame, `df`, and our graph is assigned to the `gml_graph` variable.

We're ready to instantiate `CausalModel`:

```
model = CausalModel(
    data=df,
    treatment='X',
    outcome='Y',
    graph=gml_graph
)
```

To make sure everything works as expected, let's plot the model:

```
model.view_model()
```

This should result in a visualization similar to the one in *Figure 7.2*:

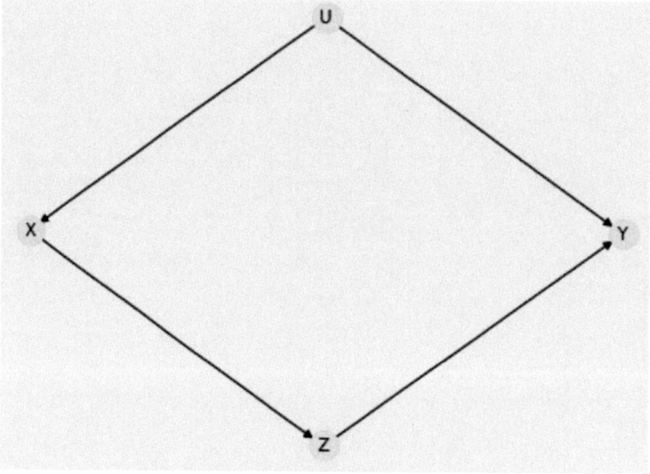

Figure 7.2 – A visualization of our model

In this section, we've learned how to create a GML graph to model our problem and how to pass this graph into the `CausalModel` object. In the next section, we'll see how to use DoWhy to automatically find estimands for our graph.

Step 2 – identifying the estimand(s)

This short section is all about finding estimands with DoWhy. We'll start with a brief overview of estimands supported by the library and then jump straight into practice!

DoWhy offers three ways to find estimands:

- Back-door
- Front-door
- Instrumental variable

We know all of them from the previous chapter. To see a quick practical introduction to all three methods, check out my blog post *Causal Python — 3 Simple Techniques to Jump-Start Your Causal Inference Journey Today* (Molak, 2022; `https://bit.ly/DoWhySimpleBlog`).

Let's see how to use DoWhy in order to find a correct estimand for our model.

It turns out it is very easy! Just see for yourself:

```
estimand = model.identify_effect()
```

Yes, that's all!

We just call the `.identify_effect()` method of our `CausalModel` object and we're done!

Let's print out our estimand to see what we can learn:

```
print(estimand)
```

This results in the following output:

```
Estimand type: nonparametric-ate

### Estimand : 1
Estimand name: backdoor
No such variable(s) found!

### Estimand : 2
Estimand name: iv
No such variable(s) found!

### Estimand : 3
```

```
Estimand name: frontdoor
Estimand expression:
Expectation(Derivative(Y, [Z])*Derivative([Z], [X]))
Estimand assumption 1, Full-mediation: Z intercepts (blocks) all
directed paths from X to Y.
Estimand assumption 2, First-stage-unconfoundedness: If U→{X} and
U→{Z} then P(Z|X,U) = P(Z|X)
Estimand assumption 3, Second-stage-unconfoundedness: If U→{Z} and U→Y
then P(Y|Z, X, U) = P(Y|Z, X)
```

We see that DoWhy prints out three different estimands. There's the estimand's name and information if a given type of estimand has been found for our model.

For the estimand that has been found, there's information about it printed out; for estimands that haven't been found, there's a `No such variable(s) found!` string printed out.

You can see that DoWhy has found only one estimand for our graph: `frontdoor`. As you might remember from the previous chapter, this is the correct one for our model!

Before we finish this section, I want to reiterate one thing. The capabilities of DoWhy are really great, yet it will only be able to find estimands for us if our model is identifiable using one of the three supported methods. For more advanced identification strategies, check out the **grapl-causal** library created by Max Little of the University of Birmingham and MIT (`https://bit.ly/GRAPLCausalRepo`).

In this section, we learned how to find estimands automatically using DoWhy. Now, we're ready to compute the estimates!

Step 3 – obtaining estimates

In this section, we'll compute causal effect estimates for our model.

Computing estimates using DoWhy is as simple as it can be. To do it, we need to call the `.estimate_effect()` method of our `CausalModel` object:

```
estimate = model.estimate_effect(
    identified_estimand=estimand,
    method_name='frontdoor.two_stage_regression')
```

We pass two arguments to the method:

- Our identified estimand
- The name of the method that will be used to compute the estimate

You might recall from *Chapter 6* that we needed to fit two linear regression models, get their coefficients, and multiply them in order to obtain the final causal effect estimate. DoWhy makes this process much easier for us.

Let's print out the result:

```
print(f'Estimate of causal effect (
    linear regression): {estimate.value}')
```

This gives us the following output:

```
Estimate of causal effect (linear regression): -0.4201729192182768
```

That's almost identical to the true causal effect of -0.42!

Note that we haven't set the random seed, so your results might slightly differ.

Currently, DoWhy only supports one estimator for the front-door criterion (`frontdoor.two_stage_regression`), but many more estimators are available in general. We'll introduce some of them soon.

In this short section, we learned how to compute causal estimates using DoWhy.

Let's think about how to validate our causal model.

Step 4 – where's my validation set? Refutation tests

In this section, we'll discuss ideas regarding causal model validation. We'll introduce the idea behind refutation tests. Finally, we'll implement a couple of refutation tests in practice.

How to validate causal models

One of the most popular ways to validate machine learning models is through **cross-validation** (CV). The basic idea behind CV is relatively simple:

1. We split the data into k folds (subsets).
2. We train the model on $k - 1$ folds and validate it on the remaining fold.
3. We repeat this process k times.
4. At every step, we train on a different set of $k - 1$ folds and evaluate on the remaining fold (which is also different at each step).

Figure 7.3 presents a schematic visualization of a five-fold CV scheme:

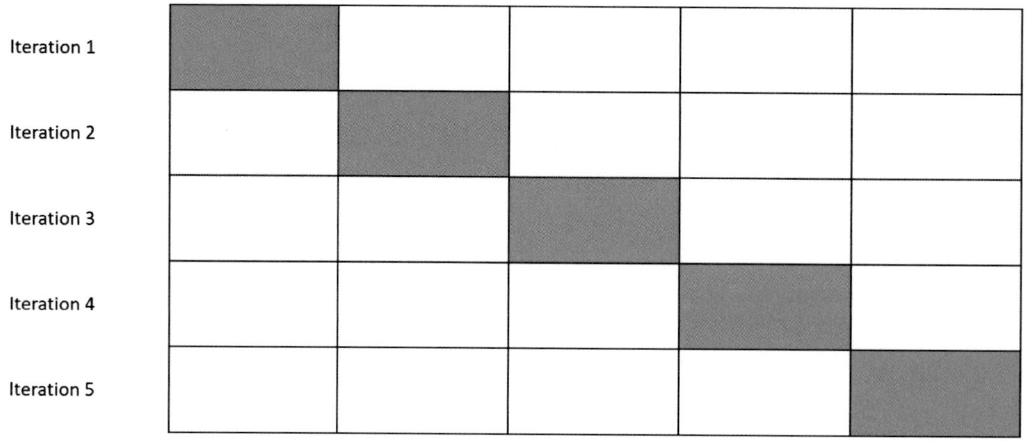

Figure 7.3 – Schematic of five-fold CV

In *Figure 7.3*, the blue folds denote validation sets, while the white ones denote training sets. We train a new model at each iteration using white folds for training and evaluate using the remaining blue fold. We collect metrics over iterations and compute a statistic summary (most frequently, the average).

CV is a widely adopted method to estimate prediction errors in statistical learning (yet it turns out that it's much less understood than we tend to think; Bates et al., 2021).

It would be great if we could use CV for causal models as well! Its simplicity and accessibility of implementations would make model evaluation really easy!

Unfortunately, this approach cannot provide us with any guarantees regarding the causal structure of the model (although it can be useful when working with and evaluating causal estimators, assuming that we know the correct causal structure; more on this in *Chapter 10*).

Why?

Although CV can provide us with some information about the estimator fit, this approach will not work in general as a causal model evaluation technique. The reason is that CV operates on rung 1 concepts. Let's think of an example.

Do you recall **Markov equivalence classes** (**MECs**), which we discussed in *Chapter 5*? All graphs within one MEC encode the same statistical independence structure. One consequence of this is that unless we intervene on critical nodes, all graphs belonging to the same MEC could generate virtually the same observational data. This means that we could have a wrong causal model that behaves very well in terms of CV prediction errors. This is problematic. Is there anything we can do to mitigate the limitation of CV?

Introduction to refutation tests

In 1935, the Austrian philosopher Karl Popper published his seminal book *Logik der Forschung* (Popper, 1935; rewritten English version: Popper, 1959). In the book, Popper wrestles with the idea of induction – generalizing knowledge from a finite sample of observations. He concludes (following our friend David Hume from *Chapter 1*) that sentences such as *all Xs are A* that are trying to capture the underlying principles of some phenomenon of interest can never be unambiguously proven. For instance, the sentence *the sun always rises in the east* might always be true for me in my lifetime, yet we can imagine a scenario where one day it does not. We have never observed this scenario, but it is physically possible.

Compare this example with another one: *the train always passes the station within five minutes after I hear the morning weather forecast on the radio* (do you remember Hume's association-based definition of causality?). Popper says that we never observe all *X*s and therefore it's impossible to *prove* a theory. He finds this problematic because he wants to see a difference between science and non-science (this is known as the **demarcation problem**). To solve this tension, Popper proposes that instead of proving a theory, we can try to disprove it.

His logic is simple. He says that "all *X*s are *A*" is logically equivalent to "no *X* is not-*A*." Therefore, if we find *X* that is not *A*, we can show that the theory is false. Popper proposes that scientific theories are *falsifiable* – we can define a set of conditions in which the theory would fail. On the other hand, non-scientific theories are *non-falsifiable* – for instance, the existence of a higher intelligent power that cannot be quantified in any systematic way.

Can Popperian ideas help us with evaluating causal models?

Let's get Popperian!

Every statistical model can be thought of as a hypothesis regarding some process. In particular, a *causal model* is a hypothesis regarding some *data-generating process*. In this sense, any model is an embodiment of a micro-theory of some real-world phenomenon and such a theory can be falsified.

Refutation tests aim to achieve this by modifying the model or the data. There are two types of transformations available in DoWhy (Sharma & Kiciman, 2020):

- Invariant transformations
- Nullifying transformations

Invariant transformations change the data in such a way that the result should not change the estimate. If the estimate changes significantly, the model fails to pass the test.

Nullifying transformations change the data in a way that should cause the estimated effect to be zero. If the result significantly differs from zero, the model fails the test.

The basic idea behind refutation tests is to modify an element of either the model or a dataset and see how it impacts the results.

For instance, a *random common cause refuter* adds a new confounding variable to the dataset and controls for it. If the original model is correctly specified, we expect that such an addition will *not lead to significant changes* in the model estimates (therefore, this test belongs to the *invariant transformations* category). We'll see a couple of refutation tests in action in this chapter.

Now, let's see how one of them – the *data subset refuter* – works.

Let's refute!

Let's apply some refutation tests to our model. Note that in DoWhy 0.8, not all tests will work with front-door estimands.

We apply `data_subset_refuter` in the following way:

```
refute_subset = model.refute_estimate(
    estimand=estimand,
    estimate=estimate,
    method_name="data_subset_refuter",
    subset_fraction=0.4)
```

This test removes a random subset of the data and re-estimates the causal effect. In expectation, the new estimate (on the subset) should not significantly differ from the original one. Let's print out the results:

```
print(refute_subset)
```

This gives us the following output:

```
Refute: Use a subset of data
Estimated effect:-0.4201729192182768
New effect:-0.41971603098814647
p value:0.98
```

As you can see, the original and newly estimated effects are very close and the p-value is high, indicating that there's likely no true difference between the two estimates. This result does not falsify our hypothesis and perhaps makes us a bit more confident that our model might be correct.

In this section, we discussed the basic challenges of validating causal models. We introduced the logic behind refutation tests and learned how to apply them in practice using DoWhy.

In the next section, we'll practice our DoWhy causal inference skills and see more refutation tests in action.

Full example

This section is here to help us solidify our newly acquired knowledge. We'll run a full causal inference process once again, step by step. We'll introduce some new exciting elements on the way and – finally – we'll translate the whole process to the new GCM API. By the end of this section, you will have the confidence and skills to apply the four-step causal inference process to your own problems.

Figure 7.4 presents a graphical model that we'll use in this section:

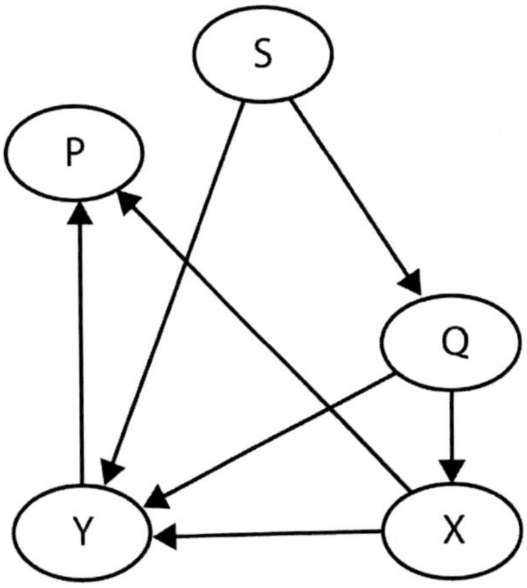

Figure 7.4 – A graphical model that we'll use in this section

We'll generate 1,000 observations from an SCM following the structure from *Figure 7.4* and store them in a data frame:

```
SAMPLE_SIZE = 1000

S = np.random.random(SAMPLE_SIZE)
Q = 0.2*S + 0.67*np.random.random(SAMPLE_SIZE)
X = 0.14*Q + 0.4*np.random.random(SAMPLE_SIZE)
Y = 0.7*X + 0.11*Q + 0.32*S +
    0.24*np.random.random(SAMPLE_SIZE)
P = 0.43*X + 0.21*Y + 0.22*np.random.random(SAMPLE_SIZE)

# Build a data frame
df = pd.DataFrame(np.vstack([S, Q, X, Y, P]).T,
    columns=['S', 'Q', 'X', 'Y', 'P'])
```

Great, now we're ready to build a graph.

Step 1 – encode the assumptions

As the graph in *Figure 7.4* is big enough to make writing its GML definition manually daunting, we'll automate it with two simple `for` loops. Feel free to steal this trick and use it in your own projects:

```
nodes = ['S', 'Q', 'X', 'Y', 'P']
edges = ['SQ', 'SY', 'QX', 'QY', 'XP', 'YP', 'XY']

gml_string = 'graph [directed 1\n'

for node in nodes:
    gml_string += f'\tnode [id "{node}" label "{node}"]\n'

for edge in edges:
    gml_string += f'\tedge [source "{edge[0]}" target
        "{edge[1]}"]\n'

gml_string += ']'
```

Let's unpack this code quickly:

1. First, we define two lists: a list of nodes (`nodes`) and a list of edges (`edges`).
2. Next, we create the `gml_string` variable, which contains the opening bracket, `[`, the `directed` keyword, and our graph's ID (number 1).
3. Then, we run the first `for` loop over the nodes. At each step, we append a new line to our `gml_string` representing a node and specifying its ID and label (we've also added tabulation and newlines to make it more readable, but this is not necessary).
4. After the first loop is done, we run the second `for` loop over edges. We append a new line at each step again. This time, each line contains information about the edge source and target.
5. Finally, we append the closing bracket, `]`, to our `gml_string`.

Let's print out our definition to see whether it's as expected:

```
print(gml_string)
```

This gives us the following output:

```
graph [directed 1
  node [id "S" label "S"]
  node [id "Q" label "Q"]
  node [id "X" label "X"]
  node [id "Y" label "Y"]
  node [id "P" label "P"]
  edge [source "S" target "Q"]
```

```
    edge [source "S" target "Y"]
    edge [source "Q" target "X"]
    edge [source "Q" target "Y"]
    edge [source "X" target "P"]
    edge [source "Y" target "P"]
    edge [source "X" target "Y"]
]
```

Beautiful! The GML part is correct.

Let's instantiate the `CausalModel` object:

```
model = CausalModel(
    data=df,
    treatment='X',
    outcome='Y',
    graph=gml_string
)
```

Let's visualize the model to make sure that our graph's structure is as expected:

```
model.view_model()
```

You should see a plot similar to the one in *Figure 7.5*:

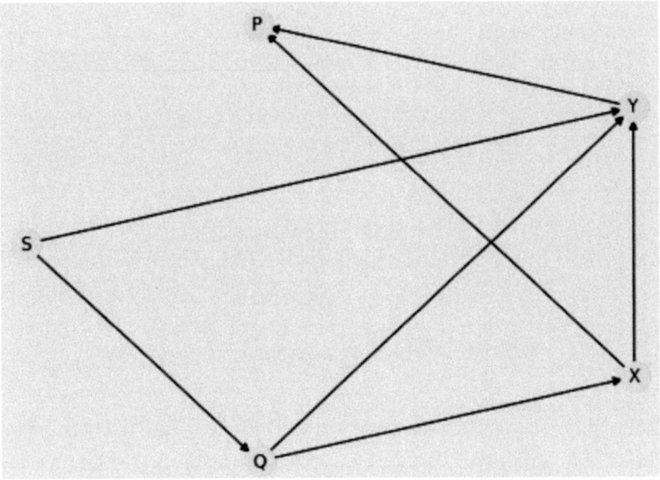

Figure 7.5 – A visualization of our DoWhy CausalModel

The graph in *Figure 7.5* has the same set of nodes and edges that the graph in *Figure 7.4* has. It confirms that our GML definition is correct.

We're now ready to find the estimand(s) for our model.

Step 2 – getting the estimand

Before we move on to coding, can you figure out what estimand we expect here? How many confounders are there between *X* and *Y*? What will happen if we control for *Q*? Or for *P*? Or for *S*?

Let's see what DoWhy's view on this is:

```
estimand = model.identify_effect()
print(estimand)
```

The estimand output is the following:

```
Estimand type: nonparametric-ate

### Estimand : 1
Estimand name: backdoor
Estimand expression:
 d
────(E[Y|Q])
d[X]
Estimand assumption 1, Unconfoundedness: If U→{X} and U→Y then
P(Y|X,Q,U) = P(Y|X,Q)

### Estimand : 2
Estimand name: iv
No such variable(s) found!

### Estimand : 3
Estimand name: frontdoor
No such variable(s) found!
```

We can see that DoWhy proposed one valid estimand – `backdoor`. Although our graph looks a bit complex, it contains only one back-door path. Controlling for *Q* deconfounds the relationship between *X* and *Y*.

Step 3 – estimate!

Although our SCM is pretty simple and we could model it using linear regression, we'll use a more advanced estimator this time. Along the way, we'll learn how to leverage DoWhy's integration with other packages in the Python machine learning ecosystem to build advanced multicomponent estimators.

First, let's import some models from scikit-learn. We picked `LassoCV` and `GradientBoostingRegressor`. Both are rather overkill for our simple problem, but we picked them on purpose so we can see DoWhy's flexibility and integration capabilities in action:

```
from sklearn.linear_model import LassoCV
from sklearn.ensemble import GradientBoostingRegressor
```

Now, let's build an estimator.

We will use a DML estimator from the EconML package. DML is a family of methods for estimating causal effects that was originally proposed by Victor Chernozhukov and colleagues (Chernozhukov et al., 2016).

Behind the scenes, DML fits *three machine learning models* to compute de-biased estimates of treatment effects. First, it predicts the outcome from the controls. Then, it predicts the treatment from the controls. Finally, it fits the model that regresses residuals from the second model on the residuals from the first model.

We will discuss DML in greater detail in *Chapter 10.*

Let's see how to leverage the power of DML using DoWhy:

```
estimate = model.estimate_effect(
    identified_estimand=estimand,
    method_name='backdoor.econml.dml.DML',
    method_params={
        'init_params': {
            'model_y': GradientBoostingRegressor(),
            'model_t': GradientBoostingRegressor(),
            'model_final': LassoCV(fit_intercept=False),
        },
        'fit_params': {}}
)
```

Let's unpack this code:

1. First, we provided the `estimate_effect()` method with the *estimand.*
2. After that, we pointed to what method we want to use. Here, we've chosen one of EconML's DML estimators. As you can see, we haven't even imported EconML in our session. We passed a `'backdoor.econml.dml.DML'` string instead. This is an example of the deep integration between DoWhy and EconML.
3. Then, we defined the models we want to use for each of the three stages of DML estimation. We use regression models only as our treatment and outcome are both continuous.
4. We left the `fit_params` dictionary empty because we didn't want to specify any initial parameters for our models.

Let's see how well DML handled the task:

```
print(f'Estimate of causal effect (DML): {estimate.value}')
```

This results in the following output:

```
Estimate of causal effect (DML): 0.6998599202773215
```

Good job! The true effect is `0.7` and so we are really close!

Before we move further, let's see a simpler model in action.

A simple linear regression would likely be sufficient to model our problem in this section.

For the sake of comparison, let's see the results of linear regression:

```
estimate_lr = model.estimate_effect(
    identified_estimand=estimand,
    method_name='backdoor.linear_regression')

print(f'Estimate of causal effect (linear regression): {
    estimate_lr.value}')
```

This gives us the following:

```
Estimate of causal effect (linear regression): 0.688147600764658
```

In this comparison, a complex DML model did a slightly better job than a simple linear regression, but it's hard to say whether this effect is anything more than noise (feel free to refit both models a couple of times to see how stable these results are; you can also re-generate or bootstrap the data to get even more reliable information).

Before we jump to refutation tests, I want to share one more thing with you. We had enough data to feed a complex DML estimator and the results are really good, but if you have a smaller dataset, a simpler method could be a better choice for you. If you're not sure what to choose, it's always a great idea to run a couple of quick experiments to see which methods are behaving better for your problem (or a similar problem represented by simulated data).

Step 4 – refute them!

As we've just seen, our DML model worked pretty well.

Let's check how robust it is.

We'll start by adding a random common cause:

```
random_cause = model.refute_estimate(
    estimand=estimand,
    estimate=estimate,
    method_name='random_common_cause'
)
print(random_cause)
```

This results in the following:

```
Refute: Add a random common cause
Estimated effect:0.6981455013596706
New effect:0.6691543110272069
p value:0.1399999999999999
```

We see that there is a difference between the estimated effect (0.69814...) and the new effect (0.66915...), yet according to the provided *p*-value, this difference is not significant at the customary 0.05 level. If we accept this rule, we need to agree that the model has passed the test.

Let's try one more refutation test. This time, we'll replace our treatment variable with a random placebo variable:

```
placebo_refuter = model.refute_estimate(
    estimand=estimand,
    estimate=estimate,
    method_name='placebo_treatment_refuter'
)
print(placebo_refuter)
```

This gives us the following:

```
Refute: Use a Placebo Treatment
Estimated effect:0.6981455013596706
New effect:0.0
p value:2.0
```

This result is a clear indication that the placebo treatment had zero effect, which is the expected result for a healthy model.

It seems that our model passed both tests! Note that the first test (random common cause) belonged to the category of *invariant transformations*, while the second (placebo treatment) belonged to the category of *nullifying transformations*.

At the time of writing this chapter (September 2022), there are more refutation tests available for back-door criterion than there are for the front-door criterion.

For an up-to-date list of refutation tests available in DoWhy, visit `https://bit.ly/DoWhyRefutation`.

Now, let's switch to the experimental GCM API.

Extra – full example using the GCM API

The purpose of this subsection is to demonstrate the flexibility in structuring the causal inference process. APIs and tools will change with time, but a good understanding of the basics and the ability to translate your skills between different APIs, systems, or platforms are universal.

> **Note on the GCM API**
>
> At the time of writing (September 2022), the GCM API is still experimental. This means that there might be some changes to this API that will break the backward compatibility.

To work with the GCM API, we need to import `networkx` and the `gcm` subpackage:

```
import networkx as nx
from dowhy import gcm
```

We will reuse the data from our previous example. I'll put the data-generating code here as a refresher:

```
SAMPLE_SIZE = 1000

S = np.random.random(SAMPLE_SIZE)
Q = 0.2*S + 0.67*np.random.random(SAMPLE_SIZE)
X = 0.14*Q + 0.4*np.random.random(SAMPLE_SIZE)
Y = 0.7*X + 0.11*Q + 0.32*S
    + 0.24*np.random.random(SAMPLE_SIZE)
P = 0.43*X + 0.21*Y + 0.22*np.random.random(SAMPLE_SIZE)

df = pd.DataFrame(np.vstack([S, Q, X, Y, P]).T,
    columns=['S', 'Q', 'X', 'Y', 'P'])
```

The next step is to generate the graph describing the structure of our data-generating process. The GCM API uses `nx.DiGraph` rather than GML strings as a graph representation.

Let's generate a graph:

```
edges = ['SQ', 'SY', 'QX', 'QY', 'XP', 'YP', 'XY']
graph_nx = nx.DiGraph([(edge[0],
    edge[1]) for edge in edges])
```

We used list comprehension to automate the edge creation process. This is an analog of what we've done earlier with the two `for` loops. That said, defining a graph with NetworkX is simpler because we don't need to specify all the nodes explicitly.

To make sure that everything is as expected, let's plot the graph (*Figure 7.6*):

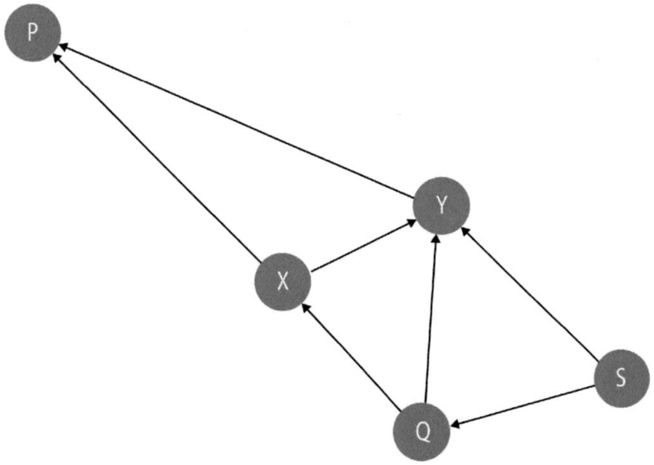

Figure 7.6 – A networkx representation of our graph

Now, let's define a causal model. It's very simple with the GCM API:

```
causal_model = gcm.InvertibleStructuralCausalModel(
    graph_nx)
```

There are many different causal models available in the GCM API. We picked the invertible SCM, since this is the only model that allows us to generate counterfactuals without manually providing values for all noise variables.

Now it's time to define causal mechanisms for each variable:

```
causal_model.set_causal_mechanism('S', gcm.EmpiricalDistribution())
causal_model.set_causal_mechanism('X', gcm.AdditiveNoiseModel(gcm.
ml.create_linear_regressor()))
causal_model.set_causal_mechanism('Y', gcm.AdditiveNoiseModel(gcm.
ml.create_linear_regressor()))
causal_model.set_causal_mechanism('P', gcm.AdditiveNoiseModel(gcm.
ml.create_linear_regressor()))
causal_model.set_causal_mechanism('Q', gcm.AdditiveNoiseModel(gcm.
ml.create_linear_regressor()))
```

We use `gcm.EmpiricalDistribution()` for `S` because it's the only variable that does not have parents among endogenous variables. For all other variables, we set the causal mechanism to an additive causal model and use linear regression to model it.

We'll learn more about **additive noise models** (**ANMs**) in *Part 3*, *Causal Discovery*. For a detailed discussion on ANMs, check out Peters et al. (2017).

Let's fit the model to the data and estimate causal effects strengths:

```
gcm.fit(causal_model, df)
gcm.arrow_strength(causal_model, 'Y')
```

This results in the following:

```
{('Q', 'Y'): 0.0006632517083816319,
 ('S', 'Y'): 0.008486091866545382,
 ('X', 'Y'): 0.006866684034567223}
```

As you can see, the GCM API returns estimates for all the variables with the incoming edges to the variable of interest (`Y` in our case; see *Figure 7.6* for reference).

These results are different from what we've seen before. The reason for this is that the GCM API by default returns results in terms of the outcome variable variance change given we remove the edge from the source variable. This behavior can be changed and you can define your own estimation functions. To learn more, refer to the GCM API documentation, available here: `https://bit.ly/DoWhyArrowStrength`.

A great feature of the GCM API is that when you create and fit a model, you can easily answer different types of causal queries using this model.

For instance, you can generate counterfactuals:

```
gcm.counterfactual_samples(
    causal_model,
    {'X': lambda x: .21},
    observed_data=pd.DataFrame(data=dict(X=[.5],
    Y=[.75], S=[.5], Q=[.4], P=[.34])))
```

This gives us the following result (*Figure 7.7*):

	S	Q	X	Y	P
0	0.5	0.4	0.21	0.539558	0.169005

Figure 7.7 – Counterfactuals from our GCM when X is set to 0.21

To learn more about the GCM API, please refer to the documentation.

Wrapping it up

In this chapter, we discussed the Python causal ecosystem. We introduced the DoWhy and EconML libraries and practiced the four-step causal inference process using DoWhy's CausalModel API. We learned how to automatically obtain estimands and how to use different types of estimators to compute causal effect estimates. We discussed what refutation tests are and how to use them in practice. Finally, we introduced DoWhy's experimental GCM API and showed its great capabilities when it comes to answering various causal queries. After working through this chapter, you have the basic skills to apply causal inference to your own problems. Congratulations!

In the next chapter, we'll summarize common assumptions for causal inference and discuss some limitations of the causal inference framework.

References

Bates, S., Hastie, T., & Tibshirani, R. (2021). *Cross-validation: what does it estimate and how well does it do it?*. arXiv preprint. `https://doi.org/10.48550/ARXIV.2104.00673`

Battocchi, K., Dillon, E., Hei, M., Lewis, G., Oka, P., Oprescu, M., & Syrgkanis, V. (2019). *EconML: A Python Package for ML-Based Heterogeneous Treatment Effects Estimation*. `https://github.com/microsoft/EconML`

Blobaum, P., Götz, P., Budhathoki, K., Mastakouri, A., & Janzing, D. (2022). *DoWhy-GCM: An extension of DoWhy for causal inference in graphical causal models*. arXiv.

Chernozhukov, V., Chetverikov, D., Demirer, M., Duflo, E., Hansen, C., Newey, W., & Robins, J. (2016). *Double/Debiased Machine Learning for Treatment and Causal Parameters*. arXiv preprint. `https://doi.org/10.48550/ARXIV.1608.00060`

Molak, A. (2022, September 27). *Causal Python: 3 Simple Techniques to Jump-Start Your Causal Inference Journey Today*. Towards Data Science. `https://towardsdatascience.com/causal-kung-fu-in-python-3-basic-techniques-to-jump-start-your-causal-inference-journey-tonight-ae09181704f7`

Peters, J., Janzing, D., & Schölkopf, B. (2017). *Elements of Causal Inference: Foundations and Learning Algorithms*. MIT Press.

Popper, K. (1935). *Logik der Forschung*. Springer.

Popper, K. (1959). *The Logic of Scientific Discovery*. Basic Books.

Sharma, A. & Kiciman, E. (2020). *DoWhy: An End-to-End Library for Causal Inference*. arXiv preprint. arXiv:2011.04216.

Shimoni, Y., Karavani, E., Ravid, S., Bak, P., Ng, T. H., Alford, S. H., Meade, D., & Goldschmidt, Y. (2019). *An Evaluation Toolkit to Guide Model Selection and Cohort Definition in Causal Inference*. arXiv preprint. arXiv:1906.00442.

8

Causal Models – Assumptions and Challenges

Welcome to *Chapter 8*.

In *Chapter 7*, we demonstrated how to leverage the power of the DoWhy library to estimate causal effects. The goal of this chapter is to deepen our understanding of when and how to use causal inference methods.

We'll review some of the assumptions that we introduced earlier in *Chapter 5* and we'll discuss some more assumptions in order to get a clearer picture of the challenges and limitations that we might face when working with causal models.

By the end of this chapter, you will have a good understanding of the challenges that you may face when implementing causal models in real life and possible solutions to these challenges.

In this chapter, we will cover the following:

- The challenges of causal inference methods
- Identifiability
- Positivity assumption
- Exchangeability/ignorability assumption
- Modularity (independent mechanisms)
- Consistency
- SUTVA
- Selection bias

I am the king of the world! But am I?

So far, we've seen what we can achieve by using causal models on observational data and we promised that we'll see them do even more impressive things. All this might feel pretty powerful!

In this section, we're going to discuss important challenges that we might face when using causal inference methods in practice.

We'll start by sketching a broader context. After that, we'll explicitly define the concept of **identifiability**. Finally, we'll discuss some popular challenges faced by practitioners:

- A lack of a priori knowledge of causal graphs
- Insufficient sample sizes
- Difficulties with verifying the assumptions

In between

Ancient Greek mythology provides us with a story of Ikaros (also known as Icarus) and his father, the Athenian inventor Daidalos (also known as Daedalus). Daidalos wants to escape from Crete – a Greek island where he's trapped. He builds two sets of wings using feathers and wax. He successfully tests his wings first before passing the other set to his son.

Before they fly, Daidalos advises his son not to fly too low, nor too high: *"for the fogs about the earth may weigh you down and the blaze from the sun are going to melt your feathers apart"* (Graves, 1955). Ikaros does not listen. He's excited by his freedom. Consumed by ecstatic feelings, he ascends toward the sun. The wax in his wings starts melting and – tragically – he falls into the sea and drowns.

The history of causality starts in a place of big dreams and seemingly impossible goals. From broad Aristotelian concepts of four causes, through the ages of religious and philosophical reflection, through David Hume's ideas, up to modern econometrics and Pearl's *do*-calculus, we've come a long way, and, just like Daidalos, we learned to fly.

It's likely that we haven't yet reached the *Causal Promised Land* and that we will continue to learn and grow in our causal journey in the coming years.

In the meantime, we have an amazing set of causal tools in our hands. In order to use them effectively, we need the awareness of their strengths and their limitations. The path is somewhere *in between*. By knowing the assumptions behind causal methods and the challenges that we might face on our way, we can improve our businesses and our communities, bringing more growth, more knowledge, and more insights.

Understanding the assumptions that we discuss in this chapter will help you achieve two things:

- Become a better (data) scientist (even if your primary goal is not to conduct causal analyses)
- Learn how to effectively use causality without over- or undervaluing its potential

Ready?

Let's go!

Identifiability

One of the core concepts that we'll use in this chapter is **identifiability**. The good news is that you already know what identifiability is.

We say that a causal effect (or any other causal quantity) is **identifiable** when it can be computed unambiguously from a set of (passive) observations summarized by a distribution $P(V)$ and a causal graph G (Pearl, 2009).

In other words, if we have (1) enough information to control for *non-causal* information flow in the graph and (2) enough data to estimate the effect of interest, the effect is identifiable.

Let's unpack that.

Do you remember *Chapter 6* and our conversation on *d*-separation and *do*-calculus?

The first condition is achievable by blocking all the paths that are *leaking* non-causal information using the rules of *do*-calculus and the logic of *d*-separation. This is often possible using the back-door criterion, the front-door criterion, instrumental variables, or the general rules of *do*-calculus.

That said, sometimes it is just impossible.

The important thing is *not* to pretend that it's possible when we know it's not. In such a case, using causal methods can bring more harm than good. One of the main challenges is that sometimes we simply don't know. We'll learn more about this in the last part of this section.

The second condition has two faces.

First, any estimator needs to have a large enough sample size to return meaningful estimates. Second, we need to make sure that the probability of every possible value of treatment in our dataset (possibly conditioned on all important covariates) is greater than 0. This is known as the **positivity assumption** and we'll discuss it in the next section.

Now, let's talk about a couple of challenges causal data scientists face.

Lack of causal graphs

In a recent survey that I conducted on LinkedIn, I asked the participants to imagine that they could ask a world-class causality expert one question. 28% chose to ask a question related to obtaining causal graphs in real-world scenarios.

The lack of a causal model can be a major challenge in implementing causal inference techniques in practice.

There are three things that people usually do to obtain a causal graph for a problem with an unknown causal structure:

- Use domain expertise
- Use causal discovery techniques
- Use a combination of both of the above

High quality trustworthy **domain expertise** is often the least risky option yet might be the hardest to obtain. **Causal discovery methods** are usually cheaper, but verifying their results can be challenging.

In many cases, a combination of domain knowledge and structure learning algorithms might be the best option. Some causal discovery methods allow us to easily incorporate our domain knowledge and then they perform the search over the remaining parts of graph search space for us (more on this topic in *Part 3, Causal Discovery*). This can lead to truly amazing results, yet there are no guarantees.

If your data comes from a **natural experiment**, you can also try some of the methods from the field of econometrics, such as **synthetic controls, regression discontinuity, or difference-in-differences**. We'll briefly discuss one of them (with a Bayesian flavor) in *Chapter 11*.

Not enough data

An insufficiently large sample size is not a uniquely causal problem. Any statistical parameter estimate becomes biased under an insufficiently large sample size.

Depending on the method we choose, some causal methods might require more data than others. If we use the **double machine learning** (**DML**) technique with neural network estimators, we need to be prepared for neural-network-style sample sizes.

Nonetheless, sample size can also be an issue in the case of very simple models. I conducted a simple experiment so we could see it in action. The full code for this experiment is in the notebook for *Chapter 8* (`https://bit.ly/causal-ntbk-08`). Here we only present the methodology and the results.

Let's take the graphical model from the previous chapter (check *Figure 8.1* for a refresher).

Understanding the sample size – methodology

Let's take four different sample sizes (30, 100, 1,000, and 10,000), and for each sample size, generate 20 datasets from the model presented in *Figure 8.1*. We fit two models for each dataset: one based on simple linear regression and one based on a DML estimator, powered by two gradient-boosting models and a cross-validated lasso regression:

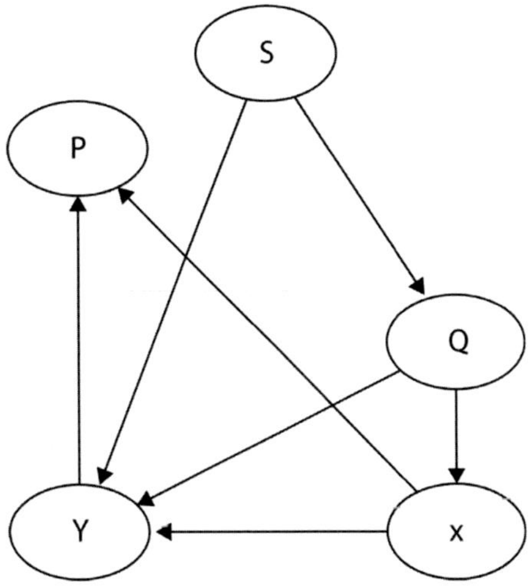

Figure 8.1 – The graphical model that we use in the experiment

Understanding the sample size – results

The results are presented in *Figure 8.2*. We see sample size on the *x* axis and percentage error on the *y* axis. 100% error means that the coefficient returned by the model was twice the size of the true coefficient; negative 100% means that the estimated effect was 0 (the true effect minus 100% of the true effect is 0):

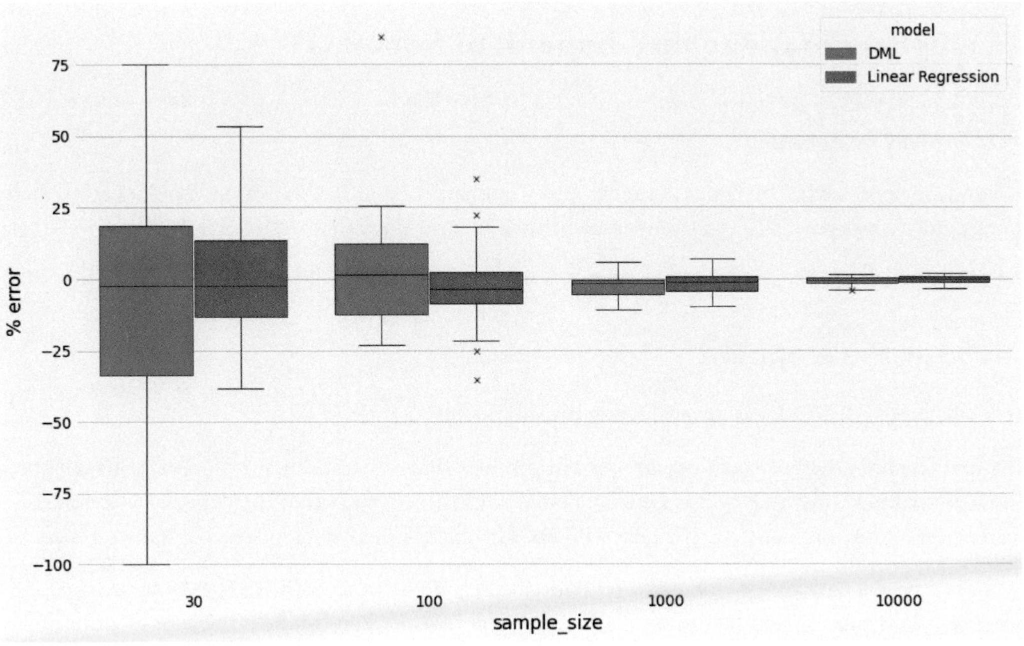

Figure 8.2 – The results of the sample size experiment

As we can see, for the smallest sample size, both models perform pretty poorly (despite the fact that the causal effect is identifiable in graphical terms). That said, the error variance of the DML model is significantly higher than the error variance of the simple linear model. At 100 observations, both models' performance match closely, and at 1,000 and 10,000 observations, the performance seems to converge. Note that we used a back-door criterion to identify estimands in this experiment. Back-door is computationally simple and much less challenging than front-door or other approaches.

To make the most out of smaller sample sizes, a good idea would be to bootstrap your results, if you can afford it.

Unverifiable assumptions

In some cases, it might be very difficult to find out whether you're meeting your assumptions. Let's start with confounding.

Imagine that you're trying to use the back-door criterion for your problem. In certain cases, you'll be able to rule out the possibility that there are other unobserved variables introducing confounding between your treatment and your outcome, but in many cases, it might be very difficult. In particular, when your research involves human interactions, financial markets, or other complex phenomena, making sure that the effects of interest are identifiable can be difficult if not impossible. That's likely one of the reasons for the huge popularity of **instrumental variable** techniques in contemporary applied econometrics. Although good instruments have a reputation of being notoriously hard to find, they might be easier to find than the certainty that we meet the back-door criterion.

An elephant in the room – hopeful or hopeless?

Some people reading about the challenges in causal inference from observational data might ask, *"Is there anything we can do?"*

I like the idea presented by James Altucher and Claudia Altucher in their book, *The Power of No*: if you cannot come up with 10 creative ideas, you should come up with 20 (Altucher & Altucher, 2014).

Let's see whether there's anything we can do to overcome these obstacles.

Let's eat the elephant

Let's talk about creative ideas for evaluating causal models.

The first level of creativity is to use the refutation tests that we described in the previous chapter. You already know how they work. One challenge with these tests is that they check for the overall correctness of the model structure, but they do not say much about how good the obtained estimate is.

By the way, if you have an idea for a new refutation test, go to `https://bit.ly/DoWhyRepo` and propose it in the discussion section or open a new pull request. You can help the causal community to move one step forward!

The second level of creativity is available when you have access to historical data coming from randomized experiments. You can compare your observational model with the experimental results and try to adjust your model accordingly.

The third level of creativity is to evaluate your modeling approach on simulated data with known outcomes. This might sound easy, but… if we had a reliable simulator of the process of interest, would we need machine learning in the first place?

Instead of building a simulator, we can try to learn it using generative neural networks. One such approach – **RealCause** – has been proposed by Brady Neal and colleagues (Neal et al., 2020). This approach certainly does not solve all your problems but can help you be more realistic, at least to an extent (for example, you can understand how your estimator behaves under **positivity assumption violation**).

An important fact about RealCause is that it generates realistic data distributions. It has been demonstrated that synthetic data can lead us astray when assessing the performance of causal models (Reisach et al., 2021; Curth et al., 2021). The good news is that the Python implementation of RealCause is open sourced and available at `https://bit.ly/RealCause`.

The fourth level of creativity is **sensitivity analysis**. In certain cases, we might have some idea about the magnitude of possible hidden confounding. In these cases, we can bound the error and check whether the estimated causal effect still holds if the confounders' influence reaches the maximum level that we think is reasonable to assume.

In other words, we can virtually check whether our effect would still hold in the worst-case scenario. Sensitivity analysis for regression models can be performed using the Python PySensemakr package (Cinelli and Hazlett, 2020; `https://bit.ly/PySensemakr`) or even using the online Sensemakr app (`https://bit.ly/SensemakrApp`).

Even better, the sensitivity analysis framework has been recently extended for a broad class of causal models (check Chernozhukov et al. (2022) for details).

In this section, we talked about the challenges that we can face when working with causal models and we discussed some creative ways to overcome them. We talked about the lack of causal graphs, insufficient sample sizes, and uncertainty regarding assumptions. We've seen that although there might not be a universal cure for all causal problems, we can definitely get creative and gain a more realistic understanding of our position.

In the next section, we'll discuss the positivity assumption.

Positivity

In this short section, we're going to learn about the **positivity assumption**, sometimes also called **overlap** or **common support**.

First, let's think about why this assumption is called *positivity*. It has to do with (strictly) **positive probabilities** – in other words, probabilities greater than zero.

What needs to have a probability greater than zero?

The answer to that is the probability of your treatment given all relevant control variables (the variables that are necessary to identify the effect – let's call them Z). Formally:

$$P(T = t|Z = z) > 0$$

The preceding formula must hold for all values of Z that are present in the population of interest (Hernán & Robins, 2020) and for all values of treatment T.

Let's imagine a simple example. In our dataset, we have 30 subjects described by one continuous feature Z. Each subject either received or did not receive a binary treatment T , and each subject has some continuous outcome Y. Additionally, let's assume that in order to identify the causal effect, we need to control for Z, which confounds the relationship between T and Y.

We can estimate the causal effect by computing:

$$E[Y|do(T = 1)] - E[Y|do(T = 0)]$$

Using the adjustment formula (Pearl et al., 2016), to compute these quantities from observational data, we need to control for Z.

Now imagine an extreme case where the support of Z (in other words, values of Z) does not overlap at all with the treatment values (hence the names *overlap* and *common support*; Neal, 2020). *Figure 8.3* presents a graphical representation of such a case:

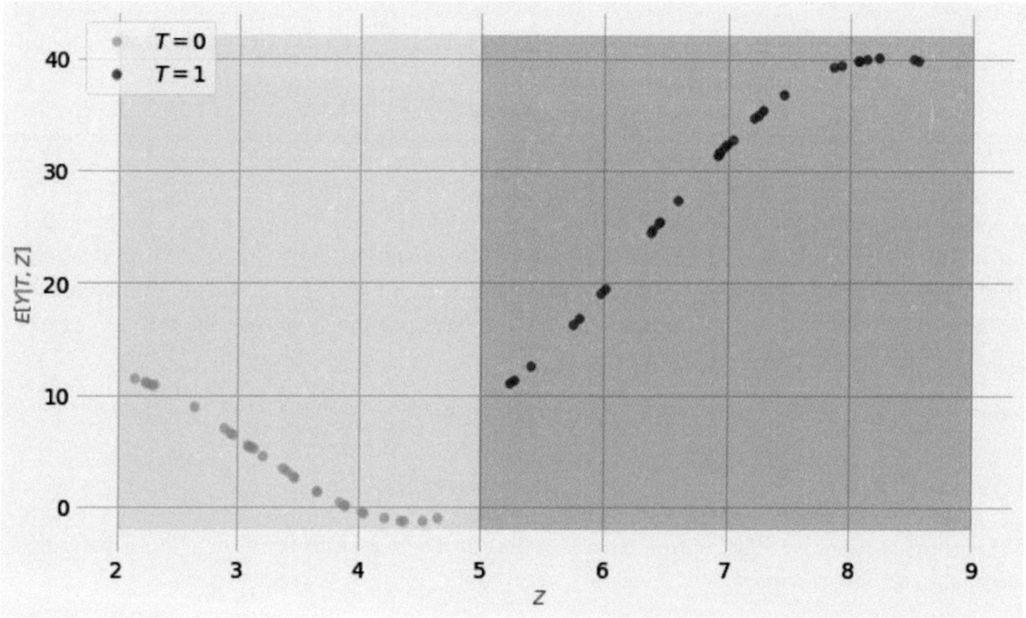

Figure 8.3 – Positivity violation example

In order to estimate the causal effect of the treatment T given Z, our estimator would need to extrapolate the red dots to the left (in the range between 2 and 5, where the support of Z for $T = 0$ is) and the blue dots to the right (in the range between 5 and 9, where the support of Z for $T = 1$ is). It's highly unlikely that any machine learning model would perform such an extrapolation realistically. *Figure 8.4* presents a possible extrapolation trajectory:

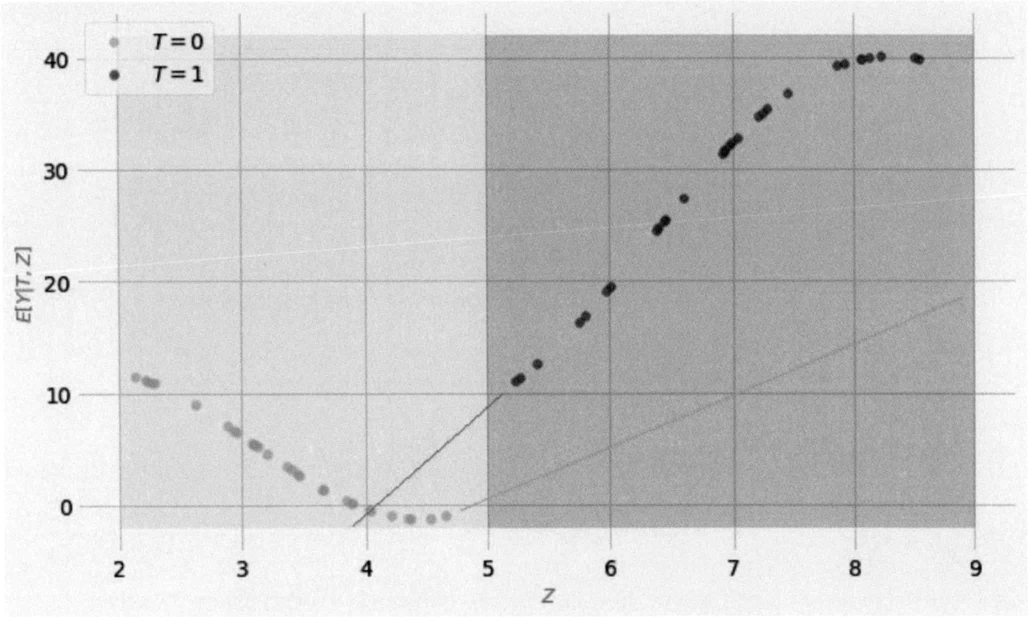

Figure 8.4 – Possible extrapolation trajectories (lines)

The red and blue lines in *Figure 8.4* represent possible extrapolation trajectories. How accurate do they seem to you?

To me, not very. They look like simple linear extrapolations, not capturing the non-linear qualities of the original functions.

Let's compare it to *Figure 8.5* where positivity is *met*:

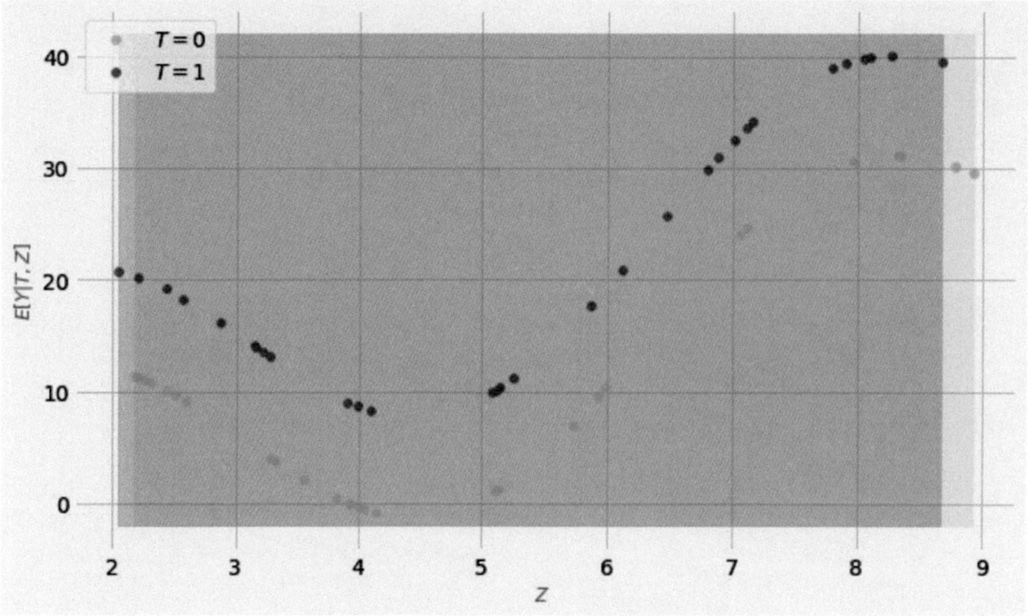

Figure 8.5 – Positivity assumption met

As you can see, here the model has a much easier task as it only needs to interpolate between the points.

Our example is very simple: we only have one confounder. In the real world, the data is often multidimensional, and making sure that $P(T = t|Z = z) > 0$ becomes more difficult. Think about a three-dimensional example. How about a 100-dimensional example?

As a side note, extrapolation and interpolation in high-dimensional spaces bring their own challenges (what does it mean to interpolate in an extremely high-dimensional space?). If this idea seems interesting to you, you might want to check the paper *Learning in High Dimension Always Amounts to Extrapolation* (Balestriero et al., 2021) or listen to episode 86 of the *Machine Learning Street Talk* podcast with two of the authors of this paper – Randall Balestriero and Yann LeCun (Machine Learning Street Talk, 2022).

In this section, we learned about the positivity assumption. We demonstrated two cases using a one-dimensional example: when the assumption is violated and when it holds. We also discussed how positivity is related to estimation and briefly noted the challenges that we can face in higher dimensions.

In the next section, we'll discuss the exchangeability assumption.

Exchangeability

In this section, we'll introduce the **exchangeability** assumption (also known as the **ignorability** assumption) and discuss its relation to confounding.

Exchangeable subjects

The main idea behind exchangeability is the following: the treated subjects, had they been untreated, would have experienced the same average outcome as the untreated did (being actually untreated) and vice versa (Hernán & Robins, 2020).

Formally speaking, exchangeability is usually defined as:

$\{Y^0, Y^1\} \perp\!\!\!\perp T|Z$

In the preceding formula, Y^0 and Y^1 are counterfactual outcomes under $T = 0$ and $T = 1$ respectively, and Z is a vector of control variables. If you're getting a feeling of confusion or even circularity when thinking about this definition, you're most likely not alone. According to Pearl (2009), many people see this definition as difficult to understand.

At the same time, the core idea behind it is simple: the treated and the untreated need to share all the relevant characteristics that can influence the outcome.

Can we express this in simpler terms?

Exchangeability versus confounding

Exchangeability is an idea that comes from the **potential outcomes** framework. Potential outcomes is a causal framework introduced by Donald Rubin in the 1970s (Rubin, 1974), but the core ideas go back to the 1920s and Polish statistician Jerzy Neyman's master thesis (Neyman, 1923).

In fact, the potential outcomes framework aims to achieve the same goals as SCM/*do*-calculus-based causal inference, just using different means (see Pearl, 2009, pp. 98-102, 243-245).

Pearl argues that both frameworks are logically equivalent and can be used interchangeably or symbiotically, pointing out that graphical models can help clearly address challenges that might be difficult to spot using the potential outcomes formalism (see `https://bit.ly/POvsSCM` for examples). I wholeheartedly agree with the latter.

We will not go deep into exchangeability/ignorability definitions here. Instead, we'll assume that – in general – *exchangeability* can be reduced to *unconfoundedness*. This means that we can achieve exchangeability using any of the deconfounding techniques we have introduced so far. This view is not always accepted, but further details are beyond the scope of this book.

For a more detailed discussion on the relationship between exchangeability and confounding, see Pearl (2009, pp. 196-199, 341-344) and Hernán & Robins (2020, pp. 27-31).

In this section, we discussed the exchangeability assumption. We introduced the potential outcomes definition of exchangeability and sketched its connection to the concept of confounding. In the next section, we're going to discuss three other assumptions that you can find in the causality literature.

...and more

In this short section, we'll introduce and briefly discuss three assumptions: the **modularity assumption**, **stable unit treatment value assumption** (**SUTVA**), and the **consistency assumption**.

Modularity

Imagine that you're standing on the rooftop of a tall building and you're dropping two apples. Halfway down, there's a net that catches one of the apples.

The net performs an *intervention* for one of the apples, yet the second apple remains unaffected.

That's the essence of the **modularity assumption**, also known as the **independent mechanisms assumption**.

Speaking more formally, if we perform an intervention on a single variable X, the structural equation for this variable will be changed (for example, set to a constant), yet *all other* structural equations in our system of interest will remain *untouched.*

Modularity assumption is central to *do*-calculus as it's at the core of the logic of interventions.

Let's see an example.

Consider the following SCM $\mathcal{S}$:

$X := \mathcal{N}(0, 1)$

$Z := \mathcal{N}(0, 1)$

$R := X + Z$

$Y := R + X$

Figure 8.6 presents a graphical representation of $\mathcal{S}$.

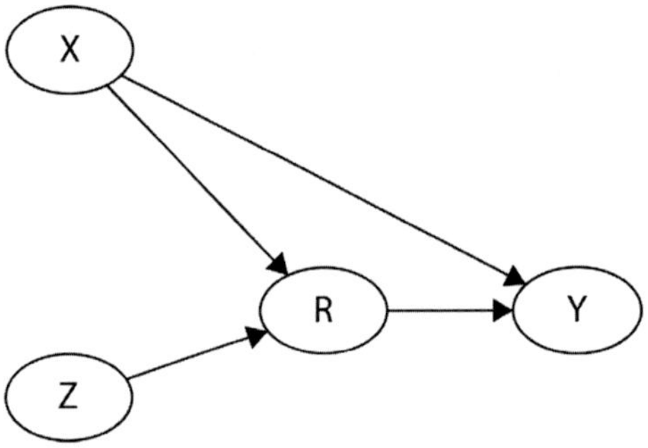

Figure 8.6 – The modularity example SCM $\mathcal{S}$

The modularity assumption says that if we intervene on node R by setting its value to r, the only equation that will change in $\mathcal{S}$ is the following:

$R := r$

All the other structural equations will remain the same.

The SCM $\mathcal{S}$ after the intervention, let's call it $\mathcal{S}_M$ (we often add a subscript M (modified) to denote an SCM after intervention), is presented in *Figure 8.7*:

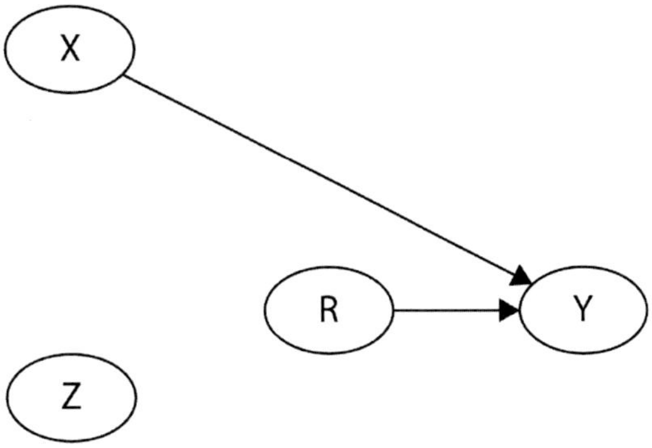

Figure 8.7 – The modified SCM $\mathcal{S}_M$

There are no longer edges from X and Z to R because we forced R to take value r and therefore any change in X or Z won't affect the value of R (this is known as a **perfect intervention**).

At the same time, the edge from X to Y is untouched (despite our intervention on R, changes in X will still affect the value of Y) in accordance with the modularity assumption.

Removing edges from the graph when we intervene on (a set of) variable(s) is sometimes called **graph mutilation**. I don't like this name too much. A more neutral term is **graph modification**.

From a graphical perspective, modularity can be summarized in the following way:

- When we perform a perfect intervention on node V, all V's incoming edges are deleted in the modified graph
- No incoming edges to other (unintervened) nodes are modified

Another way to think about modularity is that changes caused by interventions are *local*: only the mechanism for the intervened variables change (we remove the incoming edges), but other mechanisms in the system remain unchanged.

Modularity might seem challenging to understand at first, but at its core, it's deeply intuitive.

Let's imagine a world where modularity does not hold.

In this world, you'd make an intervention on your web page by changing the button shape and as a result, your web page will also automatically be translated into Portuguese, while your computer will automatically start playing Barbra Streisand songs and your lawyer will immediately color their hair green – all without any other changes in the world besides your button shape. Such a world might be interesting but hard to navigate in terms of understanding causal mechanisms.

In this sense, modularity is a common sense assumption.

To summarize, the modularity assumption states that when we perform a (perfect) intervention on one variable in the system, the only *structural* change that takes place in this system is the removal of this variable's incoming edges (which is equivalent to the modification of its structural equation) and the rest of the system remains *structurally* unchanged.

SUTVA

The SUTVA is another assumption coming from the potential outcomes framework.

The assumption states that the fact that one unit (individual, subject, or object) receives treatment does not influence any other units.

This assumption might often be challenged in the context of interacting subjects. For instance, if one person in a household decides to start psychotherapy, other household members will likely also be affected (when one person changes their thinking and/or behavior, their environment usually reacts to this change in one way or another). Similarly, if you encourage some users of a social network to send more messages, the recipients of these messages are also likely to start sending more messages (not because they were encouraged by you, but rather because they want to respond to the senders).

At the experimental level, researchers are trying to overcome these challenges using various techniques such as cluster-level (rather than individual-level) randomization or so-called *ego-randomization* (Gui et al., 2015; Saint-Jacques et al., 2018). Some of these techniques can also be applied to observational data.

Consistency

The last assumption that we're going to discuss in this section is the **consistency** assumption. Consistency comes from the potential outcomes framework.

The assumption is also known as *no multiple versions of treatment* and is sometimes included as the second part of the SUTVA assumption (yes, I know, this might be confusing).

Let's get to the point.

Imagine that the treatment is to *win a car*. There are two levels of treatment: you either get a car or don't.

Some people in the treatment group win a brand-new electric BMW while others get a rusty, 20-year-old Mazda without wheels. If our outcome variable is the level of excitement, we'd expect that on average the same person's level of excitement would differ between the two versions of treatment. That would be an example of a violation of consistency as we essentially encode two variants of treatment as one.

Another way of looking at consistency comes from Pearl and Mackenzie. In their interpretation, consistency means that the experiment is "*free of placebo effect and other imperfections*" (Pearl & Mackenzie, 2019, p. 281).

If you only take two things out of our discussion on consistency, it should be these:

- Treatments should be well defined
- There should not be *hidden versions* of treatments

These are the two essential characteristics of consistency.

In this section, we discussed three assumptions: modularity (independent mechanisms), SUTVA, and consistency. The first one comes from the graphical/*do*-calculus framework, while the remaining two have their source in the potential outcomes framework.

In the next section, we'll shed some new light on the topic of unobserved variables.

Call me names – spurious relationships in the wild

Don't you feel that when we talk about spurious relationships and unobserved confounding, it's almost like we're talking about good old friends now? Maybe they are trouble sometimes, yet they just feel so familiar it's hard to imagine the future without them.

We will start this section with a reflection on naming conventions regarding bias/spurious relationships/confounding across the fields. In the second part of the section, we'll discuss selection bias as a special subtype of spuriousness that plays an important role in epidemiology.

Names, names, names

Oh boy! Reading about causality across domains can be a confusing experience! Some authors suggest using the term **confounding** only when there's a **common cause** of the treatment and the outcome (Peters et al., 2017, p. 172; Hernán & Robins, 2020, p. 103); others allow using this term also in other cases of **spuriousness** (Pearl & Mackenzie, 2019, p. 161).

Another term popular in the literature is **selection bias**. Definitions of selection bias differ between fields. Hernán & Robins (2020) advocate for a clear distinction between confounding (understood by them in terms of *common causes*) and selection bias (understood in terms of *common outcomes*).

Note that in the field of econometrics, the term *selection bias* might be used to describe any type of confounding bias.

Although it might be challenging sometimes, it's good to understand which convention a person you talk to (or read) uses.

Let's review what Hernán and Robins (2020) call a selection bias and learn two valuable lessons.

Should I ask you or someone who's not here?

It's 1943. American military planes are engaged in numerous missions and many of them are not coming back home. The ones that are coming back are often damaged.

An interesting fact is that the damage does not look random. It seems that there's a clear pattern to it. Bullet holes are concentrated around the fuel system and fuselage, but not so much around the engines.

The military engineers decide to consult a renowned group of statisticians called the **Statistical Research Group** (**SRG**) to help them figure out how to optimally distribute the armor so that the places that are at the highest risk of damage are protected.

A person who was faced with this question was Abraham Wald, a Hungarian-born Jewish mathematician, who worked at Columbia University and was a part of the SRG at the time.

Instead of providing the army with the answer, Wald asked a question.

It was a seemingly simple one: "*Where are the missing holes?*"

Missing holes?

What Wald meant were the holes that we've never observed. The ones that were in the planes that never came back.

DAG them!

What Wald pointed out is so-called **survivorship bias**. It's a type of selection bias where the effects are estimated only on a subpopulation of survivors with an intention to generalize them to the entire population. The problem is that the population might differ from the selected sub-sample. This bias is well known in epidemiology (think about disease survivors, for instance).

Let's put a hypothetical SCM together to represent the problem that Wald was facing.

Figure 8.8 is a graphical representation of this SCM:

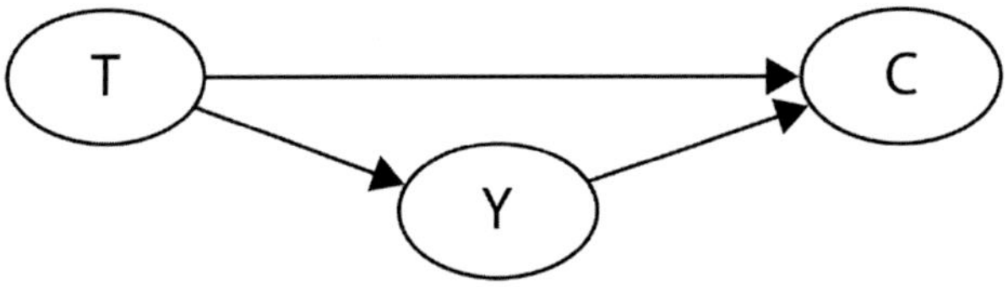

Figure 8.8 – An SCM representation of Wald's problem

We have three nodes: T, Y, and C. T represents the treatment, the number of enemy bullets shot at the engines, Y stands for the severity of plane damage, and C is a binary variable encoding whether a plane came back home (1) or not (0).

Note that what we do by only looking at planes that came back home is *implicitly conditioning on C*.

Two factors influence C: the number of bullets shot at the engines (T) and the overall damage severity (Y), which also depends on T. If the number of bullets shot at the engines is high enough, the plane is not coming back home regardless of other damage. It can also be the case that the number of bullets shot at engines is not that high, but the overall damage is so severe that the plane does not make it anyway.

Note that conditioning on C opens a spurious path, $T \rightarrow C \leftarrow Y$. This is precisely the source of bias because C is a *collider* on this path and – as you might remember – conditioning on a collider opens the information flow (as opposed to conditioning on chains and forks).

Let's translate our example into Python to see how this logic works on an actual dataset.

First, let's define the sample size and the set of structural assignments that defines our SCM:

```
SAMPLE_SIZE = 1000

# A hypothetical SCM
T = np.random.uniform(20, 110, SAMPLE_SIZE)
Y = T + np.random.uniform(0, 40, SAMPLE_SIZE)
C = (T + Y < 100).astype('int')
```

Let's put all the variables in a `pandas` DataFrame for easier manipulation:

```
df = pd.DataFrame(np.stack([T, Y, C]).T, columns=['T',
    'Y', 'C'])
```

Finally, let's condition on C and plot the results:

```
# Compare average damage (biased vs unbiased)
plt.figure(figsize=(8, 4))

plt.hist(df[df['C'] == 1]['Y'], label='Came back = 1',
    color=COLORS[0], alpha=.5)
plt.hist(df[df['C'] == 0]['Y'], label='Came back = 0',
    color=COLORS[1], alpha=.5, bins=25)

plt.xlabel('$Damage$ $severity$', alpha=.5, fontsize=12)
plt.ylabel('$Frequency$', alpha=.5, fontsize=12)

plt.legend()
plt.show()
```

Figure 8.9 presents the output of this block:

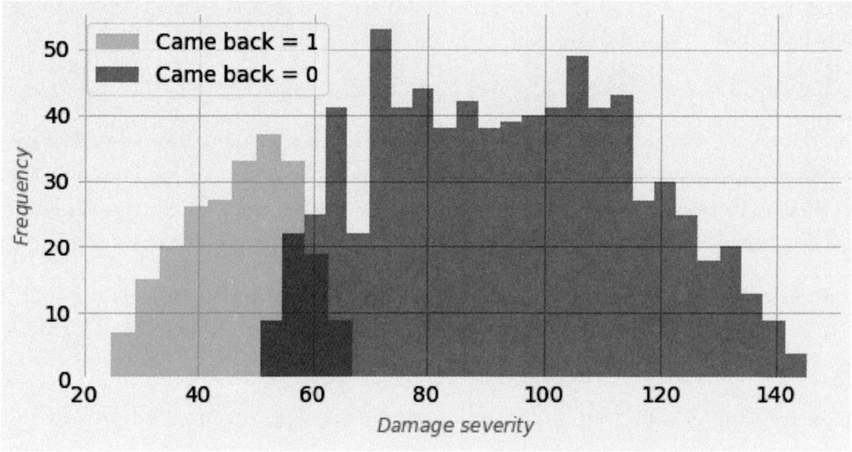

Figure 8.9 – A histogram of plane damage conditioned on C

The data in blue represents the damage severity for the planes that came back home. The data in red denotes the damage severity of the planes that did not come back.

As you can see, the severity is much higher for the planes that did not make it back home and there's only a small overlap between the two sets around the value of **60**.

Although our example is simplified (we don't take the damage location into account in our histogram), the conclusion is the same as Wald's – what matters the most are the *missing holes*, not the ones that we've observed. The first lesson is: look at what's missing.

If you want to understand the original solution proposed by Wald, you can find it in Wald (1980).

More selection bias

The DAG in *Figure 8.8* represents just one possible combination of nodes leading to selection bias. Before we conclude this chapter, let's see some more examples. I picked something a bit spicier this time. Let's start with *Figure 8.10*:

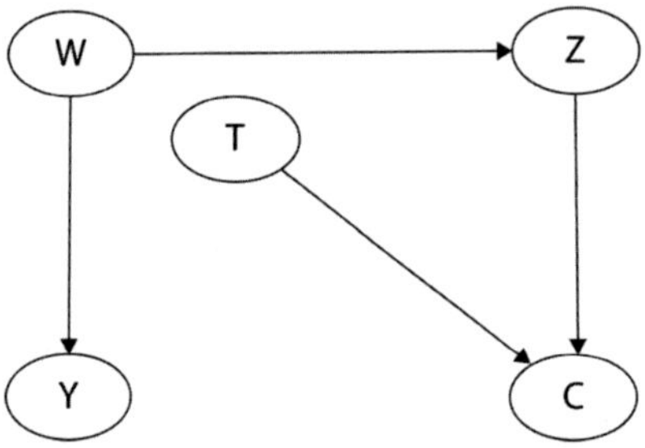

Figure 8.10 – An example of selection bias

The DAG in *Figure 8.10* is interesting. There is no connection between treatment T and the outcome Y, yet conditioning on C opens a path between the two. This is sometimes called **selection bias under the null** (Hernán and Robins, 2020).

Let's see one more example (*Figure 8.11*):

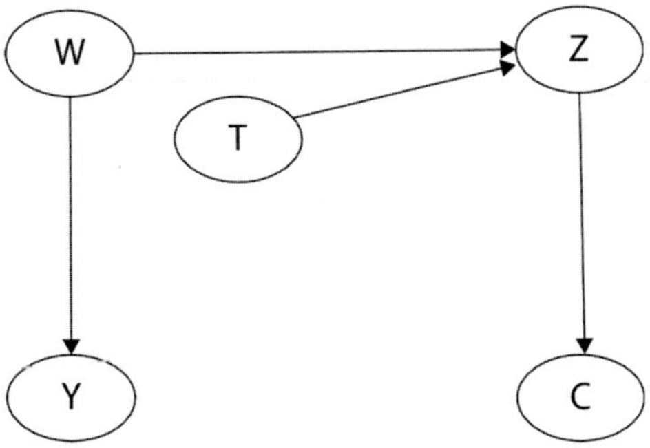

Figure 8.11 – An example of selection bias without the edge between T and C

The DAG in *Figure 8.11* is even more interesting. There are no edges directly connecting T and C or Y and C. Can you guess what's the source of spuriousness here?

Note that C is a child of Z. Controlling for C (by using it as a selection criterion) partially opens the path $T \rightarrow Z \leftarrow W \rightarrow Y$. We say *partially* because C usually *contains* some of Z's variability.

This is a fact worth remembering – conditioning *on descendants* (yes, it's not only about children) of *colliders* usually partially *opens the path* on which the collider resides (in very special cases, conditioning on descendants could leave the path closed, but these cases are rather rare). The second lesson is look further than you think is necessary.

In this section, we discussed the concepts of selection bias, confounding, and spuriousness. We showed that naming conventions regarding these concepts differ across disciplines and subfields.

In the second part of the section, we focused on selection bias and recalled the story of Abraham Wald. We cast this story into the language of DAGs and translated it into Python to see how selection bias works in practice.

Two lessons we learned in this section are look at what's missing and look further than you think is necessary.

Wrapping it up

In this chapter, we talked about the challenges that we face while using causal inference methods in practice. We discussed important assumptions and proposed potential solutions to some of the discussed challenges. We got back to the topic of confounding and showed examples of selection bias.

The four most important concepts from this chapter are identifiability, the positivity assumption, modularity, and selection bias.

Are you ready to add some machine learning sauce to all we've learned so far?

References

Altucher, J., Altucher C. A. (2014). *The Power of No: Because One Little Word Can Bring Health, Abundance, and Happiness.* Hay House.

Balestriero, R., Pesenti, J., and LeCun, Y. (2021). *Learning in High Dimension Always Amounts to Extrapolation.* arXiv, abs/2110.09485.

Cinelli, C., Hazlett, C. (2020). *Making Sense of Sensitivity: Extending Omitted Variable Bias. Journal of the Royal Statistical Society, Series B: Statistical Methodology* 81(1), 39-67.

Curth, A., Svensson, D., Weatherall, J., and van der Schaar, M. (2021). *Really Doing Great at Estimating CATE? A Critical Look at ML Benchmarking Practices in Treatment Effect Estimation. Proceedings of the Neural Information Processing Systems Track on Datasets and Benchmarks.*

Chernozhukov, V., Cinelli, C., Newey, W., Sharma, A., and Syrgkanis, V. (2022). *Long Story Short: Omitted Variable Bias in Causal Machine Learning (Working Paper No. 30302; Working Paper Series).* National Bureau of Economic Research.

Donnely, R. (2022, October 2). *One of the big challenges with causal inference is that we can't easily prove which approach produced the best estimate of the true causal effect... [Post]. LinkedIn.* `https://www.linkedin.com/posts/robert-donnelly-4376579_evaluating-the-econometric-evaluations-of-activity-6979849583241609216-7iXQ?utm_source=share&utm_medium=member_desktop`

Graves, R. (1955). Daedalus and Talus. *The Greek Myths.* Penguin Books.

Gordon, B. R., Moakler, R., and Zettelmeyer, F. (2022). *Close Enough? A Large-Scale Exploration of Non-Experimental Approaches to Advertising Measurement.* arXiv. `https://doi.org/10.48550/ARXIV.2201.07055`

Gui, H., Xu, Y., Bhasin, A., and Han, J. (2015). *Network A/B Testing: From Sampling to Estimation.* Proceedings of the 24th International Conference on World Wide Web, 399–409. `https://doi.org/10.1145/2736277.2741081`

Hernán M. A., Robins J. M. (2020). *Causal Inference: What If.* Boca Raton: Chapman & Hall/CRC.

Intellectual Ventures. (March 10, 2016). *Failing for Success: The Wright Brothers.* `https://www.intellectualventures.com/buzz/insights/failing-for-success-the-wright-brothers/`

Library of Congress. (n.d.). *Collection. Wilbur and Orville Wright Papers at the Library of Congress*. https://www.loc.gov/collections/wilbur-and-orville-wright-papers/articles-and-essays/the-wilbur-and-orville-wright-timeline-1846-to-1948/1901-to-1910/

Machine Learning Street Talk. (2022, January 4). *#61: Prof. YANN LECUN: Interpolation, Extrapolation and Linearisation (w/ Dr. Randall Balestriero)* [Video]. YouTube. https://www.youtube.com/watch?v=86ib0sfdFtw

Neal, B. (2020, September 7). 2.7 - Positivity/Overlap and Extrapolation [Video]. YouTube. https://www.youtube.com/watch?v=4xc8VkrF98w

Neal, B., Huang, C., and Raghupathi, S. (2020). *RealCause: Realistic Causal Inference Benchmarking*. arXiv, abs/2011.15007.

Neyman, J. (1923). *Sur les applications de la theorie des probabilites aux experiences agricoles: Essai des principes*.

Pearl, J. (2009). *Causality*. Cambridge, UK: Cambridge University Press.

Pearl, J., Glymour, M., and Jewell, N. P. (2016). *Causal inference in statistics: A primer*. Wiley.

Pearl, J., and Mackenzie, D. (2019). *The Book of Why*. Penguin.

Peters, J., Janzing, D., and Schölkopf, B. (2017). *Elements of Causal Inference: Foundations and Learning Algorithms*. MIT Press.

Reisach, A.G., Seiler, C., & Weichwald, S. (2021). *Beware of the Simulated DAG! Varsortability in Additive Noise Models*. arXiv, abs/2102.13647.

Rubin, D. B. (1974). *Estimating causal effects of treatments in randomized and nonrandomized studies. Journal of Educational Psychology*, 66(5), 688–701.

Saint-Jacques, G., Varshney, M., Simpson, J., and Xu, Y. (2019). *Using Ego-Clusters to Measure Network Effects at LinkedIn*. arXiv, abs/1903.08755.

Wald, A. (1980). *A Reprint of 'A Method of Estimating Plane Vulnerability Based on Damage of Survivors'*. Center for Naval Analyses.

9

Causal Inference and Machine Learning – from Matching to Meta-Learners

Welcome to *Chapter 9*!

In this chapter, we'll see a number of methods that can be used to estimate causal effects in non-linear cases. We'll start with relatively simple methods and then move on to more complex machine learning estimators.

By the end of this chapter, you'll have a good understanding of what methods can be used to estimate non-linear (and possibly heterogeneous (or *individualized*)) causal effects. We'll learn about the differences between four different ways to quantify causal effects: **average treatment effect** (ATE), **average treatment effect on the treated** (ATT), **average treatment effect on the control** (ATC), and **conditional average treatment effect** (CATE).

In this chapter, we will cover the following key topics:

- ATE, ATT, ATC, and CATE
- Matching
- Propensity scores
- Inverse probability weighting
- Meta-learners

The basics I – matching

In this section, we'll discuss the basics of **matching**. We'll introduce ATE, ATT, and ATC. We'll define a basic matching estimator and implement an (approximate) matching estimator using DoWhy's four-step causal process.

Matching is a family of methods for estimating causal effects by matching similar observations (or *units*) in the treatment and non-treatment groups. The goal of matching is to make comparisons between similar units in order to achieve as precise an estimate of the true causal effect as possible.

Some authors, including Stuart (2010) and Sizemore & Alkurdi (2019), suggest that matching should be treated as a *data preprocessing step*, on top of which any estimator can be used. This view is also emphasized by Andrew Gelman and Jennifer Hill: *"Matching refers to a variety of procedures that restrict and reorganize the original sample"* (Gelman & Hill, 2006).

If you have enough data to potentially discard some observations, using matching as a preprocessing step is typically beneficial. One important point here is that it only makes sense for observational data (without unobserved confounding) but *not* for experimental data.

To keep consistency with other methods, we will use matching as a complete causal estimator in this chapter.

Types of matching

There are many variants of matching. First, we have *exact* versus *inexact (approximate) matching*. The former requires that treated observations and their respective untreated pairs have *exactly the same values* for *all relevant variables* (which includes confounders). As you can imagine, this might be extremely hard to achieve, especially when your units are complex entities such as humans, social groups, or organizations (Stuart, 2010). Inexact matching, on the other hand, allows for pairing observations that are *similar*. Many different metrics can be used to determine the similarity between two observations. One common choice is **Euclidean distance** or its generalizations: **Mahalanobis distance** (`https://bit.ly/MahalanobisDistance`) and **Minkowski distance** (`https://bit.ly/MinkowskiDistance`). Matching can be performed in the *raw feature space* (directly on your input variables) or other spaces, for instance, the *propensity score* space (more on propensity scores in the next section). One thing that you need to figure out when using *inexact matching* is the maximal distance that you'll accept to match two observations – in other words: how *close* is *close enough*.

More on matching

A detailed discussion of different variants of matching is beyond the scope of this book. If this particular family of methods seems interesting to you, you can start with a great summary article by Elizabeth A. Stuart (Stuart, 2010; `https://bit.ly/StuartOnMatching`) or a (more recent) blog post by Samantha Sizemore and Raiber Alkurdi from the Humboldt University in Berlin (Sizemore & Alkurdi, 2019; `https://bit.ly/SizemoreAlkurdi`). The latter contains code examples in R, leverages some more recent machine learning methods (such as XGBoost), and provides you with an experimental evaluation of different approaches. To learn about matching in the multiple treatment scenarios, check out Lopez & Guttman (2017) for similarities between matching and regression, Angrist & Pischke (2008, pp. 51–59) for matching in the historical context of subclassification, Cunningham (2021, pp. 175–198) or Facure (2020, Chapter 10).

As is the case for all other methods we have discussed so far, matching requires that the relationship between the treatment and the outcome is *unconfounded*. Therefore, we need to make sure that all confounders are observed and present in the matching feature set if we want to obtain unbiased estimates of causal effects. Moreover, it's good to draw a **directed acyclic graph** (**DAG**) to make sure we don't introduce bias by controlling for **colliders**.

Note that matching does not care about linearity in the data – it can be used for linear as well as non-linear data.

Treatment effects – ATE versus ATT/ATC

Using matching, we can compute a variety of causal effects. So far in the book, when computing treatment effects, we implicitly and consistently chose ATE. Let's define ATE formally:

$$ATE = \frac{1}{N}\sum_i \tau_i$$

In the preceding formula, N is the total number of observations, and τ_i is the treatment effect for the unit i defined as:

$$\tau_i = Y_i^1 - Y_i^0$$

The superscripted Y_i in the preceding formula stands for *counterfactual outcomes* for the unit i: Y_i^1 is the outcome under treatment and Y_i^0 is the outcome under no treatment. Of course, both of these outcomes cannot be observed at the same time for the same unit (remember **the fundamental problem of causal inference** from *Chapter 2*?), and that's the reason why we need to estimate them.

Another quantity that we can estimate is ATT. It is defined in the following way:

$$ATT = \frac{1}{N_{T=1}}\sum_{i_{T=1}} \tau_i$$

ATT looks very similar to *ATE*. The key difference is that we do not sum over *all observations* but rather only over the *treated units* (units that received the treatment). In the preceding formula, $N_{T=1}$ represents the number of units that received the treatment (hence $T=1$), and $i_{T=1}$ represents the indices of these units.

ATC is a mirror reflection of ATT; the only thing we need to change is the value of T:

$$ATC = \frac{1}{N_{T=0}} \sum_{i_{T=0}} \tau_i$$

Note that ATE is the *average* of *ATT* and *ATC*.

Matching estimators

The type of causal effect that we want to estimate will influence the definition of the matching estimator itself.

A basic matching estimator for ATT can be defined as follows:

$$\hat{\tau}_{ATT} = \frac{1}{N_{T=1}} \sum_{i_{T=1}} Y_i - Y_{j(i)}$$

In the preceding formula, Y_i stands for the value of the outcome of the i-th treated observation, and $Y_{j(i)}$ represents the outcome of a matched observation from the *untreated group* (I borrowed the $Y_{j(i)}$ notation from Scott Cunningham (2021)).

The matching estimator for ATE can be defined in the following way:

$$\hat{\tau}_{ATE} = \frac{1}{N} \sum_{i} \left(2T_i - 1\right)\left(Y_i - Y_{j(i)}\right)$$

This time, we iterate over *all observations* and find matches for them within the other group. For each treated observation *i*, we match an untreated observation, *j(i)*, and vice versa. Note that in the ATT estimator, *j(i)* always belonged to the untreated group, while *i* was always treated. When estimating ATE, *i* can be treated or untreated, and *j(i)* simply belongs to the other group (if *i* is treated, *j(i)* is not and vice versa).

The $\left(2T_i - 1\right)$ part of the ATE equation is a neat mathematical trick. T_i represents the treatment value for observation *i*. If the treatment is 1, then the value of this expression will also be 1. When the treatment is 0, then the value is -1. Therefore, the expression flips the sign of the remaining part of the equation. This sign flipping helps us keep the result of the $\left(Y_i - Y_{j(i)}\right)$ part correct regardless of the unit *i*'s actual treatment status.

Note that this formula only works for binary treatments (it needs to be further adapted to work with multiple-level treatments; for some further ideas on this, check out Lopez & Gutman, 2017).

Let's see a quick example. Imagine that we only have two units in our dataset, represented in *Table 9.1*:

Unit	Covariate	Treatment	Outcome
A	33	1	9
B	33	0	1.5

Table 9.1 – Example data

Let's compute a matching ATE for this dataset. For the first unit, we have the following equation:

$(2 \times 1 - 1)(9 - 1.5) = 1 \times 7.5 = 7.5$

For the second observation, we have the following equation:

$(2 \times 0 - 1)(1.5 - 9) = -1 \times -7.5 = 7.5$

Now, we sum both results, which gives us *15*, and divide by the total number of observations, which gives us *7.5*. Et voila! Note how the sign-flipping trick makes the subtraction operation order invariant. For clarity, the computation with color coding is also presented in *Figure 9.1*.

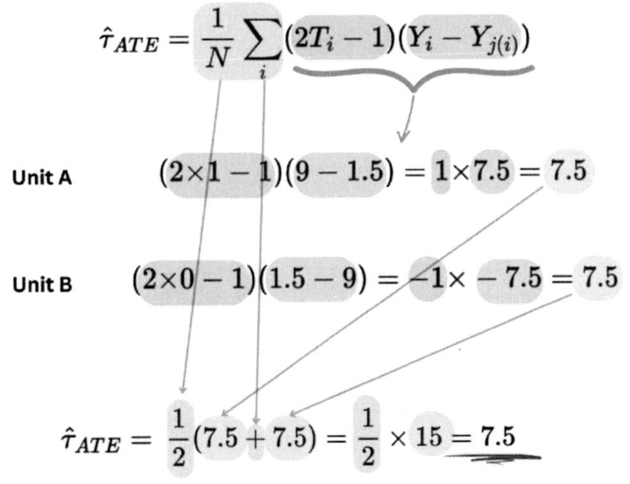

Figure 9.1 – Visual representation of matching formula computations with data from Table 9.1

Now, you might ask, what if we have observations without good matches in our dataset? The traditional answer to this question is that we need to discard them! In case of approximate (inexact) matching, you can try extending your criteria of similarity in order to retain some of these observations, but keep in mind that this will likely increase the bias in your estimates (especially if your sample size is small).

What if we end up with more than one good match per observation? Do we also need to discard it?

It turns out that we can be more efficient than that! One thing we can do to avoid discarding the observations is to average over them. For each *i*, we collect all *j(i)*s that meet our similarity criteria and simply take the average of their outcomes. This is presented formally as follows:

$$\hat{\tau}_{ATE} = \frac{1}{N}\sum_i \left(2T_i - 1\right)\left(Y_i - \left(\frac{1}{M}\sum_m Y_{j_m(i)}\right)\right)$$

In the preceding formula, *M* is the number of samples that we matched to sample *i*. We could also compute an analogous quantity for ATT.

Implementing matching

Great, we're ready to get some data and see matching in action! We'll follow DoWhy's four-step procedure and use the approximate matching estimator.

The code for this chapter can be found in the `Chapter_09.ipynb` notebook (`https://bit.ly/causal-ntbk-09`).

For our analysis, we'll use a simplified synthetic dataset (*n=200*) inspired by the famous dataset used in Robert LaLonde's seminal paper *Evaluating the Econometric Evaluations of Training Programs with Experimental Data* (1986). Our dataset consists of three variables:

- A binary indicator of a training program participation
- The subject's age
- The subject's yearly earnings 18 months after the training took place (in **United States Dollar** (**USD**))

We're interested in estimating the effect of training on participants' earnings 18 months after the training.

First, let's read in the data (we omit library imports here for a better reading experience – please refer to the notebook for the more details):

```
earnings_data = pd.read_csv(r'./data/ml_earnings.csv')
```

Let's print out a couple of rows:

```
earnings_data.head()
```

	age	took_a_course	earnings
0	19	False	110579.0
1	28	False	142577.0
2	22	True	130520.0
3	25	True	142687.0
4	24	False	127832.0

Figure 9.2 – The first five rows of the earnings dataset

We can see in *Figure 9.2* that the data has expected data types. Note that DoWhy (0.8) requires that the treatment variable is encoded as Boolean.

Let's try to group subjects by age:

```
earnings_data.groupby(['age', 'took_a_course']).mean()
```

35	**False**	172134.250000
	True	180404.500000
36	**False**	175240.666667
37	**False**	181514.000000
	True	187627.000000
38	**False**	185546.333333
39	**False**	187253.666667

Figure 9.3 – Selected rows of the data grouped by age

Although we only printed out a couple of rows in *Figure 9.3*, you can see that for some age groups (for instance, 36 or 38), there are observations only for one of the values of the treatment. This means that we won't be able to compute the exact effects for these groups. We'll leave it to our matching estimator to handle this for us, but first, let's compute the naïve estimate of the causal effect of training on earnings using the treatment and control group means:

```
treatment_avg = earnings_data.query('took_a_course==1')[
    'earnings'].mean()
cntrl_avg = earnings_data.query('took_a_course==0')[
    'earnings'].mean()

treatment_avg - cntrl_avg
```

This gives us the following result:

```
6695.57088285231
```

The naïve estimate of the effect of our training is a bit over 6,695 USD per year.

Let's see whether, and, if so, how the approximate matching estimate differs.

Step 1 – representing the problem as a graph

Let's start by constructing a **graph modeling language** (GML) graph:

```
nodes = ['took_a_course', 'earnings', 'age']
edges = [
    ('took_a_course', 'earnings'),
    ('age', 'took_a_course'),
    ('age', 'earnings')
]
```

```
# Generate the GML graph
gml_string = 'graph [directed 1\n'

for node in nodes:
    gml_string += f'\tnode [id "{node}" label "{node}"]\n'

for edge in edges:
    gml_string += f'\tedge [source "{edge[0]}" target
        "{edge[1]}"]\n'

gml_string += ']'
```

Because we know the data-generating process, we know that age is a confounder, and we encode this knowledge by adding an edge from age to both the treatment and the outcome.

Let's wrap our graph in DoWhy's `CausalModel` object:

```
model = CausalModel(
    data=earnings_data,
    treatment='took_a_course',
    outcome='earnings',
    graph=gml_string
)
```

As a sanity check, let's view the model:

```
model.view_model()
```

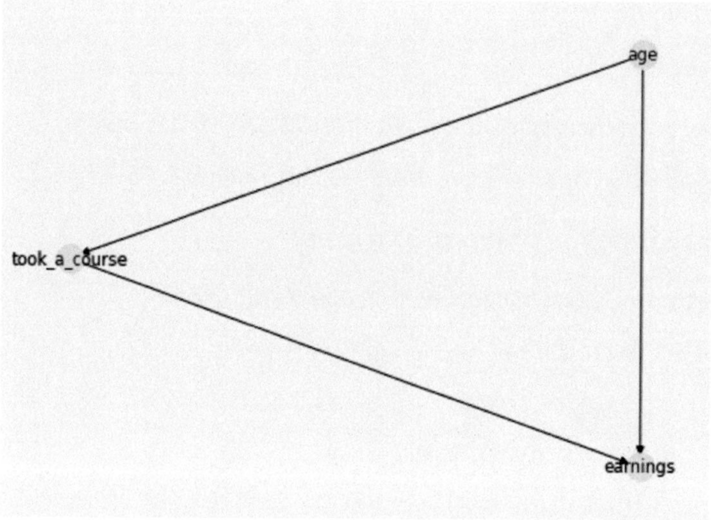

Figure 9.4 – A graphical representation of the earnings data model

The model looks as expected. Let's move to step 2.

Step 2 – getting the estimand

In order to get the estimand, we call the `.identify_effect()` method on our model object:

```
estimand = model.identify_effect()
```

Now, let's print it:

```
print(estimand)
```

This gives us the following output:

```
Estimand type: nonparametric-ate

### Estimand : 1
Estimand name: backdoor
Estimand expression:
       d
────────────────(E[earnings|age])
d[took_a_course]
Estimand assumption 1, Unconfoundedness: If U→{took_a_course} and
U→earnings then P(earnings|took_a_course,age,U) = P(earnings|took_a_
course,age)

### Estimand : 2
Estimand name: iv
No such variable(s) found!

### Estimand : 3
Estimand name: frontdoor
No such variable(s) found!
```

We correctly identified the `backdoor` estimand.

Let's compute the effect!

Step 3 – computing the effect

In order to compute the effect, we need to specify a couple of details. First, we need to pass the estimator's name. We want to use matching, so we'll pick DoWhy's `backdoor.distance_matching` estimator. We'll set target units to ATE (for consistent comparisons with other methods) and the distance metric to Minkowski with `p` set to `2` (which is equivalent to simple Euclidean distance):

```
estimate = model.estimate_effect(
    identified_estimand=estimand,
```

```
    method_name='backdoor.distance_matching',
    target_units='ate',
    method_params={'distance_metric': 'minkowski', 'p': 2})
```

One thing I'd like to add here is that we haven't standardized our matching variable (`age`). This is fine because we have just one variable, yet in a multivariable case, many people would recommend normalizing or standardizing your variables to keep their scales similar. This helps to avoid a scenario where variables with larger values disproportionally outweigh other variables in the distance computation. Many machine learning resources follow this advice, and it's often considered a standard practice in multivariate problems involving distance computations.

Contrary to this recommendation, Harvard's Gary King has repeatedly recommended *not* to standardize your variables for matching (and not to use standardized distance metrics such as Mahalonobis either) because – as he says – *it throws away the substance* (for instance: King, 2018, p. 12). I am not entirely convinced by this argument, but I'll leave it to you to decide for yourself. While making the decision, keep in mind that Gary King spent a significant amount of time working with matching. Much more time than I did.

OK, back to our effect computation, let's see our estimate:

```
estimate.value
```

This gives us:

```
10118.445
```

Now, let's reveal the true effect size! The true effect size for our data is 10,000 USD. This means that matching worked pretty well here! The absolute percentage error is about 1.2%, which is a great improvement over the naïve estimate that resulted in 33% of absolute percentage error!

Let's see how well our matching estimator will handle our attempts to refute it!

Step 4 – refuting the estimate

For brevity, we'll only run one refutation test here. In the real world, we optimally want to run as many tests as available:

```
refutation = model.refute_estimate(
    estimand=estimand,
    estimate=estimate,
    method_name='random_common_cause')
```

Let's print out the results:

```
print(refutation)
```

We get the following output:

```
Refute: Add a random common cause
Estimated effect:10118.445
New effect:10311.769699999999
p value:0.42
```

We see that the new effect is slightly higher than the estimated one. Nonetheless, a high p value indicates that the change is not statistically significant. Good job!

In this section, we defined exact and approximate matching estimators. We discussed three types of causal effects: ATE, ATT, and ATC. We implemented an approximate matching estimator as a part of DoWhy's four-step causal process and discussed some practical tips and implications on the way.

Now, let's see what challenges we may meet on our way when using matching.

The basics II – propensity scores

In this section, we will discuss **propensity scores** and how they are sometimes used to address the challenges that we encounter when using matching in multidimensional cases. Finally, we'll demonstrate why you should not use propensity scores for matching, even if your favorite econometrician does so.

Matching in the wild

Let's start with a mental experiment. Imagine that you received a new dataset to analyze. This data contains 1,000 observations. What are the chances that you'll find at least one exact match for each row if there are 18 variables in your dataset?

The answer obviously depends on a number of factors. How many variables are binary? How many are continuous? How many are categorical? What's the number of levels for categorical variables? Are variables independent or correlated with each other?

To get an idea of what the answer can be, let's take a look at *Figure 9.5*:

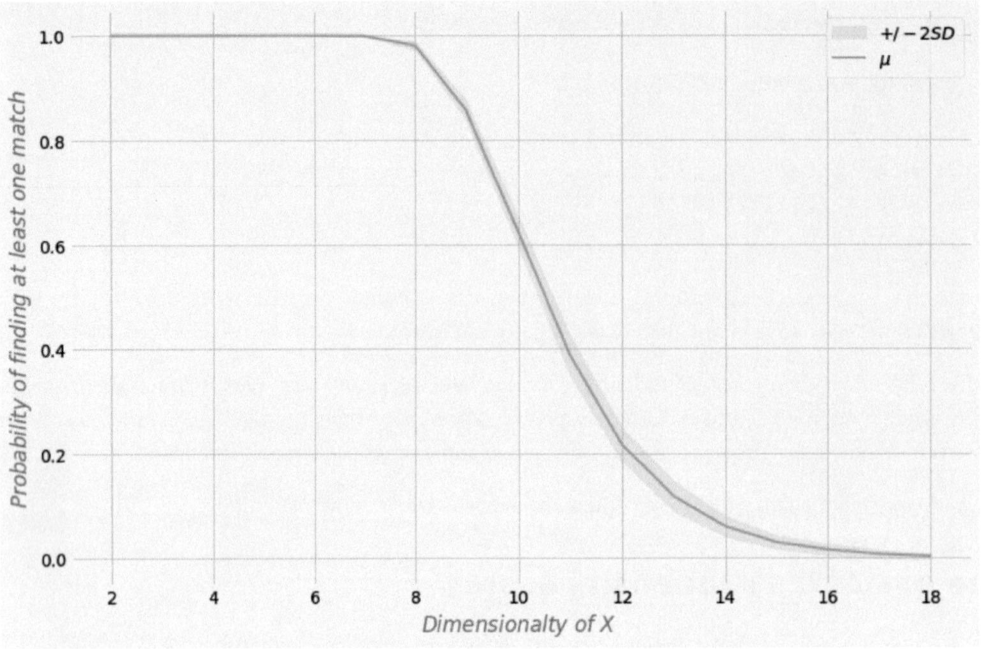

Figure 9.5 – The probability of finding an exact match versus the dimensionality of the dataset

In *Figure 9.5*, the x axis represents the dataset's dimensionality (the number of variables in the dataset), and the y axis represents the probability of finding at least one exact match per row.

The blue line is the average probability, and the shaded areas represent +/- two standard deviations.

The dataset has been generated using independent Bernoulli distributions with $p = 0.5$. Therefore each variable is binary and independent. This is an extremely simple setting.

As you can see, the probability of finding an exact match in an 18-dimensional binary random dataset is *essentially zero*. In the real world, we rarely operate on purely binary datasets, and for continuous data, multidimensional matching becomes even more difficult. This poses a serious challenge for matching, even in an approximate case.

How can we address this?

Reducing the dimensionality with propensity scores

Propensity scores are estimates of the probability that a given unit will be assigned to a treatment group based on their characteristics.

This is represented formally as follows:

$\hat{e}(X) = P(T = 1|X = x)$

According to the propensity score theorem (Rosenbaum & Rubin, 1983), if we have unconfoundedness given X, we will also have unconfoundedness given the propensity score, assuming positivity.

Sounds good!

Why not use this property to solve the high-dimensionality challenge? Propensity scores are unidimensional and so now we can match on just one number [sic!] rather than a high-dimensional vector.

This sounds really good!

Propensity score matching (PSM)

Unfortunately, there are numerous challenges with this approach:

- First, propensity scores reduce the dimensionality of our data and – by definition – force us to throw information away.
- Second, two observations that are *very different* in their original feature space may have *the same propensity score*. This may lead to matching on *very different* observations and hence, biasing the results.
- Third, PSM leads to a paradox. The main goal of PSM is to approximate randomized assignment to the treatment and control groups.

In the binary case, the optimal propensity score would be 0.5. Let's think about it.

What happens in the ideal scenario when all observations have the optimal propensity score of 0.5? The position of every observation in the propensity score space becomes identical to any other observation.

How do we match observations?

We've seen this in the formulas before – we either take the best match or we average over the best matches, yet now *every point* in the dataset is an equally good match!

We can either pick one at random or average on all the observations! Note that this kills the essence of what we want to do in matching – compare the observations that are the most similar. This is sometimes called the **PSM paradox**. If you feel like digging deeper into this topic, check out King (2018), King & Nielsen (2019), or King's YouTube video here: `https://bit.ly/GaryKingVideo`.

Other approaches to matching (that work)

Researchers have proposed numerous alternatives to approximate matching and PSM. One solution, proposed by Iacus and colleagues is called **coarsened exact matching** (**CEM**); Iacus et al., 2012). Other methods include **dynamic almost matching exactly** (**DAME**); Liu et al., 2018) and **adaptive hyper-box matching** (**AHB**); Morucci et al., 2020). Some of these methods are available in Python, others only in R. Check out Duke University's *Almost Matching Exactly Lab* web page for more details (`https://bit.ly/AlmostMatchingExactly`). To learn more about CEM, check out Gary King's page (`https://bit.ly/GaryKingCEM`).

Before we conclude this section, I want to reiterate an important and often overlooked truth about PSM. Over time, some researchers have suggested that PSM can be used to *deconfound non-experimental data with hidden confounding* (for instance, Deheija & Wahba, 2002).

Unfortunately, *this is not the case*. Setting aside the other challenges discussed earlier, PSM *requires unconfoundedness* (no hidden confounding).

Otherwise, we risk arbitrary bias in the estimates. It seems to me that the belief that propensity scores can deconfound confounded data is still alive among some communities. I hope that this book will contribute to promoting a healthy view of PSM.

In this section, we learned what propensity scores are, how to use them for matching, and why they *should not* be used for this purpose. We discussed the limitations of the PSM approach and reiterated that PSM is not immune to hidden confounding.

Can propensity scores be useful in other contexts?

Inverse probability weighting (IPW)

In this section, we'll discuss IPW. We'll see how IPW can be used to de-bias our causal estimates, and we'll implement it using DoWhy.

Many faces of propensity scores

Although propensity scores might not be the best choice for matching, they still might be useful in other contexts. *IPW* is a method that allows us to control for confounding by creating so-called **pseudo-populations** within our data. Pseudo-populations are created by upweighting the underrepresented and downweighting the overrepresented groups in our dataset.

Imagine that we want to estimate the effect of drug D. If males and females react differently to D and we have 2 males and 6 females in the treatment group and 12 males and 2 females in the control group, we might end up with a situation similar to the one that we've seen in *Chapter 1*: the drug is good for everyone, but is harmful to females and males!

This is Simpson's paradox at its best (if you want to see how we can deconfound the data from *Chapter 1* using IPW, check out the `Extras` notebook: `https://bit.ly/causal-ntbk-extras-02`).

Formalizing IPW

The formula for a basic IPW ATE estimator is as follows:

$$\hat{\tau}_{ATE_{IPW}} = \frac{1}{N_{T=1}} \sum_{i_{T=1}}^{N_{T=1}} \frac{y_i}{\hat{e}(X_i)} - \frac{1}{N_{T=0}} \sum_{j_{T=0}}^{N_{T=0}} \frac{y_j}{1 - \hat{e}(X_j)}$$

In the preceding formula, we follow the convention that we used earlier in this chapter: $N_{T=1}$ represents the number of units that received the treatment and $N_{T=0}$ represents the number of units that did not receive the treatment. Lowercase $y_{i;j}$ represents the outcome for unit *i* (or *j* respectively), and $\hat{e}(X_{i;j})$ is the (estimated) *propensity score* for unit *i* (or *j*) defined as the probability of treatment given the characteristics of the unit:

$$\hat{e}(X_i) = P(T_i = 1 | X_i)$$

Note that similarly to the previously discussed methods, we need to include *all confounders* in *X* if we want to obtain causally unbiased estimates of the treatment effect.

Implementing IPW

For this exercise, we'll use the same earnings dataset that we used in the previous section. This allows us also to reuse the graph and the estimand that we found in the previous section and the only thing we need to redo is to re-compute the estimate using the appropriate estimator. We'll use DoWhy's `backdoor.propensity_score_weighting` method. Behind the scenes, the estimator uses **weighted least squares** (**WLS**) regression, which weights each treated sample by the inverse of its propensity score ($\hat{e}(X_i)$) and each untreated sample by the inverse of $1 - \hat{e}(X_i)$.

The IPW WLS estimator is straightforward to implement in DoWhy:

```
estimate = model.estimate_effect(
    identified_estimand=estimand,
    method_name='backdoor.propensity_score_weighting',
    target_units='ate')
```

Let's see the results:

```
estimate.value
```

This gives us the following output:

```
10313.5668311203
```

Compared to the matching estimate (10118.445), the result is slightly worse. The absolute percentage error for the IPW estimator is 3.1% – over twice the error of the matching estimator (1.2%).

Note that it's not necessarily always the case that matching performs better than IPW. That said, some authors have reported that IPW underperforms compared to other methods (for instance, Elze et al., 2017; but note that this is an observational study that might suffer from other sources of bias).

IPW – practical considerations

Before we conclude the section on IPW, let's discuss a couple of practical aspects regarding the method:

- If you're using WLS as an estimator for IPW, remember that WLS is basically a linear regression model (with additional weighting), and it's not capable of modeling non-linear relationships out of the box.
- When propensity scores are close to 0 or 1, the weights either explode or go toward 1 (which is equivalent to no weighting; when all weights are equal to 1, WLS becomes a regular linear regression). This can be detrimental to your model. Some people filter out all observations with propensity scores less than .01 or greater than .99; others set the thresholds to .05 and .95, respectively.
- You need a model to compute your propensity scores before you can perform weighting. Logistic regression is a common choice because its probability estimates are (usually) well calibrated, other models might return biased probabilities, and you might want to scale their outputs using one of the available methods such as Platt scaling or isotonic regression (Niculescu-Mizil & Caruana, 2005). Although there is an opinion that probability scaling *is not* necessarily very important for IPW, recent research by Rom Gutman, Ehud Karavani, and Yishai Shimoni from IBM Research has shown that good calibration significantly reduces errors in causal effect estimates, especially when the original classifier lacks calibration (Gutman et al., 2022). This is particularly important when you use expressive machine learning models to estimate your propensity scores. You might want to use such models if you want your propensity scores to reflect higher-order relationships (interactions) in your dataset that simple logistic regression cannot capture (unless you perform some feature engineering).

It's time to conclude our section on propensity scores, but it's definitely not the last time we see them.

In this section, we learned how propensity scores can be used to weight observations in order to compute causal effects. We defined a basic IPW averaging estimator and implemented IPW using DoWhy and WLS. Finally, we discussed several aspects important to consider when working with IPW in practice.

In the next section, we'll introduce **S-Learner** – the first estimator of a bigger meta-learner family.

Let's go!

S-Learner – the Lone Ranger

With this section, we begin our journey into the world of **meta-learners**. We'll learn why ATE is sometimes not enough and we'll introduce **heterogeneous treatment effects** (**HTEs**) (also known as

conditional average treatment effects or **individualized treatment effects**). We'll discuss what *meta-learners* are, and – finally – we'll implement one (*S-Learner*) to estimate causal effects on a simulated dataset with interactions (we'll also use it on real-life experimental data in *Chapter 10*).

By the end of this section, you will have a solid understanding of what CATE is, understand the main ideas behind meta-learners, and learn how to implement S-Learner using DoWhy and EconML on your own.

Ready?

The devil's in the detail

In the previous sections, we computed two different types of causal effects: *ATE* and *ATT*. Both ATE and ATT provide us with information about the estimated average causal effect in the population.

However, it's important to remember that people and other complex entities (such as animals, social groups, companies, or countries) can have different individual reactions to the same treatment.

A cancer therapy might work very well for some patients while having no effect on others. A marketing campaign might work great for most people unless you target software developers.

Your best friend Rachel might enjoy your edgy jokes, yet your brother Artem might find them less appealing.

When we deal with a situation like this, ATE might hide important information from us. Imagine that you want to estimate the influence of your jokes on people's moods. You tell a joke to your friend Rachel, and her mood goes up from a 3 to a 5 on a 5-point scale.

This gives us the **individual treatment effect** (**ITE**) for Rachel, which is 2. Now, you say the same joke to Artem, and his mood decreases from a 3 to a 1. His ITE is -2.

If we were to calculate the ATE based on these two examples, we would get the effect of 0 since the ITEs for Rachel and Artem cancel each other out.

However, this doesn't tell us anything about the actual impact of the joke on Rachel or Artem individually.

In this case, the ATE hides the fact that the joke had a positive effect on Rachel's mood and a negative effect on Artem's mood. To fully understand the effect of the joke, we need to look at the ITE for each individual.

Unfortunately, in many cases, ITE might be very difficult or even impossible to estimate as we would need to know individual-level counterfactuals to estimate it.

Let's see whether there's anything we can do about it.

Mom, Dad, meet CATE

One solution to this challenge is to calculate CATE; also known as HTE. When computing CATE, we not only look at the treatment but also at a set of variables defining the individual characteristics of each unit that might *modify* the way the treatment impacts the outcome (if you thought about *interactions* or *moderation*, that's a great intuition).

For instance, it might be the case that your jokes are perceived as funnier by people familiar with a specific context. Let's assume that Rachel studied philosophy. It's likely that your jokes about the German philosopher Immanuel Kant will be funnier to her than they will be to Artem, who is interested in different topics and has never heard of Kant. CATE can help us capture these differences.

In other words, CATE gives us a more nuanced understanding of the effect of the treatment on units with *different characteristics*. This can be especially useful in cases where ATE hides important differences between units, as in our example with the joke.

In general, CATE for binary treatment can be defined in the following way:

$$CATE = \mathbb{E}[Y|T = 1, X] - \mathbb{E}[Y|T = 0, X]$$

In the preceding formula, $\mathbb{E}[]$ represents the expected value operator, Y is the outcome, T is the treatment, and X represents a (set of) feature(s) describing the population units. Translating this to our example, Y would represent the joke receiver's mood, T indicates whether you said a joke or not, and X is a vector of the population unit's characteristics (e.g., whether they studied philosophy or not).

CATE versus ITE

CATE versus ITE: while some researchers suggest that CATE can be treated as an estimate of ITE and it can be viewed as such from some perspectives (e.g., Künzel et al., 2019; p. 3), we'll choose to talk about estimated individual CATE rather than about ITE. On why CATE is different from ITE, check out Vegetabile (2021) and Mueller & Pearl (2020). Also, note that the *individualized* treatment effect (a synonym for CATE) is different from ITE in this literature.

Jokes aside, say hi to the heterogeneous crowd

Heterogeneous treatment effects are a challenge in fields such as medicine and marketing, where different groups of people may respond differently to the same treatment (such as a drug or marketing content). Let's take Jakub Czakon's analysis of Hacker News comments on marketing to software developers (`https://bit.ly/DevsMarketingBlog`). Jakub's analysis showed that developers might react differently to marketing content compared to the general population.

In particular, many reactions captured in the analysis were marked by strong negative emotions, including disgust towards the marketed product and even the company behind it.

The idea that people might react differently to the same content is often presented in a matrix sometimes called the **uplift model matrix** that you can see in *Figure 9.6*:

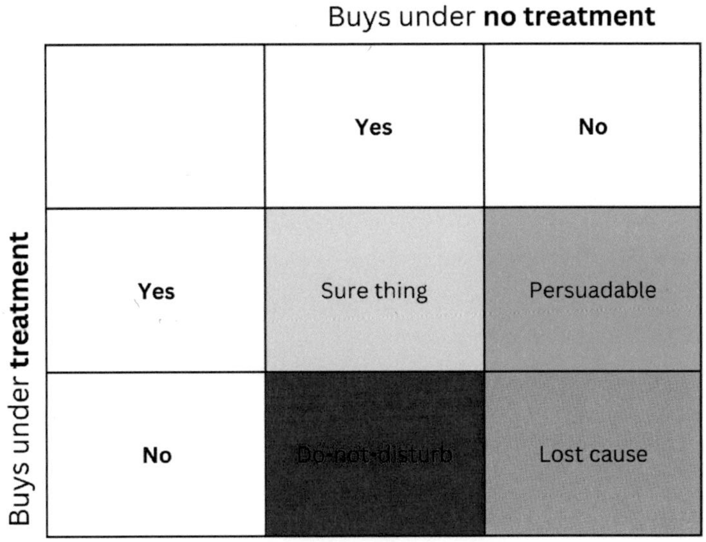

Figure 9.6 – The uplift model matrix

In *Figure 9.6*, rows represent reactions to content when the treatment (e.g., an ad) is presented to the recipient. Columns represent reactions when no treatment is applied.

The four colored cells represent a summary of the treatment effect dynamics. **Sure thing** (green) buys regardless of the treatment. **Do not disturb** (red) might buy without the treatment, but they won't buy if treated (e.g., Czakon's developers). **Lost cause** (gray) won't buy regardless of the treatment status, and **Persuadable** (blue) would not buy without the treatment but might buy when approached.

If you're a marketer with a limited budget, you want to focus on marketing to the blue group (Persuadable) and avoid marketing to the red group (Do not disturb) as much as possible.

Marketing to the Sure thing and Lost cause groups will not hurt you directly but won't give you any benefit while consuming the budget.

Analogously, if you're a doctor, you want to prescribe a drug to people who can benefit from it and want to avoid prescribing it to people whom it can hurt.

In many real-world scenarios, the outcome variable might be probabilistic (e.g., the probability of purchase) or continuous (e.g., the amount of spending). In such cases, we cannot define discrete groups as in *Figure 9.6* anymore, and we focus on finding the units with the *highest expected increase* in the outcome variable between untreated and treated conditions. This difference between the outcome under treatment versus under no treatment is sometimes referred to as **uplift**.

Waving the assumptions flag

To model heterogeneous effects correctly, we need to be sure that our data comes from a **randomized controlled trial** (**RCT**) or that we are able to control for all **relevant confounders**. Hidden confounding might lead to arbitrary bias in the estimates. We should also make sure that we meet the **positivity assumption**.

Assuming that your data comes from an RCT, you should start by checking whether the design of your study did not lead to *leakage*. Leakage refers to a situation where some aspects of your RCT design or the randomization process itself lead to the non-random assignment of units to the control and experimental groups.

One simple way to do it is to build a surrogate model that predicts your treatment variable based on the predictors you use, formally presented as follows:

$T \sim X$

The performance of such a model should be essentially random.

Note that this method is informative only when *leakage* variables are observed. In real-world scenarios, it might be the case that leakage is driven by an unobserved variable that is independent of any other observed variable.

In such a case, we won't be able to discover leakage using the preceding method, and the only way to avoid it is to carefully design your experiment, making sure that *leakage* does not happen.

You're the only one – modeling with S-Learner

S-Learner is the name of a simple approach to model HTEs. S-Learner belongs to the category of so-called meta-learners. Note that *causal meta-learners* are not directly related to the concept of *meta-learning* used in traditional machine learning. Meta-learners, as we define them here, take one or more traditional machine learning models called **base-learners** (Künzel et al., 2019) and use them to compute the causal effect. In general, you can use any machine learning model of sufficient complexity (tree-based, neural network, and more) as a base-learner as long as it's compatible with your data.

How complex does my model need to be?

When we defined CATE, we said that we were interested in the interactions between the treatment and the unit's characteristics. Alternatively, heterogeneous treatment effect can be expressed as a difference in the functional forms between the heterogeneous strata. In many real-life cases we won't know which one is the case. Hence, the minimal practical requirement for our model in order to model CATE is that it can handle interactions between two or more features.

This can be achieved either by building an architecture that allows for modeling interactions or by manually providing a model with interaction features. In the latter case, even a simple regression will be sufficient to model CATE, though, at scale, manual feature generation might be a challenging task (both epistemologically and technically).

> In the former case, we need to make sure that the architecture is expressive enough to handle feature interactions. Tree-based models deal well with this task. Classic neural networks of sufficient depth can also model interactions, but this might be challenging sometimes.
>
> Interactions are naturally expressed as multiplication, and in neural networks, multiplication must be modeled solely by a combination of additive layers and non-linear activations. Zou et al. (2020) have demonstrated that adding an explicit interaction layer makes neural networks learn interactions better.

S-Learner is the simplest possible meta-learner, which only uses a **single** base-learner (hence its name: *S(ingle)*-Learner). The idea behind S-Learner is beautifully simple: train a single model on the full training dataset, including the treatment variable as a feature, predict both potential outcomes for the observation of interest, and subtract the results to obtain CATE.

After the training, a step-by-step prediction procedure for S-Learner is shown as follows:

1. Pick the observation of interest.
2. Fix the treatment value for this observation to 1 (or `True`).
3. Predict the outcome using the trained model.
4. Take the same observation again.
5. This time, fix the value of the treatment to 0 (or `False`).
6. Generate the prediction.
7. Subtract the value of the prediction without treatment from the value of the prediction with treatment.

Formally, we can express the same as follows:

$$\hat{\tau}_{CATE_i} = \mu(X_i, T = 1) - \mu\left(X_i, T = 0\right)$$

In the preceding formula, μ represents your model of choice (base-learner), so that $\hat{y}_i = \mu\left(X_i, T = t\right)$, X_i is a vector of unit i characteristics, and T represents the treatment.

That's all.

You can easily build it yourself using any relevant model. Nonetheless, we'll use DoWhy here to continue familiarizing ourselves with the API and to leverage the power of convenient abstractions provided by the library.

We'll start with an enhanced version of the synthetic earnings dataset (`ml_earnings_interaction_train.csv` and `ml_earnings_interaction_test.csv` from `https://bit.ly/causal-repo-data`).

The enhanced dataset contains an additional variable (`python_proficiency`) that interacts with the treatment. This means that the size of the effect of training on earnings depends on the Python proficiency level in this dataset.

The causal graph for the dataset is presented in *Figure 9.7*:

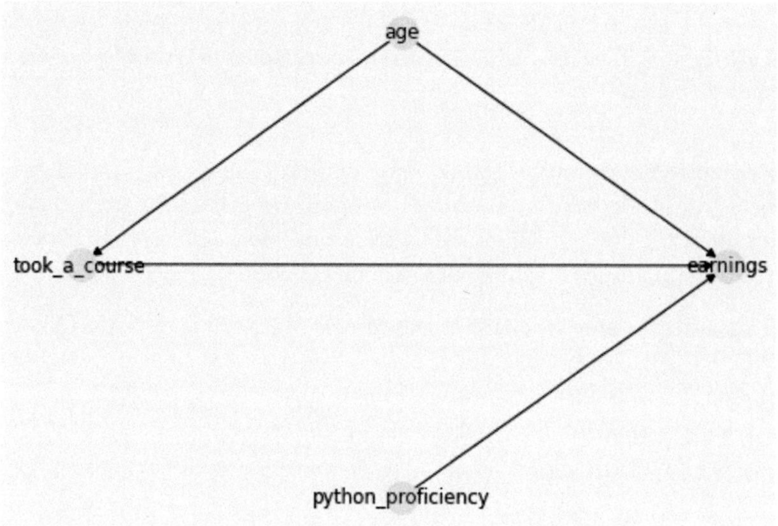

Figure 9.7 – The causal graph (DAG) for the enhanced earnings dataset

Let's read in the data. We'll use the train and test sets here so that we can evaluate the model's performance:

```
earnings_interaction_train = pd.read_csv(
    r'./data/ml_earnings_interaction_train.csv')
earnings_interaction_test = pd.read_csv(
    r'./data/ml_earnings_interaction_test.csv')
```

Let's examine the shapes:

```
earnings_interaction_train.shape, earnings_interaction_test.shape
```

This gives us the following output:

```
((5000, 4), (100, 4))
```

Our train set consists of `5000` observations, and the test set consists of `100` observations.

On train-test splits and validating causal models

Note that classic train-test splits and cross-validation schemes are *not suitable for evaluating causal models in terms of the correctness of the causal structure.*

Why?

Because they say nothing about how correct our *estimand* is. In other words, they are not informative when it comes to potential hidden confounding, selection bias, or any other structurally invoked bias (you can also think about cross-validation as a *rung 1* method).

That said, in our case, the traditional train-test split is useful. We know the true causal structure, and so we're not interested in evaluating the *estimand*, but rather – assuming we have a correct estimand – we want to know how well our models *estimate* the effect, and – as we know from traditional machine learning literature – cross-validation and train-test splits can help us with that.

Figure 9.8 presents the first five rows of the training dataset:

	age	python_proficiency	took_a_course	earnings
0	23	0.632318	True	139267.0
1	20	0.602551	False	115569.0
2	21	0.518225	False	119142.0
3	25	0.945161	False	130291.0
4	30	0.636251	True	164209.0

Figure 9.8 – The first five rows of the enhanced earnings dataset (train)

Let's review the test partition as well (*Figure 9.9*):

	age	python_proficiency	took_a_course	true_effect
0	30	0.223877	True	11120.0
1	23	0.394152	True	11970.0
2	37	0.214638	True	11073.0
3	21	0.869069	True	14345.0
4	41	0.833934	True	14169.0

Figure 9.9 – The first five rows of the enhanced earnings dataset (test)

As you can see, the test set's structure is different. We don't see the `earnings` column. Instead, we have a new column called `true_effect`. Clearly, knowing the true effect is the privilege of synthetic data, and we won't get it with the real-world data!

Nevertheless, we want to use it here to demonstrate important aspects of our models' performance.

We're now ready to create a model.

First, let's instantiate the `CausalModel` object (note we're omitting the GML graph construction here for brevity; check out the notebook for the full code):

```
model = CausalModel(
    data=earnings_interaction_train,
    treatment='took_a_course',
    outcome='earnings',
    effect_modifiers='python_proficiency',
    graph=gml_string
)
```

Let's identify the effect:

```
estimand = model.identify_effect()
```

Finally, let's get the estimate:

```
estimate = model.estimate_effect(
    identified_estimand=estimand,
    method_name='backdoor.econml.metalearners.SLearner',
    target_units='ate',
    method_params={
        'init_params': {
            'overall_model': LGBMRegressor(
                n_estimators=500, max_depth=10)
        },
        'fit_params': {}
    })
```

We have some new stuff here. Let's unpack it!

First, take a look at the `method_name` argument. We're using an EconML `SLearner` estimator, but we don't even import EconML (another great example of the deep integration between DoWhy and its sister library).

We use ATE as our target units.

Next, we have the `method_params` parameter. That's an important one. We pass a Python dictionary here. The structure of this dictionary depends on the method we pass to `method_name`.

The dictionary has two first-level keys:

- `init_params`
- `fit_params`

The expected values for these keys are also dictionaries. The former defines estimator-level details such as the base-learner model class or model-specific parameters. In other words, everything that's needed to initialize your estimator.

The latter defines parameters that can be passed to the causal estimator's `.fit()` method. One example here could be the `inference` parameter, which allows you to switch between bootstrap and non-bootstrap inference modes.

If you're unsure what keys are expected by your method of choice, check out the EconML documentation here `https://bit.ly/EconMLDocs`.

In our example, we use a LightGBM model (Ke et al., 2017) as a base learner. It's efficient and blazingly fast, and gives very good results in many cases. We do not pass any `fit` parameters to the estimator as we want to use the default values this time.

Let's check whether S-Learner did a good job. Note that we're passing the refutation step in print for brevity, but the model behaved well under a random common cause and placebo refuters (check out this chapter's notebook for details).

First, let's generate predictions for the test set:

```
effect_pred = model.causal_estimator.effect(
    earnings_interaction_test.drop(['true_effect',
    'took_a_course'], axis=1))
```

Note that we're dropping the `treatment` column (`took_a_course`) and the true effect column.

The `treatment` column is irrelevant (and usually not available) at prediction time. The fact that it is present in our dataset is an artifact of how we generated the data.

The true effect column will be useful at the evaluation stage, which we'll perform in a second.

Let's isolate the true effect values:

```
effect_true = earnings_interaction_test['
    true_effect'].values
```

Let's compute the **mean absolute percentage error** (**MAPE**) and plot the predicted values against the true effect:

```
mean_absolute_percentage_error(effect_true, effect_pred)
```

This gives us the following as output:

```
0.0502732092578003
```

Slightly above 5%! It's a pretty decent result in absolute terms (of course such a result might be excellent or terrible in a particular context, depending on your use case)!

Let's plot the true effect against predicted values. *Figure 9.10* presents the results:

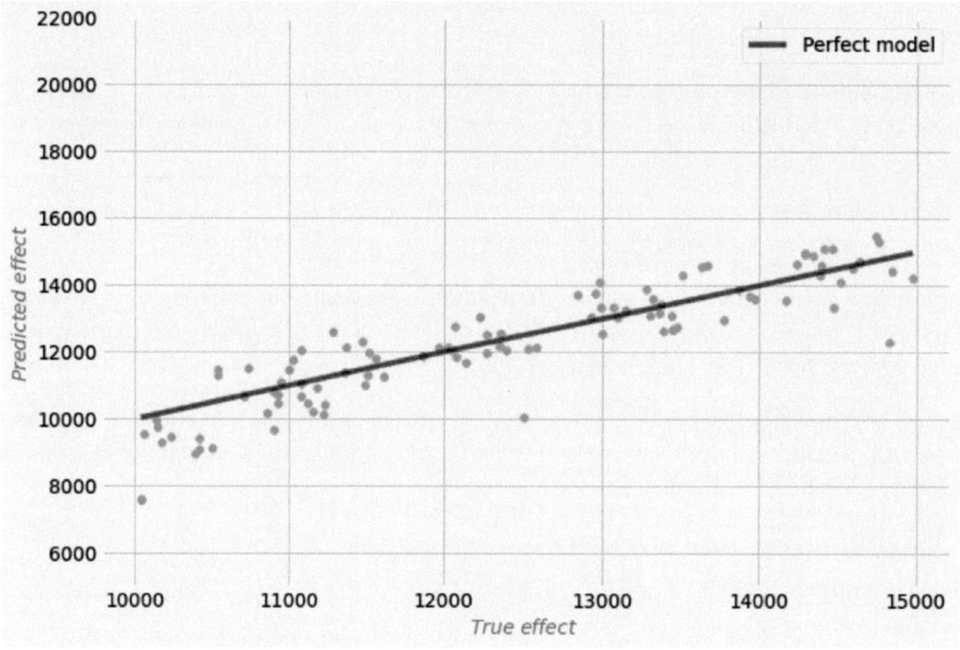

Figure 9.10 – True effect (x axis) versus predicted effect (y axis) for S-Learner trained on full data

The *x* axis in *Figure 9.10* represents the values of the true effect for each of the observations in the test set. The *y* axis represents the predicted values, and the red line represents the results of a (hypothetical) perfect model (with zero error).

We can see that there are some observations where our S-Learner underestimates the effect (the three points that are way below the line), but its overall performance looks good!

Now I want to share with you something that I feel is often overlooked or discussed only briefly or in abstract terms by many practitioners.

What happens when the dataset is small?

Small data

Let's train the same S-Learner once again but on a small subset of the training data (100 observations).

You can find the code for this training and evaluation in the notebook.

For the model trained on 100 observations, the MAPE is equal to 35.9%! That's over seven times larger than for the original dataset. *Figure 9.11* presents the results:

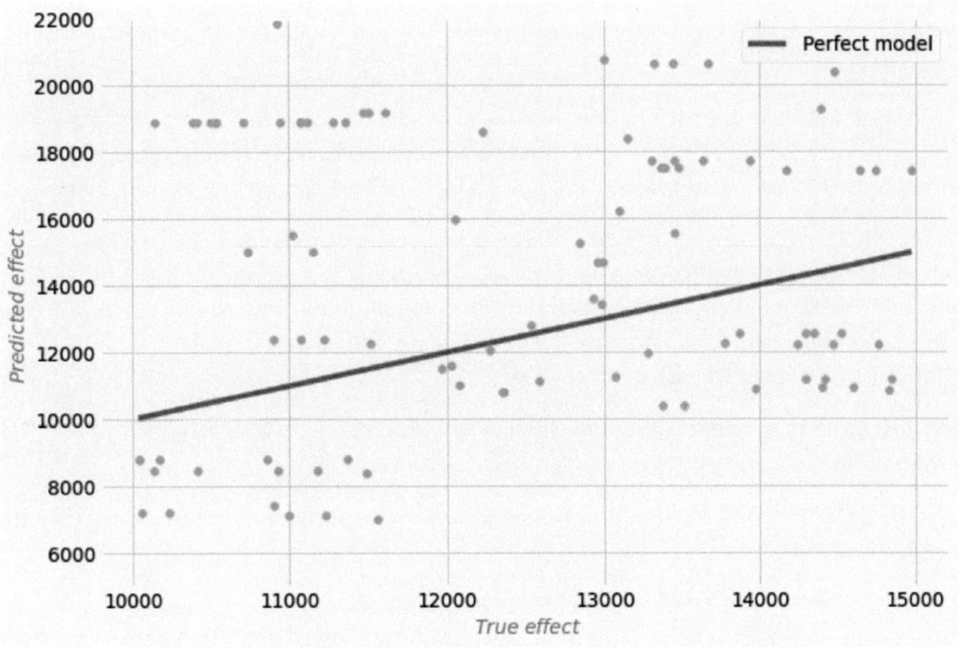

Figure 9.11 – The results for S-Learner trained on 100 observations

As you can see, this model is very noisy to the extent that it's almost unusable.

The question of defining a "safe" dataset size for S-Learner and other causal models is difficult to answer. Power calculations for machine learning models are often difficult, if possible at all. For our earnings dataset, 1,000 observations are enough to give us a pretty sensible model (you can check it out in the notebook by changing the sample size in `model_small` and re-running the code), but for another – perhaps more complex – dataset, this might not be enough.

If your case resembles an A/B test, you can try one of the A/B test sample size calculators (`https://bit.ly/SampleSizeCalc`). Otherwise, you can try computing the power for an analogous linear model using statistical power computation software (e.g., *G*Power*; `https://bit.ly/GPowerCalc`) and then heuristically adjust the sample size to your model complexity.

That said, these methods can provide you only with *very rough* estimates.

S-Learner's vulnerabilities

S-Learner is a great, flexible, and relatively easy-to-fit model. The simplicity that makes this method so effective is also a source of its main weakness.

S-Learner treats the `treatment` variable (pun not intended) as any other variable. Let's see what we might risk here.

In our example, we used LightGBM, a tree-based model, in which the basic estimator unit is a decision tree.

Decision trees utilize criteria such as *Gini Impurity* or *information gain* to determine which variables to split on in order to predict the outcome effectively (for an explanation of how decision trees work, check out Josh Starmer's great video: `https://bit.ly/DecisionTreesSQ`). If a particular variable has little impact on the outcome compared to other variables, it may be omitted by the model.

Therefore, if the treatment effect is small, the S-Learner model may decide to ignore the treatment completely, resulting in the predicted causal effect being nullified. One heuristic solution to this problem is to use deeper trees to increase the probability of the split on treatment, yet keep in mind that this can also increase the risk of overfitting.

Other base learners with regularization, such as *lasso regression*, might also learn to ignore the treatment variable.

To overcome this problem, researchers proposed another meta-learner model called **T-Learner** (Künzel et al., 2019).

In this section, we introduced *HTE* (also known as *CATE*). We defined *meta-learners* and learned how to implement *S-Learner* using DoWhy and EconML. We showed how sample size can affect the performance of this class of models and discussed the main vulnerability of S-Learner – the potential to underestimate causal effects.

Let's see what T-Learner has to offer.

T-Learner – together we can do more

In this section, we'll learn what T-Learner is and how it's different from *S-Learner*. We'll implement the model using DoWhy and EconML and compare its performance with the model from the previous section. Finally, we'll discuss some of the drawbacks of *T-Learner* before concluding the section.

Forcing the split on treatment

The basic motivation behind T-Learner is to overcome the main limitation of S-Learner. If S-Learner can learn to ignore the treatment, why not make it impossible to ignore the treatment?

This is precisely what T-Learner is. Instead of fitting one model on all observations (treated and untreated), we now fit two models – one only on the *treated units*, and the other one only on the *untreated units*.

In a sense, this is equivalent to forcing the first split in a tree-based model to be a split on the treatment variable. *Figure 9.12* presents a visual presentation of this concept:

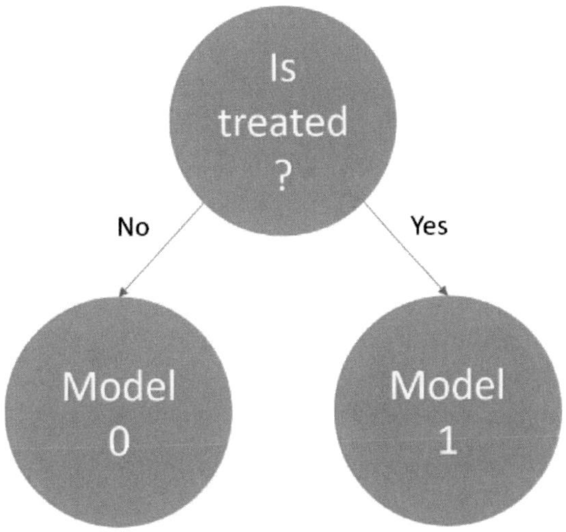

Figure 9.12 – The graphical intuition behind the T-Learner forced split

T-Learner in four steps and a formula

If you'd like to implement T-Learner from scratch using the base learner(s) of choice and predict the treatment effect, these are four steps you'd need to take:

1. Split your data on the `treatment` variable into two subsets.
2. Train two models – one on each subset.
3. For each observation, predict the outcomes using both models.
4. Subtract the results of the *untreated* model from the results of the *treated* model.

Note that now there is *no chance* that the treatment is ignored as we encoded the treatment split as *two separate models.*

Now, let's define the T-Learner estimator formally:

$$\hat{\tau}_{CATE_i} = \mu_1(X_i) - \mu_0(X_i)$$

In the preceding formula, μ_1 represents our model of choice trained on the *treated units only* (we will use LightGBM again), μ_0 represents our model of choice trained on the *untreated units only*, and X_i is a vector of unit i characteristics. Note that we did not use treatment variable T in the formula. The reason for this is that T is now *structurally* encoded into the meta-learner architecture in the form of *two separate models*, where each model represents one value of treatment.

Implementing T-Learner

We'll reuse the *same graph* and the *same estimand* as we used for S-Learner and focus on the estimate. We'll use the original (large) dataset.

Compared to the S-Learner, there are two essential differences in the code:

- First, we use EconML's `TLearner` class as our method (`method_name`)
- Second, instead of just one model, we need to fit two models now, and this is reflected in the structure of the `init_params` dictionary

Rather than the `overall_model` key, we use the `models` key that takes a list of models as a value:

```
estimate = model.estimate_effect(
    identified_estimand=estimand,
    method_name='backdoor.econml.metalearners.TLearner',
    target_units='ate',
    method_params={
        'init_params': {
            'models': [
                LGBMRegressor(n_estimators=200,
                    max_depth=10),
                LGBMRegressor(n_estimators=200,
                    max_depth=10)
            ]
        },
        'fit_params': {}
    })
```

Let's estimate the effect and retrieve the true effect value:

```
effect_pred = model.causal_estimator.effect(
    earnings_interaction_test.drop(['true_effect',
    'took_a_course'], axis=1))
effect_true = earnings_interaction_test[
    'true_effect'].values
```

Note that we repeat exactly the same steps as before. Let's compute the MAPE:

```
mean_absolute_percentage_error(effect_true, effect_pred)
```

This results in the following output:

```
0.0813365927834967
```

The error is higher than the one for S-Learner. The MAPE is now above 8%!

Let's look into the results by plotting the true effect versus the predicted effect in *Figure 9.13*:

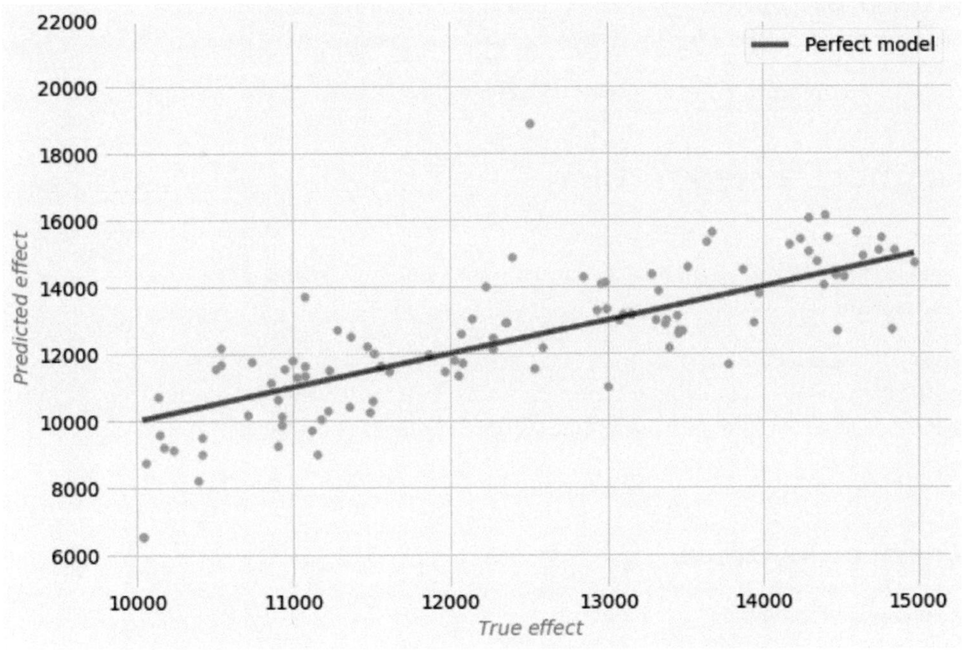

Figure 9.13 – The results of the T-Learner model trained on full data

The results look much worse than the ones in *Figure 9.10*. Didn't we just say that T-Learner was created as an improvement over S-Learner?

T-Learner focuses on improving just *one aspect* where S-Learner *might* (but does not have to) fail. This improvement comes at a price. Fitting two algorithms to two different data subsets means that each algorithm is trained on fewer data, which can harm the fit quality.

It also makes T-Learner less data-efficient (you need twice as much data to teach each T-Learner's base learner a representation of quality comparable to that in S-Learner).

This usually results in a higher variance in the T-Learner estimator relative to S-Learner. In particular, the variance might become quite extreme in cases where one treatment arm has much fewer observations than the other.

This is often the case in modern-day online A/B testing, where a company sends only a minor percentage of the traffic to a new version of the site or service in order to minimize risk. In such a case you might want to use a simpler model for the treatment arm with a smaller number of observations (yes, we don't have to use the same architecture for both base learners).

To summarize, T-Learner can be helpful when you expect that your treatment effect might be small and S-Learner could fail to recognize it. It's good to remember that this meta-learner is usually more data-hungry than S-Learner, but the differences decrease as the overall dataset size becomes larger.

Is there a way to improve T-Learner's data efficiency?

X-Learner – a step further

In this section, we'll introduce **X-Learner** – a meta-learner built to make better use of the information available in the data. We'll learn how X-Learner works and implement the model using our familiar DoWhy pipeline.

Finally, we'll compute the effect estimates on the full earnings dataset and compare the results with S- and T-Learners. We'll close this section with a set of recommendations on when using X-Learner can be beneficial and a summary of all three sections about meta-learners.

Let's start!

Squeezing the lemon

Have you noticed something?

Every time we built a meta-learner so far, we estimated two potential outcomes separately (using a single model in the case of S-Learner, and two models in the case of T-Learner) and then subtracted them in order to obtain CATE.

In a sense, we never tried to use our *estimators* to actually *estimate* CATE. We were rather estimating both potential outcomes separately and then *postprocessing* them *into* CATE.

Hey, but wait! Did we just say *estimate CATE*? How can we possibly do that if we never actually observe both potential outcomes necessary to compute CATE?

Great question!

X-Learner is aiming to estimate CATE directly and, by doing so, it leverages the information that S-Learner and T-Learner have previously discarded. What information is that?

S-Learner and T-Learner were learning a so-called **response function** or how units respond to the treatment (in other words, the response function is a mapping from features X and treatment T to outcome y). At the same time, none of the models used the actual outcome to model CATE. Can this be done?

Let's see.

Reconstructing the X-Learner

In this subsection, we'll reconstruct the logic behind the original X-Learner step by step.

...and gosh, hold on, as this will be a ride!

Seatbelts fastened?

1. The first step is easy, plus you already know it. It's precisely what we did for T-Learner.

   We split our data on the `treatment` variable so that we obtain *two separate subsets*: the first containing *treated* units only, and the second one containing *untreated* units only. Next, we train two models: one on each subset. We call these models μ_1 and μ_0, respectively.

2. Now, we're going to do something important. For each observation in our dataset, we will compute its estimated individual treatment effect (it won't be the "real" ITE in the counterfactual sense that we discussed back in *Chapter 2*, but it will be useful; we'll call them **imputed treatment scores**).

   How are we supposed to compute it though?

   Twofold.

   First, we take all observations that were *treated*.

   We know something about them! For each of the *treated units*, we know one of their counterfactual outcomes, namely $y_i(1)$ because that's precisely their *actual* outcome ($y_i(1) = y_i$).

   Hopefully, this makes sense. We know what outcome to expect under the treatment from the treated units because we simply *see* this outcome recorded in the data.

   The challenge is that we don't see the *other outcome* for the *treated* units – we don't know how they would behave if we didn't treat them.

   Happily, we can use one of our models to estimate the outcome under *no treatment*.

   Let's do it and write it down formally. We'll call the obtained imputed treatment scores $\hat{d}$ (for the estimated difference).

   We will use superscript notation to indicate whether the score was computed for the treated versus untreated units. The score for the *treated* units is computed in the following way:

   $$\widehat{d_i^1} = y_i - \mu_0(X_i)$$

   Second, we take all the *untreated* observations and compute the "mirror" score for them:

   $$\widehat{d_j^0} = \mu_1(X_j) - y_j$$

   We indexed the first formula using i and the second using j to emphasize that the subsets of observations used in the first and second formulas are *disjoint* (because we split the dataset on the treatment in the beginning).

3. In the third step, we're going to train two more models (hold on, that's not the end!). These models will learn to predict the imputed scores $\widehat{d_{i;j}}$ from units' feature vectors $X_{i;j}$.

   You might ask – why do we want to predict $\hat{d}$ from X if we've just computed it?

   Great question! The truth is that if we're only interested in *quantifying* the causal effects for an existing dataset, we don't have to do it.

   On the other hand, if we're interested in *predicting causal effects* for new observations *before* administering the treatment, then this becomes necessary (because we won't know *any* of the potential outcomes required for computations in *step 2* before administering the treatment).

   This scenario is prevalent in personalized medicine when we want to decide whether some drug or therapy will be beneficial to our patient and in marketing when we want to understand which individuals are *persuadable* (*Figure 9.5*) in order to allocate our campaign budget effectively.

   Going back to our models. We said that we'll train two of them. Let's call these models v_0 and v_1. These second-stage models are also known in the literature as **second-stage base learners**. We'll train the first model to predict $\hat{\hat{d}}_0$, and the second one to predict $\hat{\hat{d}}_1$:

   $\hat{\hat{d}}_0 = v_0(X_i)$

   $\hat{\hat{d}}_1 = v_1(X_j)$

   We call the new predicted quantities $\widehat{\widehat{d_{0;1}}}$ (with a double hat) because this quantity is an estimate of an estimate.

4. Finally, we compute our final CATE estimates based on the second-stage models' outputs. Want to breathe a sigh of relief? We're almost there. In the final computation, we weight the outputs of v_0 and v_1 by *propensity scores*. Let's call our estimate $\hat{\tau}_{CATE}$ and describe it with a formula:

   $\hat{\tau}_{CATE} = \hat{e}(X_i)\, v_0(X_i) + (1 - \hat{e}(X_i))\, v_1(X_i)$

   Note that we now call $v_{0;1}$ models on all available observations (although we trained these models using disjoint data subsets split on the treatment). This makes sense because, for new observations, we usually won't have any treatments recorded, and even if so, we're likely interested in predicting CATE *before* administering any treatment.

Now, let's briefly discuss the logic behind the weighting part. We weight the output of v_0 by the unit's propensity score (which is the probability of this unit getting the treatment).

Let's recall that v_0 is a model trained on the units that were untreated. We knew their *actual outcome* under no treatment, but we needed to *predict* their *potential outcome* under treatment in order to train v_0.

The importance of the output of $v_0(X_i)$ in the final model $\hat{\tau}_{CATE}$ increases when the propensity score $\hat{e}(X_i)$ increases. This means that we give more weight to $v_0(X_i)$ when it's more likely that X_i gets the treatment. Why is that?

The intuition is that when it's highly likely that X_i gets the treatment, then observations such as X_i are prevalent in the dataset and we can assume that we have good quality fit of the μ_1 model. Note that we use μ_1 to compute $\widehat{d_j^0}$, which we then use (indirectly) to train v_0. In other words, we want to prioritize high-quality estimates over the poor-quality ones.

This logic is not bullet-proof, though. Perhaps this is the reason why the authors propose that we can use other weighting functions instead of propensity scores or even *"choose [the weights to be] (...) 1 or 0 if the number of treated units is very large or small compared to the number of control units"* (Künzel et al., 2019).

Let's summarize what we've learned so far! X-Learner requires us to fit five models in total (if we count the propensity score model).

First-stage base learners μ_0 and μ_1 are identical to the two models we use in T-Learner. The former (μ_0) is trained solely on untreated, while the latter (μ_1), solely on the treated units. Second-stage base learners are trained on the actual outcomes from the dataset and outputs from the first-stage models.

Finally, we train the propensity score model and compute $\hat{\tau}_{CATE}$, weighting the outputs of v_0 and v_1 by propensity scores.

X-Learner – an alternative formulation

Recently, I learned from Rob Donnelly of Arena AI that he has his own simplified formulation of X-Learner. Rob says that this simplified version works better than the full version in certain cases. I found it interesting, and so I want to share it with you as well.

Here are the steps to build Rob's X-Learner:

1. We start exactly the same as before. We split our data on the `treatment` variable, which gives us two subsets: the subset of all *treated observations* and a subset of all *untreated observations*.

   We fit two separate models, one to each subset of the data. These are our first-stage base learners μ_0 and μ_1.

2. In step 2, we use the models μ_0 and μ_1 alongside the actual outcomes from the dataset in order to compute the *imputed scores*:

   $$\widehat{d_j^0} = \mu_1(X_j) - y_j$$
   $$\widehat{d_i^1} = y_i - \mu_0(X_i)$$

   Again, this step is identical to what we've done before. Note that now we have CATE estimates for all observations (regardless of their original treatment values), let's call it $\hat{d}$.

3. In step 3, we fit the final model, let's call it η, that learns to predict $\hat{d}$ directly from X:

   $\hat{\hat{d}}_i = \eta(X_i)$

   We used a double hat for $\hat{\hat{d}}_i$ again because it's an estimate of an estimate.

That's all! Rob's X-Learner only needs three models (μ_0, μ_1, and η) compared to five models in the classic X-Learner (μ_0, μ_1, v_0, v_1, and $\hat{e}$). This is a great simplification!

Implementing X-Learner

Now, understanding how X-Learner works, let's fit it to the data and compare its performance against its less complex cousins.

We'll reuse the graph and the estimand that we created previously and only focus on the estimate:

```
estimate = model.estimate_effect(
    identified_estimand=estimand,
    method_name='backdoor.econml.metalearners.XLearner',
    target_units='ate',
    method_params={
        'init_params': {
            'models': [
                LGBMRegressor(n_estimators=50,
                    max_depth=10),
                LGBMRegressor(n_estimators=50,
                    max_depth=10)
            ],
            'cate_models': [
                LGBMRegressor(n_estimators=50,
                    max_depth=10),
                LGBMRegressor(n_estimators=50,
                    max_depth=10)
            ]
        },
        'fit_params': {},
    })
```

Note that we now have a new key in the `init_params` object: `cate_models`. We use it to specify our *second-stage base learners*. If you don't specify the CATE models, EconML will use the same models that you provided as your first-level base learners. It's also good to mention that if you want to use identical models for μ_0, μ_1, v_0, and v_1, it's sufficient if you only specify it once:

```
estimate = model.estimate_effect(
    identified_estimand=estimand,
    method_name='backdoor.econml.metalearners.XLearner',
```

```
    target_units='ate',
    method_params={
        'init_params': {
            'models': LGBMRegressor(n_estimators=50,
                      max_depth=10),
        },
        'fit_params': {},
    })
```

EconML will duplicate this model behind the scenes for you.

If we want to explicitly specify the propensity score model, this can also be done by adding the `propensity_model` key to the `init_params` dictionary and passing the model of choice as a value.

Now, let's see how X-Learner performs.

We generate predictions and assign the true effect values to a variable exactly as before:

```
effect_pred = model.causal_estimator.effect(
    earnings_interaction_test.drop(['true_effect',
    'took_a_course'], axis=1))
effect_true = earnings_interaction_test['true_effect'
    ].values
```

Let's compute the MAPE:

```
mean_absolute_percentage_error(effect_true, effect_pred)
```

This gives us the following result as an output:

```
0.036324966995778
```

The MAPE for X-Learner is 3.6%. That's more than twice as good as T-Learner's 8.1% and around 32% better than S-Learner's 5.2%!

Good job, X-Learner!

Figure 9.14 presents the results visually:

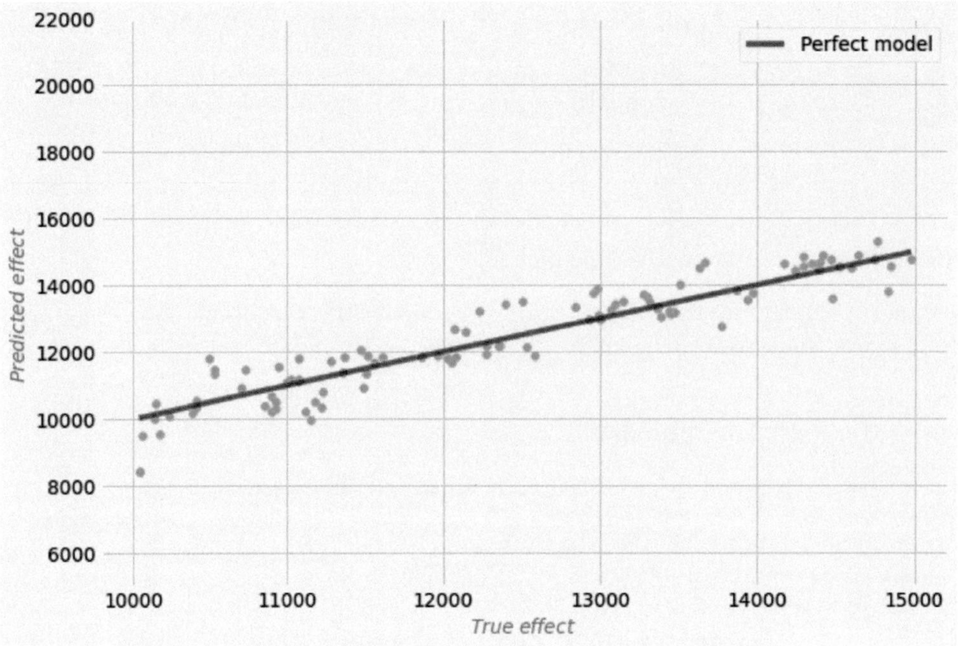

Figure 9.14 – X-Learner results

We can see that most points are focused around the red line. We don't see clear outliers as in the case of S-Learner (*Figure 9.10*), and the overall error is much smaller than in the case of T-Learner (*Figure 9.13*). A pleasant view. The results for all three meta-learners on our dataset are summarized in *Table 9.2*:

Estimator	MAPE
S-Learner	5.2%
T-Learner	8.1%
X-Learner	3.6%

Table 9.2 – A summary of meta-learners' results

When X-Learner shines and when it doesn't

Due to its weighting capabilities between the two sub-models (v_0 and v_1), X-Learner can really shine when the dataset is highly imbalanced. It can work really well when you want to test a new variant of your web page, but you're only willing to show it to a small number of users to minimize the risk in case they don't like this new variant.

On the other hand, when your dataset is very small, X-Learner might not be a great choice, as fitting each additional model comes with some additional noise, and we might not have enough data to overpower this noise with signal (in such a case, it might be better to use a simpler – perhaps linear – model as your base learner).

Take a look at *Figure 9.15*, which presents the results of X-Learner trained on just 100 observations from our training data:

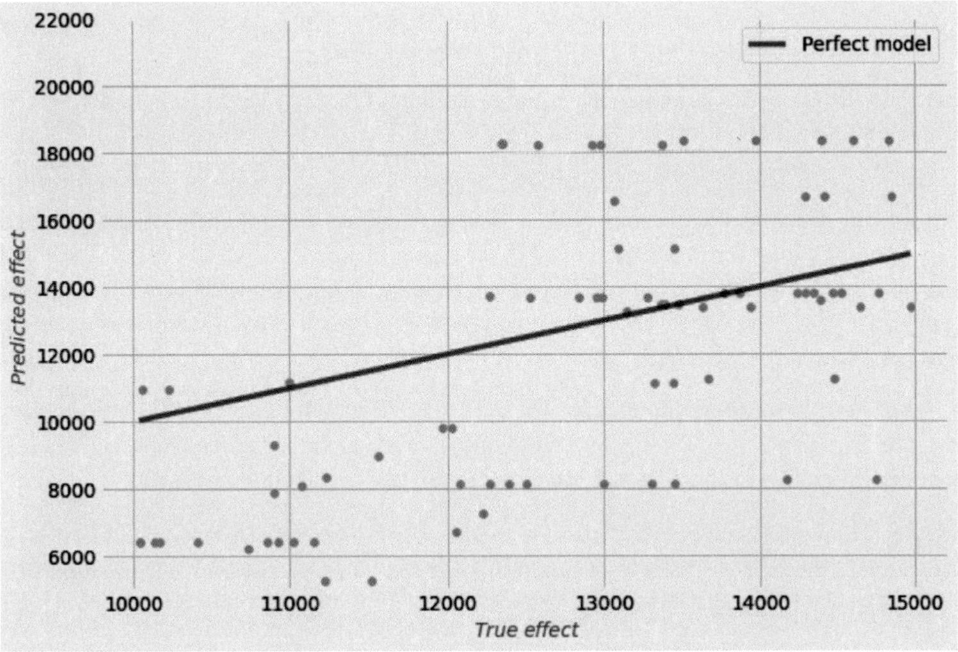

Figure 9.15 – X-Learner's results on small data

At first sight, the results in *Figure 9.15* look slightly more structured than the ones for S-Learner on small data (*Figure 9.11*), but the MAPE is slightly higher (39% versus 36%).

That said, X-Learner usually outperforms S- and T-Learners when CATE is complex (e.g., highly non-linear).

As a closing remark, meta-learners can be extended to multi-level treatment scenarios. In other words, these models can be used in a setting where we have more than two mutually exclusive treatments (e.g., sending three different promotional email variants or testing four new therapies). We'll see the multi-level treatment scenario in action in the next chapter.

It's time to conclude our journey with X-Learner for now (we'll see it again soon, though).

In this section, we introduced the X-Learner model. We analyzed its building blocks: first- and second-stage base learners and weighting, and we showed how to connect them. We discussed the logic behind the weighting mechanism. We presented Rob Donnelly's alternative simplified version of X-Learner. Finally, we evaluated the model against S- and T-Learners, achieving a superior performance on our data, and talked about when using X-Learner can be beneficial.

Wrapping it up

Congrats on finishing *Chapter 9*!

We presented a lot of information in this chapter! Let's summarize!

We started with the basics and introduced the matching estimator. On the way, we defined ATE, ATT, and ATC.

Then, we moved to propensity scores. We learned that propensity score is the probability of being treated, which we compute for each observation. Next, we've shown that although it might be tempting to use propensity scores for matching, in reality, it's a risky idea. We said that propensity scores can shine in other scenarios, and we introduced propensity score weighting, which allows us to construct sub-populations and weight them accordingly in order to deconfound our data (it does not help when we have unobserved confounding).

Next, we started our journey with meta-learners. We said that ATE can sometimes hide important information from us and we defined CATE. This opened the door for us to explore the world of HTEs, where units with different characteristics can react differently to the same treatment.

We presented a simple yet often very effective model called S-Learner, which uses a single base-learner in order to learn the patterns in the data. This model is later used to generate estimated counterfactual outcomes, which allow us to compute individualized CATE for each observation.

We learned that S-Learner might sometimes ignore the treatment variable and therefore underestimate (or nullify) causal effects.

We introduced T-Learner as an antidote to this problem. T-Learner uses two models (hence the name *T(wo)-Learner*), and this very structure prevents it from ignoring the treatment. This comes at a price of decreased data efficiency, and T-Learner underperformed on our data compared to S-Learner.

To overcome these difficulties, we introduced X-Learner, which takes T-Learner's logic to the next level by explicitly using the actual outcomes in the training. We introduced and implemented the original version of X-Learner (Künzel et al., 2019) and discussed a simplified version proposed by Rob Donnelly.

X-Learner outperformed both T-Learner and S-Learner on our data. We said that X-Learner might be a great choice when the data is imbalanced between the treatment and control groups. We've also shown that a small data regime might be challenging for X-Learner.

Looking at meta-learners, it's difficult to unambiguously pick one winner. Each model can perform well in certain circumstances but underperform its counterparts in another context.

X-Learner seems like a safe bet in most cases where the sample size is sufficiently large. S-Learner is a great starting point in many settings as it's simple and computationally friendly.

In the next chapter, we'll see more architectures that can help us model heterogeneous treatment effects.

Hope you're ready for another ride!

References

Abrevaya, J., Hsu, Y., & Lieli, R.P. (2014). *Estimating Conditional Average Treatment Effects. Journal of Business & Economic Statistics*, 33, 485–505.

Angrist, J. D., & Pischke, J.-S. (2008). *Mostly harmless econometrics*. Princeton University Press.

Dehejia, R. H., & Wahba, S. (2002). *Propensity score-matching methods for nonexperimental causal studies*. The *Review of Economics and Statistics*, 84(1), 151–161.

Elze, M. C., Gregson, J., Baber, U., Williamson, E., Sartori, S., Mehran, R., Nichols, M., Stone, G. W., & Pocock, S. J. (2017). *Comparison of Propensity Score Methods and Covariate Adjustment: Evaluation in 4 Cardiovascular Studies*. Journal of the American College of Cardiology, 69(3), 345–357. `https://doi.org/10.1016/j.jacc.2016.10.060`

Facure, M., A. (2020). *Causal Inference for The Brave and True*. `https://matheusfacure.github.io/python-causality-handbook/landing-page.html`

Gelman, A., & Hill, J. (2006). *Analytical methods for social research: Data analysis using regression and multilevel/hierarchical models*. Cambridge University Press.

Gutman, R., Karavani, E., & Shimoni, Y. (2022). *Propensity score models are better when post-calibrated*. arXiv.

Hernán M. A., Robins J. M. (2020). *Causal Inference: What If*. Boca Raton: Chapman & Hall/CRC.

Iacus, S., King, G., & Porro, G. (2012). *Causal Inference without Balance Checking: Coarsened Exact Matching. Political Analysis*, 20, 1–24.

Ke, G., Meng, Q., Finley, T., Wang, T., Chen, W., Ma, W., Ye, Q., & Liu, T. (2017). *LightGBM: A Highly Efficient Gradient Boosting Decision Tree*. NIPS.

King, G. (2018). *Gary King on Simplifying Matching Methods for Causal Inference*. [Speech transcript]. Retrieved from `http://ntupsr.s3.amazonaws.com/psr/wp-content/uploads/2018/10/02-1-Gary-King-compressed.pdf`.

King, G., & Nielsen, R. (2019). *Why Propensity Scores Should Not Be Used for Matching. Political Analysis*, 27 (4).

Künzel, S.R., Sekhon, J.S., Bickel, P.J., & Yu, B. (2017). *Meta-learners for Estimating Heterogeneous Treatment Effects using Machine Learning*. arXiv: Statistics Theory.

LaLonde, R.J. (1986). *Evaluating the Econometric Evaluations of Training Programs with Experimental Data. The American Economic Review*, 76, 604–620.

Liu, Y., Dieng, A., Roy, S., Rudin, C., & Volfovsky, A. (2018). *Interpretable Almost Matching Exactly for Causal Inference*. arXiv: Machine Learning.

Lopez, M. J., & Gutman, R. (2017). *Estimation of Causal Effects with Multiple Treatments: A Review and New Ideas. Statistical Science*, 32(3), 432–454.

Morucci, M., Orlandi, V., Roy, S., Rudin, C., & Volfovsky, A. (2020). *Adaptive Hyper-box Matching for Interpretable Individualized Treatment Effect Estimation*. arXiv, abs/2003.01805.

Niculescu-Mizil, A., & Caruana, R. (2005). *Predicting good probabilities with supervised learning*. Proceedings of the 22nd international conference on Machine learning.

Pearl, J. (2009). *Causality*. Cambridge University Press.

Pearl, J., Glymour, M., & Jewell, N. P. (2016). *Causal inference in statistics: A primer*. Wiley.

Pearl, J., & Mackenzie, D. (2019). *The Book of Why*. Penguin.

Peters, J., Janzing, D., & Schölkopf, B. (2017). *Elements of Causal Inference: Foundations and Learning Algorithms*. MIT Press.

Rosenbaum, P.R., & Rubin, D.B. (1983). *The central role of the propensity score in observational studies for causal effects. Biometrika*, 70, 41–55.

Sizemore, S., Alkurdi, R. (August 18, 2019). *Matching Methods for Causal Inference: A Machine Learning Update. Seminar Applied Predictive Modeling* (SS19). Humboldt-Universität zu Berlin. `https://humboldt-wi.github.io/blog/research/applied_predictive_modeling_19/matching_methods/`

Stuart E. A. (2010). *Matching methods for causal inference: A review and a look forward. Statistical science: a review journal of the Institute of Mathematical Statistics*, 25(1), 1–21.

Vegetabile, B.G. (2021). *On the Distinction Between "Conditional Average Treatment Effects" (CATE) and "Individual Treatment Effects" (ITE) Under Ignorability Assumptions*. arXiv, abs/2108.04939.

Zou, D., Zhang, L., Mao, J., & Sheng, W. (2020*). Feature Interaction based Neural Network for Click-Through Rate Prediction*. arXiv, abs/2006.05312.

10

Causal Inference and Machine Learning – Advanced Estimators, Experiments, Evaluations, and More

Welcome to *Chapter 10*!

We closed the previous chapter by discussing meta-learners. We started with a single model S-Learner and finished with a complex X-Learner that required us to train five machine learning models behind the scenes!

Each new model was an attempt to overcome the limitations of its predecessors. In this chapter, we'll continue to walk the path of improvement. Moreover, we'll integrate some of the approaches introduced in the previous chapter in order to make our estimates better and decrease their variance.

In this chapter, we'll learn about **doubly robust** (**DR**) methods, **double machine learning** (**DML**), and Causal Forests. By the end of this chapter, you'll have learned how these methods work and how to implement them using EconML by applying them to real-world experimental data. You'll also have learned about the concept of counterfactual explanations.

In this chapter, we'll cover the following topics:

- Doubly robust methods
- Double machine learning
- Targeted maximum likelihood estimator
- Causal Forests
- Heterogeneous treatment effects with experimental data
- Counterfactual explanations

Doubly robust methods – let's get more!

So far, we've discussed a broad range of methods that can be used to estimate causal effects. In earlier chapters, we discussed linear regression; in later chapters, we discussed matching, propensity score weighting, and the meta-learner framework. The latter allowed us to go beyond the limitations of linear regression by plugging arbitrary machine learning models as base learners. Meta-learners turned out to be very flexible as they offer all the benefits of contemporary machine learning.

Do we need another thing?

As we learned, propensity scores alone can be used to deconfound the data (as in propensity score weighting; note that this only holds for observed confounding). The same is true for regression models, where we can deconfound the data by simply controlling for the right variable(s) by including them in the regression formula. Propensity score models are sometimes referred to as **treatment models** (as they aim to predict the treatment from confounders) and regression models are referred to as **outcome models** (as they aim to predict the outcome from the treatment and other relevant variables; note that we use the term *regression models* in a broad sense, which includes but is not limited to linear regression).

Isn't the fact that both *treatment* and *outcome* models can be used to achieve the same goal interesting?

Let's see.

A graphical approach is usually helpful when we want to examine questions like this. *Figure 10.1* presents two **directed acyclic graphs** (**DAGs**):

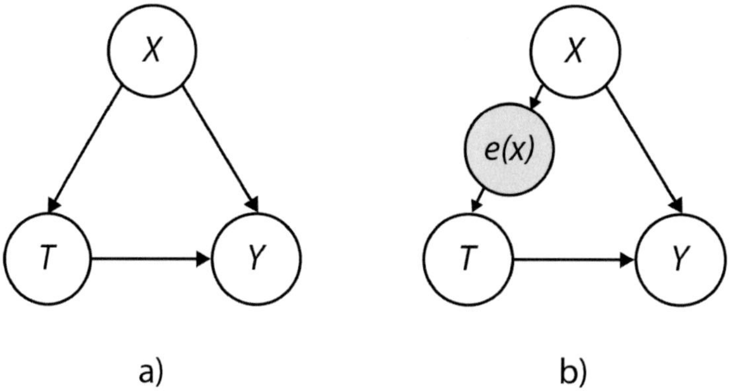

Figure 10.1 – Two models – without and with a propensity score

In panel **a)**, we see a model with a treatment, T, an outcome, Y, and a confounder, X. In panel **b)**, we see the same model, but with the propensity score, $e(X)$, added on the path between X and T. As a refresher, the propensity score is defined as follows:

$$e(X) = P(T|X)$$

Adding a new node representing the propensity score to the graph is possible thanks to the **propensity score theorem** that we learned about in the previous chapter.

The theorem states that if we have unconfoundedness given X, we will also have unconfoundedness given the propensity score of X, assuming positivity (Rosenbaum & Rubin, 1983). Thanks to this, we can use the propensity score as a full mediator of the relationship between X and T. Note that this gives us a possibility to close the backdoor path between T and Y in three ways (*Figure 10.1*; panel *b)*):

- By controlling for X
- By controlling for $e(X)$
- By controlling for both of them

Each of these ways will deconfound the relationship between the treatment and the outcome.

Interestingly, although all three ways to deconfound the data are equivalent from a graphical point of view, they might lead to different estimation errors. In particular, although the *estimands* obtained using X and $e(X)$ are equivalent ($P(Y|T,X) = P(Y|T, e(X))$), the *estimators* estimating these quantities might have different errors. In particular, in certain cases, one of the models might be correct with a near-zero error, while the other might be misspecified with arbitrary bias.

What if we could combine both estimators in a way that would allow us to automatically choose the better model?

It turns out that this is exactly what DR methods do. We get a model that automatically *switches* between the outcome model and the treatment model. The bias of DR estimators scales as the *product* of the errors of the *treatment* and *outcome* models (Hernán & Robins, 2020; p. 229).

Let's reiterate this – the DR estimator will give asymptotically unbiased estimates whenever one of the models (outcome or treatment) is correctly specified. This is a really powerful property!

Moreover, DR methods can be seen as a subset of the meta-learner framework, meaning that we can use arbitrary estimators in order to compute the outcome and treatment models. DR estimators are guaranteed to be consistent when either of the models (*treatment* or *outcome*) is correct, but not necessarily both models. DR is a large-sample property, which means that if our sample size is small, we might not get the benefits.

Doubly robust is not equal to bulletproof...

Although theoretically speaking, the treatment and outcome models are equivalent in the DR estimator, some practitioners and researchers report that misspecification of the outcome model leads to a significant bias *even if* the *treatment* model is *correct* (Li, 2021).

Moreover, when both models (treatment and outcome) are even moderately misspecified, DR estimators can have high bias and high variance (Kang & Schafer, 2007).

...but it can bring a lot of value

If both models – outcome and treatment – are correct, the DR estimator will have a smaller variance than **inverse probability weighting (IPW)**, at least in large samples (Li, 2021).

Speaking from experience, it will usually also have a smaller variance than the meta-learners introduced in the previous chapter. This observation is supported by theory. The DR estimator can be decomposed as an S-Learner with an additional adjustment term (for details, see Courthoud, 2022).

The secret doubly robust sauce

Although many advances in DR estimators are fairly recent (see Tan et al., 2022), the method's origins date back to the 1994 paper *Estimation of Regression Coefficients When Some Regressors are not Always Observed* by Robins et al. (1994). Interestingly, the authors originally considered the method in the context of the missing data problem.

To be fair, the basic idea of double robustness dates back even earlier – to Cassel et al.'s 1976 paper. Cassel and colleagues (1976) proposed an estimator virtually identical to what we call the DR estimator today, with the difference that they only considered a case with known (as opposed to estimated) propensity scores.

> **Causal inference and missing data**
>
> The fundamental problem of causal inference (Holland, 1986) that we introduced in *Chapter 2* is that we can never observe all potential outcomes at the same time. One view on causal inference that stems from this perspective is that it is a missing data problem. This idea inspired researchers and practitioners to use causal methodologies for data imputation purposes (e.g., Mohan & Pearl, 2021) and vice versa. For an overview, check out Ding & Li (2018).

We're now ready to define a basic DR estimator formally (Facure, 2020):

$$\hat{\tau}_{ATE} = \frac{1}{N}\sum_i \left(\frac{T_i(Y_i - \mu_1(X_i))}{\hat{e}(X_i)} + \mu_1(X_i) \right) - \frac{1}{N}\sum_i \left(\frac{(1 - T_i)(Y_i - \mu_0(X_i))}{1 - \hat{e}(X_i)} + \mu_0(X_i) \right)$$

In the preceding formula, T_i is the treatment for unit i, $\hat{e}(X_i)$ is the estimate of the propensity score, μ_0 and μ_1 are models that estimate $E[Y|X, T = t]$ with $t = 0$ and $t = 1$, respectively, and Y is the outcome variable. Note that we define an estimator for the **average treatment effect** (**ATE**) here, but DR methods can be applied to estimate **conditional average treatment effects** (**CATE**) as well.

Let's unpack the formula.

We'll set the stage in the following way:

1. Divide the big formula into two chunks (on the left of the main minus sign and on the right).
2. Focus on the part inside the brackets on the left.
3. Develop the intuition for this part.
4. Generalize this intuition to the entire formula.

We've supplied a color-coded formula in *Figure 10.2* to make the process easier to understand.

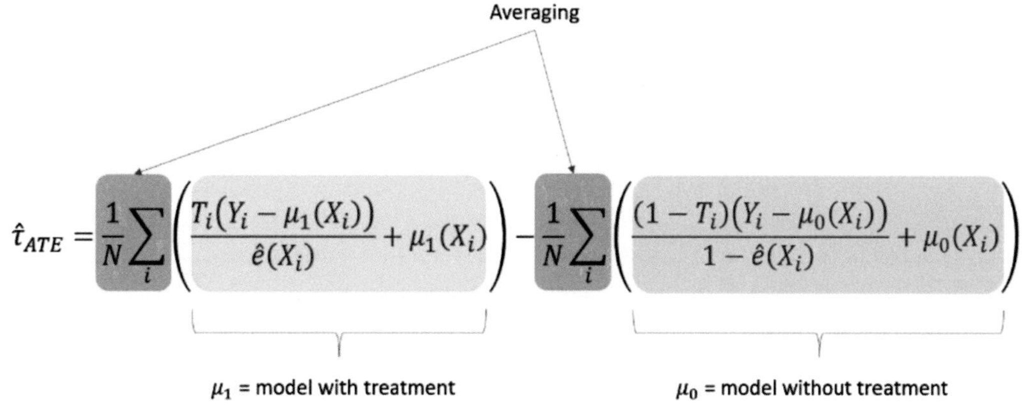

Figure 10.2 – A color-coded formula for the DR estimator

The two main parts of the formula in *Figure 10.2* represent models under treatment (left; orange) and under no treatment (right; green). The purple parts represent averaging.

Let's focus on the orange part first.

Let's say that our model, μ_1, returns a perfect prediction for observation X_i, but our propensity estimate, $\hat{e}(X_i)$, is way off. In such a case, this prediction will be equal to Y_i. Therefore, $Y_i - \mu_1(X_i)$ will be 0. This will make the whole fraction expression ($\frac{T_i(Y_i - \mu_1(X_i))}{\hat{e}(X_i)}$) in the orange part in *Figure 10.2* equal to 0, leaving us with $\mu_1(X_i)$ after the plus sign. Because μ_1 returned a perfect prediction, $\mu_1(X_i)$ is a perfect estimate and we're happy to use it.

Note that the same logic holds for the green part of the formula in *Figure 10.2*.

We can also show that in the case of a misspecified outcome model, the opposite will happen – the outcome model will be weighted down to 0 and the treatment model will take the lead in the estimate. Showing this mechanism requires some algebraic transformations, which we will skip here. If you're interested in more details, Chapter 12 of Matheus Facure's online book contains an accessible explanation: `https://bit.ly/DoublyRobust`.

Doubly robust estimator versus assumptions

As with all the methods discussed in the previous chapter, the DR estimator works properly when there's no hidden confounding (i.e., X contains all the variables we need to control for and no variables that introduce bias). For precise estimates of CATE, we also need to include relevant effect modifiers in X.

Additionally, note that *positivity assumption* violations might lead to high variance for DR estimators (Li, 2020).

DR-Learner – crossing the chasm

DR-Learner (*DR* comes from *doubly robust*) is a DR meta-learner model. EconML offers a couple of variants of DR-Learner. The simplest one is the linear variant implemented in the `LinearDRLearner` class. This model is in fact more complex than the DR estimator we described earlier.

It uses **cross-fitting** and **orthogonalization** (we'll discuss both terms in the next section) and an additional model to estimate CATE directly. For `LinearDRLearner`, this additional model defaults to linear regression, but this can be changed to an arbitrary model in another class called `DRLearner`.

The code for the following experiments can be found in the notebook for *Chapter 10* (`https://bit.ly/causal-ntbk-10`).

We will continue with the same data that we used for meta-learners in the previous chapter and so we'll skip the graph creation and estimand identification steps here. You can find the full pipeline implemented in the notebook accompanying this chapter.

As in the case of meta-learners, we'll use DoWhy's CausalModel API to call EconML's estimators.

Let's compute our estimate using `LinearDRLearner`:

```
estimate = model.estimate_effect(
    identified_estimand=estimand,
    method_name='backdoor.econml.dr.LinearDRLearner',
    target_units='ate',
    method_params={
        'init_params': {
            # Specify treatment and outcome models
            'model_propensity': LogisticRegression(),
            'model_regression': LGBMRegressor(n_estimators=
```

```
                    1000, max_depth=10)
            },
            'fit_params': {}
        })
```

First, we use `'backdoor.econml.dr.LinearDRLearner'` as a method name. We specify the ATE as a target unit (but CATE estimates will still be available to us) and pass model-specific parameters as a dictionary. Here, we only use two parameters to specify the outcome model (`'model_regression'`) and the treatment model (`'model_propensity'`). We picked simple logistic regression for the latter and an LGBM regressor for the former.

As a reminder, logistic regression is often the go-to method for propensity score modeling as its probability output is well calibrated. Its limitation is that it cannot model interactions directly, so if you expect that interaction terms might be important for your propensity model, you might want to specify interaction terms explicitly in your dataset (you can do so by multiplying the features that interact with each other and adding the result as a new feature(s) to your dataset) or go for another model.

In the latter case, remember to scale the probability output.

Let's generate predictions:

```
effect_pred = model.causal_estimator.effect(
    earnings_interaction_test.drop(['true_effect',
    'took_a_course'], axis=1))

effect_true = earnings_interaction_test['true_effect'
    ].values
```

Now, we're ready to evaluate our model. Let's check the value of the **mean absolute percentage error** (**MAPE**):

```
mean_absolute_percentage_error(effect_true, effect_pred)
```

This gives us the following result:

```
0.00623739241153059
```

This is *six times* lower than X-Learner's error in the previous chapter (3.6%)!

Let's plot the predictions versus the true effect (*Figure 10.3*):

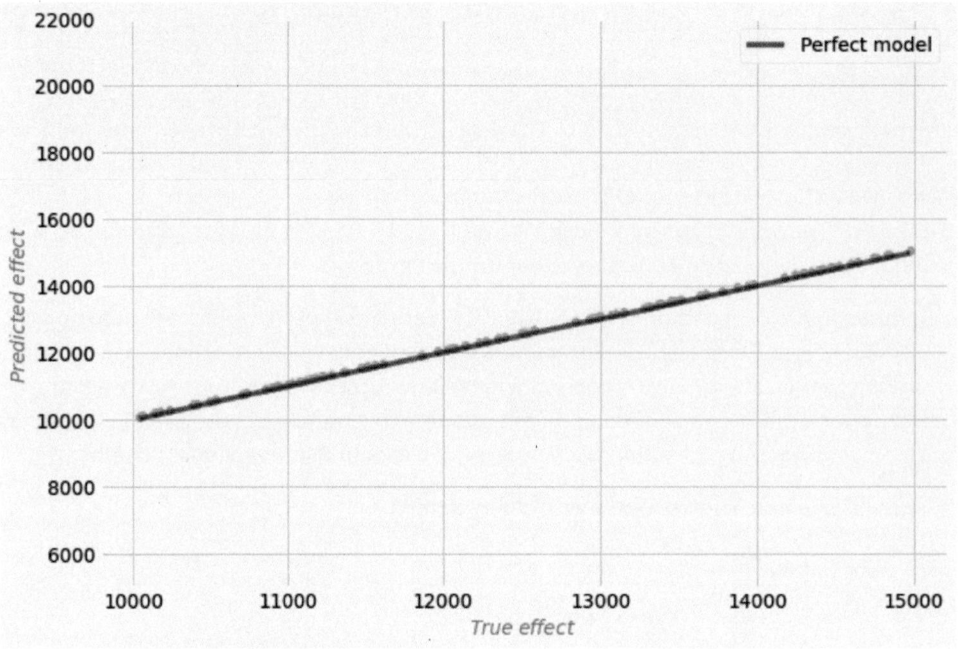

Figure 10.3 – True versus predicted effect for the linear DR-Learner model

This looks pretty impressive!

Let's think about what could help the model get such a good fit.

As we said earlier, DR methods can be a benefit when both models – outcome and treatment – are well specified. This is the case in our example. This allows the model to achieve a small variance compared to the meta-learners in the previous chapter.

The bias is also very small, although you can see in the plot that the model slightly, but systematically, overestimates the true effect.

Note that the scale of the plot plays a role in forming our impressions regarding the model's performance. For ease of comparison, we kept the ranges for both axes identical to the ones in the previous chapter. To an extent, this can mask the model's errors visually, but it does not change the fact that the improvements over meta-learners from *Chapter 9* are significant.

Let's address one more question that some of us might have in mind – we used a model called `LinearDRLearner`. Why do we call it linear if we used a non-linear boosting model as an outcome model? The answer is that the orthogonalization procedure that we'll describe in the next section allows us to model non-linearities in the data while preserving linearity in causal parameters.

This setting is a good-enough fit for a broad category of problems, yet if you need more flexibility, you can use the `DRLearner` class and choose an arbitrary non-linear final model.

Note that using super-powerful models might sometimes be overkill. To illustrate this, let's use `DRLearner` with a relatively deep boosting regressor as a final model and apply it to our data:

```
estimate = model.estimate_effect(
    identified_estimand=estimand,
    method_name='backdoor.econml.dr.DRLearner',
    target_units='ate',
    method_params={
        'init_params': {
            'model_propensity': LogisticRegression(),
            'model_regression': LGBMRegressor(
                n_estimators=1000, max_depth=10),
            'model_final': LGBMRegressor(
                n_estimators=500, max_depth=10),
        },
        'fit_params': {}
    })
```

This model's MAPE is over 7.6% – over 10 times higher than for a simple linear DR-Learner. *Figure 10.4* presents the results:

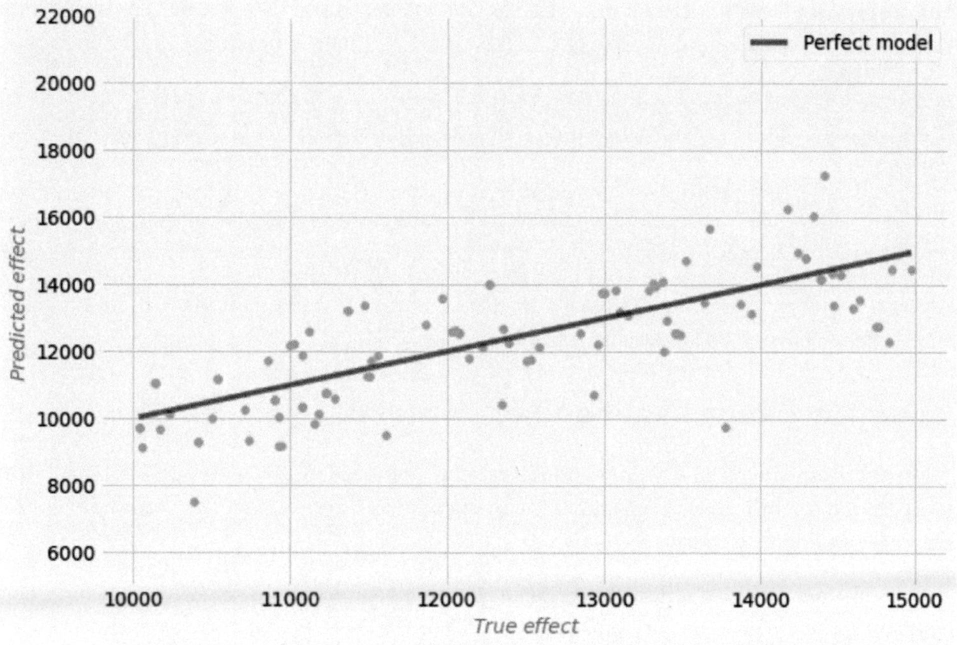

Figure 10.4 – True versus predicted effect for the non-linear DR-Learner model

As we can see, the non-linear model has a much higher variance on the test set. Try to decrease the number of estimators and the maximum depth in the final model and see how it affects the error.

Spoiler alert – you should expect some improvements!

DR-Learners – more options

EconML provides us with a total of four different DR-Learners. On top of the two that we've discussed before, we also have `SparseLinearDRLearner`, which uses debiased lasso regression (Bühlmann & van de Geer, 2011; van de Geer et al., 2013) as a final stage algorithm, and `ForestDRLearner`, which uses *Causal Forest* as the final stage algorithm.

We'll now discuss them briefly.

`SparseLinearDRLearner` uses an L1-penalized regression, which means that the algorithm can effectively perform automatic feature selection by weighting the coefficients for some features down to 0. A sparse linear DR-Learner will be a good choice whenever the number of features is large.

It shines in particular when the number of features is close to or larger than the number of observations, where a regular linear DR-Learner would fail. The model will also provide you with valid confidence intervals. Its main limitation is that – similar to `LinearDRLearner` – it expects that the treatment effect is linear.

`ForestDRLearner` uses the Causal Forest algorithm (Wager & Athey, 2018) as the final model. We'll discuss Causal Forests in greater detail later in this chapter. Forest DR-Learner is great at handling multidimensional data, and unlike `SparseLinearDRLearner` is not limited to linear cases.

If obtaining confidence intervals is important to you, `ForestDRLearner` can provide them through bootstrapping. Note that this will significantly impact computation times for the model, in particular in large samples.

We will discuss how to obtain confidence intervals for estimators that do not support such an option natively later in the chapter.

Now, let's see another interesting DR estimator that can bring advantages under (limited) positivity violations (Porter et al., 2011) or smaller sample sizes.

Targeted maximum likelihood estimator

DR estimators come in various shapes and tastes. One popular DR method is called TMLE. It was originally introduced by van der Laan and Rubin in their paper *Targeted Maximum Likelihood Learning* (van der Laan & Rubin, 2006).

TMLE is a semi-parametric method and allows us to use machine learning algorithms while yielding asymptotic properties for statistical inference. In other words, we can use complex machine learning models but retain some of the convenience of traditional statistical methods, including generating valid confidence intervals without bootstrapping. Moreover, TMLE uses an extra *targeting* step to optimize the bias-variance trade-off when estimating the causal effect.

Note that some of TMLE's properties are similar to these of DR-Learner or DML (which we will discuss in the next section). A detailed comparison between the three is beyond the scope of this book, but you'll find links to the resources containing detailed TMLE and DML comparisons at the end of the next section.

In this section, we'll explain the mechanics behind TMLE, so you can understand the main factors contributing to its uniqueness.

Note that the TMLE estimator we introduce in this chapter works for binary treatments and binary outcomes only. The method can be extended to continuous outcomes under certain conditions (Gruber & van der Laan, 2010).

As TMLE isn't currently available in EconML, we won't implement it here. Instead, we'll look into the algorithm mechanics step by step and share the resources demonstrating how to use it in other Python packages, such as IBM's `causallib` or `zEpid`.

TMLE can be used with any machine learning algorithm and in this sense can be treated as a *meta-learner*.

There are eight steps to implement TMLE:

1. Train a model, μ, that models $Y \sim X + T$, where Y is a binary outcome, X is a feature matrix, and T is a binary treatment. Arbitrary machine learning models compatible with the outcome and features can be used here.
2. Generate the following predictions (note that all $\hat{y}$s are probabilities, not labels):

   A. For each observation, predict the outcome for the actual treatment value:

   $$\hat{y}_t = \mu(X, T = t)$$

   B. For each observation, predict the outcome under no treatment:

   $$\hat{y}_0 = \mu(X, T = 0)$$

   C. For each observation, predict the outcome under treatment:

   $$\hat{y}_1 = \mu(X, T = 1)$$

3. Estimate the propensity score for each observation: $\hat{e}(X) = P(T = 1|X)$.
4. Compute the following quantity:

   $$H(T, X) = \frac{1_{\{T=1\}}}{\hat{e}(X)} - \frac{1_{\{T=0\}}}{1 - \hat{e}(X)}$$

where $1_{\{T=t\}}$ is an indicator function (refer to *Chapter 2* (the *Associations* section) for a definition). The quantity, $H(T, X)$, is known in the literature as the **clever covariate** and it will help us update our estimates to reduce bias.

5. Estimate the **fluctuation parameter**, which will help us calculate the variance necessary to obtain confidence intervals for our estimates. This can be achieved by doing the following:

   A. Fitting a logistic regression model:

   $$y(T, X, \hat{y}_t) = Y \sim [-1 + logit(\hat{y}_t)] + H(T, X)$$

   In the preceding formula, $[-1 + logit(\hat{y}_t)]$ means *do not fit intercept* (-1)*; instead, use a fixed vector* $logit(\hat{y}_t)$.

   By saying *fixed vector*, we mean that we take a *whole vector of values* (in this case, a vector of predictions coming from the model, $\mu(X, T = t)$), and use this vector as an intercept, instead of using just a single number (scalar). Specifically, the intercept value for each row in our dataset is the prediction of the $\mu(X, T = t)$ model for that particular row.

   B. Obtaining the coefficient for $H(T, X)$ from the preceding logistic regression model. We call this coefficient the *fluctuation parameter* and use $\hat{\epsilon}$ to denote it.

6. Update the predictions from *step 2* using the fluctuation parameter, $\hat{\epsilon}$. We'll use asterisk notation for the updated predictions:

   A. $\hat{y}_t^* = expit(logit(\hat{y}_t) + \hat{\epsilon}H(T = t, X))$

   B. $\hat{y}_0^* = expit(logit(\hat{y}_0) + \hat{\epsilon}H(T = 0, X))$

   C. $\hat{y}_1^* = expit(logit(\hat{y}_1) + \hat{\epsilon}H(T = 1, X))$

   The *expit* function is the inverse of the *logit* function. We need it here to go back from *logits* to *probabilities*. To learn more about *logit* and *expit*, check out this great blog post by Kenneth Tay: `https://bit.ly/LogitExpit`.

7. Compute the estimate of the ATE (this can be also adapted for CATE):

   $$\hat{\tau}_{ATE} = \frac{1}{N}\sum_i \hat{y}_1^* - \hat{y}_0^*$$

8. Compute the confidence intervals:

   A. Calculate the values of the **influence function** ($\widehat{IF}$):

   $$\widehat{IF} = (Y - \hat{y}_t^*)H(T, X) + \hat{y}_1^* - \hat{y}_0^* - \hat{\tau}_{ATE}$$

   B. Compute the estimate of the standard error:

   $$\widehat{SE} = \sqrt{\frac{var(\widehat{IF})}{N}}$$

A. Get the 95% intervals:

$$CI_{lower} = \hat{\tau}_{ATE} - 1.96\,\widehat{SE}$$

$$CI_{upper} = \hat{\tau}_{ATE} + 1.96\,\widehat{SE}$$

That's the mechanics of TMLE.

Following the formulas, you can relatively easily implement it from scratch yourself in Python, but you don't have to!

TMLE has already been implemented in IBM's causallib library by Ehud Karavani, as well as in zEpid – an epidemiology analysis library created by computational epidemiologist Paul Zivich.

You can find causallib's documentation for TMLE here: `https://bit.ly/TMLEDocs`. An example notebook can be found here: `https://bit.ly/CausallibTMLEExample`. The documentation for zEpid's implementation of TMLE can be found here: `https://bit.ly/zEpidTMLEDocs`.

For an excellent visual introduction to TMLE, check out the series of blog posts by Katherine Hoffman: `https://bit.ly/KatHoffmanTMLE`. Her great work helped me structure this section more clearly and I hope this will also translate into more clarity for you.

It's time to conclude this section.

We learned that DR methods rely on two models: the *outcome model* and the *treatment model* (also called the *propensity model*). Both models can be estimated using any compatible machine learning technique – whether linear models, tree-based methods, or neural networks.

The core strength of DR models is that even if only one model (e.g., the outcome model) is specified correctly, they will still give consistent estimates. When both models (outcome and treatment) are specified correctly, DR estimators tend to have very low variance, which makes them even more attractive.

TMLE – an extension of the classic DR estimator – offers us the advantages of parametric models and good statistical properties while allowing us to use flexible machine learning models as base learners. Moreover, it can outperform other DR methods under positivity violations and can be an advantage for smaller sample sizes. Perhaps that's one of the reasons TMLE has gained significant traction lately, even though the original idea dates back to 2006.

In the next section, we'll dive into another exciting area of causal inference, called *double machine learning*, which offers some improvements over the DR framework.

If machine learning is cool, how about double machine learning?

The title of this section is inspired by Brady Neal's video (`https://bit.ly/BradyNealDML`) where he (jokingly) suggests that DML "*is maybe twice as cool*" as regular machine learning. Let's see!

DML, also known as **debiased machine learning** or **orthogonal machine learning**, is another causal framework with the root *double* in its name. In DML – similarly to DR methods – we fit two models that estimate different parts of the relationships in the data.

DML can be implemented using arbitrary base estimators, and in this sense, it also belongs to the meta-learner family. At the same time, unlike S-, T- and X-Learners, the framework comes with a strong theoretical background and unique architectural solutions.

In this section, we'll introduce the main concepts behind DML. After that, we'll apply it to our `earnings` dataset using DoWhy's API. We'll discuss some popular myths that have arisen around DML and explore the framework's main limitations. Finally, we'll compare it to DR estimators and present some practical guidelines for when to choose DML over DR-Learner.

Why DML and what's so double about it?

Similar to DR methods, DML also uses two estimators in order to model data, yet it does it slightly differently. Before we jump into the technicalities, let's discuss what the main motivations behind DML are.

DML was first proposed by MIT statistician and economist Victor Chernozhukov and colleagues (Chernozhukov et al., 2018). The authors' motivation was to build a causal estimator that can leverage the flexibility of non-parametric machine learning models while achieving low bias and offering *valid confidence intervals* (note how similar these ideas are to what we saw for TMLE).

In particular, the authors built DML in a way that makes it **root-n consistent**. We say that an estimator is consistent when its error goes down with the sample size. Intuitively, root-n consistency is an indicator that the estimation error goes to 0 at a rate of $\frac{1}{\sqrt{n}}$ when the sample size (n) goes to infinity.

> **More on consistency**
>
> Estimator **consistency** is important (not only in causality) because it tells us whether the estimator will converge to the true value with a large enough sample size. Formally, we say that a consistent estimator will *converge in probability* to the true value.
>
> Although consistency is an asymptotic property, consistent estimators usually show good behavior in practice (with finite and realistic sample sizes).
>
> *Inconsistent* estimators, on the other hand, have a non-zero probability of non-convergence even for infinitely large samples.
>
> For a lightweight introduction to consistency, root-n consistency, and convergence in probability, check out Kenneth Tay's blog post: `https://bit.ly/RootNConsistency`.

OK, so we have a consistent estimator that gives us the flexibility of machine learning and valid confidence intervals. How do we achieve these properties?

It turns out that there are two main sources of bias that we need to address.

The first comes from a mechanism that we usually see as beneficial in machine learning: **regularization**. Regularization is a set of techniques that helps machine learning models avoid overfitting. It turns out that it can lead to bias when we apply machine learning techniques to treatment effect estimation, preventing us from achieving *root-n consistency*.

The second source of bias comes from overfitting. Let's start by addressing the latter.

Overfitting bias

DML solves the second problem using cross-fitting. The idea is as follows:

1. We split the data into two random partitions, D_0 and D_1.
2. We fit the models (remember, we have two of them) on D_0 and estimate the quantity of interest on D_1.
3. Next, we fit the models on D_1 and estimate on D_0.
4. Finally, we average the two estimates and this gives us the final estimate.

This procedure might remind you of *cross-validation*. Cross-fitting and cross-validation both stem from the same idea of masking parts of the data, where masked partitions serve as a proxy for (future) unseen data. At first glance, cross-fitting and cross-validation have different goals (bias correction versus model evaluation), but the mechanics of both methods are virtually identical.

Most implementations of DML estimators perform cross-fitting on two partitions by default. From a theoretical point of view, the number of partitions (or *folds* as we call them in the context of *cross-validation*) has no impact on the estimator's performance (asymptotically). That said, *in practice*, DML tends to work better with four or five partitions than with just two, especially on smaller datasets. Although this is not a rule, these differences seem to have a *relatively systematic* character (Chernozhukov et al., 2018, p. C24).

Regularization bias

After crossing overfitting bias off our to-do list, we're now ready to tackle **regularization bias**.

DML addresses this challenge using a technique called **orthogonalization**. The procedure is inspired by the **Frisch-Waugh-Lovell** (**FWL**) theorem.

To get an understanding of FWL, let's start with the following linear regression equation:

$$Y = \beta_1 T + \beta_2 X + \epsilon$$

FWL states that we can obtain β_1 not only by fitting the model described by the preceding formula but also by carrying out the following steps:

1. Regress T on X using linear regression: $\hat{t} = \gamma X$.
2. Regress Y on X using linear regression: $\hat{y} = \psi X$.

3. Compute the residuals from regressions from points 1 and 2:

   A. $\delta_T = T - \hat{t}$

   B. $\delta_Y = Y - \hat{y}$

4. Regress residuals δ_Y on residuals δ_T using linear regression: $\hat{\delta}_T = \alpha_1 \delta_Y$.

It turns out that the coefficient, α_1, from the last equation is *equal to* the coefficient, β_1, from the original regression equation (note that if you code it yourself, you may get minor differences between β_1 and α_1; they might come from numerical imprecisions and/or the implementation details of the packages you use). For a proof of the FWL theorem, including R code examples, check out `https://bit.ly/FWLProof`.

Orthogonalization is a modification of the FWL procedure that allows us to use arbitrary machine learning models instead of linear regression in *steps 1* and *2* (note that the last model from *step 4* remains linear in the linear DML estimator (Chernozhukov et al., 2018); this limitation does not apply to non-parametric DML).

The core strengths of DML come from its ability to model complex non-linear relationships in the data. Let's re-write the original linear regression equation to allow for non-linearities. This will allow us to demonstrate the power of DML more clearly. We will start with a so-called *partially linear model*:

$$Y = \theta T + f_Y(X) + \epsilon_Y$$

$$T = f_T(X) + \epsilon_T$$

In the preceding formulas, Y is the outcome, T is the treatment, $f_Y(.)$ and $f_T(.)$ are arbitrary and possibly non-linear functions, X is a set of predictors that *includes the confounders*, and the ϵs represent error terms. In this formulation, θ is the causal parameter that we want to estimate.

By applying orthogonalization, we can separate the estimation of the causal parameter, θ, from estimating the so-called **nuisance parameter** that models the impact of non-causal predictors in the model (the nuisance parameter in our partial linear model is represented by $f_Y(.)$, which is a function; that's why the nuisance parameter is sometimes also referred to as the **nuisance function**).

The last step of the orthogonalization procedure (which is analogous to the last step of FWL) will provide us with an estimate of the θ parameter that is *free* of the *regularization bias*!

Moreover, this means that we can get the benefits of parametric statistical inference and don't care about the exact functional form of the nuisance parameter. This gives us great flexibility!

Before we conclude this subsection, let's summarize the key points. DML uses two machine learning models in order to estimate the causal effect. These models are sometimes called the *treatment* and the *outcome* models (as they were in the case of DR methods), but note that the treatment model in DML does not estimate the propensity score, but rather models treatment directly.

Additionally, we fit one more model to estimate the causal parameter, θ, from the residuals. This model is known as the *final model*. In linear DML, this model is – by design – a linear regression, but in generalized, non-parametric DML, an arbitrary machine learning regressor can be used.

DML is an estimator with low variance and bias and can provide us with valid confidence intervals. It also natively supports both discrete and continuous treatments.

DML with DoWhy and EconML

Let's implement a linear DML estimator and apply it to our data. We'll skip graph creation, model initialization, and estimand identification steps as they are identical to what we've done for previous models. Note that this modular logic offered by DoWhy makes experimentation with various methods seamless, as problem definition and estimand identification are completely independent of the estimation step.

To use linear DML, we need to pass `'backdoor.econml.dml.LinearDML'` to the `method_name` parameter. Notice that we also introduce an additional argument, `'discrete_treatment'`, and set it to `True`. This argument is passed to the model as a part of the `'init_params'` dictionary. We need to specify it because EconML DML estimators default to continuous treatment, while our treatment is binary:

```
estimate = model.estimate_effect(
    identified_estimand=estimand,
    method_name='backdoor.econml.dml.LinearDML',
    target_units='ate',
    method_params={
        'init_params': {
            # Define outcome and treatment models
            'model_y': LGBMRegressor(
                n_estimators=500, max_depth=10),
            'model_t': LogisticRegression(),
            # Specify that treatment is discrete
            'discrete_treatment': True
        },
        'fit_params': {}
    })
```

Let's predict on test data:

```
effect_pred = model.causal_estimator.effect(
    earnings_interaction_test.drop(['true_effect',
    'took_a_course'], axis=1))
effect_true = earnings_interaction_test['true_effect'
    ].values
```

Let's compute the error:

```
mean_absolute_percentage_error(effect_true, effect_pred)
```

This gives us the following:

```
0.0125345885989969
```

This error is roughly twice higher than the error for the linear DR-Learner.

Let's plot the results (*Figure 10.5*).

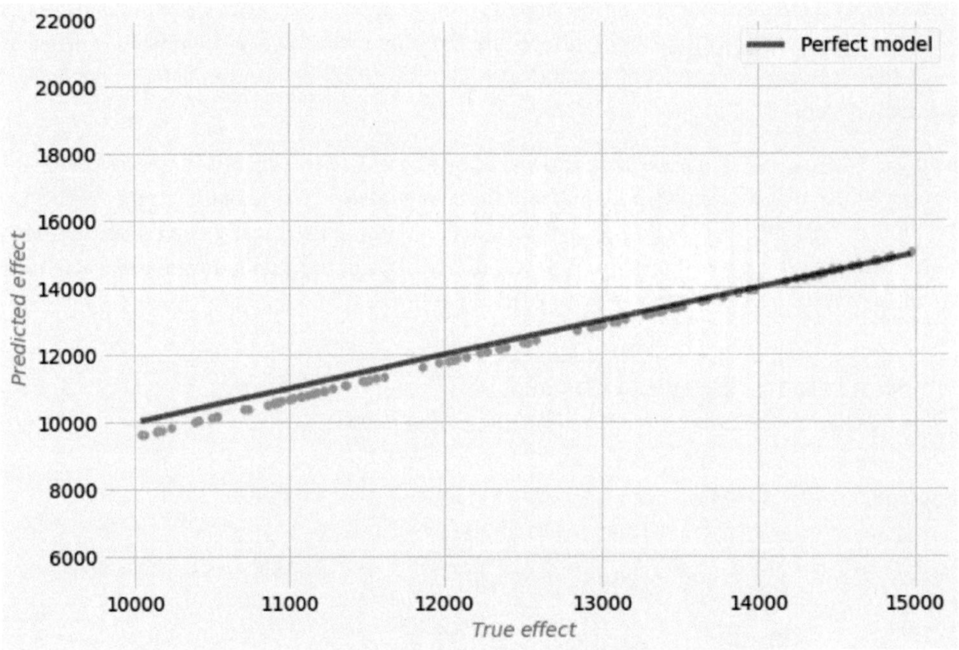

Figure 10.5 – The true versus predicted effect for linear DML

It seems that DML comes with a slightly biased estimate. In particular, the model underestimates the lower effect values (see the blue dots below the red line for lower values of the true effect in *Figure 10.5*).

Let's try to reduce the complexity of the outcome model and increase the number of cross-fitting folds:

```
estimate = model.estimate_effect(
    identified_estimand=estimand,
    method_name='backdoor.econml.dml.LinearDML',
    target_units='ate',
    method_params={
        'init_params': {
            # Define outcome and treatment models
            'model_y': LGBMRegressor(n_estimators=50,
                max_depth=10),
            'model_t': LogisticRegression(),
            # Specify that treatment is discrete
            'discrete_treatment': True,
            # Define the number of cross-fitting folds
            'cv': 4
        },
        'fit_params': {
        }
    })
```

Let's get predictions and calculate the error:

```
effect_pred = model.causal_estimator.effect(
    earnings_interaction_test.drop(['true_effect',
    'took_a_course'], axis=1))
effect_true = earnings_interaction_test['true_effect'
    ].values
mean_absolute_percentage_error(effect_true, effect_pred)
```

This results in the following:

```
0.00810075098627887
```

That's better, but the results are still slightly worse than for the best DR-Learner.

Let's plot the results (*Figure 10.6*).

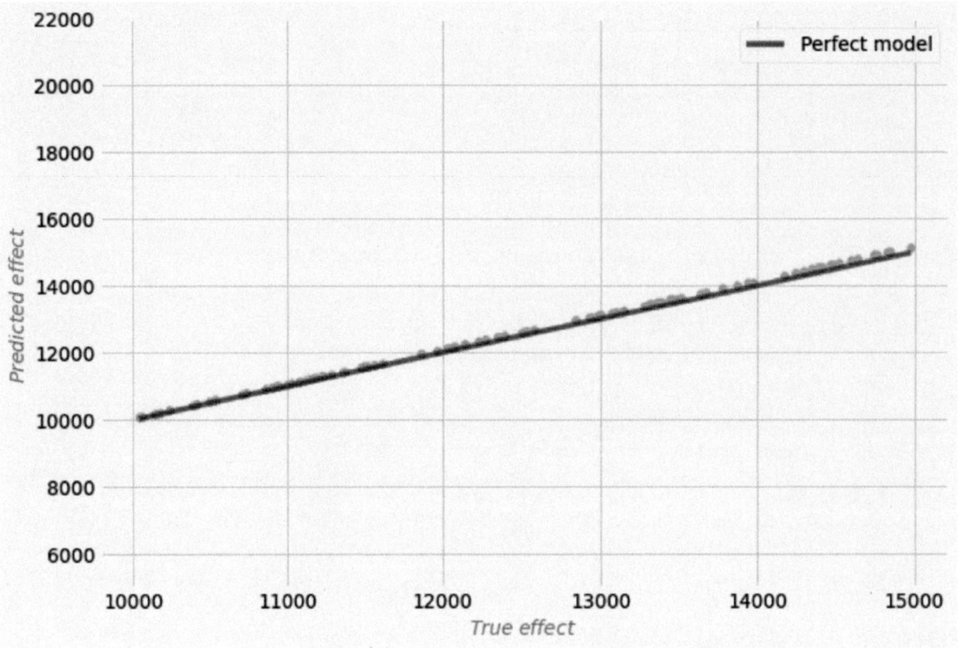

Figure 10.6 – The true versus predicted effect for linear DML with less complex models and four cross-fitting folds

These results look much better, but the model seems to systematically overestimate the effect.

Now, you might be puzzled about this whole process. Isn't there a fundamental challenge to all we're doing?

We changed some of the parameters of the base models and observed improved results – great – but this is only possible when we have simulated data, isn't it?

Is there anything we can do when simulated data is unavailable?

Hyperparameter tuning with DoWhy and EconML

Yes. One path we can take in order to optimize our models is to tune the hyperparameters of the outcome and treatment models.

Hyperparameter tuning can improve our estimators' fit to the data and their generalization to new instances (note that it cannot help with the estimand).

There are two main ways to run hyperparameter tuning with DoWhy and EconML.

The first is to wrap the models in one of the sklearn cross-validation classes, `GridSearchCV`, `HalvingGridSearchCV`, or `RandomizedSearchCV`, and pass the wrapped models into the constructor.

Let's try it!

This time, we'll use the LGBM classifier instead of logistic regression to predict the treatment. We hope that with some hyperparameter tuning, we can outperform the model with logistic regression.

Now's also a good moment for a reminder. In DML, the treatment model does not estimate propensity scores but rather predicts treatment values directly. In this setting, probability calibration – important for propensity scores – is not that critical and so using a more complex model might be beneficial, despite the fact that its probabilities might be less well calibrated than in the case of logistic regression.

Ready to code?

We'll start by defining our outcome (`model_y`) and treatment (`model_t`) models and wrapping them in a grid search wrapper:

```
model_y = GridSearchCV(
    estimator=LGBMRegressor(),
    # Define the model's parameter search space
    param_grid={
        'max_depth': [3, 10, 20, 100],
        'n_estimators': [10, 50, 100]
    },
    # Define GridSearch params
    cv=10, n_jobs=-1, scoring='neg_mean_squared_error'
)

model_t = GridSearchCV(
    estimator=LGBMClassifier(),
    # Define the model's parameter search space
    param_grid={
        'max_depth': [3, 10, 20, 100],
        'n_estimators': [10, 50, 100]
    },
    # Define GridSearch params
    cv=10, n_jobs=-1, scoring='accuracy'
)
```

We set `GridSearchCV`'s `cv` parameter to `10`. This parameter determines how many folds will be used to tune the hyperparameters of our treatment and outcome models. Note that this is different from the DML estimator's `cv` parameter, which controls the number of folds for cross-fitting. It's good to remember this distinction as both parameters control different functionalities.

Now, let's estimate the effects. Doing so is straightforward. We simply pass wrapped `model_y` and `model_t` objects to the `init_params` dictionary:

```
estimate = model.estimate_effect(
    identified_estimand=estimand,
    method_name='backdoor.econml.dml.LinearDML',
    target_units='ate',
    method_params={
        'init_params': {
            # Pass models wrapped in GridSearchCV objects
            'model_y': model_y,
            'model_t': model_t,
            # Set discrete treatment to `True`
            'discrete_treatment': True,
            # Define the number of cross-fitting folds
            'cv': 4
        },
        'fit_params': {
        }
    })
```

After computing the results, we obtain the following:

```
0.0017934682521269
```

The MAPE value is only 0.17%. This is much better than anything we've seen so far!

In particular, this result is more than 3.5 times better than the result of our best DR-Learner.

Let's examine the results visually (*Figure 10.7*).

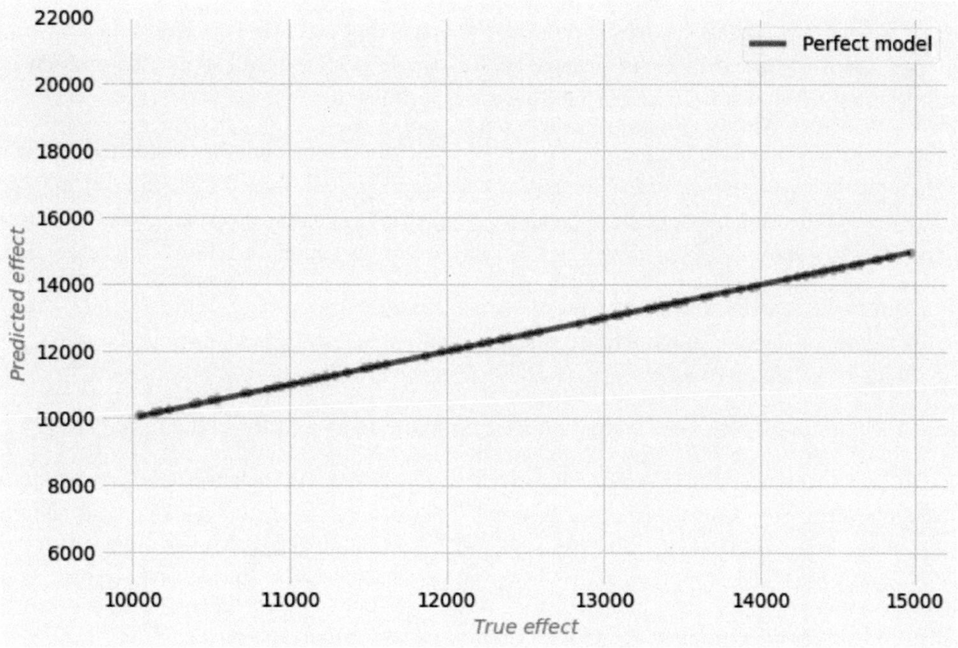

Figure 10.7 – DML results after hyperparameter tuning

These results look very good!

The tuned model did a really good job! To the extent that such a small error might seem unrealistic.

When looking at *Figure 10.7*, we should remember two things. First, we're working with a relatively simple synthetic dataset, which should be easily solvable by a powerful enough model. Second, for comparability, we keep the same value ranges for both axes in the plot that we used for the previous models. This (to an extent) hides the fact that the model has *some error*.

If you see results like this in real life, don't forget about **Twyman's law**. The law has multiple variants (Kohavi et al., 2020) and states that any figure or statistic that looks interesting is most likely wrong. Twyman's law can be a valuable reminder to retain healthy skepticism in our work.

As we've just seen, tuning hyperparameters for CATE models can bring significant improvements. At the beginning of this section, we said that there are two ways to tune hyperparameters with DoWhy and EconML.

Let's discuss the second way now.

The second way to tune hyperparameters is to do it in advance using your favorite hyperparameter tuning framework, such as Hyperopt or Optuna, and then simply use the best models found.

There are two main advantages to this approach. The first is that you're *not limited* to the grid search or random search options available in sklearn. With Hyperopt, Optuna, and some other frameworks, you can leverage the power of more efficient Bayesian optimization.

Note that the cross-validation procedure or a separate validation set should be used when tuning the hyperparameters in order to minimize the risk of leakage and overfitting. The second reason to tune your parameters independently – perhaps even more important – is that while passing sklearn wrappers to EconML, only a subset of the data will be used for tuning. This might be statistically less stable.

As an additional remark, I want to comment once again on *cross-validation*. In *Chapter 7*, we said that *cross-validation* is not a suitable technique to validate structural aspects of causal models, yet it can be useful for validating the estimation part.

This also includes hyperparameter tuning for base estimators that we carried out in this section.

The idea of hyperparameter tuning brings more interesting questions. For instance, if the outcome model is tuned and trained on a particular dataset, how will it perform on the data that is out of distribution? Wouldn't it be reasonable to expect that a causal model would handle this task smoothly? At the end of the day, we've learned about a causal structure that goes beyond associations in the dataset, right?

The answer depends on a number of factors. Let's discuss two important ones.

First, the answer depends on which models we use. For instance, tree-based models *do not extrapolate* beyond the maximum value in the training set. Let's imagine that you only have one predictor in your problem, X, and all values of X in your training dataset are bounded between 0 and 1,000. Additionally, let's assume that the outcome, Y, is always two times X.

This is a very simple problem, but if you test your tree-based model on data where X ranges from 1,000 to 2,000 (that is, all values are outside the training range), the prediction for all observations will be a constant value that is no greater than the maximum outcome seen in the training dataset (which would be 1000*2 = 2000).

This behavior comes from the fact that trees learn a set of rules from the data (e.g., if $4.5 < x < 5.5$, then $y = 10$) and they would need to essentially *make up* the rules for data that is outside the training range. The fact that we're using a causal DML model will not surpass this limitation.

If we use a linear regression model or a neural network, on the other hand, these models will extrapolate. This brings us to the second factor.

The extrapolation can only be correct under certain limited circumstances – when the relationship between X and Y is linear or, in the case of neural networks, when the activation function is *similar* to the target function (Xu et al., 2021).

In this scenario, using DML will also not surpass the limitations of the outcome and treatment models.

These limitations are extremely important in any production system and should be taken into account at the early stages of the system design.

Is DML a golden bullet?

We just discussed some of the general limitations of machine learning models. Accepting them as they are, let's take a closer look at the DML framework itself.

DML is a great and flexible method and tends to work very well in a broad set of circumstances; yet – like any other method – it has its own set of constraints. We will discuss the main ones here.

We already know that one of the assumptions behind DML is a lack of hidden confounding. In their 2022 paper, Paul Hünermund and colleagues showed that not meeting this assumption leads to significant biases that are similar in magnitude to biases that we get from other, much simpler methods, such as LASSO (Hünermund et al., 2022). These findings are consistent with the results obtained by Gordon et al. (2022) in a large-scale study that benchmarked DML using high-dimensional non-experimental data from the Facebook Ads platform. Note that DML is sensitive to not only unobserved common causes of treatment and outcomes but also other bad control schemes that allow for non-causal information flow in the graph. This is also true for other causal models (for a comprehensive overview of bad control schemes, check out Cinelli et al., 2022).

While it might not be particularly surprising to some of you that DML can lead to biased results when hidden confounding cannot be excluded, there are two ideas I'd like to highlight here.

It can be tempting for some researchers and practitioners to transfer their insights from the fields of deep learning and big data to the domain of causal inference. Let's discuss why such an approach might backfire.

First, those familiar with deep learning will recognize that in certain cases, increasing the training sample size can lead to significant model performance improvements. In causal machine learning, this approach can also be helpful when the base models do not have enough data to learn a useful mapping or when the original data does not provide enough diversity to satisfy the positivity assumption. That said, when these conditions are met, adding more observations *cannot help* in reducing *causal bias* that arises from *unmet causal assumptions*.

The reason for this is that causal bias comes from ill-defined structural relationships between variables, not from an insufficient amount of information within a dataset. In other words, causal bias is related to the *estimand* misspecification and not to the statistical *estimate*.

Secondly, sometimes, in particular in big data settings, practitioners of traditional machine learning might benefit from adding more features to the model. For many tech companies, it's not unusual to use hundreds or even thousands of variables for predictive tasks. The logic behind adding more features to a statistical model relies on the assumption that having more features translates to more predictive power, which in turn translates to better predictions. This reasoning might lead to beneficial outcomes when using modern machine learning techniques.

The causal setting is different. As we know, adding arbitrary features to the model might result in opening non-causal paths in the DAG. This can introduce confounding and lead to biased estimates of causal parameters.

In practice, it might be better to include a smaller set of variables in your model and make sure that they do not introduce unwanted confounding. This might be easier said than done, yet in cases where it's unclear which variables to include, this approach can be treated as a hypothesis-generating process that can be iteratively improved over time.

If you cannot exclude the possibility of unobserved confounding in your setting and you cannot afford to perform an experiment (for ethical, financial, or other reasons), DML can still be useful for you. Chernozhukov et al. (2022) proposed a general framework for finding confidence bounds under unobserved confounding. The method, belonging to a broader family of sensitivity analysis methods, allows us to assess how stable the effect would be under hidden confounding of different strengths.

This solution can bring a lot of value to business decision-making, providing us with potentially actionable insights in light of difficult or impossible-to-meet assumptions.

Doubly robust versus DML

Before we conclude this section, let's make a quick comparison between DR-Learner and DML. Both methods can lead to good results. Both offer smart solutions for reducing the bias and variance of causal estimates. After reading this chapter, you might wonder: which one should I choose in practice?

I cannot give you a definitive answer that will guarantee that one model always outperforms the other, but we can look into some recommendations together. Hopefully, these recommendations will help you make decisions in your own use cases.

The first key difference between the models is that DML works for categorical and continuous treatments, while DR-Learner (similarly to TMLE) is – by design – limited to categorical treatments. This might sort some stuff out for you right away.

Now, let's focus on the particular implementations available in EconML. As we said before, `DRLearner` is more than just a simple DR estimator as it uses orthogonalization and cross-fitting under the hood. In a sense, you can think of `DRLearner` as a DR estimator on steroids as it incorporates various modern techniques in order to minimize error. One thing that remains unchanged is that DR correction is at the heart of the method. That's one of the reasons why it behaves differently compared to EconML's DML methods.

The main advantage of the DR method is that the error of the final estimate is only affected by the product of errors of the outcome model and the treatment model (Hernan & Robins, 2020). DR methods might perform better whenever the outcome model is misspecified.

On the other hand, DR-Learner will usually have higher variance than DML. Jane Huang from Microsoft suggests that this might become particularly noticeable when "*there are regions of the control space (...) in which some treatment has a small probability of being assigned*" (Huang et al., 2020). In this scenario, "*DML method could potentially extrapolate better, as it only requires good overlap on average to achieve good mean squared error*" (Huang et al., 2020). Note that TMLE could also perform well in the latter case. Another setting where DML might outperform DR-Learner is under sparsity in a high-dimensional setting, as demonstrated by Zachary Clement (Clement, 2023; note that in this case, DR-Learner's results could be potentially improved by adding lasso regularization to the final model).

In addition, a comparison between DML and TMLE might interest you. As we mentioned earlier, a detailed discussion on this topic is beyond the scope of this book, yet great resources are available. To start, check out van der Laan & Hejazi (2019) and Díaz (2020).

What's in it for me?

It's difficult to point out just one algorithm that would be guaranteed to unconditionally work better than other solutions.

That said, given the results of our experiments in this and the previous chapter, we might get the impression that DML outperforms other methods. This impression is somewhat biased as we did not tune hyperparameters for the remaining methods. On the other hand, DML is often recommended as the go-to method for continuous treatments. DR methods cannot compete in this category. S-Learner can be adapted to work with continuous treatment, but the current version of EconML does not support this feature.

If you cannot benchmark a wide array of methods and you're convinced that your data contains heterogeneous treatment effects, my recommendation would be to start with S-Learner, in particular if computational resources are an issue. T-Learner and X-Learner might be good to add to the mix if your treatment is discrete.

If computational resources are not an issue, DML (continuous or discrete treatment) and DR-Learner or TMLE (discrete treatment) will usually be good shots. That said, it's always good to have a simpler model as a benchmark. It's very easy to plug in complex base estimators to DML or DR/TMLE and get carried away, not knowing that the complexity pulls us far away from the best results we could achieve.

In the next section, we'll discuss one more family of methods that might be worth considering.

Before this, let's summarize the current section.

In this section, we introduced DML. We discussed the key concepts that constitute the uniqueness of the method: orthogonalization and cross-fitting. We demonstrated how to perform hyperparameter tuning for submodels using DoWhy and EconML. Then, we discussed the weaknesses of DML, finishing with a comparison between DR-Learner and DML.

Causal Forests and more

In this short section, we'll provide a brief overview of the idea behind **Causal Forests**. We'll introduce one of the EconML classes implementing the method. An in-depth discussion on Causal Forests and their extensions is beyond the scope of this book, but we'll point to resources where you can learn more about forest-based causal estimators.

Causal Forest is a tree-based model that stems from the works of Susan Athey, Julie Tibshirani, and Stefan Wager (Wager & Athey, 2018; Athey et al., 2019). The core difference between regular random forest and Causal Forest is that Causal Forest uses so-called **causal trees**. Otherwise, the methods are similar and both use resampling, predictor subsetting, and averaging over a number of trees.

Causal trees

What makes causal trees different from regular trees is the **split criterion**. Causal trees use a criterion based on the estimated treatment effects, using so-called **honest splitting**, where the splits are generated on training data, while leaf values are estimated using a hold-out set (this logic is very similar to cross-fitting in DML). For a more detailed overview, check out Daniel Jacob's article (Jacob, 2021), Mark White's blog post (`https://bit.ly/CausalForestIntro`), or the chapter on Causal Forests in White & Green (2023). For a high-level introduction, check out Haaya Naushan's blog post (`https://bit.ly/CausalForestHighLvl`). For a deep dive, refer to Wagner & Athey (2018) or Athey et al. (2019).

Forests overflow

EconML offers a wide variety of estimators that build on top of the idea of Causal Forests. The methods share many similarities but may differ in significant details (for instance, how first-stage models are estimated). This might translate to significant differences in computational costs. To understand the differences between the different estimator classes, check out the EconML documentation page here: `https://bit.ly/EconMLCausalForestDocs`.

Advantages of Causal Forests

Causal Forest models are a good choice when dealing with high-dimensional data. They provide valid confidence intervals while being non-parametric and offering high flexibility.

To start with Causal Forests, the `CausalForestDML` class from the `dml` module will likely be the best starting point in most cases. EconML also offers a *raw* version of Causal Forest - `CausalForest` - which can be found in the `grf` module. The latter class does not estimate the *nuisance parameter*. You might want to use this basic implementation in certain cases, but keep in mind that this might lead to suboptimal results compared to `CausalForestDML`.

Causal Forest with DoWhy and EconML

To use Causal Forest with DML orthogonalization, we simply pass the method's name to the `method_name` parameter. You might also want to make your own choice of the outcome and treatment models. This is done exactly in the same way as we did for the DML estimator. If your treatment is discrete, don't forget to include `discrete_treatment': True` in the `init_params` dictionary. Here's a code example for reference:

```
estimate = model.estimate_effect(
    identified_estimand=estimand,
    method_name='backdoor.econml.dml.CausalForestDML',
    target_units='ate',
    method_params={
        'init_params': {
            'model_y': LGBMRegressor(n_estimators=50,
                max_depth=10),
            'model_t': LGBMClassifier(n_estimators=50,
                max_depth=10),
            'discrete_treatment': True,
            # Define the num. of cross-fitting folds
            'cv': 4
        },
        'fit_params': {
        }
    }
)
```

This model's error is around 4.6% – a result comparable to S- and X-Learners. Note that we did not tune hyperparameters for this model.

Figure 10.8 presents the results of the model:

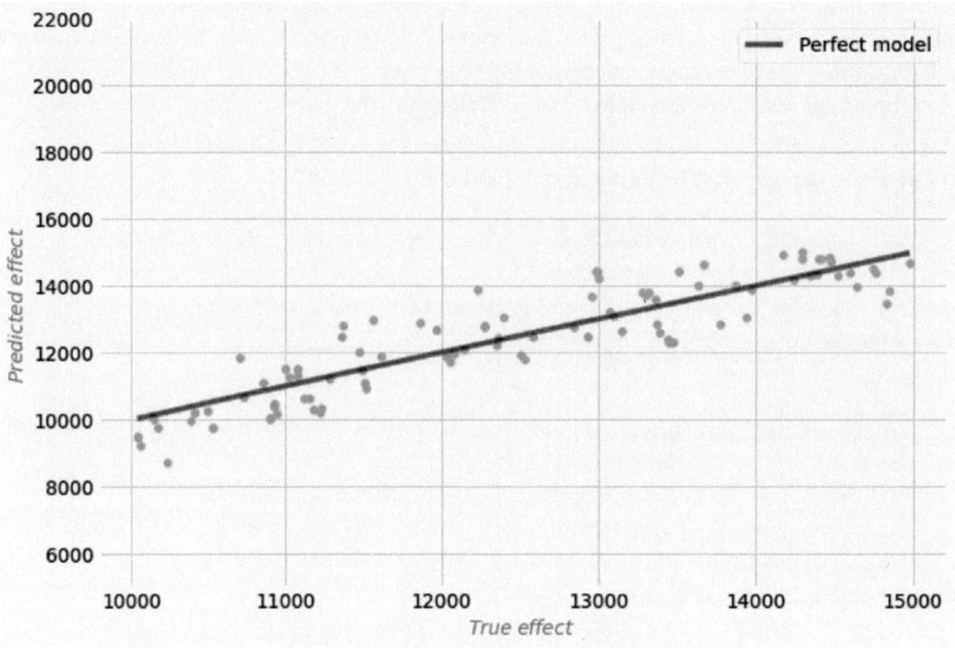

Figure 10.8 – Results for Causal Forest with DML (untuned)

Before we conclude this section, let's summarize the results of all CATE models on the machine learning earnings interaction dataset from *Chapter 9* and *Chapter 10* in a single table. *Table 10.1* presents this summary:

Estimator	MAPE
S-Learner	5.02%
T-Learner	8.13%
X-Learner	3.63%
Linear DR-Learner	0.62%
Linear DML	1.25%
Linear DML (tuning)	0.17%
Causal Forest	4.60%

Table 10.1 – A summary of the results for all models from Chapter 9 and Chapter 10 on the machine learning earnings interaction dataset

In this section, we discussed the core differences between classic random forest and Causal Forests. We said that the main difference between the two algorithms lies in how the trees are constructed. We pointed to resources where you can learn more about methods based on Causal Forests. Finally, we implemented `CausalForestDML` – a method that extends the basic Causal Forest with nuisance parameter estimation – and summarized the results for all CATE models on the machine learning earnings interaction dataset.

In the next section, we'll discuss estimating heterogeneous treatment effects from experimental data.

Ready?

Heterogeneous treatment effects with experimental data – the uplift odyssey

Modeling treatment effects with experimental data is usually slightly different in spirit from working with observational data. This stems from the fact that experimental data is assumed to be unconfounded by design (assuming our experimental design and implementation were not flawed).

In this section, we'll walk through a workflow of working with experimental data using EconML. We'll learn how to use EconML's basic API and see how to work with discrete treatments that have more than two levels. Finally, we'll use some causal model evaluation metrics in order to compare the models.

The title of this section talks about heterogeneous treatment effects – we already know what they are, but there's also a new term: *uplift*. **Uplift modeling** and **heterogeneous (aka conditional) treatment effect modeling** are closely related terms. In marketing and medicine, *uplift* simply means the quantity of change in some outcome in a treatment group (or subject) as compared to a control group – in other words, the treatment effect. Although uplift can be calculated for an entire treatment group, it can also be estimated for individual subjects or subgroups. In the latter case, it's synonymous with conditional (heterogeneous) treatment effects.

The data

In this section, we'll use the data from Kevin Hillstrom's *MineThatData* challenge (`https://bit.ly/KevinsDataChallenge`).

Before we start, I want to take a moment to express my gratitude for Kevin's generosity. Kevin agreed that we could use his dataset in the book. I appreciate this and believe that Kevin's decision will help us all become better causal data scientists, one step at a time. Thank you, Kevin!

Now, let's understand how the dataset is structured. The data comes from a randomized email experiment on 64,000 customers.

The treatment has three levels and was administered randomly:

- 1/3 of the customers received an email campaign featuring men's merchandise (treatment 1)
- 1/3 received an email campaign featuring women's merchandise (treatment 2)
- 1/3 received no campaign (control)

The features include the time since the last purchase (*recency*), the amount of dollars spent in the past year (*history*), indicators of the type of merchandise bought in the past year (*mens* or *womens*), an indicator of whether the customer was new in the past 12 months (*newbie*), what channel they purchased from previously (*channel*), and what type of area they live in (*rural*, *suburban*, *urban*; *zip_code*). Treatment is a three-level discrete variable describing which email campaign the customer received (*men's*, *women's*, or *control*). Finally, we have three outcome variables: *visit*, *conversion*, and *spending*.

We'll use *spending* as our target. It records a customer's spending within the two weeks following the delivery of the email campaign.

Let's read in the data.

We'll read the main dataset from a CSV file and the treatment mapping from a JSON file:

```
hillstrom_clean =
    pd.read_csv(r'./data/hillstrom_clean.csv')

with open(r'./data/hillstrom_clean_label_mapping.json',
    'r') as f:
    hillstrom_labels_mapping = json.load(f)
```

Our treatment has three levels. I stored the mapping in a dictionary serialized as a JSON object.

Let's see a couple of rows from our dataset (*Figure 10.9*):

	recency	history	mens	womens	newbie	visit	conversion	spend	zip_code__rural
0	10	142.44	1	0	0	0	0	0.0	0
1	6	329.08	1	1	1	0	0	0.0	1
2	7	180.65	0	1	1	0	0	0.0	0
3	9	675.83	1	0	1	0	0	0.0	1
4	2	45.34	1	0	0	0	0	0.0	0

	zip_code__surburban	zip_code__urban	channel__multichannel	channel__phone	channel__web	treatment
	1	0	0	1	0	1
	0	0	0	0	1	0
	1	0	0	0	1	1
	0	0	0	0	1	2
	0	1	0	0	1	1

Figure 10.9 – The first five rows of the Hillstrom dataset

We cut the display in *Figure 10.9* into two parts for readability. As you can see, there are many sparse binary features in the data. Roughly half of them are one-hot-encoded multi-level categorical features: zip code area and channel.

The *zip code* and *channel* variables are represented as fully one-hot-encoded sets of variables. This means that for each row, the set of variables representing a channel (or zip code area) will have exactly one column with the value 1.

This makes one of the columns redundant as its value can be unambiguously inferred from the values of the remaining columns in the set (if `channel__web` and `channel__phone` are both 0, `channel__multichannel` has to be 1 – by definition of one-hot-encoding).

Note that this setting with redundant information will introduce multicollinearity into the data. Although this might not be a problem for the tree-based methods, it will impact linear models' convergence and performance.

To address this in advance, let's drop the redundant columns:

```
hillstrom_clean = hillstrom_clean.drop(['zip_code__urban',
    'channel__web'], axis=1)
```

The data is technically ready.

Let's examine its properties.

Testing the waters – how unconfounded are you, my dear?

We expect that experimental data is unconfounded due to randomization, yet sometimes experimental data might be biased. This can be the case for a number of reasons: technical glitches, invalid procedures, treatment leakage, and more.

We cannot fully test whether randomization was valid (there is no easy way to spot arbitrary unobserved confounding), but we can test whether observed variables can predict treatment. If this were the case, we'd have an indicator that the randomization or data collection process was flawed.

One practical way to perform this check is to split your data in half: train a model that predicts the treatment from covariates on one half of the data and predict treatment values on the other half. Our model's performance should essentially be random.

Let's implement this process.

First, let's split the data into treatment, outcome, and feature vectors:

```
hillstrom_X = hillstrom_clean.drop(['visit', 'conversion',
    'spend', 'treatment'], axis=1)
hillstrom_Y = hillstrom_clean['spend']
hillstrom_T = hillstrom_clean['treatment']
```

Second, let's check whether the treatments are distributed uniformly in our data as expected:

```
sample_size = hillstrom_clean.shape[0]
hillstrom_T_.value_counts() / sample_size
```

We get the following output:

```
1    0.334172
2    0.332922
0    0.332906
Name: treatment, dtype: float64
```

All values are close to 33.3%, which indicates that the treatments were distributed uniformly.

Third, let's perform a train-test split for the randomness checks:

```
X_train_eda, X_test_eda, T_train_eda, T_test_eda =
    Train_test_split(hillstrom_X, hillstrom_T_eda,
        test_size=.5)
```

Let's verify the split's quality. We expect that roughly 33% of observations should be assigned to each treatment group:

```
T_test_eda.value_counts() / T_test_eda.shape[0]
```

We get the following:

```
0     0.335156
2     0.333250
1     0.331594
Name: treatment, dtype: float64
```

This looks good!

Fourth, let's fit the classifier that aims to predict treatment *T* from features *X*:

```
lgbm_eda = LGBMClassifier()
lgbm_eda.fit(X_train_eda, T_train_eda)
```

One side remark that I want to share with you here is that, in general, for the LGBM classifier, it might be better for us not to one-hot encode our categorical features (such as zip area or channel). The model handles categorical data natively in a way that can improve the results over one-hot-encoded features in certain cases.

That said, we'll continue with one-hot-encoded features as they give us more flexibility at later stages (other models might not support categorical features natively) and we don't expect significant improvements in our case anyway.

Fifth, let's predict on the test data and calculate the accuracy score:

```
T_pred_eda = lgbm_eda.predict(X_test_eda)
accuracy_score(T_test_eda, T_pred_eda)
```

If there's no confounding in the data, we expect to get an accuracy of around 33%. The result is as follows:

```
0.33384375
```

This looks good!

Finally, we can generate empirical confidence intervals to see whether this score falls within them:

```
random_scores = []

test_eda_sample_size = T_test_eda.shape[0]

for i in range(10000):
    random_scores.append(
```

```
        (np.random.choice(
            [0, 1, 2],
            test_eda_sample_size) == np.random.choice(
            [0, 1, 2],
            test_eda_sample_size)).mean())

np.quantile(random_scores, .025), np.quantile(random_scores, .975)
```

We compare how often two random vectors of three mutually exclusive values are the same. For each draw, we compare as many vectors as we have observed in our test set. We repeat this procedure 10,000 times and calculate 0.025 and 0.975 quantiles. This gives us 95% confidence intervals:

```
(0.32815625, 0.33850078125)
```

The accuracy score that we obtained for our model lies within the boundaries of these intervals. This gives us more confidence that the data is not observably confounded.

See *Figure 10.10* for reference.

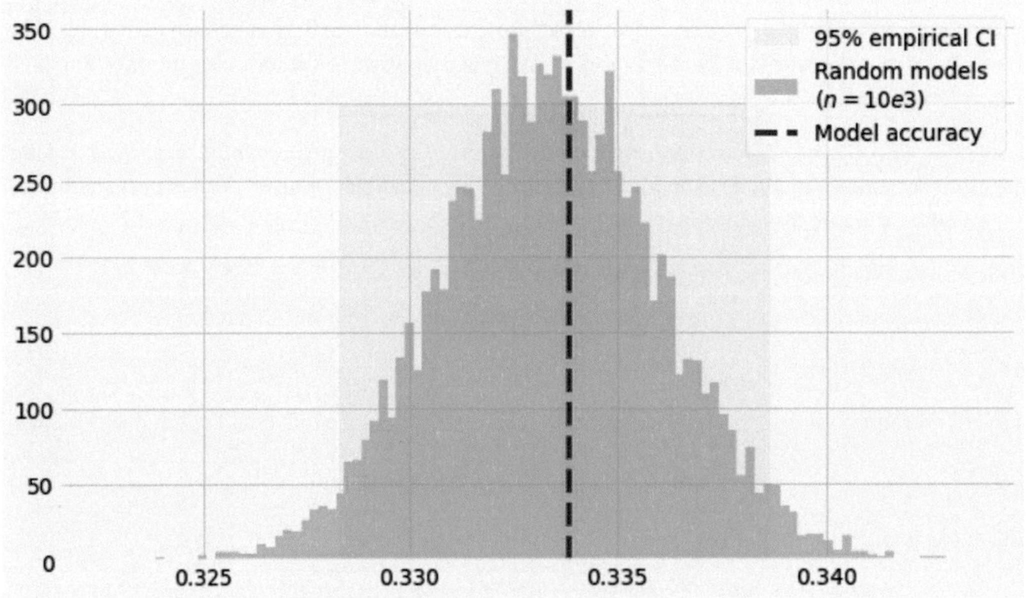

Figure 10.10 – Empirical distribution of random models versus model accuracy

Another similar way to check randomization under observed variables is to use a **classifier two-sample test** (**C2ST**; Diemert et al., 2018; Lopez-Paz & Oquab, 2016). The procedure is very similar, with the difference that the C2ST compares the *loss* of a classifier trained on the actual data with the distribution of losses of a classifier predicting random noise, instead of comparing accuracies.

C2STs based on different types of classifiers might perform better in certain cases or for certain data types (e.g., images). Check out Lopez-Paz & Oquab (2016) for details.

Choosing the framework

We started this section with the statement that modeling treatment effects in experimental data differs from working with observational data.

We already got a taste of some of the differences in the workflow. Instead of starting the process by defining a graph, we performed randomization checks. The fact that we do not explicitly define a graph means that we won't explicitly look for the estimand and that there's no clear basis for performing refutation tests.

These differences make it a natural choice to work with EconML estimators directly (rather than using DoWhy's four-step process) when we use experimental data.

We're almost ready to start, but before we open the toolbox, let me share something with you.

We don't know half of the story

I was recently skimming through a paper discussing *selection models*. These models are used by statisticians who perform meta-analyses to assess how much the effect of interest might be skewed due to research that was *not* published.

As researchers and practitioners, we are used to working with materials demonstrating successful outcomes. Research papers and blog posts rarely focus on challenges and failures and not many journals (though there are exceptions) are willing to publish negative results. Though understandable from a psychological standpoint, this bias toward discussing successful results has its price.

Those of us who've worked with meta-analyses know about the tools we use in order to assess **publication bias**. Those of us working in the industry will have perhaps seen junior data scientists surprised by the messiness of real-world data, something they never found in their handbooks and courses. Moreover, most of us have likely been in a similar position at least once – surprised at how far away real-world data can be from our expectations.

This surprise comes partially from the fact that the world is complex, yet the way we structure incentives in the education system and the publish-or-perish culture also play a role here.

In this section, we'll see how things should look when everything works smoothly, but we'll also see what happens when they don't.

I hope this approach will be beneficial to you.

Now, let's get some more context and begin our journey into the wild!

Kevin's challenge

As we said in the beginning, the data that we're about to use comes from an online experiment, but this is only half of the story. The data was released as part of a challenge organized by Kevin back in 2008. The challenge also included a series of questions, among others – *if you could eliminate 10,000 customers from the campaign, which 10,000 should that be?*

This and the other questions posed by Kevin are very interesting and I am sure they stir up a sense of excitement in anyone interested in marketing.

Check out the full list of Kevin's questions here: `https://bit.ly/KevinsDataChallenge`.

Although most, if not all, of these questions can be answered with the tools we'll use in this section (plus some clever analytics), we'll ask a simpler question instead: which of the models would help us make decisions that would translate to the best financial results?

The fact that this question might seem simpler does not make our endeavor easier.

There are a number of challenges that we'll need to overcome:

- First, we have more than one treatment. This makes model evaluation more challenging than in a binary case.
- Second, although the dataset is relatively large (64,000 observations), the conversion rate is low.

Let's take a look at the label mapping to find out how to work with the treatment:

```
hillstrom_labels_mapping
```

This gives us the following:

```
{'control': 0, 'womans_email': 1, 'mens_email': 2}
```

`0` represents the control group assignment, `1` represents women's emails, and `2` represents men's emails.

Let's check how many people bought something under both treatments:

```
(hillstrom_Y[hillstrom_T > 0] > 0).sum()
```

We get the following:

```
456
```

This is roughly 0.7% of the entire dataset.

Let's open the toolbox!

Opening the toolbox

In this section, we'll use six algorithms: S-Learner, T-Learner, X-Learner, DR-Learner, linear DML, and Causal Forest with DML. We'll compare their performance from three different angles: computational cost, ability to sort true uplift, and average expected outcome. If some of these sound cryptic to you, don't worry; we'll explain them on the way.

Let's start by instantiating the models. First, we'll create a function that returns an instance of the LGBM model to make the code a bit more readable:

```
def create_model(model_type, n_estimators=100, max_depth=10, learning_
rate=.01):
    if model_type == 'regressor':
        return LGBMRegressor(
            n_estimators=n_estimators,
            max_depth=max_depth,
            learning_rate=learning_rate)
    elif model_type == 'classifier':
        return LGBMClassifier(
            n_estimators=n_estimators,
            max_depth=max_depth,
            learning_rate=learning_rate)
    else:
        raise NotImplementedError(
            f'Model type `{model_type}` not implemented.')
```

The function returns an instance of an LGBM regressor or LGBM classifier, depending on the argument we pass to the `model_type` parameter.

Let's instantiate our causal models:

```
s_learner = SLearner(
    overall_model=create_model('regressor')
)

x_learner = XLearner(
    models=[
        create_model('regressor'),
        create_model('regressor'),
        create_model('regressor'),
    ],
    cate_models=[
        create_model('regressor'),
        create_model('regressor'),
        create_model('regressor'),
```

```
    ]
)

t_learner = TLearner(
    models=[
        create_model('regressor'),
        create_model('regressor'),
        create_model('regressor'),
    ]
)

dml = LinearDML(
    model_y=create_model('regressor'),
    model_t=create_model('classifier'),
    discrete_treatment=True,
    cv=5
)

dr = DRLearner(
    model_propensity=LogisticRegression(),
    model_regression=create_model('regressor'),
    model_final=create_model('regressor'),
    cv=5,
)

cf = CausalForestDML(
    model_y=create_model('regressor'),
    model_t=create_model('classifier'),
    discrete_treatment=True,
    cv=5
)
```

This is very similar to what we were doing before when using DoWhy wrappers. The main difference is that we now pass model parameters directly to model constructors rather than encoding them in an intermediary dictionary.

Note that for linear DML and Causal Forest, we set `discrete_treatment` to `True`. We don't do so for meta-learners and DR-Learner because these models only allow discrete treatments (S-Learner can be generalized to continuous treatments, but the current version of EconML does not support that). Also note that our `create_model()` function returns estimators with the same set of pre-defined parameters for each base learner.

First things first

We want to assess the performance of our models and so we'll divide our data into training and test sets.

As a reminder – we won't be able to compute an error metric like we'd do in the case of traditional supervised learning. We'll need to use different approaches, but having a test set will still be beneficial for us.

We'll use scikit-learn's `train_test_split` function to perform the split:

```
X_train, X_test, y_train, y_test, T_train, T_test =
    train_test_split(
    hillstrom_X,
    hillstrom_Y,
    hillstrom_T,
    test_size=.5
)
```

We set the test size to 0.5. The reason I chose this value is that although our dataset has 64,000 observations, only a tiny fraction of subjects actually converted (made a purchase). Let's see how many conversion instances we have in each of the splits:

```
(y_train[T_train > 0] > 0).sum(),
(y_test[T_test > 0] > 0).sum()
```

This gives us the following:

```
(227, 229)
```

That's only 227 converted observations in training and 229 in the test set. This is not a very large number for machine learning methods. The trade-off here is between having enough observations to effectively train the models and having enough observations to effectively evaluate the models. Our case is pretty challenging in this regard.

Nonetheless, let's fit the models and see how much we can get out of them.

We'll fit the models in a loop to save ourselves some space and time. Speaking of time, we'll measure the fitting time for each of the algorithms to get a sense of the differences between them in terms of computational cost.

Let's start by creating a dictionary that aggregates all the models:

```
models = {
    'SLearner': s_learner,
    'TLearner': t_learner,
    'XLearner': x_learner,
    'DRLearner': dr,
```

```
    'LinearDML': dml,
    'CausalForestDML': cf
}
```

Let's iterate over the dictionary and fit the models:

```
for model_name, model in models.items():
    start = time.time()
    model.fit(
        Y=y_train,
        T=T_train,
        X=X_train,
        inference='bootstrap'
    )
    stop = time.time()
    print(f'{model_name} fitted in {stop - start:0.4f}
        seconds.')
```

This gives us the following output:

```
SLearner fitted in 0.1730 seconds.
XLearner fitted in 0.8588 seconds.
TLearner fitted in 0.2894 seconds.
DRLearner fitted in 2.0550 seconds.
LinearDML fitted in 4.0384 seconds.
CausalForestDML fitted in 6.3661 seconds.
```

From this output, we can get a sense of the computational costs related to each model. It would be great to repeat this experiment a couple of times to get more reliable estimates of the differences between the models. I did this in advance for you. *Table 10.2* contains rough estimates of how much computational time each of the methods needs compared to the S-Learner baseline:

Model	**Time** **(multiplier compared to S-Learner)**
S-Learner	1x
T-Learner	2x
X-Learner	5x
DR-Learner	13x
LinearDML	27x
CausalForestDML	39x

Table 10.2 – Relative training times of six different EconML CATE estimators

In *Table 10.2*, the right column displays the time taken by each model to complete its training in comparison to the S-Learner baseline. For instance, *2x* means that a model needed twice as much time as S-Learner to finish the training.

All the models were trained on the three-level treatment scenario, using the same dataset, with identical base estimators and default hyperparameters.

T-Learner needs twice as much training time as S-Learner, and Causal Forest with DML needs a stunning 39 times more time! Just to give you an understanding of the magnitude of this difference: if S-Learner trained for 20 minutes, Causal Forest would need 13 hours!

Computational cost becomes an important factor whenever we design a production-grade system. Causal Forest with DML might easily become prohibitively expensive on very large datasets, especially if we add hyperparameter tuning to the mix.

Our models are trained. Let's think about how to evaluate them.

Uplift models and performance

There's a significant body of literature on evaluating uplift models. The most popular metrics include the **Qini coefficient** (Radcliffe, 2007) and the **Area Under the Uplift Curve** (**AUUC**; Rzepakowski & Jaroszewicz, 2010).

The Qini coefficient is a single-scalar model quality summary that is based on a comparison between the Qini curve for an actual model and a random model. The Qini curve shows the cumulative number of positive outcomes scaled by the number of treated units.

The AUUC is based on a similar idea – it measures the area under the cumulative uplift curve. We plot uplift on the *y* axis against the percentage of observed units (the cumulative percentage of our sample size) *sorted by* model predictions on the *x* axis and calculate the area under the curve.

The AUUC and Qini are very popular and you can find many open source implementations for these metrics (for instance, in the `uplift-analysis` package: `https://bit.ly/UpliftAnalysis`). Both metrics were originally designed for scenarios with binary treatments and binary outcomes. Another popular choice for uplift model performance assessment is the **uplift by decile** (or uplift by percentile) plot.

You might be wondering – why are we talking about metrics and plots that are *cumulative* or *per decile*? The answer is related to the nature of the problem we're tackling: we never observe the true uplift (aka the true causal effect).

Let's take a look at *uplift by decile* and explain it step by step. It turns out that we can generalize it naturally to continuous outcomes. That's good news!

Uplift by decile

When we run an experiment, we can never observe all potential outcomes for a given unit at the same time. Each unit or subject can either receive treatment, T, or not receive it.

When we run a randomized experiment, we try to overcome this inherent limitation by computing group effects, assuming that the results will be generalizable (we could validly ask to what extent and under what conditions, but we will skip these questions here).

In other words, if we take a group of subjects and randomly assign them to experimental conditions, we hope that we can learn something about the general effect of the treatment.

Uplift by decile draws from the same source.

We divide the dataset into bins and assume we can learn something about the true effect within each bin. We leverage this information to assess the quality of our models.

How exactly do we do this?

1. First, we generate predictions from our models.
2. Next, we sort the predictions from the highest to the lowest predicted uplift.
3. We bin our predictions into deciles (in case of smaller datasets or when it's impossible to split the data into deciles, quantiles of smaller granularity can also be used, for example, quartiles).
4. We split the observations in our dataset into 10 bins according to the deciles we've just calculated.
5. Within each decile, we compute the average outcome for the units that were originally treated and the average outcome for the units that were originally in the control group.
6. Within each decile, we subtract the average outcome for untreated from the average outcome for treated.

   These differences are our estimates of the *true uplift* within each decile.
7. We use a bar plot to visualize these estimates against the deciles, ordered from the top to the bottom decile (left to right).

Figure 10.11 presents an example of an uplift by decile plot:

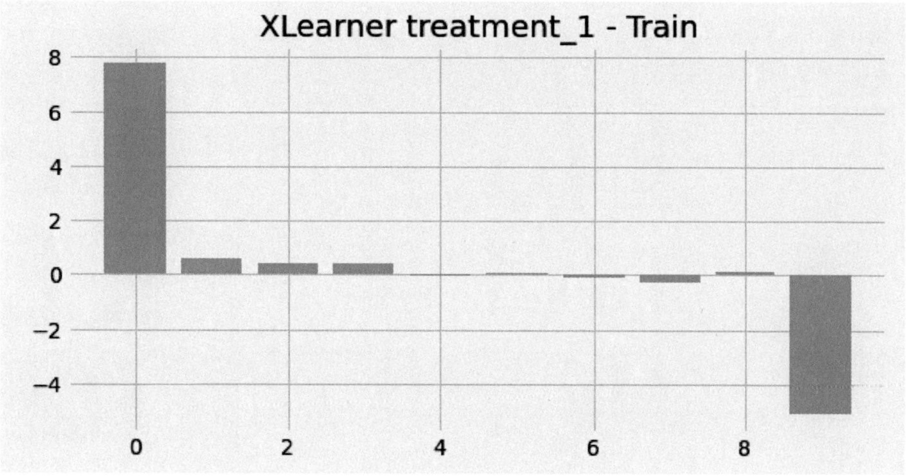

Figure 10.11 – An example of an uplift by decile plot

Let's take a closer look at *Figure 10.11*. The *x* axis represents deciles. The *y* axis represents our estimated average true uplift.

The *true meaning* of this plot comes from the fact that the deciles are *not* sorted by the *estimated true uplift* that we actually see in the plot but rather by our *predicted uplifts* (which are not visible in the plot).

How does this make sense?

We expect that the output of a good model will correlate with the true uplift – we'd like to see a high estimated true uplift in the top deciles (on the left) and a low estimated true uplift in the bottom deciles (on the right).

Figure 10.11 presents the results from a really good model as we can see that higher values are on the left and lower values are on the right.

In the case of a perfect model, the values on the *y* axis should *monotonically* go down from left to right. We see that in *Figure 10.11*, this is not entirely the case, with minor deviations on the fifth and eighth ticks (note that the *x* axis is 0-indexed), but overall, the pattern indicates a very good model.

Uplift by decile can be a good way to quickly visually assess the model, yet it doesn't provide us with the means to quantitatively compare various models.

We will use another tool for this purpose, but first, let's plot uplift by decile for all of our models. *Figure 10.12* presents the results:

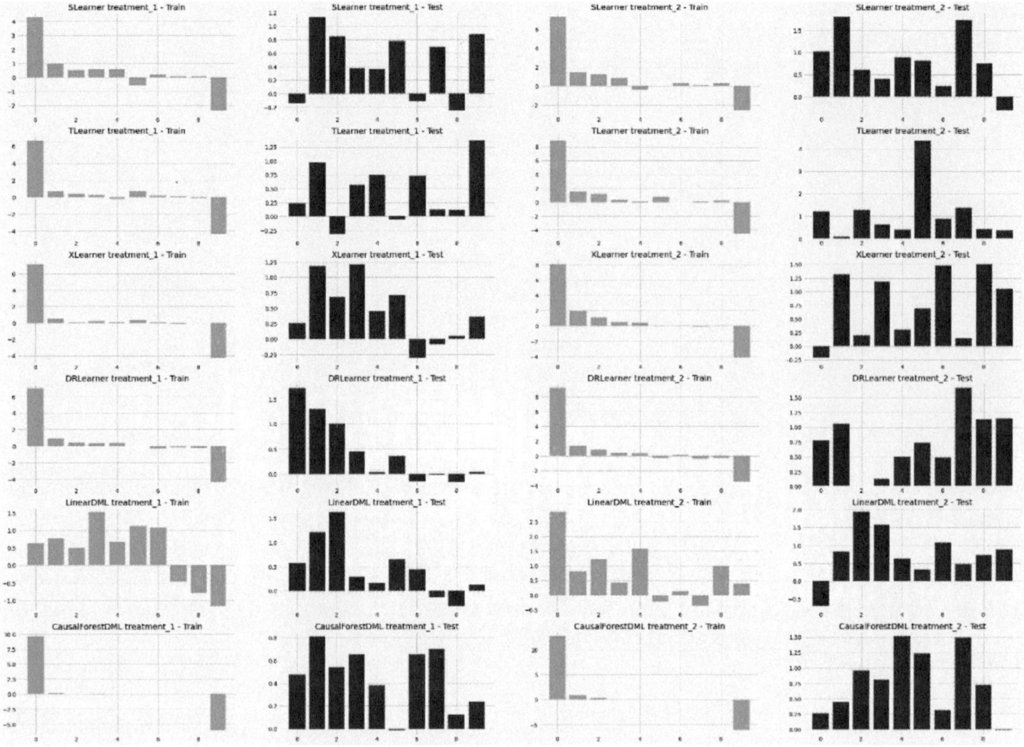

Figure 10.12 – Uplift by decile plots

Each row in *Figure 10.12* corresponds to one model. The leftmost two columns present the results for treatment 1, and the rightmost two columns for treatment 2. Blue plots represent the evaluation on training data, while red ones the evaluation on the test data. Note that the *y* axes are not normalized. We did this on purpose to more clearly see the patterns between different models.

According to the criteria that we discussed earlier, we can say that most models perform very well on the training data. One exception is linear DML, with a less clear downward pattern. One reason for this might be the fact that the last stage in linear DML is… linear, which imposes a restriction on the model's expressivity.

When it comes to the test set, the performance of most models drops significantly. Most cells in the plot indicate poor performance. DR-Learner for treatment 1 is a strong exception, but the same model for treatment 2 gives almost a reversed pattern!

There might be a couple of reasons for this poor performance on the test set:

- First, our models might be overfitting to the training data. This can be related to the fact that there is not enough data for the models to build a generalizable representation.
- The second side of the same coin is that the architectures we used might be too complex for the task (note that we picked hyperparameters arbitrarily, without tuning the models at all).
- Finally, there might be some instability in the per-decile estimates of true uplift, yet the results on the train set suggest that this is likely not the main issue.

The fact that uplift per decile plots do not look favorable does not necessarily imply that our models are not useful.

Let's compute a metric that will help us assess whether the models can bring us some real value.

Expected response

The **expected response metric** was introduced by Yan Zhao and colleagues in their 2017 paper *Uplift Modeling with Multiple Treatments and General Response Types* (Zhao et al., 2017). The method works in multiple-treatment scenarios and with continuous outcomes, which is perfect for our case.

Although the metric is focused on the outcome rather than on uplift, it's a valid way to evaluate uplift models. The metric computes the expected average outcome of a model by combining information from all the treatments. That's very handy.

At the same time, the metric is also useful from a decision-making point of view as it gives us a good understanding of what average return on investment we can expect by employing a chosen model.

Intuitively, the metric works for uplift models because we use previously unseen data to check the expected return on investment for a given model. This information can be used to compare two or more models under unconfoundedness and obtain information on the expected performance of out-of-sample data.

Before we explain how the expected response metric works, let's get some context. Uplift models can be understood as **action recommendation systems**.

Imagine we have k different treatments. For each observation in the dataset, we can obtain k effect estimates – one for each treatment. We can pick the highest estimate for each observation and treat it as a predicted optimal treatment.

Now to the explanation.

The idea behind the *expected response* is simple. For each observation in the test set, we check whether the predicted treatment was the same as the actual treatment. If so, we divide the value of the outcome for this observation by the probability of the treatment and store it. Otherwise, we set the value to 0 and store it. Finally, we average over the stored values and the obtained score is our *expected response* for a given model.

This basically gives us a treatment-weighted average outcome that we expect to get if we administer treatments according to the model's recommendations.

I put the formula for the expected response metric in the notebook for this chapter. We'll skip it here, but feel free to explore the notebook and play with the implementation and the formula.

Now, let's see the results for the expected response (the full code is in the notebook):

```
Expected response on train:

SLearner: 2.004509358884219
TLearner: 2.499033323345889
XLearner: 2.3844783394170035
DRLearner: 2.357949913732327
LinearDML: 1.5596898804820036
CausalForestDML: 2.9583483277085936

------------------------------
Expected response on test:

SLearner: 1.3498049695400602
TLearner: 1.2108070097957537
XLearner: 1.2901946274863276
DRLearner: 1.500974856751045
LinearDML: 1.3496321556492639
CausalForestDML: 1.3114730998145985
```

We see that the metric for all models significantly dropped between the train and test sets. The smallest difference can be observed for the linear DML model. This is congruent with what we observed in the uplift by decile plot – linear DML performed relatively poorly on the training data and slightly worse on the test data.

The best model on the test set according to the *expected response* is DR-Learner. This also translates – at least partially – to what we observed in the plot. DR-Learner had a pretty clear downward trend for treatment 1. Perhaps this good performance on treatment 1 allowed the model to compensate for the worse performance on treatment 2.

Other metrics for continuous outcomes with multiple treatments

Radcliffe proposed a version of Qini that is applicable to continuous outcome problems (Radcliffe, 2007), but it does not work with multiple treatments.

A multi-treatment generalization has been proposed by Gubela & Lessmann (2020). Check out their article for more details: `https://bit.ly/MultiTreatQini`.

Confidence intervals

We said before that one of the advantages of linear DML is its ability to provide us with valid confidence intervals. How can we obtain them in practice?

With EconML, it's very easy. We simply call the `.effect_interval()` method on the fitted estimator. The method returns a two-tuple of numpy arrays. The first array contains the lower bounds and the second the upper bounds of the confidence intervals.

Let's implement it!

```
models['LinearDML'].effect_interval(X=X_test, T0=0, T1=1)
```

The output is as expected:

```
(array([-1.41417908, -0.40901173, -1.50891344, ..., -0.27946152,
-0.8185368 , -0.92689394]),
 array([0.88022207, 1.03706657, 3.34888932, ..., 2.47925003,
1.75716167, 1.51788005]))
```

Based on the confidence intervals, we can decide whether there are observations that we'd like to exclude from targeting. Let's see how many intervals contain 0:

```
ints = np.stack(models['LinearDML'].effect_interval(
    X=X_test, T0=0, T1=1, alpha=.05)).T
# What % of effects contains zero?
(np.sign(ints[:, 0]) == np.sign(ints[:, 1])).sum() /
    ints.shape[0]
```

This gives us the following:

```
0.100875
```

Out of all the test observations, confidence intervals for 10% of them contain 0. Removing these observations from our action recommendation set could perhaps further improve the model's performance.

To obtain confidence intervals for methods that do not support them natively, pass `inference='bootstrap'` to the model's `.fit()` method. Note that this will result in a significant increase in training time. The number of bootstrap samples can be adjusted by using the `BootstrapInference` object. For more details, check out `https://bit.ly/EconMLBootstrapDocs`.

Kevin's challenge's winning submission

At the beginning of this section, we said that the data we were using was part of a challenge. The submission that Kevin Hillstrom picked as the winning one came from Nicholas Radcliffe.

Does this name ring a bell for you?

If it sounds oddly familiar, it might be because we've already seen it (that is, the last name) in this chapter. Nicholas Radcliffe is not only the author of the winning submission in Kevin's challenge but also the person who originally proposed the Qini coefficient (and the Qini curve).

If you're interested in uplift modeling and marketing, you might find Nicholas' submission interesting or even inspiring. The document describing Nicholas' approach is available here: `https://bit.ly/NicksSolution`.

Before we close this section, I want us to think about a question that I received from one of the members of the **causalpython.io** community.

When should we use CATE estimators for experimental data?

Organizations – both commercial and non-commercial – usually decide to perform experiments in order to answer particular questions. A commercial organization might ask questions such as what impact a change in our funnel page design will have on our sales. A university research team might be interested in learning how a change in communication style from the municipality will impact citizens' engagement in an important public initiative.

These questions can often be answered using randomized experiments and – in many cases – traditional statistical analyses.

A two-sample sample *t-Test* (Student, 1908) is a popular choice for analyzing the data from binary treatment experiments. For more complex designs, perhaps involving hierarchical structures, *mixed-effect models* can be used (e.g., Baayen et al., 2008; Barr, 2008). We also have a large variety of methods in between, including (but not limited to) regression analysis and – closely related to the latter – ANOVA.

All these methods can help us make valid conclusions from experimental data.

> **Experiments, treatment effects, and generalization**
>
> What *valid conclusions* from experiments really mean and what the generalizability guarantees are are beyond the scope of this book. If you're interested in understanding the intricacies of the relationships between experimental results, the ATE, and transportability (the generalizability of results beyond the test (sub)population), this Twitter conversation involving Judea Pearl, Frank Harrell, and Stephen Senn, among others, might be interesting to you: `https://bit.ly/GeneralizationDiscussion`.

Machine learning methods come in handy when the feature space is large and when relationships and interactions in the data can take arbitrary functional forms. CATE methods in particular give us additional flexibility by enabling us to predict individualized responses to a (potentially high) number of treatments under high model complexity. These quasi-counterfactual capabilities go beyond what traditional statistical methods can offer us.

Uplift (CATE and HTE) modeling techniques have been proven to bring value in numerous industrial settings from marketing and banking to gaming and more.

The main price that we pay for the flexibility offered by CATE machine learning models is the difficulty of computing the sample size necessary to establish the desired statistical power. In *Chapter 9*, we discussed some ideas of how to overcome this limitation.

The main advantage of CATE machine learning models is that they give us a way to non- or semi-parametrically distinguish the units that can benefit from obtaining our treatment (*persuadables*) from those that will most likely not benefit from it (*sure things* and *lost causes*) and those who will likely not benefit but can additionally get hurt or hurt us (*do not disturbs*; check *Chapter 9* and *Table 9.5* for a refresher).

More ways to determine the sample size for complex models

When it comes to estimating statistical power for complex models, there's a smart trick that I recently learned from Frank Harrell (`https://bit.ly/FrankHarrell`). If you can afford a pilot study or you have some historical data that represents a problem similar to the one that you're interested in, you can find a subgroup in your data that is as homogenous as possible. You can estimate the sample size for this group using some of the traditional statistical power tools. Finally, scale your overall sample size so that this subgroup is properly powered relative to the entire sample (Harrell, 2023).

Model selection – a simplified guide

Before closing this section, I want to share a simple table with you, where we summarize key information about the models we discussed in this chapter. I hope that this will help you get the most out of this chapter.

Table 10.3 summarizes important aspects of various EconML estimators that can help you guide your implementation decisions:

Model name	Treatment type	Confidence intervals	Linear treatment assumed	Multiple outcomes	Training speed (relative to S-Learner)
`SLearner`	Categorical (can be adapted to continuous)	Only by bootstrapping	No	Yes	1x
`TLearner`	Categorical	Only by bootstrapping	No	Yes	2x
`XLearner`	Categorical	Only by bootstrapping	No	Yes	5x
`DRLearner`	Categorical	Only by bootstrapping	No	No	13x
`LinearDML`	Categorical, continuous	Natively	Yes	Yes	27x
`CausalForestDML`	Categorical, continuous	Bag-of-little-bootstraps or by (conventional) bootstrapping	Yes	Yes	39x

Table 10.3 – Comparison of selected EconML estimators

For an even more comprehensive comparison between EconML estimators, check out this documentation page: `https://bit.ly/EconMLComparison`.

For more performance comparisons between various machine learning methods for CATE (meta-learners, DR, and more) on experimental data, check Jacob (2021).

Now, it's time to conclude this section.

We started this section with a brief discussion on using CATE models with experimental data and the EconML workflow tailored to experimental scenarios.

After that, we introduced the Hillstrom dataset and tested whether our data is unconfounded under observed variables. We fitted six different models and compared their performance from a computational cost point of view.

We introduced popular evaluation tools for uplift models: the Qini coefficient, the AUUC, and uplift by decile. We used the latter and the generalized *expected response metric* to compare our models' performance.

Finally, we showed how to obtain confidence intervals from EconML estimators, discussed when using CATE machine learning models with experimental data can be beneficial, and shared a comprehensive causal estimator comparison table.

In the next short section, we'll discuss the idea of using machine learning for counterfactual explanations.

Extra – counterfactual explanations

Imagine that you apply for a loan from your bank. You prepared well – you checked your credit score and other variables that could affect the bank's decision. You're pretty sure that your application will be approved.

On Wednesday morning, you see an email from your bank in your inbox. You're extremely excited! You open the message, already celebrating and ready to welcome the success!

There's a surprise in the email.

Your loan application has been rejected.

You call the bank. You ask questions. You want to understand why. At the end of the day, its decision impacts some of your most important plans!

The only response you get from the customer service representative is that *you did not meet the criteria*. "*Which criteria?*" you ask. You don't get a satisfying answer.

You'd like to make sure that you meet the criteria the next time you re-apply, yet it seems that no one can tell you *how* to improve!

Bad faith or tech that does not know?

Does the lack of answers come from bank employees' unwillingness to help?

Not necessarily. Some organizations might not be technically ready to answer questions like ours. How could we help them change this?

Let's recall the idea behind S-Learner.

First, we train a single model on our data. Then, we generate predictions for different values of the treatment variable and perform a simple subtraction. This idea is very flexible. What if we extended it to other variables that we did not treat as the treatment before?

Theoretically (depending on the setting), this could mess up the causal character of the model.

Do we care?

If our goal is to answer the question *What should be done?* in order to *change the output of the model*, we actually do not.

Why?

We're performing an *intervention on the model* and we're interested in the *model's behavior*, not in how accurately it represents an underlying process.

Interventions such as this provide us with valid results *given our goal*.

In a sense, this approach is even simpler than S-Learner as we're only interested in finding minimal changes to the data that would result in the expected change of the outcome, so we don't even need to calculate the causal effect. There are some challenges that come with this approach, though.

What if we need to change more than one feature in order to influence the outcome because there's an interaction between these features? What if there are many ways to change the outcome and some are much easier, but we've only found the hardest one?

To address this and other issues, Microsoft released an open source package called **Diverse Counterfactual Explanations** (**DiCE**; Mothilal et al., 2020). The basic intuition behind DiCE is that it searches for a set of changes in the input features that lead to the outcome change, at the same time maximizing the proximity to the original values and diversity (finding many different solutions to the same problem to let us choose the best one). If you want to learn more about DiCE, check out the introductory blog post by Amit Sharma (`https://bit.ly/DiCEIntro`) and DiCE's GitHub repository (`https://bit.ly/DiCERepo`).

Note that depending on the industry sector and geopolitical region, usage of methods such as the ones we discussed previously might be difficult due to particular regulatory requirements. DiCE offers a smart set of tools that can help when sensitive data is at stake.

In cases where complex machine learning models might be difficult to apply due to interpretability requirements, logic similar to that we discussed at the beginning of this section can be implemented with simple linear models.

In this short extra section, we discussed basic ideas behind counterfactual model explanations and introduced DiCE – an open source Python library that helps analysts perform counterfactual inferences easily in more complex cases.

Wrapping it up

Congratulations! You just reached the end of *Chapter 10*.

In this chapter, we introduced four new causal estimators: DR-Learner, TMLE, DML, and Causal Forest. We used two of them on our synthetic earnings dataset, comparing their performance to the meta-learners from *Chapter 9*.

After that, we learned about the differences in workflows between observational and experimental data and fit six different models to the Hillstrom dataset. We discussed popular metrics used to evaluate uplift models and learned how to use confidence intervals for EconML estimators. We discussed when using machine learning models for heterogeneous treatment effects can be beneficial from an experimental point of view. Finally, we summarized the differences between different models and closed the chapter with a short discussion on counterfactual model explanations.

In the next chapter, we'll continue our journey through the land of causal inference with machine learning, and with *Chapter 12*, we'll open the door to the last part of the book, dedicated to causal discovery. See you!

References

Athey, S., Tibshirani, J., & Wager, S. (2018). *Generalized random forests. The Annals of Statistics*, 47(2). 1148-1178.

Balestriero, R., Pesenti, J., & LeCun, Y. (2021). *Learning in High Dimension Always Amounts to Extrapolation.* arXiv, abs/2110.09485.

Barr, D. J. (2008). *Analyzing "visual world" eyetracking data using multilevel logistic regression.* J. Mem. Lang. 59, 457-474.

Baayen, R. H., Davidson, D. J., and Bates, D. M. (2008). *Mixed-effects modeling with crossed random effects for subjects and items.* J. Mem. Lang. 59, 390-412.

Bühlmann, P. & van de Geer, S. A. (2011). *Statistics for High-Dimensional Data.* Springer.

Cassel, C.M., Särndal, C., & Wretman, J. H. (1976). *Some results on generalized difference estimation and generalized regression estimation for finite populations.* Biometrika, 63, 615-620.

Chernozhukov, V., Chetverikov, D., Demirer, M., Duflo, E., Hansen, C., Newey, W., & Robins, J. M. (2018). *Double/debiased machine learning for treatment and structural parameters.* The Econometrics Journal, 21(1), C1-C68. `https://academic.oup.com/ectj/article/21/1/C1/5056401`.

Chernozhukov, V., Cinelli, C., Newey, W., Sharma, A., & Syrgkanis, V. (2022). *Long Story Short: Omitted Variable Bias in Causal Machine Learning (Working Paper No. 30302; Working Paper Series).* National Bureau of Economic Research. `https://doi.org/10.3386/w30302`.

Cinelli, C., Forney, A., & Pearl, J. (2022). *A crash course in good and bad controls.* Sociological Methods & Research, 00491241221099552.

Clement, Z. (2023, February 8). *Estimating causal effects under sparsity using the econml package.* Medium. `https://medium.com/@clementzach_38631/estimating-causal-effects-under-sparsity-using-the-econml-package-153b787cb2b1`.

Courthoud, M. (2022, July 19). *Understanding AIPW, the Doubly-Robust Estimator.* Towards Data Science; Medium. `https://towardsdatascience.com/understanding-aipw-ed4097dab27a`.

Diemert, E., Betlei, A., Renaudin, C., & Amini, M. R. (2018). *A Large Scale Benchmark for Uplift Modeling*. KDD.

Ding, P. & Li, F. (2018). *Causal Inference: A Missing Data Perspective*. Statist. Sci. 33(2), 214-237.

Díaz, I. (2020). *Machine learning in the estimation of causal effects: targeted minimum loss-based estimation and double/debiased machine learning, Biostatistics, 21(2). 353-358.* `https://doi.org/10.1093/biostatistics/kxz042`.

Facure, M. A. (2020). *Causal Inference for The Brave and True*. `https://matheusfacure.github.io/python-causality-handbook/landing-page.html`.

Gordon, B. R., Moakler, R., & Zettelmeyer, F. (2022). *Close Enough? A Large-Scale Exploration of Non-Experimental Approaches to Advertising Measurement*. arXiv. `https://doi.org/10.48550/ARXIV.2201.07055`.

Green, J. & White, M. H., II. (2023). *Machine Learning for Experiments in the Social Sciences*. Cambridge University Press.

Gruber, S. & van der Laan, M. J. (2010). *A Targeted Maximum Likelihood Estimator of a Causal Effect on a Bounded Continuous Outcome*. The International Journal of Biostatistics, 6(1), 26. `https://doi.org/10.2202/1557-4679.1260`.

Gubela, R. & Lessmann, S. (2020). *Uplift Forest for Multiple Treatments and Continuous Outcomes*. International Conference on Information Systems.

Harrell, F. [@f2harrell]. (2023, March 2). *This is a difficult case. Sometimes one must have pilot data to do meaningful calculations*. [Tweet]. Twitter. `https://twitter.com/f2harrell/status/1631281762075590656`.

Hernán M. A. & Robins J. M. (2020). *Causal Inference: What If*. Boca Raton: Chapman & Hall/CRC.

Holland, P. (1986). *Statistics and Causal Inference*. Journal of the American Statistical Association, 81, 945-960.

Huang, J., Yehdego, D., & Siddarth, K. (2020, November 5). *Causal inference (Part 2 of 3): Selecting algorithms*. Medium. `https://medium.com/data-science-at-microsoft/causal-inference-part-2-of-3-selecting-algorithms-a966f8228a2d`.

Hünermund, P., Louw, B., & Caspi, I. (2022). *Double Machine Learning and Automated Confounder Selection – A Cautionary Tale*. arXiv. `https://doi.org/10.48550/ARXIV.2108.11294`.

Jacob, D. (2021). *CATE meets ML - Conditional Average Treatment Effect and Machine Learning*. Accounting Technology & Information System eJournal.

Kang, J. D. Y. & Schafer, J. L. (2007). *Demystifying Double Robustness: A Comparison of Alternative Strategies for Estimating a Population Mean from Incomplete Data*. Statist. Sci. 22(4), 523-539.

Kennedy, E. H. (2020). *Towards optimal doubly robust estimation of heterogeneous causal effects.* arXiv: Statistics Theory. `https://arxiv.org/abs/2004.14497`.

Kohavi, R., Tang, D., & Xu, Y. (2020). Twyman's Law and Experimentation Trustworthiness. *In Trustworthy Online Controlled Experiments: A Practical Guide to A/B Testing (pp. 39-57).* Cambridge: Cambridge University Press.

Li, F. (2020). *Comment: Stabilizing the Doubly-Robust Estimators of the Average Treatment Effect under Positivity Violations.* Statist. Sci. 35(3), 503-510. `https://doi.org/10.1214/20-STS774`.

Li, F. (2021). STA 640 — *Causal Inference. Chapter 3.5. Doubly Robust and Augmented Estimators [Course materials].* Department of Statistical Science. Duke University. `http://www2.stat.duke.edu/~fl35/teaching/640/Chap3.5_Doubly%20Robust%20Estimation.pdf`.

Lopez-Paz, D. & Oquab, M. (2016). *Revisiting classifier two-sample tests.* arXiv.

Mohan, K. & Pearl, J. (2021). *Graphical Models for Processing Missing Data.* Journal of the American Statistical Association, 116, 1023-1037.

Mothilal, R. K., Sharma, A., & Tan, C. (2020). *Explaining machine learning classifiers through diverse counterfactual explanations.* Proceedings of the 2020 Conference on Fairness, Accountability, and Transparency, 607-617.

Oprescu, M., Syrgkanis, V., & Wu, Z. S. (2019). *Orthogonal Random Forest for Causal Inference.* Proceedings of the 36th International Conference on Machine Learning, in Proceedings of Machine Learning Research, 97, 4932-4941. `https://proceedings.mlr.press/v97/oprescu19a.html`.

Porter, K. E., Gruber, S., van der Laan, M. J., & Sekhon, J. S. (2011). *The Relative Performance of Targeted Maximum Likelihood Estimators.* The International Journal of Biostatistics, 7(1), 31. `https://doi.org/10.2202/1557-4679.1308`.

Radcliffe, N. (2007). *Using control groups to target on predicted lift: Building and assessing uplift model.* Direct Marketing Analytics Journal, 3, 14-21.

Robins, J. M., Rotnitzky, A., & Zhao, L. P. (1994). *Estimation of Regression Coefficients When Some Regressors are not Always Observed.* Journal of the American Statistical Association, 89, 846-866.

Rosenbaum, P. R. & Rubin, D. B. (1983). *The central role of the propensity score in observational studies for causal effects.* Biometrika, 70, 41-55.

Rzepakowski, P. & Jaroszewicz, S. (2010). *Decision Trees for Uplift Modeling.* 2010 IEEE International Conference on Data Mining, 441-450.

Schuler, M. S. & Rose, S. (2017). *Targeted maximum likelihood estimation for causal inference in observational studies.* American Journal of Epidemiology, 185(1), 65-73.

Student. (1908). *The probable error of a mean.* Biometrika, 1-25.

Tan, X., Yang, S., Ye, W., Faries, D. E., Lipkovich, I., & Kadziola, Z. (2022). *When Doubly Robust Methods Meet Machine Learning for Estimating Treatment Effects from Real-World Data: A Comparative Study.* arXiv. `https://doi.org/10.48550/ARXIV.2204.10969`

van de Geer, S.A., Buhlmann, P., Ritov, Y., & Dezeure, R. (2013). *On asymptotically optimal confidence regions and tests for high-dimensional models.* Annals of Statistics, 42, 1166-1202.

van der Laan, M. & Hejazi, N. (2019, December 24). *CV-TMLE and double machine learning. vanderlaan-lab.org.* `https://vanderlaan-lab.org/2019/12/24/cv-tmle-and-double-machine-learning/`

van der Laan, M. & Rubin, D. (2006). *Targeted Maximum Likelihood Learning.* The International Journal of Biostatistics, 2(1). `https://doi.org/10.2202/1557-4679.1043`

Wager, S. & Athey, S. (2018). *Estimation and Inference of Heterogeneous Treatment Effects using Random Forests.* Journal of the American Statistical Association, 113(523), 1228–1242. `https://doi.org/10.1080/01621459.2017.1319839`

Xu, K., Li, J., Zhang, M., Du, S. S., Kawarabayashi, K., & Jegelka, S. (2020). *How Neural Networks Extrapolate: From Feedforward to Graph Neural Networks.* arXiv, abs/2009.11848.

Zhao, Yan, Xiao Fang, and David Simchi-Levi. *Uplift Modeling with Multiple Treatments and General Response Types.* Proceedings of the 2017 SIAM International Conference on Data Mining (June 9, 2017): 588–596.

11

Causal Inference and Machine Learning – Deep Learning, NLP, and Beyond

You've come a long way! Congratulations!

Chapter 11 marks an important turning point in our journey into causality. With this chapter, we'll conclude our adventure in the land of causal inference and prepare to venture into the uncharted territory of causal discovery.

Before we move on, let's take a closer look at what deep learning has to offer in the realm of causal inference.

We'll start by taking a step back and recalling the mechanics behind two models that we introduced in *Chapter 9* – S-Learner and T-Learner.

We'll explore how flexible deep learning architectures can help us combine the advantages of both models, and we'll implement some of these architectures using the PyTorch-based CATENets library.

Next, we'll explore how causality and **natural language processing** (**NLP**) intersect, and we'll learn how to enhance modern Transformer architectures with causal capabilities, using Huggingface Transformers and PyTorch.

After that, we'll take a sneak peek into the world of econometrics and quasi-experimental time series data, learning how to implement a Bayesian synthetic control estimator using CausalPy.

Ready?

In this chapter, we will cover the following:

- Conditional average treatment effects (ATEs) with deep learning
- Causal NLP with Transformers
- Bayesian synthetic control

Going deeper – deep learning for heterogeneous treatment effects

Since modern deep learning started gaining traction in the early 2010s, we have seen a continuous progression of breakthroughs. From AlexNet (Krizhevsky et al., 2012), which revolutionized computer vision, through Word2vec (Mikolov et al., 2013), which changed the face of NLP forever, to Transformers (Vaswani et al., 2017) and modern generative architectures (e.g. Radford et al., 2021, and Rombach et al., 2022), which fueled the generative AI explosion of 2022-2023.

Although the core idea behind (supervised) deep learning is associative in its nature and, as such, belongs to rung one of the **Ladder of Causation**, the flexibility of the framework can be leveraged to improve and extend existing causal inference methods.

In this section, we will introduce deep learning architectures to model **heterogeneous treatment effects** (aka **conditional treatment effects** (**CATE**)). We'll discuss the advantages of using deep learning to model CATE and implement two key architectures, using the PyTorch-based CATENets library (Curth & van der Schaar, 2021a).

CATE goes deeper

Differentiable deep learning architectures make it easy to arrange information flows in virtually any possible way. This opens the door to a whole new world of possibilities.

In *Chapter 9*, we introduced **S-Learner** and **T-Learner** algorithms. We saw that one of the advantages of S-Learner compared to T-Learner is sample efficiency.

S-Learner uses a single base-learner model and trains it with all available data. Meanwhile, T-Learner uses treated observations and control observations to train two separate base models.

One of the advantages of T-Learner is that by learning two separate response functions, it can be more effective in modeling these functions when they significantly differ.

What if we could combine the advantages of both models in one single architecture?

TARNet

The **Treatment-Agnostic Representation Network** (**TARNet**) is a neural network architecture, introduced by Uri Shalit from Technion (back then at NYU) and his colleagues in the 2017 ICML paper *Estimating individual treatment effect: generalization bounds and algorithms* (Shalit et al., 2017).

The architecture consists of a block of shared layers, trained using all available data, and two disjoint regression heads, trained using treated or control data, respectively. Intuitively, this architecture combines the sample efficiency of S-Learner thanks to shared layers and the flexibility of T-Learner thanks to disjoint regression heads.

Note that this solution also combats the greatest weakness of S-Learner – namely, the risk that a treatment variable will not be taken into account in the shared representation.

Figure 11.1 presents the TARNet architecture symbolically:

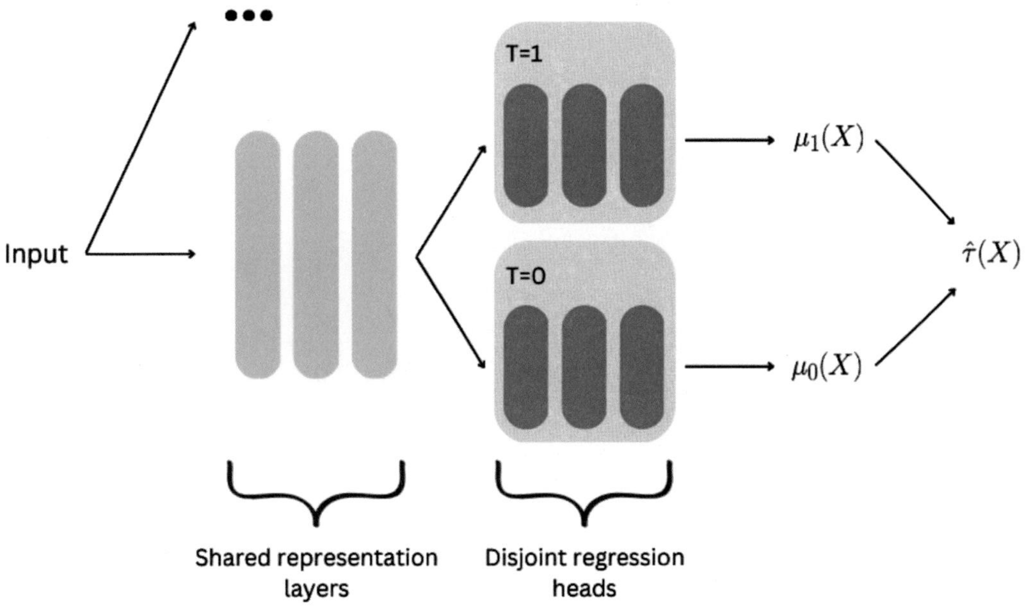

Figure 11.1 – A simplified TARNet architecture

As you can see in *Figure 11.1*, the first layers of TARNet (*shared representation layers*) leverage all the data. Then, the information flow is split between treatment- and control-specific heads (*disjoint regression heads*). The output from these heads are used to compute CATE.

In addition to what we see in *Figure 11.1*, TARNet uses an extra component that computes the discrepancy between the treatment and control covariate representations, which can be used to balance these representations when needed, analogously to the **propensity score** (marked symbolically by three dots in *Figure 11.1*, with details skipped for the clarity of presentation).

TARNet has been demonstrated to perform competitively or outperform a number of other architectures (Shalit et al., 2017, and Curth & van der Schaar, 2021a).

SNet

SNet (Curth & van Der Schaar, 2021a) is a deep learning-based architecture that can be thought of as a generalization of TARNet (and other architectures such as DragonNet (Shi et al., 2019) and DR-CFR (Hassanpour & Greiner, 2020)).

SNet consists of a set of parallel early layers trained on all data. In particular, SNet learns five different representations and feeds them to three disjoint heads – two regression heads (representing the outcome model) and one propensity score head (representing the treatment model).

The *S* in SNet's name comes from the fact that the information from the early representations in the network is shared between the latter task-specific heads.

Figure 11.2 presents the SNet architecture symbolically:

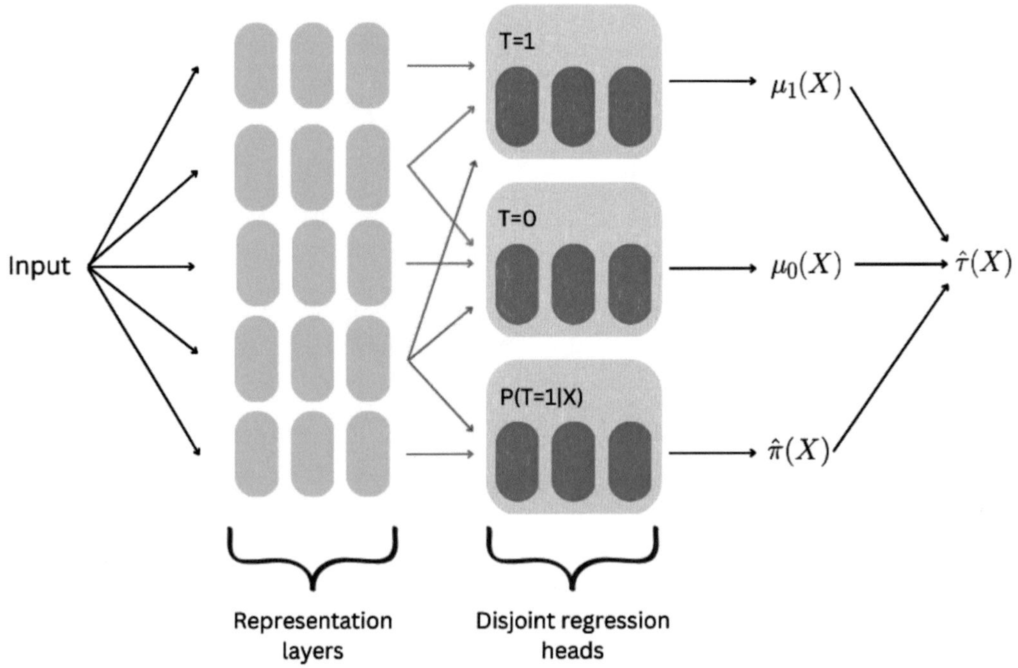

Figure 11.2 – A simplified SNet architecture

In *Figure 11.2*, we can see that the signal from each of the five representation layers (yellow) flows to a different set of regression heads. Blue arrows indicate flow to just a single head, while green and orange arrows indicate flow to multiple heads.

As all representations are learned jointly, the distinction between them might not be well identified. The authors add a regularization term to the model objective that "*enforces orthogonalization of inputs to (...) different layers*" (Curth & van der Schaar, 2021).

The authors demonstrate that SNet outperforms TARNet and neural network versions of T-Learner and DR-Learner over multiple synthetic and semi-synthetic datasets.

SNet's additional flexibility might come at a price of more challenges when fitting the algorithm, as might be the case with any complex architecture.

We will now implement TARNet and SNet using the **CATENets** library.

Let's meet CATENets.

CATENets

CATENets was developed by Alicia Curth, a researcher at the van der Schaar Lab at Cambridge University, led by Mihaela van der Schaar. The library is built on top of JAX (Bradbury et al., 2018) and provides a range of deep learning architectures to estimate CATE, including TARNet and SNet.

Additionally, the library includes implementations of three original algorithms proposed by Curth and van der Schaar – SNet (Curth & van der Schaar, 2021a), FlexTENet, and OffsetNet (Curth & van der Schaar, 2021b).

Most of the models are also available as PyTorch (Paszke et al., 2017) implementations (kindly contributed by Bogdan Cebere – `https://github.com/bcebere`). We'll use these implementations in the subsequent code examples.

CATENets offers a very convenient and intuitive scikit-learn-style API.

> **PyTorch**
>
> PyTorch (Paszke et al., 2017) is an open source deep learning framework, originally developed by the Meta AI (Facebook AI) team and currently governed by the PyTorch Foundation. Version 2.0 was released in March 2023, introducing a number of features that can speed up PyTorch in numerous scenarios. In recent years, PyTorch has gained significant traction, especially in the research community. The models that we will experiment with in this chapter (CATENets and CausalBert) use PyTorch behind the scenes. In *Part 3*, *Causal Discovery*, we'll build a complete PyTorch training loop when implementing Microsoft's DECI model.

Experiments with CATENets

We'll use a simulated non-linear dataset with a binary treatment for our CATENets experiments.

You can find the code for this and the next section in the `Chapter_11.1.ipynb` notebook (`https://bit.ly/causal-ntbk-11_1`).

Let's start with the data:

```
import numpy as np

SAMPLE_SIZE = 5000
TRAIN_SIZE = 4500
N_FEATURES = 20

X = np.random.normal(0, 1, (SAMPLE_SIZE, N_FEATURES))
T = np.random.binomial(1, 0.5, SAMPLE_SIZE)

weights = np.random.gumbel(5, 10, (SAMPLE_SIZE,
    N_FEATURES - 1))

y = (50 * T * np.abs(X[:, 0])**1.2) + (weights * X[:,
    1:]).sum(axis=1)

y0 = (50 * 0 * np.abs(X[:, 0])**1.2) + (weights * X[:,
    1:]).sum(axis=1)
y1 = (50 * 1 * np.abs(X[:, 0])**1.2) + (weights * X[:,
    1:]).sum(axis=1)
effect_true = y1[TRAIN_SIZE:] - y0[TRAIN_SIZE:]
```

We generate 5,000 samples and split them into training and test sets containing 4500 and 500 observations, respectively. Our dataset has 20 features. The data is generated according to the following formula:

$$Y_i = \left(50 * T_i * abs\left(X_i^{(0)}\right)\right)^{1.2} + \sum_{d=1}^{D} w^{(d)} X_i^{(d)}$$

In the preceding formula:

- Y_i is the outcome of the i-th observation
- T_i is the treatment for the i-th observation
- $X_i^{(d)}$ is the d-th feature for the i-th observation
- $w^{(d)}$ is the weight for feature d
- $abs(.)$ is the absolute value operator

We pick weights at random, drawing from the Gumbel distribution.

As you can see in the preceding formula, the treatment effect is non-additive and non-linear (we have an absolute value and raise the interaction term to the *1.2*-th power). At the same time, only 1 out of 20 features we generated interacts with the treatment (feature $X^{(0)}$, which corresponds to `X[:, 0]` in the code snippet).

We'll use our dataset to fit S-Learner, X-Learner, DR-Learner, and Causal Forest as a baseline. Next, we'll fit TARNet and SNet.

Let's start with the necessary imports:

```
from catenets.models.torch import TARNet, SNet
from econml.metalearners import SLearner,
from econml.dr import LinearDRLearner
from econml.dml import CausalForestDML
from lightgbm import LGBMRegressor
```

We imported the `TARNet` and `SNet` classes from `catenets.models.torch` and added Causal Forest DML and the S-, X-, and DR-Learners from EconML.

We'll also import PyTorch (`torch`) and PyTorch Lightning (`pytorch_lightning`):

```
import torch
import pytorch_lightning as pl
```

Let's set the computational device using `torch`:

```
device = 'cuda' if torch.cuda.is_available() else 'cpu'
device
```

If you have a GPU installed in your system that is supported by PyTorch and you have properly configured the drivers, this will print the following:

```
'cuda'
```

Otherwise, you should see the following:

```
'cpu'
```

Computations on CPU-only machines will take more time, but we prepared the datasets in a way that should allow you to complete them in a reasonable time on a CPU.

Next, let's set the seed for reproducibility. PyTorch Lightning offers a convenience function to do so:

```
SEED = 18
pl.seed_everything(SEED)
```

Note that even using `pl.seed_everything()` does not always lead to the same results. To enforce fully the deterministic behavior of PyTorch, we would need to use `torch.use_deterministic_algorithms(True)` and freeze the randomness in data loaders. At the time of writing, this would require modifying environmental variables and CATENets code. We won't go that far and keep the results *weakly reproducible*. Be prepared for your results to differ.

To learn more about reproducibility in PyTorch, check out `https://bit.ly/PyTorchReproducibility`.

Let's fit the benchmark models first:

```
benchmark_models = {
    'SLearner': SLearner(overall_model=LGBMRegressor()),
    'XLearner': XLearner(models=LGBMRegressor()),
    'DRLearner': LinearDRLearner(),
    'CausalForest': CausalForestDML()
}

benchmark_results = {}

for model_name, model in benchmark_models.items():
    model.fit(
        X=X[:TRAIN_SIZE, :],
        T=T[:TRAIN_SIZE],
        Y=y[:TRAIN_SIZE]
    )

    effect_pred = model.effect(
        X[TRAIN_SIZE:]
    )

    benchmark_results[model_name] = effect_pred
```

We create a dictionary of models and iterate over it, fitting each model and storing the results in another dictionary called `benchmark_results`. We used LightGBM regressors for S- and X-Learner and default models for DR-Learner and Causal Forest.

Now, let's fit TARNet and SNet:

```
tarnet = TARNet(
    n_unit_in=X.shape[1],
    binary_y=False,
    n_units_out_prop=32,
    n_units_r=8,
    nonlin='selu',
)

tarnet.fit(
    X=X[:TRAIN_SIZE, :],
    y=y[:TRAIN_SIZE],
    w=T[:TRAIN_SIZE]
)
```

We need to specify a number of parameters to initialize the `TARNet` class:

- `n_unit_in` defines the number of features in our dataset. To keep the code dynamic, we pass the size of the first dimension of our dataset as an argument. This parameter is mandatory.
- `binary_y` informs the model whether the outcome is binary. Our dataset has a continuous outcome, so we set it to `False`. Internally, this parameter will control which loss function the model should use for the outcome model (binary cross-entropy for a binary outcome and mean squared error otherwise). This parameter is set to `False` by default, but I wanted to use it explicitly because it's an important one.
- `n_units_out_prop` and `n_units_r` define the number of neurons in the propensity score layer (three dots in *Figure 11.1*) and representation layers (yellow layers in *Figure 11.1*), respectively. These parameters are optional, but I wanted us to see them, as they might be useful if you decide to tune TARNet for yourself one day. For more parameters (e.g., the number of layers), check out `https://bit.ly/TARNetCode`.
- `nonlin` defines the activation function used by the network. The default value is **exponential linear unit** (ELU), but **scaled exponential linear unit** (SELU) has been shown to have an auto-normalizing effect on dense networks (Klambauer et al., 2017). This effect might not be guaranteed in more complex architectures such as TARNet, but I found SELU to work better than ELU for datasets similar to the one we use.

After initializing the model, we call the `.fit()` method and pass the data. Note that the naming convention in CATENets differs from the one we used in EconML:

- `X` takes the feature matrix (it should include all confounders if there is observational data)
- `y` takes the outcome vector
- `w` takes the treatment vector

We index the `X`, `y`, and `T` variables using the `TRAIN_SIZE` constant that we defined at the beginning (for example, `X[:TRAIN_SIZE, :]` means that we take all observations from the first one up to (but not including) the `TRAIN_SIZE` one and we take all the features (marked by the second colon after the comma)).

Note that we did not shuffle the dataset. This is because it's randomly generated.

Let's get predictions from TARNet:

```
effect_pred_tarnet = tarnet.predict(
    X=X[TRAIN_SIZE:, :]
).cpu().detach().numpy()
```

To get the predicted CATE, we use the `.predict()` method. Note that this time we pass the test dataset (starting from the `TRAIN_SIZE` observation up to the last one).

Note that we call a chain of methods on the result:

1. We call `.cpu()` to send the resulting tensor from a GPU (if you used one) to a CPU.
2. Next, we call `.detach()`, which detaches the tensor from the computational graph used by PyTorch behind the scenes (note that this graph does not have anything to do with causal graphs; it's used by PyTorch to perform computations efficiently).
3. Finally, we call `.numpy()` to cast the tensor to NumPy's `np.array` data type.

This chain is only necessary when we use a GPU, but it's harmless when working on a CPU-only machine.

Now, let's fit the SNet model.

The procedure is virtually identical to the one we used for TARNet:

```
snet = SNet(
    n_unit_in=X.shape[1],
    binary_y=False,
    n_units_out_prop=32,
    n_units_r=8,
    nonlin='selu',
)

snet.fit(
    X=X[:TRAIN_SIZE, :],
    y=y[:TRAIN_SIZE],
    w=T[:TRAIN_SIZE]
)
```

To get the predictions, we call the `.predict()` method and the CPU-detach-NumPy chain on the result:

```
effect_pred_snet = snet.predict(
    X=X[TRAIN_SIZE:, :]
).cpu().detach().numpy()
```

Great! Now we're ready to compare the results between all the models.

Figure 11.3 summarizes the results for TARNet, SNet, and our benchmark methods:

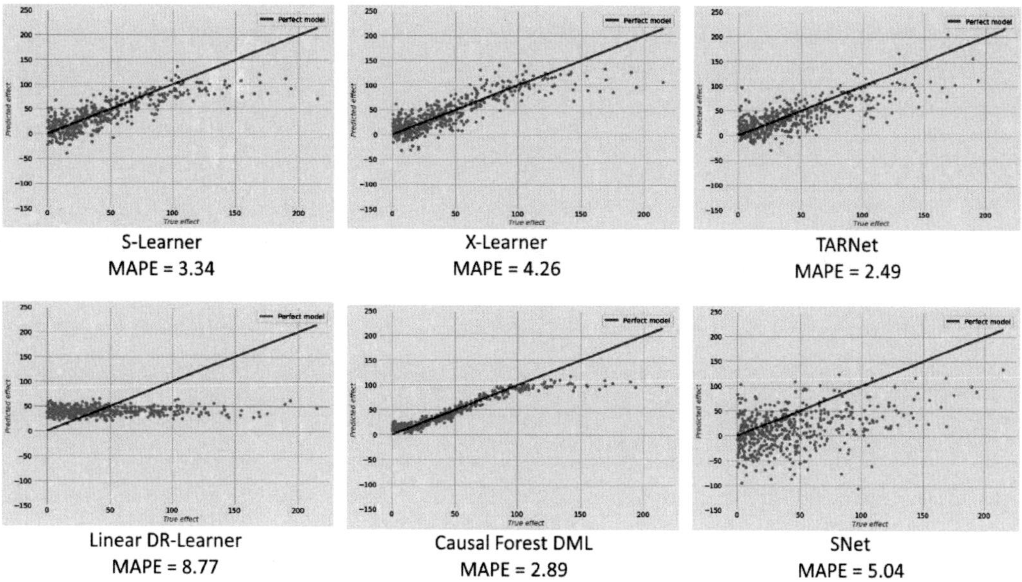

Figure 11.3 – Results for the benchmark models and deep learning models (TARNet and SNet)

As we can see in *Figure 11.3*, TARNet got the best results, achieving a **mean absolute percentage error (MAPE)** value of 2.49. SNet performed less favorably, with the highest variance out of all compared models. Perhaps the model could benefit from longer training and/or a larger sample size.

TARNet is the best at approximating low-density regions (the part in the top-right corner of each panel with a small number of points). Causal Forest DML has the lowest variance, but performs poorly in these low-density regions, giving place to TARNet.

S- and X-Learners seem to have variance comparable to TARNet, but they visibly underperform in comparison in the lower-density regions.

Finally, the linear DR-Learner fails to capture the heterogeneity of the effect. This is not surprising as the model – by definition – can only capture treatment effects linear in parameters.

Note that the results of our experiment should not be treated as a universal benchmark. We only ran one iteration for each model, but there's also a deeper reason.

As demonstrated by Curth et al. (2021), CATE models might perform very differently depending on the construction of the dataset. In particular, changing the function that modifies the treatment effect can favor some models over others.

This fact might make CATE model benchmarking on synthetic data challenging.

The authors propose a number of steps to address these challenges, such as using artificially biased experimental data to construct observational datasets. That said, each of their proposals comes with its own disadvantages (Curth et al., 2021).

In the real world, integrating expert knowledge into the process and validating model predictions with test data (using interventions and counterfactual predictions if possible) can be very helpful in addressing these challenges. This brings us to a seemingly paradoxical conclusion – it might be *easier* to evaluate a CATE model in a particular practical real-world use case than to compare its universal performance against other models on a curated benchmark.

Taking a broader perspective, perhaps we could say that this state of affairs is not unique to modeling causality, and contemporary non-causal machine learning faces similar challenges, yet they are harder to explicitly spot (for example, think about validating large language models trained on virtually all of the internet).

In this section, we introduced two deep learning-based architectures, TARNet and Snet, and implemented them using the CATENets library. We compared the results against other CATE methods and discussed the challenges in benchmarking CATE models.

In the next section, we'll see an example of adapting the Transformer architecture to causal NLP tasks.

Transformers and causal inference

"Der Gegenstand ist einfach."

Ludwig Wittgenstein (1921)

It's 1916. The flames of war consume Europe. A young Austrian man of Jewish descent arrives at a hospital in Kraków, injured in an industrial explosion. He's a volunteer soldier who served in an Austrian artillery regiment.

There's something that differentiates him from other young men in the hospital.

His backpack is full of notes.

He keeps them close, but the notes are not a diary. They consist of a set of remarks on logic, ethics, language, and religion. Some of them were taken while he was still in the trenches of the Eastern Front.

The young man's name is Ludwig Wittgenstein, and his notes will later become the basis of the only book he will publish in his lifetime – *Tractatus Logico-Philosophicus* (Wittgenstein, 1922).

The book will become one of the most significant works of 20th-century Western philosophy.

One of the core ideas of the book is that most philosophical problems are created by the misuse of language. It states that fixing language by making clear references to real-world objects and states of affairs would solve existing philosophical problems – many by showing that they are mere artifacts of language misuse.

In this section, we'll discuss the challenges of using natural language in causal inference tasks, demonstrate one of the approaches to tackling this challenge, and implement it using a PyTorch-based CausalBert model.

The theory of meaning in five paragraphs

We started this section with a quote from Wittgenstein's book. The quote (thesis 2.02 of *Tractatus Logico-Philosophicus*) was translated into English by Charles Kay Ogden as "*The object is simple*" (Wittgenstein, 1922).

The theory of meaning proposed in the book states that names that we use in language refer to *simple* (atomic) objects. Atomic objects have no complexity; they cannot be divided further or described, only named.

There's beauty in this vision. The correspondence between language and the world seems simple and elegant. One challenge to this view is that in natural languages, the same word can often denote different objects, events, or even represent entire sentences.

For instance, the Arabic word يلا (*yalla*), used extensively by Arabic and Hebrew speakers, has numerous meanings that heavily depend on the context. It can mean (among others) the following:

- Let's go!
- Hurry up!
- Please go to bed now.
- Deal!
- Go away!
- Come here!
- Let's do it!

This context dependence is common in natural languages. Moreover, the changes in the meaning of a word might have a subtle character between different usages. Wittgenstein realized this and changed his approach toward meaning in the later stages of his philosophical career.

The new approach he took in his later works might have helped us build systems such as ChatGPT, but let's take it step by step.

Making computers understand language

Working with natural language based on discrete units that we call words has been a major challenge for computer scientists for a pretty long time.

Over the years, computational linguists and computer scientists came up with many creative ways to squeeze information from natural language documents. First attempts relied on bag-of-words-type approaches and information-theoretic analyses (e.g., Zipf in 1949).

The main challenge with these approaches was that they were not able to capture the aspects of semantic similarities between words (although some of them could capture some notion of similarity on a document level).

Wittgenstein's approach toward meaning moved from the idea of words denoting objects to contextual usage. In *Philosophical Investigations* (published posthumously), Wittgenstein (1953) wrote, "*The meaning of a word is its use in the language,*" and proposed that different meanings might be codified within **language games**.

These ideas are closely related to the notion promoted by English linguist John Rupert Firth, summarized as, "*You shall know a word by the company it keeps*" (Firth, 1957).

Wittgenstein's works have likely influenced many lines of research in artificial intelligence and linguistics through a number of paths. One of these paths led to the works of his student Margaret Masterman, who applied Wittgensteinian ideas to the realm of machine translation. She founded the Cambridge Language Research Unit in 1955, and her work influenced researchers around the world (Molino & Tagliabue, 2023).

From philosophy to Python code

A 2013 seminal paper by Czech Google researcher Tomáš Mikolov and colleagues changed the face of NLP forever. The paper presented a self-supervised algorithm called **word2vec** that learned continuous dense vector representations of words, allowing the framing of semantic similarity as a distance between vectors in a continuous multidimensional space (Mikolov et al., 2013).

Although *word2vec* was not able to model **polysemy** (multiple meanings of the same word), it can be considered the first practical implementation of the core ideas proposed in Wittgenstein's later works.

Less than five years after the publication of the *word2vec* paper, **ELMo** – a model introduced by Matthew E. Peters and colleagues (Peters et al., 2018) – made modeling polysemy possible. Just a couple of months later, another model – **BERT** – was released by a team at Google (Devlin et al., 2018). BERT replaced recurrent neural networks with a multi-head attention mechanism (Vaswani et al., 2018). BERT is an example of the Transformer architecture that also gave birth to the GPT family of models (Radford et al., 2019, Brown et al., 2020, and OpenAI, 2023).

BERT has revolutionized the entire field of NLP, bringing huge improvements to most if not all known benchmarks. Its generative cousins from the GPT family made NLP a mainstream topic with media headlines.

Although modern **large language models** (**LLMs**) such as BERT or GPT-4 led to an impressive leap in what's possible in today's natural language modeling and processing, they have some limitations.

LLMs and causality

ChatGPT is a chatbot system introduced by OpenAI in November 2022 (OpenAI, 2022). The system is based on the GPT-3.5 and GPT-4 models, trained using the **reinforcement learning from human feedback** (**RLHF**) paradigm. ChatGPT is well known to produce plausible sounding short-, mid-, and even long-form texts.

It has been demonstrated that the model can successfully answer various types of causal and counterfactual questions. *Figure 11.4* presents how ChatGPT (correctly) answered the counterfactual query that we solved analytically in *Chapter 2*.

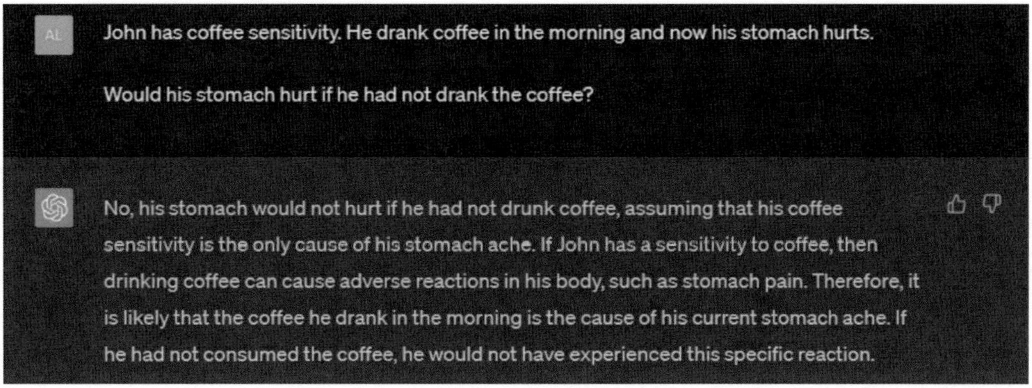

Figure 11.4 – ChatGPT's counterfactual reasoning

I find the behavior presented in *Figure 11.4* impressive, yet it turns out that under more systematic examination, the model is not entirely consistent in this realm.

The system has been thoroughly scrutinized from the causal perspective by two independent teams at Microsoft (led by Cheng Zhang) and TU Darmstadt (led by Moritz Willig and Matej Zečević). Both teams arrived at similar conclusions – the system has significant potential to answer various types of questions (including some causal questions), but cannot be considered fully causal (Zheng et al., 2023 and Willig et al., 2023).

Willig et al. (2023) proposed that ChatGPT learns a meta-SCM purely from language data, which allows it to reason causally but only in a limited set of circumstances and without proper generalization.

Zhang et al. (2023) suggested that the model could benefit from integration with implicit or explicit causal modules. Her team has even demonstrated an early example of GPT-4 integration with a causal end-to-end framework DECI (we will discuss DECI in *Part 3, Causal Discovery*).

In a more recent paper titled *Causal Reasoning and Large Language Models: Opening a New Frontier for Causality* (Kıcıman et al., 2023), Emre Kıcıman and colleagues demonstrated that GPT-based models outperform many existing models on pair-wise causal discovery, counterfactual reasoning, and in determining necessary and sufficient causes, with GPT-4 achieving an accuracy of 92.44% on the CRASS counterfactual reasoning benchmark (comparing to the 98.18% accuracy of human annotators).

Figure 11.5 presents an accuracy comparison of the CRASS counterfactual benchmark (Frohberg & Binder, 2022) between different models and human annotators.

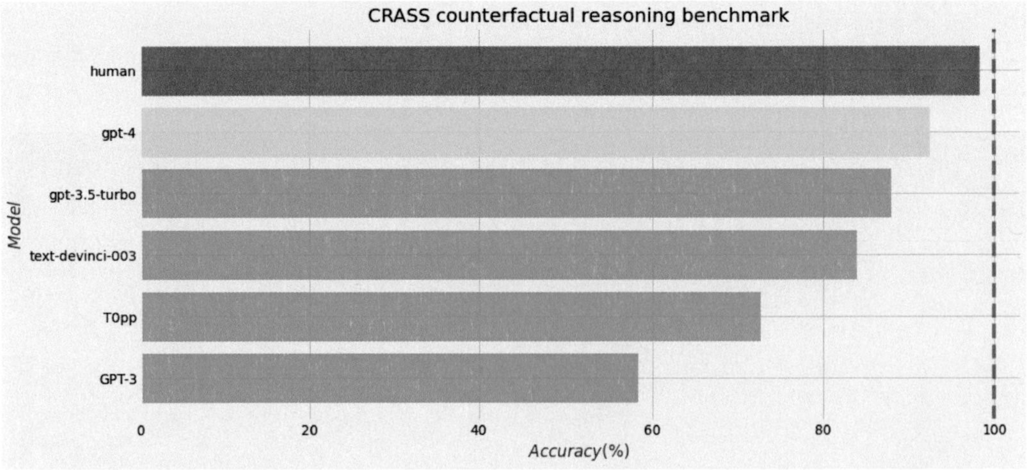

Figure 11.5 – Performance of models and humans on the CRASS counterfactual benchmark

These results are truly impressive. The main challenge that remains is related to model failure modes, which are difficult to predict and might occur "*even in tasks where LLMs obtain high accuracy*" (Kıcıman et al., 2023). This might be related to the fact that the *meta-SCM* that the model learns (as proposed by Willig et al. (2023)) is correlational in its nature, so the model might produce mistakes stochastically.

Keeping in mind that LLMs are not yet capable of systematic causal reasoning, a question that naturally arises is whether there are other ways in which they can be useful in the context of causality.

It turns out that the answer is positive.

The three scenarios

There are two main types of questions we can ask at the intersection of NLP and causality:

- Questions regarding LLMs' and/or other NLP tools' capabilities to help us answer causal queries about the world (e.g., did a writing training program improve the participants' writing clarity?)
- Questions regarding the internal causal mechanics of LLMs or other models (e.g., what changes in the output can be caused by altering the embedding space?)

We'll focus solely on the first type of question.

There are three basic scenarios where we can leverage LLMs and other NLP tools to answer causal queries when addressing the first type of question. In each of the scenarios, we will use text as a node (or a set of nodes) in a causal graph.

The three scenarios are as follows:

- Text as a treatment
- Text as an outcome
- Text as a confounder

In this subsection, we will draw from a great review article by Amit Feder and colleagues, which I wholeheartedly recommend you read if you're interested in causality and NLP (Feder et al., 2020).

Let's review the three scenarios.

Text as a treatment

Hanna is a copywriter at a top New York marketing agency. Over the last few weeks, she's been working on a high-profile project. She and her team are working on an online campaign to drive conversions for a major fashion brand.

Hanna has poured her heart into the project, painstakingly choosing words that she believes will speak to her ideal client. She's created numerous successful campaigns in the past, but deep down in her heart, she really doesn't know which aspects of her copywriting are responsible for their success.

Is it the wording? The use of metaphors? The rhythm of the copy? A combination of all of these things?

Hanna relies on her intuition to decide when the copy is good. She's often right, but quantifying the impact of the copy in a more systematic way could help her work and scale to new niches much faster. It would also give her an excellent asset that she could leverage in communication with internal and external stakeholders.

One of the examples of how Hanna's use case could be addressed comes from Reid Pryzant et al.'s paper (2017). The authors designed a neural network to isolate language aspects that influence sales and concluded that in their sample (coming from a Japanese online marketplace Rakuten), appealing to authority by using polite, informative, and seasonal language contributed most to increased sales.

Some other works that aim at discovering the features of language that impact the outcome of interest include the discovery of conversational tendencies that lead to positive mental health outcomes (Zhang et al., 2020).

These works are very interesting and open a path toward new fascinating research directions. At the same time, they come with a number of challenges.

For instance, it might be difficult to exclude confounding that is rooted internally in text. Text is a source of the treatment, but other (non-treatment) aspects of text might impact the treatment as well as the outcome (Feder et al., 2022).

Moreover, the situation can be further complicated by the fact that different readers might interpret a text differently (to see an example of a model that takes the reader's interpretation into account, check out Pryzant et al. (2021)).

Text as an outcome

Yìzé is an aspiring writer. He has a prolific imagination and produces stories with ease, but he feels that the way he writes lacks a bit of focus and clarity. He decides to enroll in a writing course at a local community college.

Measuring Yìzé's improvement in writing clarity after the course is an example of a text-as-outcome scenario.

In this scenario, the treatment can be relatively easily randomized (technically speaking), and deconfounding the observational data could be possibly much easier than in the previous case.

The main challenge in this scenario is the measure of the outcome. If we use a model to measure clarity and this model is trained on the data from our sample, the measure of clarity becomes dependent on the values of treatment for all participants. This makes the outcomes of all participants dependent on the treatments of all other participants, which violates the consistency assumption (Feder et al., 2022).

One way to deal with this challenge is to train the outcome measurement model on another sample (Egami et al., 2018). This can be relatively easily done if we have enough samples.

Text as a confounder

Finally, text can also be a confounder.

Catori and her friend Stephen both love manga and are inspired by similar characters. They pay attention to similar details and often find themselves wanting to share the same story at the same moment.

Both of them post about manga on Reddit. One day, they noticed an interesting pattern – Stephen's posts get more upvotes, and it's much more likely that his post gets an upvote within the first hour after being posted than Catori's post does. They are curious about what causes this difference.

It has been repeatedly shown that across scientific fields, female authors are cited less frequently than their male counterparts. This effect has been demonstrated in neuroscience (Dworkin et al., 2020), astronomy (Caplar et al., 2017), transplantation research (Benjamens et al., 2020), and so on.

Could the fact that Catori is perceived as female impact how other Reddit users react to her posts?

As seasoned causal learners, we know that to answer this question, we need to carefully consider a number of factors.

Catori's gender might impact the topics she chooses, her style of writing, or the frequency of using certain words. All of these choices can impact the way other participants react to her content.

Moreover, other Reddit users do not know Catori's true gender. They can only infer it from her profile information, such as her username or her avatar.

Therefore, the question here is about *perceived* genders, rather than the true gender's impact on other users' behavior.

Let's build a **directed acyclic graph** (**DAG**) representing this problem. We'll also add a node that represents whether a given post contains a picture or not.

Figure 11.6 presents the proposed DAG:

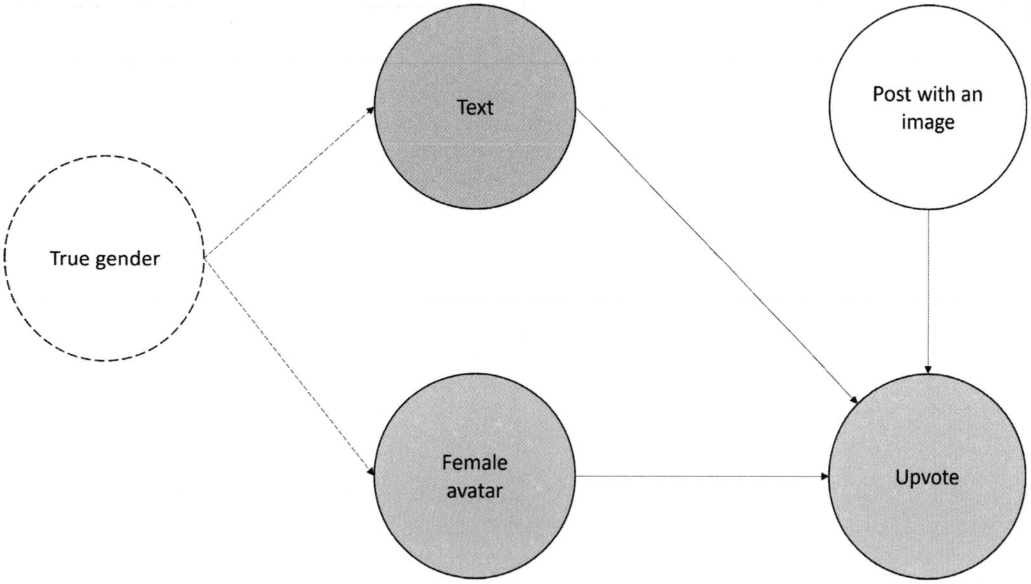

Figure 11.6 – The Reddit DAG

The blue node in *Figure 11.6* represents our treatment (*perceived gender*), and the green one is the outcome (*Upvote* – a post upvote within one hour of posting).

True gender impacts the probability that a person will use a female avatar and impacts *Text* (e.g., the topic or linguistic properties). Note that *True gender* is unobserved, which we indicate by dashed lines in *Figure 11.6.*

Additionally, we have a node indicating whether a post contains an image. In our model, this node is independent of *true* and *perceived gender.*

Note that the *True gender* node opens a backdoor path between the treatment (*Female avatar*) and outcome (*Upvote*). Luckily, its impact is mediated by *Text.* This means that by controlling for *Text,* we can block the path.

A natural question to ask here is which aspects of the text we should control for and how can we make sure that they are present in the representation of the text that we choose to use.

CausalBert

CausalBert is a model proposed by Victor Veitch, Dhanya Sridhar, and David Blei from Columbia University in their paper *Adapting Text Embeddings for Causal Inference* (Veitch et al., 2020). It leverages BERT architecture (Devlin et al., 2018) and adapts it to learn **causally sufficient embeddings** that allow for causal identification when text is a confounder or mediator.

CausalBert is conceptually similar to DragonNet (Shi et al., 2019) – a descendant of the TARNet architecture. *Figure 11.7* presents CausalBert symbolically:

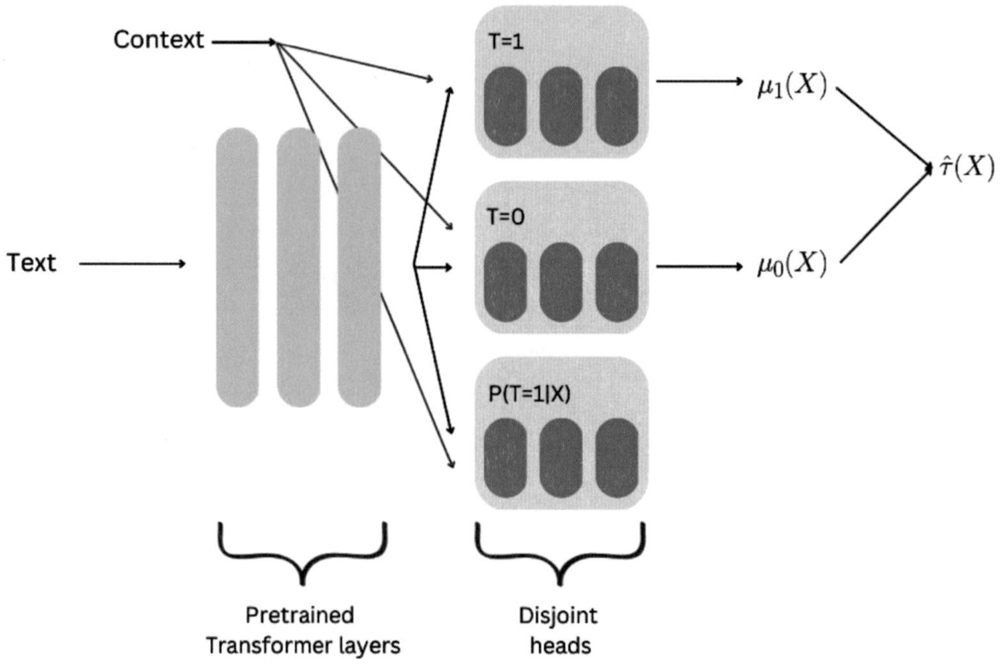

Figure 11.7 – CausalBert architecture

The yellow layers in *Figure 11.7* are pretrained Transformer layers. These layers come from the BERT model pre-trained on the original corpus. Three disjoint heads estimate the two potential outcomes and the propensity score, all starting from the same shared representation.

> **The BERT model family**
>
> Since the original BERT model was introduced in 2018, many modifications of the original architecture have been proposed. One of them is DistilBERT (Sanh et al., 2019) – a smaller, faster, and lighter version of BERT that retains about 97% of the original model's capabilities, while reducing its size by 40% and performing computations in 60% less time. CausalBert uses DistilBERT behind the scenes.

Note that the version of CausalBert presented in *Figure 11.7* is slightly different from the original version proposed by Veitch et al. (2020) and follows Reid Pryzant's PyTorch implementation. Pryzant added the possibility to include an additional categorical confounder (or context) variable, marked as *Context* in the figure.

During the training, CausalBert adapts the pretrained layers and learns the embedding, outcome, and treatment models jointly. This joint objective preserves the information in the embeddings that is predictive of the treatment and outcome and attenuates everything else. Thanks to this mechanism, we make sure that information relevant to the downstream task is preserved in the embeddings, making them sufficient to effectively control for confounding.

Note that the same mechanism is helpful when the text is a partial mediator of the treatment effect. When controlling for text in this scenario, we learn the direct effect of the treatment on the outcome (this will exclude all the information that travels through the mediator and only leave the information that flows directly from the treatment to the outcome, also known as the **natural direct effect** (**NDE**)).

Playing safe with CausalBert

The mechanism that adapts the embeddings that predict the treatment and outcome also has a darker side. Confounding and mediation scenarios are not the only ones in which text is correlated with both the treatment and outcome.

It will also happen when text is a common descendant of the treatment *and* outcome. In such a case, the text becomes a collider, and controlling for it opens a spurious path between the treatment and outcome, biasing the results.

To mitigate this risk, we should always make sure that none of the aspects of the text are a descendant of the treatment *and* outcome; neither should any aspect of the text be a descendant of the outcome alone (as this would nullify any effect of the treatment on the outcome).

For instance, if a Reddit user shares a post, observes a lack of upvote within the first 15 minutes after posting, and then edits the post in the hope of getting an upvote, the text becomes a collider between the treatment and the outcome.

On top of this, CausalBert requires standard causal inference assumptions – a lack of hidden confounding, positivity, and consistency (one type of treatment and no treatment interference between subjects; check out *Chapter 8* for more details).

CausalBert in code

We will implement CausalBert using Reid Pryzant's PyTorch implementation (`https://bit.ly/CausalBertCode`).

At the time of writing, the code in the original repository contained a small mistake that could distort the model's results. A fixed version of the code that we'll use in this section can be found in the book's repository (`https://bit.ly/CausalBertCodeBook`).

Let's start with the imports:

```
import pandas as pd
from models.causal_bert_pytorch.CausalBert import CausalBertWrapper
```

We import `pandas` to read the data and the `CausalBertWrapper` class, which implements the model and wraps it in a user-friendly API.

Next, we read in the data:

```
df = pd.read_csv('data/manga_processed.csv')
```

Our dataset has been generated according to the structure presented in *Figure 11.6*. It consists of 221 observations and 5 features:

- `text` – the text content
- `subreddit` – the subreddit name (we'll ignore this variable, as it has a single value for all posts)
- `female_avatar` – a binary variable, indicating whether a user has a female avatar in their profile
- `has_photo` – a binary indicator if a post contains an image
- `upvote` – a binary indicator of a post upvote in the 1st hour after posting (the outcome)

Texts are short Reddit-like posts, generated using ChatGPT and prompted indirectly to produce gender-stereotypical content. Both the *text* and *female avatar* indicators are confounded by an unobserved *true gender* variable, and the *text* causally impacts the outcome through linguistic features (for the data-generating process code, check out `https://bit.ly/ExtraDGPs`).

Figure 11.8 presents the first five rows of the dataset before shuffling:

	text	subreddit	female_avatar	has_photo	upvote
0	What's your favorite romance manga with a fema...	manga	1	0	1
1	As a woman, I find 'Nana' to be a very empower...	manga	1	0	0
2	Can we talk about how badass the female charac...	manga	1	0	0
3	Any other ladies here obsessed with 'Ouran Hig...	manga	1	1	0
4	Just finished reading 'Skip Beat!' and I'm in ...	manga	1	1	1

Figure 11.8 – A manga pseudo-Reddit dataset

Let's instantiate the model:

```
causal_bert = CausalBertWrapper(
    batch_size=8,
    g_weight=0.05,
```

```
    Q_weight=1.,
    mlm_weight=0.05
)
```

We pass four parameters to the constructor.

We define the batch size and three `weight` parameters. These three parameters will be responsible for weighting the components of the loss function during the training.

Here's their meaning:

- `g_weight` is responsible for weighting the part of the loss that comes from propensity score (the "*P(T=1|X)*" block in *Figure 11.7*; it's called *g*, according to the convention used in Veitch et al.'s (2018) paper)
- `Q_weight` is responsible for weighting the outcome model loss (the sub-model that predicts the actual outcome – the "*T=0*" and "*T=1*" blocks in *Figure 11.7*, called *Q* according to the paper's convention)
- `mlm_weight` weights BERT's **masked language model** (**MLM**) loss

MLM

BERT and some of its cousins are trained using the so-called MLM objective. It's a self-supervised training paradigm in which a random token in a training sequence is masked, and the model tries to predict this masked token using other tokens in the sequence. Thanks to the **attention mechanism**, the model can "*see*" the whole sequence when predicting the masked token.

As you can see, we weighted the outcome model loss (`Q_weight`) much higher than the propensity model (`g_weight`) or MLM loss (`mlm_weight`).

This setting works pretty well for our dataset, but when you work with your own data, you should tune these parameters only if you have enough samples to do so.

The low weighting of the MLM loss indicates that the texts in our dataset are likely not very different from the overall language on the internet, and the generic DistilBERT embeddings provide us with a good-enough representation for our task.

Let's train the model:

```
causal_bert.train(
    texts=df['text'],
    confounds=df['has_photo'],
    treatments=df['female_avatar'],
    outcomes=df['likes'],
    epochs=6
);
```

The `.train()` method takes five arguments:

- `texts` – an array (`pd.Series`) of texts
- `confounds` – a categorical array containing values of an additional confounding or context variable (if there's no such variable in your setting, just pass an array of zeros here)
- `treatments` – a binary treatment indicator
- `outcomes` – a binary outcome indicator
- `epochs` – the number of training epochs

After training the model, we can compute the ATE.

To do so, we call the `.inference()` method and pass texts and additional confounds as arguments. This method returns a tuple. We're interested in the 0th element of this tuple:

```
preds = causal_bert.inference(
    texts=df['text'],
    confounds=df['has_photo'],
)[0]
```

The 0th element contains an array of dimension $N \times T$, where N is the number of observations and T is the number of treatment levels (for a binary treatment $T = 2$). Entries in the first (0th) column are the probabilities that the outcome is equal to 1 under no treatment. Entries in the second (1st) column are the probabilities that the outcome is equal to 1 under the treatment.

To calculate the ATE, we subtract the entries in the first column from the entries in the second column and take the average:

```
np.mean(preds[:, 1] - preds[:, 0])
```

This gives us the following:

```
-0.62321178301562
```

This result is pretty close to the true effect of -0.7.

It indicates that perceived gender causes a significant drop in early reactions to the content published in our imaginary manga subreddit.

This conclusion is only valid if the three causal assumptions (no hidden confounding, positivity, and consistency) are met and the model is structurally sound (no aspects of the text are descendants of the treatment and outcome, nor the outcome itself).

If Catori and Stephen had doubts regarding some of these assumptions, they could run a randomized experiment on Reddit to see whether the results held.

Before we conclude this section, I want to take a step back and take a look at the topic of **fairness**. At the beginning of this section, we cited a number of papers, demonstrating a citation gender gap between female and male authors.

Although we might be tempted to make conclusions regarding gender gaps and other similar effects based on simple statistical analyses of observational data (e.g., survey data), this is usually a bad idea.

The structural aspect is crucial in fairness analyses, and ignoring it will *almost surely* lead to invalid results (including sign reversal, effect masking, or hallucinating non-existent effects). To learn more about this topic, check out the excellent works of Drago Plečko and Elias Bareinboim (Plečko & Bareinboim, 2023).

In this section, we explored the intersection of NLP and causality, starting with a discussion on the ideas of Ludwig Wittgenstein and how these and similar ideas contributed to making computers encode natural language efficiently.

We then delved into the three types of scenarios encountered at the intersection of NLP and causality – text as a treatment, text as an outcome, and text as a confounder. Next, we demonstrated an approach to adapt text embeddings for causal inference in the text-as-confounder scenario, using a Transformer-based CausalBert model.

Finally, we discussed the limitations and potential challenges that we can encounter when working with this model. We finished the chapter by sharing references to materials that discuss how we can tackle the problems of fairness from a causal perspective.

In the next section, we'll take a look at one of the ways in which we can leverage the time dimension to draw causal conclusions when experiments are not available.

Causality and time series – when an econometrician goes Bayesian

In this section, we're going to introduce a new style of thinking about causality.

We'll start this section with a brief overview of quasi-experimental methods. Next, we'll take a closer look at one of these methods – the **synthetic control estimator**. We'll implement the synthetic control estimator using an open source package, **CausalPy**, from PyMC Labs and test it on real-life data.

Quasi-experiments

Randomized controlled trials (**RCTs**) are often considered the "*gold standard*" for causal inference. One of the challenges regarding RCTs is that we cannot carry them out in certain scenarios.

On the other hand, there's a broad class of circumstances where we can observe naturally occurring interventions that we cannot control or randomize. Something *naturally* changes in the world, and we are interested in understanding the impact of such an event on some outcome of interest.

Events like this are sometimes referred to as **natural experiments**.

Such interventions do not have the power to guarantee unconfoundedness, yet sometimes, they can provide us with useful information.

A family of methods traditionally used to analyze data coming from natural experiments (also known as quasi-experiments) is known as **quasi-experimental methods**.

Traditionally, quasi-experiments are framed as time series problems. An event is observed at some point in time, and we track how some measurable quantity changes after this event compare to some baseline.

Let's make it more concrete.

Twitter acquisition and our googling patterns

On October 27, 2022, Elon Musk acquired a popular social media platform, Twitter.

The acquisition process was lengthy and marked by numerous controversies.

The day after the formal acquisition, on October 28, Musk tweeted, "*The bird is freed,*" suggesting that the acquisition had now become a reality. The tweet quickly gained significant attention from the public and media outlets alike, with many people commenting and resharing it on the platform.

Significant events in politics, economy, or art and culture can spark public attention and alter the behaviors of large groups of people, making them search for additional information.

Was Twitter's acquisition such an event?

Let's see.

To answer this question, we'll take a look at Google Trends data and compare how often users searched for Twitter before and after Elon Musk's tweet.

To perform such a comparison, we will need some baseline.

The logic of synthetic controls

With RCTs, we randomly assign units to the treatment and control groups and compare the outcomes between both groups to quantify the relative efficacy of the treatment.

In quasi-experiments, we don't have control over the treatment assignment. Moreover, the intervention is oftentimes limited to just one unit.

How can we navigate this?

First, let's notice what we already have. We have a treated unit, and we believe that we know at which point in time the treatment has been assigned.

That's valuable information, but it's not sufficient to draw conclusions.

To make a comparison, we'll also need a baseline – a control group or control unit.

A useful control unit would provide us with information about what would have happened to the treated unit if the treatment had not occurred. As we already know, this alternative outcome cannot be observed. How can we deal with this?

Recall the core idea behind meta-learners. With meta-learners, we learn response functions for treated and untreated units and then predict one or both outcomes, based on the learned representation. We use these counterfactual outcomes to compute the estimated treatment effect.

Synthetic control is different from meta-learners in a number of significant aspects, yet it bears a conceptual similarity to them.

In synthetic control (Abadie & Gardeazabal, 2003), we observe units over time. If two units are correlated over an extensive period of time, it is highly likely that either one of the units has a (direct or indirect) causal effect on the other unit, or they have a common cause that is a source of variability in both of them.

Whichever scenario of the two is the case, the two units will have some predictive power to predict each other (as long as the underlying data-generating process does not change).

Reichenbach's principle

Reichenbach's common cause principle asserts that when two variables are correlated, there must be either a causal relationship between the two, or a third variable exists (known as a Reichenbachian common cause) that causes the correlation between the two.

In a finite data regime, correlations between two variables might also occur randomly. That's why in the text we say that it's *highly likely* that the two variables are causally related or they have a common cause, rather than saying that this is *certainly* true. Random correlations between two long time series are highly unlikely, but the shorter the series, the more likely the random correlation is.

Note that some authors propose (putative) counterexamples to Reichenbach's principle (check out `https://bit.ly/ReichenbachPrinciple` for more details). The principle is also debated in quantum physics (the Einstein-Podolsky-Rosen argument – e.g., Rédei, 2002).

The main idea behind synthetic control is to find units that are correlated with our unit of interest in the pre-treatment period, learning a model that effectively predicts the behavior of the treated unit after the treatment occurs. The units that we use as predictors are called the **donor pool**.

Let's unpack it.

A visual introduction to the logic of synthetic controls

Let's take a look at *Figure 11.9*, which presents an outcome variable (**Target**, in blue) and a set of potential donor pool variables (green, red, and purple). Note that all variables are recorded over time:

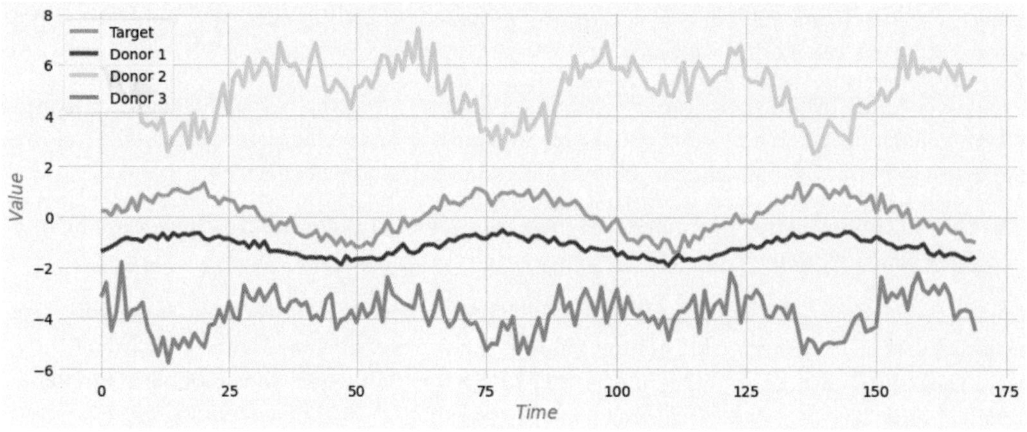

Figure 11.9 – An outcome variable (Target) and a set of potential donor variables

We're aiming to predict the outcome variable (**Target**) by using the remaining variables (**Donor 1**, …, **Donor 3**) as predictors.

The donor pool variables in *Figure 11.9* seems to be good potential predictors of **Target**, as there are visible correlation patterns between them and **Target**.

To see this in a more systematic way, *Table 11.1* presents Pearson correlation coefficients between the donor pool variables and the outcome.

Variable	**Pearson's r (donor-outcome)**	**p-value**
Donor 1	0.92	<0.0001
Donor 2	-0.60	<0.0001
Donor 3	-0.33	<0.0001

Table 11.1 – The correlation coefficients between the donor variables and the outcome

Strong significant correlation coefficients indicate that these donor pool variables will be good predictors of the outcome.

Let's see how well we can predict the outcome from these variables using simple linear regression. *Figure 11.10* presents the actual outcome variable (blue) and its predicted version (gray):

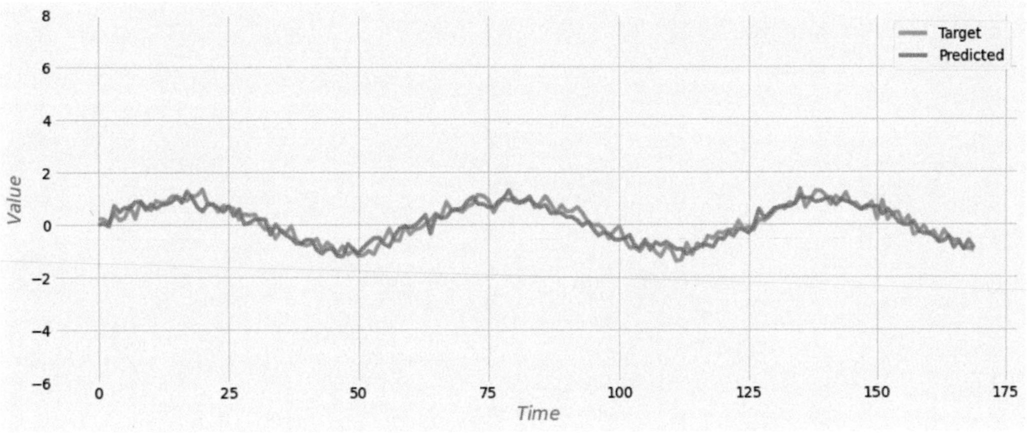

Figure 11.10 – The actual target and prediction based on donor variables

As we can see, the overall fit seems really good.

An important property of donor pool units is that they should be correlated with the treated unit in the pre-treatment period (before the treatment occurs), but they should not react to the treatment themselves.

In *Figure 11.11*, we can see a longer version of the time series from *Figure 11.9* with a treatment recorded at time **170**:

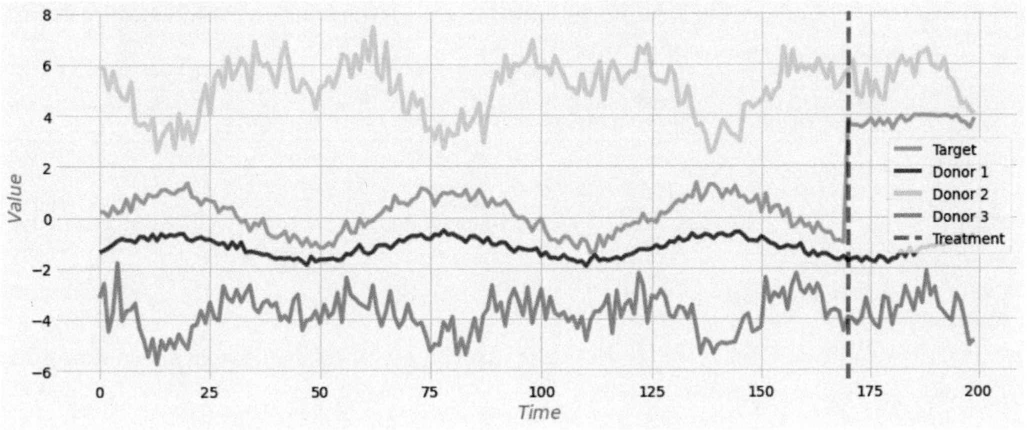

Figure 11.11 – An outcome variable (Target), a set of donor pool variables, and the treatment

As we can see, our outcome variable changed significantly after the treatment occurred, but donor variables seem to follow their previous pattern in the post-treatment period.

Let's predict the outcome variable from the donor pool variables after the occurrence of the treatment.

Figure 11.12 presents the results:

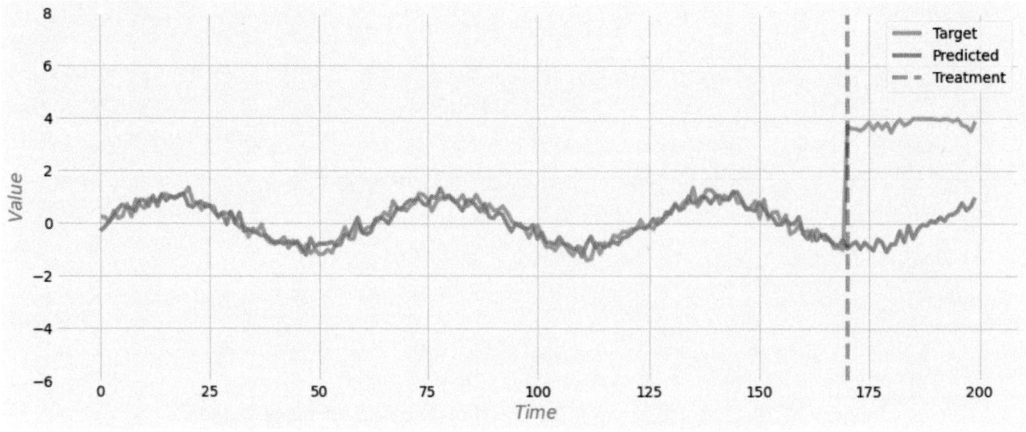

Figure 11.12 – The actual target and prediction, based on donor pool variables in the pre- and post-treatment periods

The prediction (the gray solid line in *Figure 11.12*) in the post-treatment period is our *synthetic control* unit.

Having the *actual outcome* (the blue line in *Figure 11.12*) and the predicted *counterfactual outcome* (the gray line in *Figure 11.12*), we can subtract the latter from the former to get the estimated treatment effect at any point in the post-treatment period.

Conceptually, we learn the counterfactual outcome from the donor pool variables, and then we subtract the values of this counterfactual outcome from the values of the actual outcome to obtain the estimate of the treatment effect.

Let's use this logic to see whether Elon Musk's tweet had enough impact to alter our Google search patterns.

Starting with the data

In this section, we'll use Google Trends data on search volume for different social media platforms over time.

We'll use the information on search volume for LinkedIn, TikTok, and Instagram as our donor pool units. We sampled the data with daily granularity between May 15, 2022 and November 11, 2022, with the treatment (the tweet) occurring on October 28, 2022. This gives us 181 samples (days) in total, with 166 samples (days) in the pre-treatment period. This sample size should be more than sufficient to capture predictive regularities in the dataset.

Synthetic controls in code

In the visual introduction section, all that we did was based on a simple linear regression model. In fact, the synthetic control estimator is based on the same idea.

The synthetic control estimator learns to predict the outcome variable using the donor pool variables in the pre-treatment period, and then it predicts the counterfactual version of the outcome variable in the post-treatment period.

This procedure is carried out by finding a set of weights for each of the donor pool variables that best predicts the outcome variable. The easiest way to do this is to use linear regression.

In order to decrease the risk of overfitting, the synthetic control estimator forces the weights for the donor pool variables to take values between 0 and 1 and enforces the condition that all the weights sum up to 1.

This constraints the model to learn to predict the outcome variable by interpolating between the donor pool variables, effectively reducing the risk of overfitting.

In a traditional synthetic control estimator, this constraint can be achieved by using the constrained optimization scheme (for more details, check out Facure, 2020 in *Chapter 15*).

As we will follow a Bayesian implementation, we'll use a Dirichlet prior to impose the constraints on the weights, rather than constraining the optimization scheme.

Dirichlet distribution is a multidimensional generalization of the beta distribution. Samples from the Dirichlet distribution are bounded between 0 and 1 and sum up to 1 – a perfect match for our overfitting-reducing idea!

Note that to effectively predict the outcome variable from the donor pool variables under these constraints, we need some of our donor pool variables to take values greater than the outcome and some others to take values lower than the outcome.

Intuitively, note that a weighted average of an array of values can never be lower than the minimum of this array and can never be greater than the maximum of this array, assuming that the weights are bounded between 0 and 1.

Let's take a look at *Figure 11.11* once again. Note that the green line is above, while the red and purple ones are below our outcome variable (blue). This is good.

If all your donor pool variables always take values below or above the values of your outcome, a constraint synthetic control estimator won't work. Theoretically, in such a case, you can transform your variables, but this comes with certain drawbacks (see Abadie, 2021 for details).

Ok, we're ready to do some coding!

We'll use CausalPy, a Bayesian library for quasi-experimental data, to implement the synthetic controls estimator. CausalPy builds on top of PyMC, a popular Python probabilistic programming framework that makes building and debugging Bayesian models seamless.

You can find the code for this section in the `Chapter_11.2.ipynb` notebook (`https://bit.ly/causal-ntbk-11_2`). Note that this notebook uses a separate `conda` environment. You'll find installation instructions in the repository's description or the notebook itself (whichever is more convenient for you).

Let's import the libraries:

```
import pandas as pd
import causalpy as cp
import matplotlib.pyplot as plt
```

Let's read in the data:

```
data = pd.read_csv(r'./data/gt_social_media_data.csv')
```

Figure 11.13 presents the first five rows of the dataset:

	date	twitter	linkedin	tiktok	instagram
0	2022-05-15	55	9	23	59
1	2022-05-16	54	18	20	59
2	2022-05-17	54	20	23	57
3	2022-05-18	54	20	21	55
4	2022-05-19	49	23	21	52

Figure 11.13 – The first five rows of the social media search volume dataset

The first column stores the information about the date. The remaining four columns contain information about the relative search volume for a given day.

To make our work with CausalPy smooth, we'll use `date` as the index of our data frame:

```
data.index = pd.to_datetime(data['date'])
data = data.drop('date', axis=1)
```

First, we cast it to the `pandas.Timestamp` type and overwrite the current index.

Second, we drop the original column (the date information is now stored in the index).

Let's plot the data. *Figure 11.14* presents the data, with the date of Musk's tweet marked by a black dashed line:

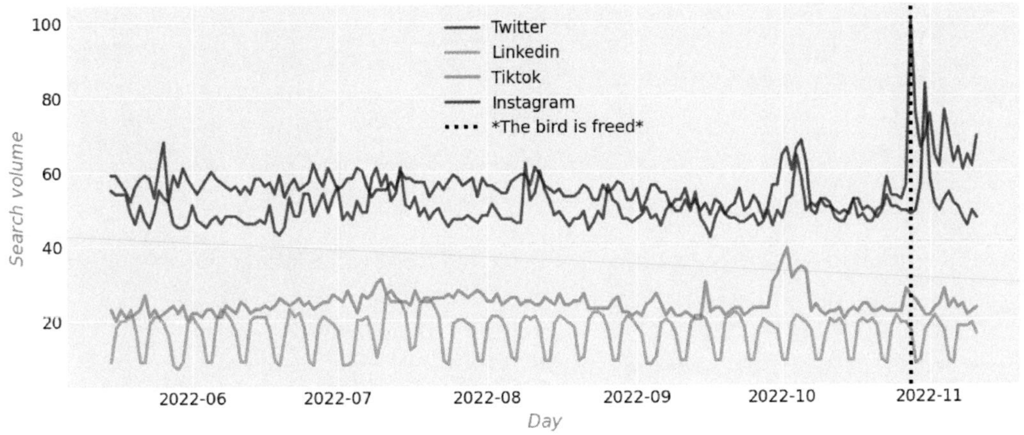

Figure 11.14 – Social media platforms search volume data

Note that Instagram's search volume is typically higher than that of Twitter, while LinkedIn and TikTok have lower search volumes compared to the latter. Twitter's line occasionally exceeds Instagram's line, which is not ideal, but as this happens rarely, we'll accept it, assuming that it won't hinder the model's ability to learn a useful representation.

To prepare the dataset for modeling, we need to store the treatment date in the same format as the dates in the index of our data frame. We will use the `pd.to_datetime()` function for this purpose:

```
treatment_index = pd.to_datetime('2022-10-28')
```

To implement the synthetic controls estimator in CausalPy, we'll use the `WeightedSumFitter()` class from the `pymc_models` module:

```
model = cp.pymc_models.WeightedSumFitter()
```

To define the model structure, we'll use the R-style regression formula (you can refer to *Chapter 3* for a refresher on R-style formulas):

```
formula = 'twitter ~ 0 + tiktok + linkedin + instagram'
```

The formula says that we'll predict `twitter` using the remaining three variables. Zero at the beginning of the formula means that we'll not fit an intercept.

Finally, we can fit the model. In CausalPy, we do it using the `SyntheticControl` class from the `pymc_experiments` module:

```
results = cp.pymc_experiments.SyntheticControl(
    data,
    treatment_index,
    formula=formula,
```

```
    model=model,
)
```

We pass the data, treatment date index, formula, and model to the constructor and assign the object to the `results` variable.

The training will start automatically.

We can now use the fitted `SyntheticControl` object to access useful information about the model.

First, let's plot the results:

```
results.plot(plot_predictors=True)
```

Figure 11.15 presents the output:

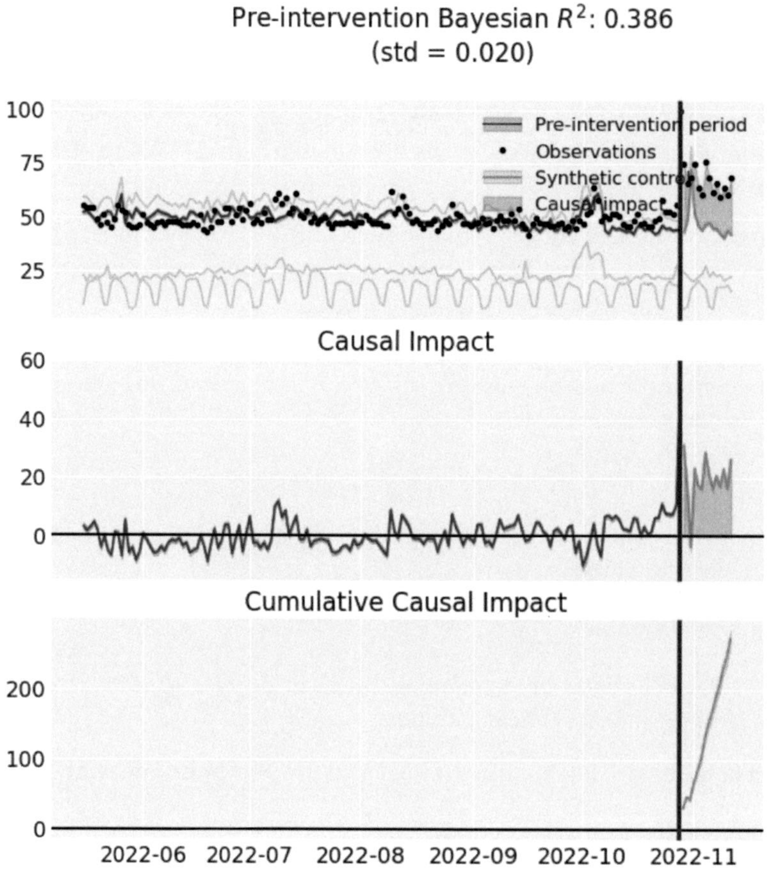

Figure 11.15 – The results of the fitted model

At the top of *Figure 11.15*, we can see the information about the pre-treatment model fit, expressed in terms of Bayesian R^2 (Gelman et al., 2018), which defines how the amount of variability in the outcome variable in the pre-treatment period is explained by the variability in the donor pool predictors.

Our donor pool predictors only explain 38.6% of the variability in the outcome before the treatment. This means that the fit has limited quality.

The top panel presents the actual values of the outcome variable (the black dots) and the predicted values of the outcome variable (the blue line). The orange line represents the predicted synthetic control, and the blue shaded area represents the estimated causal effect of the treatment. The treatment is represented as a red vertical line.

The middle panel presents the difference between the predicted and actual values of the outcome variable. If we had a model that predicted the outcome perfectly, the blue line in the middle panel of *Figure 11.15* would be a straight line fixed at zero in the entire pre-treatment period. This is because a perfect model would have zero errors.

Finally, the bottom panel presents the estimated cumulative causal impact of the treatment.

Let's take a look at how each of the donor pool predictors contributed to the prediction. This can be achieved by calling the `.summary()` method on the `results` object:

```
results.summary()
```

This gives us the following printout:

```
===============================Synthetic Control=====================
===========
Formula: twitter ~ 0 + tiktok + linkedin + instagram
Model coefficients:
tiktok                          0.08, 94% HDI [0.01, 0.18]
linkedin                        0.08, 94% HDI [0.01, 0.15]
instagram                       0.84, 94% HDI [0.81, 0.87]
sigma                           5.79, 94% HDI [5.34, 6.28]
```

The coefficient for Instagram's contribution is the highest (0.84), rendering it the strongest predictor of the outcome.

Note that none of the 94% **highest density intervals** (**HDIs**) contains zero, suggesting that all predictors were significant. You can think of the HDI as a Bayesian analog of confidence intervals (although this is a simplification; for more details, check out Martin et al., 2021).

The model fit is not perfect (as expressed by R^2), yet the overall effect seems pretty large.

To increase our confidence in the results, we could further formally test the significance of the effect (for more ideas, check out Facure, 2020 in *Chapter 15* and Chernozhukov et al., 2022), but we'll skip this procedure here.

Assuming that our model is correctly specified, we can say that we've found convincing evidence that Elon Musk's tweet increased the Google search volume for Twitter.

That's powerful!

Before we conclude, let's discuss a number of challenges.

Challenges

The donor pool size we used for this analysis is small, which may explain the low value of R^2. Many practitioners would recommend using at least between 5 to 25 variables in your donor pool as a rule of thumb. That said, smaller donor pool sizes might have certain advantages.

For instance, we can be pretty sure that we're not overfitting, which might happen with larger sizes of donor pools (Abadie, 2021).

We hypothesized that Elon Musk's tweet caused the increase in the search volume for Twitter, yet there might be other factors at work (e.g., media publications on Twitter's acquisition). We might also deal with confounding here.

The Twitter acquisition itself could have caused Musk's tweet *and* increased interest in the information about the platform. This alternative cannot be excluded based on the data alone and might be very difficult to exclude in general.

This consideration shows us an important truth about quasi-experimental methods – they *do not* automatically guarantee causal identifiability.

We should consider all the available data when working with these methods, exactly the same way we do with any other causal method. Considering a DAG that describes our problem, understanding structural relationships between variables, and investigating potential confounding are good first steps in quasi-experimental analysis.

To learn more about good practices regarding data selection and overall synthetic control methodology, check out the excellent papers from Abadie (2021) and Ferman et al. (2020).

Other great resources on synthetic controls include Scott Cunningham's book *Causal Inference: The Mixtape* (Cunningham, 2021) and *Chapter 15* of Matheus Facure's online book *Causal Inference for the Brave and True* (Facure, 2020).

This concludes our section on synthetic control and quasi-experimental methods.

In this section, we introduced quasi-experimental methods and discussed how a synthetic control estimator works. We implemented it in Python using CausalPy and discussed a number of challenges with our analysis.

Wrapping it up

We covered a lot in this chapter. We started by revisiting the S-Learner and T-Learner models and demonstrated how flexible deep learning architectures can help combine the benefits of both models. We implemented TARNet and SNet and learned how to use the PyTorch-based CATENets library.

Next, we delved into the application of causality in NLP. We used a Transformer-based CausalBert model to compute the average treatment effect of a gender avatar on the probability of getting an upvote in a simulated Reddit-like discussion forum.

Finally, we took a glimpse into the world of econometrics and quasi-experimental data and learned how to implement a Bayesian synthetic control estimator using CausalPy.

In the next chapter, we'll start our adventure with causal discovery.

See you on the other side!

References

Abadie, A. (2021). *Using Synthetic Controls: Feasibility, Data Requirements, and Methodological Aspects.* Journal of Economic Literature, 59(2), 391-425.

Abadie, A., & Gardeazabal, J. (2003). *The Economic Costs of Conflict: A Case Study of the Basque Country.* Public Choice & Political Economy Journal.

Benjamens, S., Banning, L. B. D., van den Berg, T. A. J., & Pol, R. A. (2020). *Gender Disparities in Authorships and Citations in Transplantation Research.* Transplantation Direct, 6(11), e614.

Bradbury, J., Frostig, R., Hawkins, P., Johnson, M. J., Leary, C., Maclaurin, D., Necula, G., Paszke, A., VanderPlas, J., Wanderman-Milne, S., & Zhang, Q. (2018). *JAX: composable transformations of Python+NumPy programs [Computer software]*: `http://github.com/google/jax`

Brown, T., Mann, B., Ryder, N., Subbiah, M., Kaplan, J. D., Dhariwal, P., ... & Amodei, D. (2020). *Language models are few-shot learners.* Advances in Neural Information Processing Systems, 33, 1877-1901.

Caplar, N., Tacchella, S., & Birrer, S. (2017). *Quantitative evaluation of gender bias in astronomical publications from citation counts.* Nature Astronomy, 1(6), 0141.

Chernozhukov, V., Wuthrich, K., & Zhu, Y. (2022). *A t-test for synthetic controls.* arXiv.

Cunningham, S. (2021). *Causal Inference: The Mixtape.* Yale University Press.

Curth, A., Svensson, D., Weatherall, J., & van der Schaar, M. (2021). *Really Doing Great at Estimating CATE? A Critical Look at ML Benchmarking Practices in Treatment Effect Estimation.* Proceedings of the Neural Information Processing Systems Track on Datasets and Benchmarks.

Curth, A., & van der Schaar, M. (2021a). *Nonparametric Estimation of Heterogeneous Treatment Effects: From Theory to Learning Algorithms*. Proceedings of the 24th International Conference on Artificial Intelligence and Statistics (AISTATS).

Curth, A., & van der Schaar, M. (2021b). *On Inductive Biases for Heterogeneous Treatment Effect Estimation*. Proceedings of the Thirty-Fifth Conference on Neural Information Processing Systems.

Devlin, J., Chang, M. W., Lee, K., & Toutanova, K. (2018). *Bert: Pre-training of deep bidirectional transformers for language understanding*. arXiv.

Dworkin, J. D., Linn, K. A., Teich, E. G., Zurn, P., Shinohara, R. T., & Bassett, D. S. (2020). *The extent and drivers of gender imbalance in neuroscience reference lists*. Nature Neuroscience, *23(8)*, 918-926.

Egami, N., Fong, C. J., Grimmer, J., Roberts, M. E., & Stewart, B. M. (2018). *How to make causal inferences using texts*. arXiv.

Facure, M., A. (2020). *Causal Inference for The Brave and True.*

Feder, A., Keith, K. A., Manzoor, E., Pryzant, R., Sridhar, D., Wood-Doughty, Z., ... & Yang, D. (2022). *Causal inference in natural language processing: Estimation, prediction, interpretation and beyond.* Transactions of the Association for Computational Linguistics, 10, 1138-1158.

Ferman, B., Pinto, C., & Possebom, V. (2020). *Cherry Picking with Synthetic Controls*. Journal of Policy Analysis and Management., 39, 510-532.

Firth, J. (1957). *A Synopsis of Linguistic Theory, 1930–55*. In Studies in Linguistic Analysis. Special Volume of the Philological Society. Blackwell.

Frohberg, J., & Binder, F. (2022). *CRASS: A Novel Data Set and Benchmark to Test Counterfactual Reasoning of Large Language Models*. Proceedings of the Thirteenth Language Resources and Evaluation Conference, 2126–2140. `https://aclanthology.org/2022.lrec-1.229`

Gelman, A., Goodrich, B., Gabry, J., & Vehtari, A. (2018). *R-squared for Bayesian regression models*. The American Statistician.

Hassanpour, N., & Greiner, R. (2020). *Learning disentangled representations for counterfactual regression*. International Conference on Learning Representations.

Hernán M. A., Robins J. M. (2020). *Causal Inference: What If*. Boca Raton: Chapman & Hall/CRC.

Kıcıman, E., Ness, R., Sharma, A., & Tan, C. (2023). *Causal Reasoning and Large Language Models: Opening a New Frontier for Causality*. arXiv preprint arXiv:2305.00050.

Klambauer, G., Unterthiner, T., Mayr, A., & Hochreiter, S. (2017). *Self-normalizing neural networks*. Advances in Neural Information Processing Systems, 30.

Krizhevsky, A., Sutskever, I., & Hinton, G. E. (2012). *ImageNet Classification with Deep Convolutional Neural Networks*. In: F. Pereira, C. J. Burges, L. Bottou, & K. Q. Weinberger (Eds.), Advances in Neural Information Processing Systems (Vol. 25).

Martin, O. A., Kumar, R., Lao, J. (2021). *Bayesian Modeling and Computation in Python*. Chapman and Hall/CRC.

Mikolov, T., Chen, K., Corrado, G., & Dean, J. (2013). *Efficient estimation of word representations in vector space*. arXiv.

Molino, P., & Tagliabue, J. (2023). *Witgenstein's influence on artificial intelligence*. arXiv.

OpenAI. (November 30, 2022). *Introducing ChatGPT*. OpenAI blog: `https://openai.com/blog/chatgpt`

OpenAI. (2023). *GPT-4 Technical Report*. arXiv.

Paszke, A., Gross, S., Chintala, S., Chanan, G., Yang, E., DeVito, Z., Lin, Z., Desmaison, A., Antiga, L., & Lerer, A. (2017). *Automatic differentiation in PyTorch*.

Pearl, J. (2009). *Causality*. Cambridge University Press.

Pearl, J., Glymour, M., & Jewell, N. P. (2016). *Causal inference in statistics: A primer*. Wiley.

Pearl, J., & Mackenzie, D. (2019). *The Book of Why*. Penguin.

Peters, J., Janzing, D., & Schölkopf, B. (2017). *Elements of Causal Inference: Foundations and Learning Algorithms*. MIT Press.

Peters, M. E., Neumann, M., Iyyer, M., Gardner, M., Clark, C., Lee, K., & Zettlemoyer, L. (2018). *Deep Contextualized Word Representations*. North American Chapter of the Association for Computational Linguistics.

Plečko, D., & Bareinboim, E. (2023). *Causal Fairness Analysis*. arXiv.

Pryzant, R., Chung, Y., & Jurafsky, D. (2017). *Predicting Sales from the Language of Product Descriptions*. eCOM@SIGIR.

Pryzant, R., Card, D., Jurafsky, D., Veitch, V., & Sridhar, D. (2021). *Causal Effects of Linguistic Properties*. Proceedings of the 2021 Conference of the North American Chapter of the Association for Computational Linguistics: Human Language Technologies, 4095-4109.

Pryzant, R., Shen, K., Jurafsky, D., & Wagner, S. (2018). *Deconfounded Lexicon Induction for Interpretable Social Science*. Proceedings of the 2018 Conference of the North American Chapter of the Association for Computational Linguistics: Human Language Technologies, 1, 1615–1625.

Radford, A., Kim, J. W., Hallacy, C., Ramesh, A., Goh, G., Agarwal, S., ... & Sutskever, I. (2021). *Learning transferable visual models from natural language supervision*. In International Conference on Machine Learning, 8748-8763. PMLR.

Radford, A., Wu, J., Child, R., Luan, D., Amodei, D., & Sutskever, I. (2019). *Language Models are Unsupervised Multitask Learners*.

Rédei, M. (2002). *Reichenbach's Common Cause Principle and Quantum Correlations.* In: Placek, T., Butterfield, J. (eds) Non-locality and Modality. NATO Science Series, Vol. 64. Springer, Dordrecht.

Rombach, R., Blattmann, A., Lorenz, D., Esser, P., & Ommer, B. (2022). *High-resolution image synthesis with latent diffusion models.* In Proceedings of the IEEE/CVF Conference on Computer Vision and Pattern Recognition, 10684-10695.

Sanh, V., Debut, L., Chaumond, J., & Wolf, T. (2019). *DistilBERT, a distilled version of BERT: smaller, faster, cheaper and lighter.* arXiv.

Shalit, U., Johansson, F. D., & Sontag, D. (2017). *Estimating individual treatment effect: generalization bounds and algorithms.* In International Conference on Machine Learning,. 3076-3085. PMLR.

Shi, C., Blei, D., & Veitch, V. (2019). *Adapting neural networks for the estimation of treatment effects.* Advances in Neural Information Processing Systems, 32.

Vaswani, A., Shazeer, N., Parmar, N., Uszkoreit, J., Jones, L., Gomez, A. N., Kaiser, Ł., & Polosukhin, I. (2017). *Attention is All you Need.* In: I. Guyon, U. V. Luxburg, S. Bengio, H. Wallach, R. Fergus, S. Vishwanathan, & R. Garnett (eds), Advances in Neural Information Processing Systems (Vol. 30).

Veitch, V., Sridhar, D., & Blei, D. (2020). *Adapting text embeddings for causal inference.* In Conference on Uncertainty in Artificial Intelligence, 919-928. PMLR.

Willig, M., Zečević, M., Dhami, D. S., Kersting, K. (2023). *Causal Parrots: Large Language Models May Talk Causality But Are Not Causal [ACM preprint].*

Wittgenstein, L. (1953). *Philosophical investigations.* Philosophische Untersuchungen. Macmillan.

Wittgenstein, L. (1922). *Tractatus Logico-Philosophicus.* Harcourt, Brace & Company, Inc.

Zhang, C., Bauer, S., Bennett, P., Gao, J., Gong, W., Hilmkil, A., ... & Vaughan, J. (2023). *Understanding Causality with Large Language Models*: Feasibility and Opportunities. arXiv.

Zhang, J., Mullainathan, S., & Danescu-Niculescu-Mizil, C. (2020). *Quantifying the causal effects of conversational tendencies.* Proceedings of the ACM on Human-Computer Interaction, 4(CSCW2), 1-24.

Zipf, G. K. (1949). Human behavior and the principle of least effort. Addison Wesley Press.

Part 3: Causal Discovery

In *Part 3*, we will start our journey into the world of causal discovery. We will begin with an overview of the sources of causal knowledge and a deeper look at important assumptions.

We will introduce four families of causal discovery algorithms and implement them using `gCastle`. We will move toward advanced methods and demonstrate how to train a DECI algorithm using PyTorch.

Along the way, we will show you how to inject expert knowledge into the causal discovery process, and we will briefly discuss methods that allow us to combine observational and interventional data to learn causal structure more efficiently.

We will close *Part 3* with a summary of the book, a discussion of causality in business, a sneak peek into the (potential) future of the field, and pointers to more resources on causal inference and discovery for those who are ready to continue their causal journey.

This part comprises the following chapters:

12
Can I Have a Causal Graph, Please?

Welcome to *Chapter 12*.

We will start our journey to the land of **causal discovery** here.

Most people who hear about causal discovery for the first time are truly fascinated by this topic. Other people are skeptical, yet almost no one is indifferent.

Perhaps this tendency toward stronger reactions reveals something fundamental about our own human nature. In the first chapter, we briefly discussed Alison Gopnik's research showing that even infants and small babies run experiments in order to efficiently construct world models.

In this chapter, we'll discuss three sources of causal knowledge and we'll think together about the relative advantages and disadvantages of using them.

By the end of this chapter, you'll have a clear idea about different sources of causal knowledge and will be able to discuss their core strengths and weaknesses.

In this chapter, we will cover the following:

- Sources of causal knowledge
- Scientific experiments and simulations as a source of causal knowledge
- Personal observations and domain knowledge
- Causal discovery and structure learning

Sources of causal knowledge

Malika, Illya, and Lian are 11-month-old infants playing together. Malika passes a toy car to Illya, who had dropped it accidentally. Lian is trying to grab a new teddy bear that her sister put next to the chair. If you observe Malika, Illya, and Lian, you will quickly notice that they are very motivated to explore the environment around them.

This is a good sign – one of the indicators of a healthy developmental trajectory.

There's a catch though.

How do they choose *what* to explore?

You and I, oversaturated

It's estimated that around 11 million bits of information are sent from sensory inputs to the brain every second. In adults, only about 60 bits per second can be consciously processed (Martín, 2009).

It's difficult to assess how much of the 11 million bits can be processed unconsciously. It is also difficult to translate these numbers directly into babies' processing capabilities, but it's safe to say that infants are not able to process all the information available in the environment most of the time.

One of the mechanisms that helps humans and other animals to free up some of their processing capacity is called **habituation**. Habituation is a process in which an organism's response to repeated or prolonged presentations of a stimulus decreases. In other words, we stop paying attention to things that happen around us repeatedly over and over again in a similar way.

Have you ever moved to a new house or apartment with a loud street behind the windows? If you had this experience, it's likely that it was hard not to notice the noise in the beginning.

There's a chance it was pretty annoying to you. You might have even said to yourself or your family or friends "Gosh, how loud this is!"

It is likely that in a month or so, you stopped noticing the noise. The noise became a part of the background; it became essentially *invisible*.

This is habituation at work.

Habituation appears very early in development and can be observed even in later pre-natal stages (e.g., Muenssinger et al., 2013).

The power of a surprise

Developmental psychologists took advantage of the habituation mechanism and created research paradigms such as the **violation of expectation** (**VoE**), which allow them to study how little babies learn. Researchers have shown that surprising (*unhabituated*) events can trigger multiple specific reactions such as alterations in facial expressions, pupil dilation, changes in cerebral blood flow, changes in brain electrical activity, and alterations in looking time.

Aimee Stahl and Lisa Feigenson from Johns Hopkins University have shown groups of 11-month-old infants regular toys and toys that (seemingly) violated the laws of physics. The *altered* toys went through the walls, flowed in the air, and suddenly changed location.

Infants spent more time exploring the altered toys than the regular ones. They also engaged with them differently.

The analyses have shown that babies learned about objects with unexpected behavior better, explored them more, and tested relevant hypotheses for these objects' behavior (Stahl & Feigenson, 2015).

This and other experiments (see Gopnik, 2009) suggest that even very small babies systematically choose actions that help them falsify hypotheses and build relevant causal world models. This interventional active learning approach is essential in achieving this goal.

Do you remember Malika, Illya, and Lian from the beginning of this chapter? Malika passed a toy car to Illya, who dropped it accidentally. It turns out that it's much more likely that a baby will pass a dropped object to a person who dropped it accidentally than to someone who dropped it or threw it intentionally.

World models are critical for efficient navigation in physical and social worlds, and we do not stop building them as grown-ups.

Scientific insights

Human babies have a lot to learn during their development – the laws of physics, language, and social norms. After learning the basics, most children start school. School provides most of us with a canon of current knowledge about a broad variety of topics.

To many people, learning this canon is sufficient. Others, unsettled by the answers to the questions they have or motivated by other factors, decide to dig deeper and look for the answers themselves. Some of these people become scientists.

In this section, we'll take a look at causal knowledge through the lens of scientific methods. We'll introduce some core scientific methodologies and touch upon their benefits and limitations.

The logic of science

Karl Popper, one of the 20th century's most famous philosophers of science, used to say that "*what is true in logic is true in scientific method*" (Popper, 1971). We briefly mentioned Popper's framework in *Chapter 7* and we'll refresh it now.

Popper's narrative is as follows: saying that all *X*s are *x* is usually impossible because we usually cannot observe all *X*s (and if in certain cases we can observe all *X*s, we don't need science for these cases, as we can observe all the outcomes).

Although we cannot observe all *X*s and hence we cannot definitely confirm any particular hypothesis about *X*s, we can still learn something useful.

"All *X*s are *x*" is logically equivalent to "no *X* is *not x*." Although we cannot unambiguously prove that all *X*s are *x*, finding even a single case where *X* is *not x* disproves the hypothesis that all *X*s are *x*. Disproving a hypothesis in this way is called **falsification**.

A falsifiable hypothesis is a hypothesis for which we can define an empirical test that can falsify this hypothesis. *All pigeons are white* is a falsifiable hypothesis that can be falsified by finding at least one non-white pigeon.

On the other hand, the existence of an intelligent supernatural being is usually not falsifiable unless we set a hypothesis in a very specific way, for instance, *the existence of a supernatural being guarantees that no person ever dies before their 18th birthday.*

It seems to me that not many people who advocate for the existence of supernatural beings are interested in formulating hypotheses such as this. Other, more general or more vague hypotheses in similar contexts usually turn out to be unfalsifiable.

Hypotheses are a species

In the Popperian framework, hypotheses come from theories (or tentative theories). Once generated, hypotheses should be scrutinized, i.e., put to the empirical test, which can falsify them.

If a hypothesis generated from a theory is falsified, the theory in its original shape is falsified and should be retracted. Every theory can generate many different hypotheses, yet a theory that survives the largest number of tests is *not* necessarily *more true*. It's more *fit*, in a sense, analogous to *fitness* in biological evolution.

For instance, a theory might *fit* the current data very well. The reason for that might be that we simply do not have advanced enough tooling to collect the data that *could falsify* this theory and so the theory's *fitness* does not automatically translate to its *truthfulness*. Some of these views have been since criticized and not all of them are broadly accepted today (see the callout box).

Popper and other philosophers

We present a very brief and synthetic overview of the Popperian framework here, which is certainly simplified and not complete. Although Popper's ideas are still a vital part of modern scientific culture, we should be aware that some of them have been criticized.

For instance, Thomas Kuhn has proposed an alternative model of how science develops over time (Kuhn, 1962), and other philosophers such as Imre Lakatos or Paul Feyerabend criticized Popper's views on the demarcation between science and pseudo-science and his criteria of theory rejection.

One of the (perhaps surprising) consequences of the consistent Popperism is the rejection of Darwin's theory of evolution as non-scientific (Popper himself called it *an interesting metaphysics project*; Rosenberg & McIntyre, 2020).

French physicist Pierre Duhem and American logician Willard Van Orman Quine argued independently that hypotheses cannot be empirically falsified in isolation because an empirical test needs auxiliary assumptions. Popper's theory has been also criticized as overly romantic and non-realistic (Rosenberg & McIntyre, 2020).

One logic, many ways

Scientific inquiry can take different forms depending on the object of interest of a given field.

Physicists usually design their experiments differently from psychologists. Although virtually all scientists follow (or at least do their best to follow) a set of similar basic principles, they might *do* very different things *in practice*.

For instance, physicists are interested in formulating hypotheses regarding the universal basic laws that rule the physical world. The objects they are interested in can be often described by a finite number of well-defined physical observables.

On the other hand, psychologists try to capture universal laws governing human and other animals' cognition and behavior.

The number of ways in which two individual chimpanzees or humans can differ is even difficult to quantify. Animals can be viewed as complex systems, where multiple different factors interact with each other and with the environment in a virtually infinite dance.

These differences are reflected in the choice of scientific tools that scientists in these fields make.

Controlled experiments

Physicists, chemists, and other representatives of the so-called *hard sciences* often work with controlled experiments. The *control* aspect means that the experimental environment is carefully controlled in order to minimize any interference from the outside world or – in other words – to keep the context variables constant. An extreme example of such control is projects such as the *Large Hadron Collider*

– a sophisticated experimental system consisting of a 27-kilometer-long ring of superconducting magnets placed over 100 meters under the ground and a no less sophisticated shielding system aiming to reduce unwanted outside influences.

Many experiments in *hard sciences* do not require randomization, as the objects the experimenters deal with are considered to be governed by universal principles and the observed effects are often assumed to be generalizable to other conditions. For instance, if a properly designed experiment concerning some universal principles is conducted in Paris, the results are assumed to be replicable in Kyiv, New York, and Shanghai.

Things are different in medicine, social sciences, and agriculture. The objects studied in these fields are usually complex and might significantly differ from each other along dimensions that are not observed. If the treatment and control groups differ systematically along some of these dimensions, this might lead to biased results. How to address this risk?

Randomized controlled trials (RCTs)

Randomized controlled trials (RCTs) are experiments where participants (or – more broadly – units) are randomly assigned to experimental conditions. The idea of randomization comes from the iconic British polymath Sir Ronald Aymler Fisher. Fisher used the idea of randomization in the context of agriculture. Although the idea was known before, he formalized it and popularized it through his work, starting in the 1920s.

The goal of randomization is to eliminate bias and permit valid significance testing (Hall, 2007). Contrary to popular misconception, randomization *does not* make treatment and control groups *balanced* or *homogenous* (Senn, 2020).

RCTs are often considered the *golden standard* for inferring causal relationships.

That said, the idea of randomization seems controversial to many. As expressed by Stephen Senn, "*(...) it has remained controversial ever since it was introduced by R.A. Fisher into the design of agricultural studies in the 1920s and even statisticians disagree about its value*" (Senn, 2021).

One of the challenges with RCTs pointed out by some authors is that they do not provide us with estimates of the efficacy of treatment at the individual level, but only at a group level (e.g., Kostis & Dobrzynski, 2020). Other authors suggest that this is not always problematic and that often the group-level conclusions are *surprisingly transportable* to individuals (e.g., Harrell, 2023), but as we saw in *Chapter 9*, group-level conclusions can hide important information from us.

In this section, we implicitly assumed that an RCT consists of two (or more) groups that are assigned to the treatment or control conditions in parallel. This is not the only possible RCT design. Moreover, other designs such as cross-over design might be more powerful. Further discussion on experimental designs is beyond the scope of this book. Check Harrell (2023) for a starter.

From experiments to graphs

Scientific experiments can help us understand which real-world phenomena are causally related. Although from a traditional Popperian point of view, it would be difficult to argue that science can provide us with *true* causal graphs, most people would probably agree that science can *help* us decide which causal graphs are *plausible*.

Each new hypothesis and each new experiment can potentially deepen our understanding of real-world causal systems and this understanding can be encoded using causal graphs (note that not all systems can be easily described using acyclic graphs and sometimes causality might be difficult to quantify). For instance, you might be interested in how the brightness of colors on your website impacts sales. You might design an A/B test to test this hypothesis. If the results indicate an influence of color brightness on sales, you should add an edge from brightness to sales to a graph describing the causes of sales.

Simulations

Simulations are another way to obtain causal knowledge.

Simulations usually start with a set of known (or hypothesized) low-level mechanisms. We code these mechanisms in order to observe a high-level behavior of a system of interest.

For instance, at TensorCell (`https://bit.ly/TensorCell`), a research group founded by a Polish mathematician and AI researcher Paweł Gora, we used simulators of traffic systems to optimize traffic control systems using various machine learning and reinforcement learning techniques.

Performing interventions in a simulator is typically much cheaper than performing interventions in a real-world system, yet if the simulator is precise enough, we expect to obtain valuable real-world insights from such interventions.

Interestingly, complex simulations might also become too expensive for certain purposes. For example, using a complex traffic simulator to produce inputs for a reinforcement learning agent is inefficient and very slow. At TensorCell, we used **graph neural networks** and **Transformer** models to approximate the outputs of simulators to tackle this problem.

In this section, we discussed the foundations of the scientific method and core scientific tools that can be used to generate causal knowledge. We briefly discussed how hypotheses can be put to the empirical test using experiments and what the main advantages and limitations of this approach are.

Now, let's take a look at less formal sources of causal knowledge.

Personal experience and domain knowledge

We started this chapter by talking about how babies perform experiments to build causal world models. In this section, we'll look into an adult's approach to refining and building such models.

Imagine a rainy chilly afternoon somewhere in Northern Europe. You stand at a bus stop near your favorite park. There's a large puddle on the street in front of you. You notice a car approaching from the left, driving close to the sidewalk. It seems that it will drive straight into the puddle. As the car approaches the puddle without slowing down, you instinctively jump behind the bus stop's shelter. Water hits the shelter's glass right next to your face, but fortunately, you are safe on the other side.

Your reaction was likely a result of many different factors, including a fast instinctive response to a threatening stimulus (splashing muddy water), but it was likely not entirely instinctive. You noticed a car in advance and likely simulated what will happen. A simulation like this requires us to have a world model.

In this case, your model of what will happen when a relatively hard object (a tire) moves through a puddle at a sufficient speed likely comes from various different experiences. It might have experimental components (such as you jumping into puddles as a 2-year-old and observing the effects of your interventions) and observational components (you seeing a person splashed by a car and observing the consequences).

Personal experiences

Personal experiences such as the ones that led you to simulate the car splashing you with the water can be a valid source of causal knowledge. Humans and some other animals can effectively generalize experiences and knowledge from one context to another.

That said, the generalizations are not always correct. A good example comes from the realm of clinical psychology. Children growing up in dysfunctional families might (and usually do) learn specific relational patterns (how to relate to other people in various situations).

These patterns are often carried into adulthood and *transferred* to relationships with new people, causing unstable or destructive relationship dynamics. Although the original patterns worked well in the family of origin, they do not work well in a new relationship. The model has not been updated.

Personal experiences are vulnerable to many biases, especially when they rely on observational data and are not examined critically. Daniel Kahneman and Amos Tversky collected an extensive list of such biases. Here, we'll only briefly discuss one of them.

An availability heuristic is a mental shortcut (usually used unconsciously) that relies on the data that comes to mind first (or most easily; Kahneman, 2011). For instance, if you usually see men rather than women in leadership positions, the image of a man will be cognitively more accessible for you when you think about leadership.

This might make you subconsciously associate men with leadership and manifest itself in a conscious belief that being male is related to being better equipped to take leadership positions, although the evidence suggests otherwise (e.g., Zenger & Folkman, 2020).

An availability heuristic might lead not only to faulty world models but also to interesting paradoxes. Multiple studies have shown that although women are perceived as having stronger key leadership competencies than men, they are not necessarily perceived as better leaders by the same group of people (e.g., Pew Research Center, 2008).

Domain knowledge

Domain knowledge can rely on various sources. It might be based on scientific knowledge, personal experiences, cultural transmission, or a combination of all of these.

Domain experts will usually have a deep understanding of one or more areas that they spent a significant amount of time studying and/or interacting with. They might be able to accurately simulate various scenarios within their area of expertise.

The main risks related to domain expertise as a source of causal knowledge are similar to the risks that we've discussed in terms of personal experience. Cultural transmission that takes place in everyday life and organizations can also equip us with incorrect or biased models (e.g., prayers for rain seem to assume an incorrect causal model).

On top of this, experts can be sensitive to overconfidence, especially when they have a narrow focus. It turns out that experts that are specialized in a narrow field tend to give predictions about the future that are not better than the ones provided by complete laymen and sometimes even worse, indicating inaccurate world models (Tetlock, 2005; Tetlock & Gardner, 2015).

Phillip Tetlock's research that we refer to here was specifically focused on forecasting in complex real-world scenarios. Although the conclusions might not generalize perfectly to some other areas, they definitely highlight an important risk factor in using domain expertise as a source of causal knowledge.

Summarizing, personal experiences and domain expertise can be valuable sources of causal knowledge. At the same time, they are susceptible to numerous distortions associated with heuristics and biases.

Personal experiences and domain expertise seem to be generally less trustworthy than scientific insights, but in certain cases, they might be in fact more accurate (e.g., when no scientific insights are available for a given (sub)domain or the domain is highly heterogeneous).

Causal structure learning

The last source of causal knowledge that we will discuss in this chapter is causal structure learning. **Causal structure learning** (sometimes used interchangeably with **causal discovery**) is a set of methods aiming at recovering the structure of the data-generating process from the data generated by this process. Traditional causal discovery focused on recovering the causal structure from observational data only.

Some more recent methods allow for encoding expert knowledge into the graph or learning from interventional data (with known or unknown interventions).

Causal structure learning might be much cheaper and faster than running an experiment, but it often turns out to be challenging in practice.

Many causal structure learning methods require no hidden confounding – a condition difficult to guarantee in numerous real-world scenarios. Some causal discovery methods try to overcome this limitation with some success.

Another challenge is scalability – the space of possible **directed acyclic graphs** (**DAGs**) grows super exponentially according to the number of nodes in the graph.

An exciting and relatively new research direction is to combine causal structure learning with domain knowledge and efficient experimentation.

We'll learn more about causal discovery in the next chapter.

Wrapping it up

In this chapter, we discussed three broad sources of causal knowledge: scientific insights, personal experiences and domain knowledge, and causal structure learning.

We saw that humans start to work on building world models very early in development; yet not all world models that we build are accurate. Heuristics that we use introduce biases that can skew our models on an individual, organizational, or cultural level.

Scientific experiments are an attempt to structure the process of obtaining knowledge so that we can exclude or minimize unwanted interferences and sources of distortion.

Unfortunately, experiments are not always available and have their own limitations. Causal structure learning methods can be cheaper and faster than running experiments, but they might rely on assumptions difficult to meet in certain scenarios.

Hybrid methods that combine causal structure learning, domain expertise, and efficient experimentation are a new exciting field of research.

Let's see how to implement causal discovery algorithms and how they work in practice.

See you in *Chapter 13*!

References

Gopnik, A. (2009). *The philosophical baby: What children's minds tell us about truth, love, and the meaning of life*. Farrar, Straus and Giroux.

Hall N. S. (2007). *R. A. Fisher and his advocacy of randomization. Journal of the History of Biology*, 40(2), 295–325.

Harrell, F. (2023, February 14). *Randomized Clinical Trials Do Not Mimic Clinical Practice, Thank Goodness. Statistical Thinking.* https://www.fharrell.com/post/rct-mimic/

Kahneman, D. (2011). *Thinking, fast and slow.* Farrar, Straus and Giroux.

Kostis, J. B., & Dobrzynski, J. M. (2020). *Limitations of Randomized Clinical Trials. The American Journal of Cardiology*, 129, 109–115.

Kuhn, T. S. (1962). *The structure of scientific revolutions.* University of Chicago Press.

Martín, F. M. (2009). *The thermodynamics of human reaction times.* arXiv, abs/0908.3170.

Muenssinger, J., Matuz, T., Schleger, F., Kiefer-Schmidt, I., Goelz, R., Wacker-Gussmann, A., Birbaumer, N., & Preissl, H. (2013). *Auditory habituation in the fetus and neonate: an fMEG study. Developmental Science*, 16(2), 287–295.

Pew Research Center. (2008). *Men or Women: Who's the Better Leader? A Paradox in Public Attitudes.* https://www.pewresearch.org/social-trends/2008/08/25/men-or-women-whos-the-better-leader/

Popper, K. (1959). *The Logic of Scientific Discovery.* Basic Books.

Popper, K. (1971). *Conjectural Knowledge: My Solution of the Problem of Induction.* Revue Internationale de Philosophie, 25(95/96), 167-197.

Rosenberg, A., & McIntyre, L. (2020). *Philosophy of Science: A Contemporary Introduction (4th ed.).* Routledge.

Senn, S. S. (2021). *Statistical Issues in Drug Development (3rd ed.).* Wiley.

Senn, S. S. (2020, April 20). *Randomisation is not about balance, nor about homogeneity but about randomness.* Error Statistics. https://errorstatistics.com/2020/04/20/s-senn-randomisation-is-not-about-balance-nor-about-homogeneity-but-about-randomness-guest-post/

Stahl, A. E., & Feigenson, L. (2015). *Cognitive development. Observing the unexpected enhances infants' learning and exploration.* Science (New York, N.Y.), 348(6230), 91–94.

Tetlock, P.E. (2005). *Expert Political Judgment: How Good Is It? How Can We Know?* Princeton University Press.

Tetlock, P. E., & Gardner, D. (2015). *Superforecasting: The Art and Science of Prediction.* Crown.

Zenger, J., & Folkman, J. (2020, December 30). *Research: Women Are Better Leaders During a Crisis. Harvard Business Review.* https://hbr.org/2020/12/research-women-are-better-leaders-during-a-crisis

13

Causal Discovery and Machine Learning – from Assumptions to Applications

In the previous chapter, we reviewed three classes of sources of causal knowledge and discussed their main advantages and disadvantages. In this chapter, we'll focus on the last source of knowledge mentioned in the previous chapter – **causal discovery**.

We'll start by reviewing the popular assumptions behind causal discovery. Next, we'll present four broad families of methods for causal discovery and we'll introduce **gCastle** – the main Python package that we'll use in this chapter. We'll follow with a comparison of selected methods and a practical guide on how to combine causal discovery algorithms with expert knowledge.

By the end of this chapter, you will know a broad range of causal discovery methods. You'll be able to implement them using Python and gCastle and you'll understand the mechanics and implications of combining selected methods with pre-existing domain knowledge.

In this chapter, we will cover the following:

- Assumptions for causal discovery – a refresher
- Introduction to gCastle
- Constraint-based causal discovery
- Score-based causal discovery
- Functional causal discovery
- Gradient-based causal discovery
- Encoding expert knowledge

Causal discovery – assumptions refresher

The first time we mentioned causal discovery in this book was in *Chapter 1*. In *Chapter 5*, we went a little bit deeper and discussed two assumptions that are often used for causal discovery methods: **faithfulness** and **minimality**.

In this section, we'll review these assumptions and discuss other, more general assumptions that will be useful in our causal discovery journey.

Let's start!

Gearing up

Causal discovery aims at discovering (or learning) the true causal graph from observational (and sometimes interventional or mixed) data.

In general, this task is difficult but possible under certain conditions. Many causal discovery methods will require that we meet a set of assumptions in order to use them properly.

The first general assumption is one of **causal sufficiency** (or lack of **hidden confounding**). A vast majority of causal discovery methods rely on this assumption (although not all).

Another popular assumption for causal discovery is faithfulness.

Always trying to be faithful...

The **faithfulness** assumption states that if two variables are *conditionally independent* in their distributions given a third variable, they will also be *conditionally independent* in the graph that represents the data-generating process. This is represented more formally here:

$$X \perp\!\!\!\perp_P Y|Z \Rightarrow X \perp\!\!\!\perp_G Y|Z$$

This assumption is the reverse of the **global Markov property** that we use for **causal inference** and that we discussed back in *Chapter 5*. The formula says that if X and Y are independent in their distribution given Z, they will also be independent in the graph given Z.

...but it's difficult sometimes

The faithfulness assumption might be difficult to fulfill sometimes. One reason for this is the sampling error when testing for conditional independence in the finite sample size regime (Uhler et al., 2013).

Moreover, any situation where one variable influences another through two different paths and these paths *cancel out completely* will lead to the violation of faithfulness (see *Chapter 5* for more details and see Neal Brady's video for a quick reference: `https://bit.ly/BradyFaithfulness`).

That said, the probability of encountering the latter in the real world is extremely small (Sprites et al., 2000, pp. 68-69), even if it feels easy to come up with theoretical examples (Peters et al., 2017, pp. 107-108).

Minimalism is a virtue

There might exist more than one graph or **structural causal model** (**SCM**) that entails the same distribution.

That's a challenge for recovering the causal structure as the mapping between the structure and the distribution becomes ambiguous.

The **causal minimality** assumption is designed to address this. The assumption states that the **directed acyclic graph** (**DAG**) G is minimal with respect to distribution P if, and only if, G induces P, but no proper subgraph of G induces P. In other words, if graph G induces P, removing *any* edge from G should result in a distribution that is different than P.

Although not all causal discovery methods require all three assumptions that we discussed in this section, the three are likely the most frequent over a broad set of methods. We'll talk more about this when discussing particular methods in detail.

In this section, we refreshed three popular assumptions that many causal discovery methods rely on: *sufficiency*, *faithfulness*, and *minimality*.

In the next section, we'll discuss four streams of ideas that led to the development of classic and contemporary causal discovery methods.

The four (and a half) families

In this section, we'll present an overview of the four families of causal discovery methods. By the end of this section, you should have a good grasp of the four families and their core properties.

We use the word *families* rather than a more formal term such as *type*, as the distinction between the four families we'll use might be slightly vague. We follow the categorization proposed by Glymour et al. (2019) and extend it slightly to include more recent causal discovery methods not mentioned in Glymour and colleagues' paper.

The four streams

The origins of modern causal discovery can be traced back to the works of Judea Pearl and the 1987 paper he co-authored with George Rebane. The paper described a method that recovers causal structure from statistical data, assuming that the data-generating process has a poly-tree structure (Rebane and Pearl, 1987).

The ideas that followed from this research led to two parallel research streams focused around three academic centers – the **University of California, Los Angeles** (**UCLA**), **Carnegie Mellon University** (**CMU**), and **Stanford** (Pearl, 2009):

- **Constraint-based methods**: Researchers from UCLA and CMU focused on the approach to causal discovery based on graph independencies (understood as we described them in *Chapter 5*). We refer to such methods as constraint-based methods. This research stream led to the development of algorithms such as **inductive causation** (**IC**) and its implementation in a famous software package called TETRAD.
- **Score-based method**: The work at Stanford focused on the Bayesian network approach. Early research (for example, Heckerman et al., 1995) paved the way for the development of the **greedy equivalence search** (**GES**) algorithm (Chickering, 2020) – one of the classic examples of a score-based method.
- **Functional causal discovery**: The third line of thought was inspired by **independent component analysis** (**ICA**) (Hyvärinen et al., 2001) and developed by Shohei Shimizu and colleagues. We refer to this family of algorithms as functional causal discovery. Algorithms in this family leverage various aspects of functional forms of the relationships between variables in order to determine the causal direction. A classic example representing this family is the **Linear Non-Gaussian Acyclic Model** (**LiNGAM**) algorithm (Shimizu et al., 2006).
- **Gradient-based methods**: The fourth line of thought originates from the research focused on the idea of treating the graph space search as a continuous optimization problem. We'll refer to this fourth family as gradient-based methods, as we typically use gradient descent for optimization purposes. A classic method within this family is the **NOTEARS** algorithm (Zheng et al., 2018).

This section was titled *The four (and a half) families*. What about the remaining half?

The remaining half includes hybrid methods, reinforcement-learning-based methods, and other methods that do not fit the main four categories. This is not to say that these methods are less important.

Each of the families comes with its own benefits and challenges, yet the demarcation lines between them might sometimes be blurry.

In this section, we introduced the four (and a half) families of causal discovery algorithms – constraint-based, score-based, functional, gradient-based, and other – and provided a brief historical account of the main four categories.

We'll discuss each family in greater detail, but before we start, let's introduce the main library that we'll use in this chapter – **gCastle**.

Introduction to gCastle

In this section, we'll introduce gCastle (Zhang et al., 2021) – a causal discovery library that we'll use in this chapter. We'll introduce four main modules: models, synthetic data generators, visualization tools, and model evaluation tools. By the end of this section, you'll be able to generate a synthetic dataset of chosen complexity, fit a causal discovery model, visualize the results, and evaluate the model using your synthetic data as a reference.

Hello, gCastle!

What is gCastle?

It's an open source Python causal discovery library created by Huawei's Noah's Ark Lab. The library provides us with a comprehensive selection of modern causal discovery algorithms that include classics such as the PC algorithm, as well as cutting-edge gradient- or reinforcement-learning-based methods.

The repository (`https://bit.ly/gCastleRepo`) includes example notebooks, a list of currently available models, and basic documentation.

A great strength of gCastle is that it provides us with a unified, very intuitive, and elegant API for interacting with various causal discovery models. This makes the experimentation and model comparison seamless.

The library has four main functional components:

- Synthetic data generators
- Models
- Visualization tools
- Model evaluation tools

Let's examine them!

Synthetic data in gCastle

Synthetic data is often a natural choice for benchmarking causal discovery algorithms, as not many real-world causal datasets are publicly available. gCastle provides us with the `datasets` module, which allows us to generate synthetic data easily.

gCastle's datasets module

The two main objects in the module are `DAG` and `IIDSimulation`. The former allows us to generate graphs (structure) in the form of an **adjacency matrix**. The latter generates the actual data given an adjacency matrix and a set of parameters that define the properties of **structural equations** that determine the relationships between variables.

The `DAG` object allows us to generate five different types of graphs:

- Erdős–Rényi
- Scale-free (Barabási–Albert)
- Bipartite
- Hierarchical
- Low-rank

Graph types, graph theory, and network science

The idea of distinguishing between different types of graphs comes from graph theory and was later extended by what we know today as **network science**. The latter started with the works of two Hungarian mathematicians, Paul Erdős and Alfréd Rényi, who studied so-called **random graphs** (Erdös and Rényi, 1959). More recently, network science regained popularity with the works of Albert-László Barabási and Réka Albert (for example, Barabási and Albert, 1999; Barabási, 2009).

The `IIDSimulation` object allows us to choose between linear and non-linear assignments. Linear datasets can be binary (`logistic`) or continuous. Continuous datasets can be created using one of four different noise distributions:

- Gaussian (`gauss`)
- Exponential (`exp`)
- Gumbel (`gumbel`)
- Uniform (`uniform`)

Non-linear datasets can be generated using the following:

- **Multilayer perceptron** (`mlp`)
- Two versions of **Gaussian processes** (`gp` and `gp-add`)
- Quadratic function (`quadratic`)
- Multiple index model (`mim`; Zheng et al., 2020)

There's also an additional simulator class called `THPSimulation`, which allows for simulating event sequences with **Topological Hawkes Processes** (**THP**). The discussion on THP is beyond the scope of this book. To learn more, check Cai et al. (2021).

Let's generate some data. On the way, we'll also briefly discuss scale-free graphs and the main parameters of the `IIDSimulation` object.

Generating the data with gCastle

Let's start with the imports. The code for this chapter can be found in the notebook at `https://bit.ly/causal-ntbk-13`.

We import the `DAG` and `IIDSimulation` objects from gCastle. Additionally, we import NetworkX and Matplotlib for visualizations:

```
from castle.datasets import DAG, IIDSimulation
import networkx as nx
import matplotlib.pyplot as plt
```

We set the seed to keep the code reproducible:

```
SEED = 18
np.random.seed(SEED)
```

Now, we're ready to generate our first adjacency matrix:

```
adj_matrix = DAG.scale_free(
    n_nodes=10,
    n_edges=17,
    seed=SEED
)
```

We use the `.scale_free()` method of the `DAG` object. We specify the number of nodes to be `10` and the number of edges to be `17`. We fix the random seed to the predefined value.

Scale-free networks have a number of interesting properties. They are created using a probabilistic **preferential attachment** mechanism. A node with a large number of connections is more likely to gain new connections than a node with a smaller number of connections.

This is sometimes metaphorically described as *the rich get richer*. The distribution of node degrees (number of edges per node) in scale-free networks is fat-tailed. This is because scale-free networks tend to have a few strongly connected hubs and a majority of nodes have a significantly smaller number of connections.

Although scale-free networks were known at least from the 1960s (although not necessarily under their current name), they significantly gained popularity in the late 1990s and early 2000s with the works of Albert-László Barabási and Réka Albert, who proposed that scale-free networks can be used to model the internet interlink structure and other real-world systems (Barabási and Albert, 1999; Barabási, 2009).

Graphs, networks, and adjacency matrices

In network science terms, *graph* and *network* are used interchangeably. As we discussed in *Chapter 4*, graphs can be represented as adjacency matrices, and matrices can be visualized as graphs. We extensively use this correspondence in the current chapter.

Let's plot the graph representing our adjacency matrix and see whether we can recognize the preferential attachment scheme in the plot. We'll use NetworkX for this purpose.

First, let's transform the adjacency matrix into the NetworkX directed graph object:

```
g = nx.DiGraph(adj_matrix)
```

Next, let's plot the graph `g`:

```
plt.figure(figsize=(12, 8))
nx.draw(
    G=g,
    node_color=COLORS[0],
    node_size=1200,
    pos=nx.circular_layout(g)
)
```

We set the figure size using Matplotlib and pass a number of parameters to NetworkX's `nx.draw()` method. We pass `g` as a graph, set the node color and size, and define the network layout to increase readability. The circular layout should provide good visual clarity for our relatively small graph.

To learn about other layout options in NetworkX, check `https://bit.ly/NetworkXLayouts` or the NetworkX documentation (`https://bit.ly/NetworkXDrawingDocs`).

Figure 13.1 presents the resulting graph:

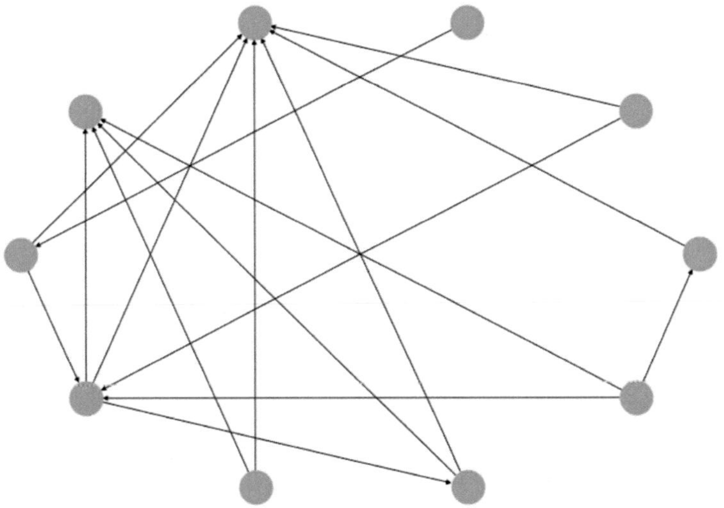

Figure 13.1 – A graph representing the adjacency matrix, g

In *Figure 13.1*, at the top, we see a highly connected node with six incoming edges. This is the effect of the preferential attachment mechanism. If we grew our graph further, the differences between highly connected nodes and less connected nodes would become even more visible. Looking at the graph in *Figure 13.1*, you can imagine how the preferential attachment mechanism would add more edges to the more connected nodes and fewer edges to the less connected ones.

We are now ready to generate some data. We'll use our adjacency matrix, `adj_matrix`, and generate 10,000 observations with linear structural assignments and Gaussian noise:

```
dataset = IIDSimulation(
    W=adj_matrix,
    n=10000,
    method='linear',
    sem_type='gauss'
)
```

The parameter `W` accepts adjacency matrices as NumPy arrays. Matrices can be (but do not have to be) weighted, `n` determines the number of samples returned, and we can choose between linear and non-linear datasets via the `method` parameter (available options are `linear` and `nonlinear`). Finally, `sem_type` determines the key characteristics of the structural assignments (`gauss`, `exp`, `mlp`, etc.).

The `dataset` object produced by `IIDSimulation` has two attributes: `X` and `B`. The former contains the actual data, and the latter contains the adjacency matrix.

We can access the generated data as follows:

```
dataset.X
```

With our dataset generated, let's learn how to fit a gCastle causal discovery model.

Fitting your first causal discovery model

gCastle offers a broad variety of causal discovery models, from classics such as PC and GES models up to recent gradient-based methods such as GOLEM.

For the sake of this demonstration, we will use the PC algorithm.

Let's start with the imports:

```
from castle.algorithms import PC
```

After importing the model class, we need to instantiate it.

```
pc = PC()
```

Training the model is extremely simple:

```
pc.learn(dataset.X)
```

The output of a causal discovery algorithm is a learned adjacency matrix. Depending on the method you use, this matrix can be either weighted or unweighted. In our case, we learned an unweighted adjacency matrix. Let's access it:

```
pc.causal_matrix
```

This will print out the learned causal matrix. We won't print it here to save space, but you can see the matrix in this chapter's notebook.

Now that we have learned the adjacency matrix, we are ready to compare it with the ground truth. First, we'll do it visually.

Visualizing the model

In the previous subsection, we visualized the adjacency matrix as a graph. Let's do the same for the true DAG and the learned DAG to compare them. *Figure 13.2* presents the result:

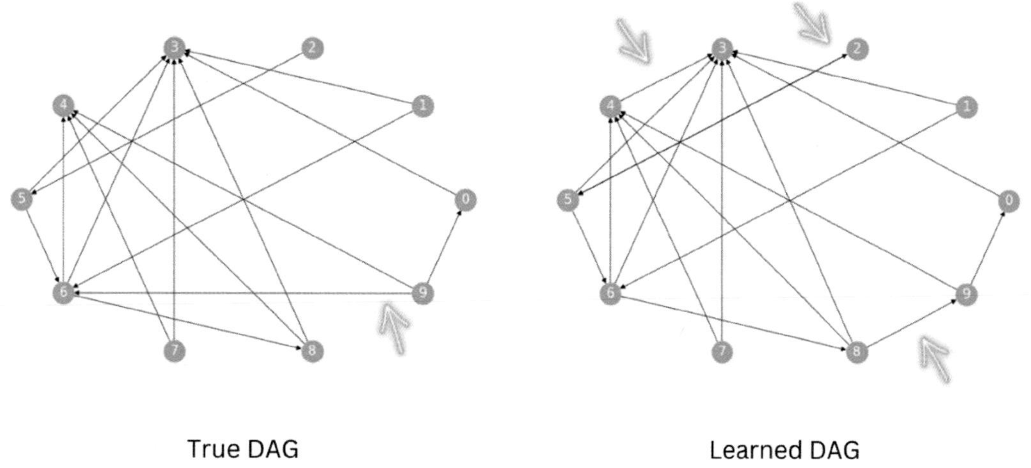

Figure 13.2 – True DAG versus learned DAG

We added yellow arrows in *Figure 13.2* to denote incorrectly identified edges. Note that the edge between nodes 2 and 5 exists in both the true and the learned DAGs, but in the learned DAG, this edge is *bidirectional*. This is a practical example of a situation where a causal discovery model returns a **complete partially directed acyclic graph** (**CPDAG**; recall our discussion on **Markov equivalence classes** in *Chapter 5*).

Comparing two graphs visually is only useful for smaller graphs. Although our graph has only 10 nodes and 17 edges, the comparison might be already challenging for some of us.

Another way to visualize adjacency matrices is to use heatmaps. Because our adjacency matrix is unweighted, a respective heatmap will be binary. In a binary heatmap, each cell can only have one of two values (`0` or `1`).

gCastle comes with a convenience object called `GraphDAG` that plots comparison heatmaps for us. Let's import `GraphDAG` and see it in action:

```
from castle.common import GraphDAG
GraphDAG(
    est_dag=pred_dag,
    true_dag=adj_matrix)
```

You can see the resulting plot in *Figure 13.3*:

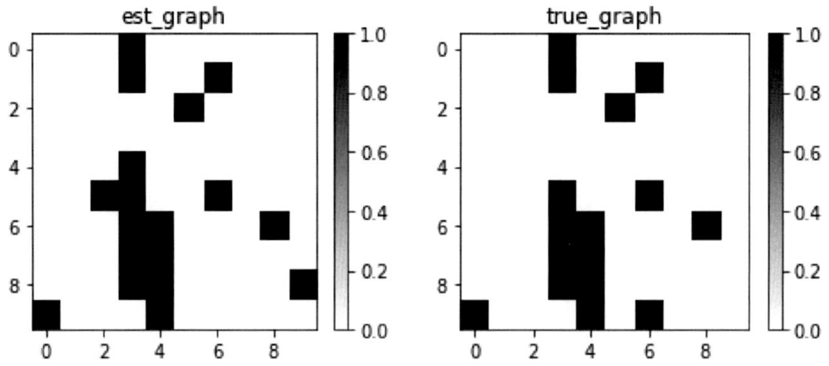

Figure 13.3 – Heatmaps representing the learned and the true adjacency matrices

After a short inspection, you should be able to spot four differences between the two matrices in *Figure 13.3*. That's congruent with our observation from *Figure 13.2*.

Although heatmaps might make it easier for us to make visual comparisons between slightly bigger graphs, they only work to a point.

Visual comparisons might be useful and even very helpful in certain cases, yet their usefulness is limited due to the limitations of our human attention, which can only track between three and seven elements at a time. That's when numerical evaluation metrics become useful.

Model evaluation metrics

gCastle comes with a dedicated object for model evaluation called `MetricsDAG`.

Let's import the object and instantiate it:

```
from castle.metrics import MetricsDAG
metrics = MetricsDAG(
    B_est=pred_dag,
    B_true=adj_matrix
)
```

The newly created `metrics` object computes a number of useful metrics for us internally. We can access them through a dictionary internally stored as an attribute called `metrics`. The values for all available metrics can be easily accessed via respective dictionary keys.

For example, to access the F1 score, we do it in the following way:

```
metrics.metrics['F1']
```

The F1 score for the PC algorithm on our graph is as follows:

```
0.8824
```

As of the time of writing (gCastle, version 1.0.3), there are nine available metrics in `MetricsDAG`.

We can access the complete metrics dictionary as follows:

```
metrics.metrics
```

This will give us the following:

```
{'fdr': 0.1176,
 'tpr': 0.9375,
 'fpr': 0.069,
 'shd': 3,
 'nnz': 17,
 'precision': 0.8333,
 'recall': 0.9375,
 'F1': 0.8824,
 'gscore': 0.75}
```

Table 13.1 presents a summary and definitions of the metrics available in gCastle 1.0.3:

Name	Acronym	Definition
False Discovery Rate	`fdr`	$\frac{rev + FP}{TP + FP}$
True Positive Rate	`tpr`	$\frac{TP}{TP + FN}$
False Positive Rate	`fpr`	$\frac{rev + FP}{TN + FP}$
Structural Hamming Distance	`shd`	No. of edge additions, flips, or deletions to get from the predicted graph to the true one
No. of Non-Negative Entries	`nnz`	$TP + FP$
Precision	`precision`	$\frac{TP}{TP + FP}$
Recall	`recall`	$\frac{TP}{TP + FN}$
F1 Score	`F1`	$2\frac{recall \cdot precision}{recall + precision}$
G-Score	`gscore`	$\max\left(0, \frac{TP - FP}{TP + FN}\right)$

Table 13.1 – Summary of metrics available in the MetricsDAG object

In *Table 13.1*, *TP* stands for the number of **true positives**, *FP* stands for the number of **false positives**, *TN* stands for the number of **true negatives**, and *FN* stands for the number of **false negatives**; *rev* represents the number of **reversed edges**.

We would count an entry in the adjacency matrix as a *true positive* if we predicted that this entry should be `1` and it is also `1` in the true graph. On the other hand, we say that an entry is a *true negative* when we predicted it to be `0` and it's also `0` in the true graph. If we predicted an entry as `1` but in fact, it's `0`, we count it as a *false positive*. If we predicted an entry as `0` but in fact, it's `1`, we count it as a *false negative*. Reversed edges are the ones that exist in the predicted and the true graph, but we mispredicted their orientation (direction).

We'll discuss how to understand some of the metrics in the subsequent sections.

There are two other useful quantities that you might want to compute when benchmarking causal discovery methods: the number of undirected edges and the **structural intervention distance** (**SID**) (Peters and Bühlmann, 2015).

We can implement the former, for instance, this way:

```
def get_n_undirected(g):
    total = 0
    for i in range(g.shape[0]):
        for j in range(g.shape[0]):
            if (g[i, j] == 1) and (g[i, j] == g[j, i]):
                total += .5
    return total
```

The latter is available in the CDT Python package (`https://bit.ly/CDTMetricsDocs`) as a wrapper for an R implementation.

Now, let's summarize what we've learned in this section.

In this section, we introduced gCastle, a causal discovery library that we will use throughout this chapter. We've discussed the four main modules of the package: the synthetic data generation module, models module, data visualization module, and model evaluation module. We introduced data simulation and model fitting APIs, and demonstrated how to use the `GraphDAG` class for visualizations and the `MetricsDAG` class for calculating relevant metrics. We defined the metrics available in gCastle and introduced two additional quantities that can help us assess our model's quality: the number of undirected edges and SID.

We'll learn more about gCastle's modules in the next sections while working with specific algorithms.

Ready?

Let's start!

Constraint-based causal discovery

In this section, we'll introduce the first of the four families of causal discovery methods – constraint-based methods. We will learn the core principles behind constraint-based causal discovery and implement the **PC algorithm** (Sprites et al., 2000).

By the end of this chapter, you will have a solid understanding of how constraint-based methods work and you'll know how to implement the PC algorithm in practice using gCastle.

Constraints and independence

Constraint-based methods (also known as **independence-based methods**) aim at decoding causal structure from the data by leveraging the independence structure between three basic graphical structures: **chains**, **forks**, and **colliders**.

Let's start with a brief refresher on chains, forks, and colliders. *Figure 13.4* presents the three structures:

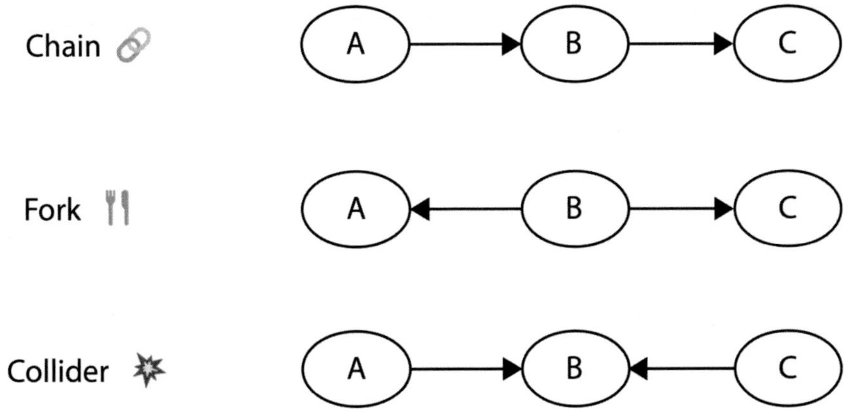

Figure 13.4 – The three basic graphical structures

In *Chapter 5*, we demonstrated that the collider structure has a unique property.

Let's take a look at *Figure 13.4* once again. Each structure consists of three variables represented by nodes *A*, *B*, and *C*. For each structure, let's imagine a model where we regress *C* on *A*.

When we control *B* in chains and forks, *A* and *C* become independent. A collider is different. When we control *B* in a collider, *A* and *C* become dependent.

This property can help us recover structural information from observational data.

Let's see how this can be useful in practice.

Leveraging the independence structure to recover the graph

We'll start with a graph. *Figure 13.5* presents the graph that we will use in this section. The graph topology follows the one from Glymour et al. (2019):

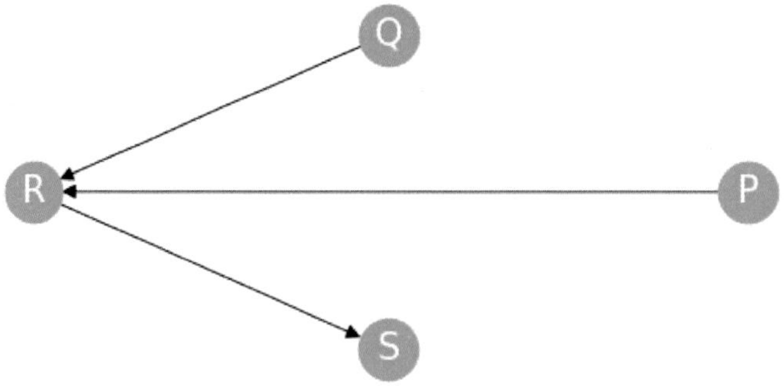

Figure 13.5 – An example graph that we'll use in this section

The graph in *Figure 13.5* consists of four nodes and three directed edges.

Let's pretend that we observe four variables that correspond to the *P*, *Q*, *R*, and *S* nodes in the graph and that we don't know the actual structure.

We'll use the **PC** algorithm to retrieve this structure from observations. The source of the algorithm's name is the first names of its creators, **Peter** (Sprites) and **Clark** (Glymour). The name likely also refers to a precursor algorithm called **IC**, proposed by Verma and Pearl in 1990.

The PC algorithm consists of five basic steps:

1. Start with a fully connected graph.
2. Delete the edges between unconditionally independent variables.
3. Iterate over all remaining variable pairs (A, B) and delete an edge between A and B if $A \perp\!\!\!\perp B|C$, where C is a conditioning set of size 1 (containing only one variable). Repeat this step for all remaining pairs (A, B), increasing the size of the conditioning set C by 1.
4. For each triple of variables, $A - B - C$, where "–" represents an undirected edge and where A and C are not adjacent, orient the edges $A \rightarrow B \leftarrow C$ whenever $A \not\perp\!\!\!\perp C|B$ (note that if the latter is true, we know that $A - B - C$ forms a collider and hence we know how to orient the edges).
5. For each triple of variables, $A \rightarrow B - C$, where A and C are not adjacent, orient the edge between B and C as $B \rightarrow C$. This is called **orientation propagation** (Glymour et al., 2019).

For a more detailed view of the PC algorithm, check Glymour et al. (2019), Sprites et al. (2000), or Le et al. (2015).

Let's apply the PC algorithm step-by-step to the graph presented in *Figure 13.5*.

We present the entire process in *Figure 13.6*:

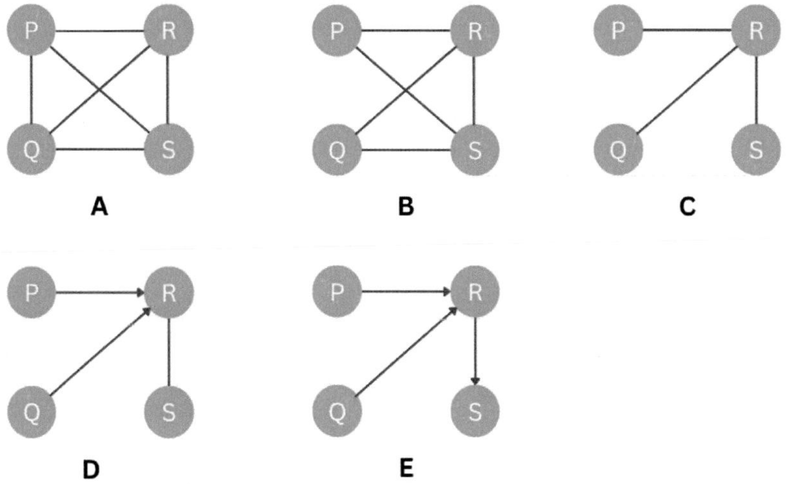

Figure 13.6 – The PC algorithm step by step

Let's examine the process in *Figure 13.6*:

1. We start with a fully connected graph (A).
2. We remove the edges between the nodes that are unconditionally independent (B). There's only one pair like this. This is the pair (P, Q).
3. We remove the edges between P and Q, and Q and S, as $P \perp\!\!\!\perp Q|R$ and $Q \perp\!\!\!\perp S|R$ (C).
4. We orient the edges $P \rightarrow R \leftarrow S$ because R is a collider between P and S (D).
5. Finally, we orient the edge between R and S because we know that R is not a collider between S and any other adjacent variable (E).

If any of the steps seem unclear to you, feel free to go through the stages in *Figure 13.6* once again and review the PC algorithm steps that we discussed earlier. If you need a deeper refresher on conditional independencies, review *Chapter 5*.

Let's generate some data according to our graph and fit the PC algorithm to recover the true structure.

We'll start by generating 1,000 observations and store them in a NumPy matrix:

```
N = 1000
p = np.random.randn(N)
q = np.random.randn(N)
r = p + q + .1 * np.random.randn(N)
s = .7 * r + .1 * np.random.randn(N)
```

```
# Store the data as a matrix
pc_dataset = np.vstack([p, q, r, s]).T
```

Now, let's instantiate and fit the algorithm:

```
pc = PC()
pc.learn(pc_dataset)
```

Let's display the predicted causal matrix alongside the true DAG:

```
GraphDAG(
    est_dag=pc.causal_matrix,
    true_dag=pc_dag)
plt.show()
```

Figure 13.7 presents the visualization:

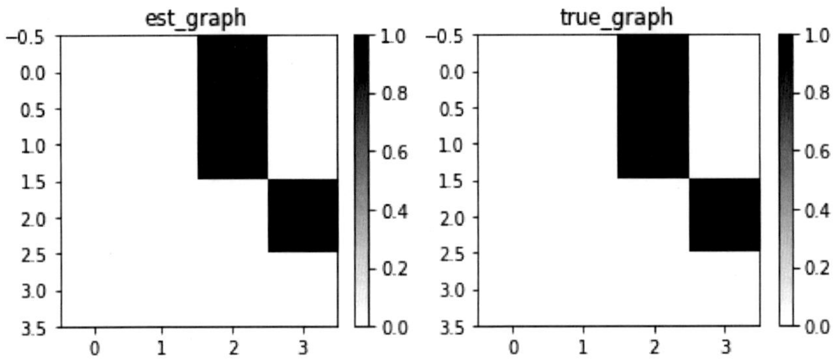

Figure 13.7 – The comparison between the DAG learned by the PC algorithm (left) and the true DAG (right)

Both DAGs in *Figure 13.7* look identical. It indicates that our model learned the underlying DAG perfectly.

In this case, it's just a pure formality; nonetheless, let's print out the metrics:

```
MetricsDAG(
    B_est=pc.causal_matrix,
    B_true=pc_dag
).metrics
```

This results in the following:

```
{'fdr': 0.0,
 'tpr': 1.0,
 'fpr': 0.0,
```

```
'shd': 0,
'nnz': 3,
'precision': 1.0,
'recall': 1.0,
'F1': 1.0,
'gscore': 1.0}
```

The metrics confirm that the model learned a perfect representation. Precision, recall, TPR, and F1 score are all equal to 1. FDR, FPR, and SHD are equal to 0. NNZ is equal to 3, indicating that there are 3 edges in the graph.

PC algorithm – hidden challenges

The PC algorithm worked very well for the data in our example. Although in general, the PC algorithm comes with theoretical guarantees of convergence to the true MEC in the large sample limit, assuming that all model assumptions are met, in certain high-dimensional cases, the *original algorithm* might return incorrect results.

The reason for this is that in certain scenarios, the algorithm might be sensitive to the order in which we perform conditional independence tests. The sensitivity has been addressed in a variant of the PC algorithm called **PC-stable** (Colombo and Maathuis, 2012).

Fortunately, implementing PC-stable is very easy with gCastle. We only need to specify a variant when initializing the object:

```
pc_stable = PC(variant='stable')
```

> **More on PC-stable**
>
> In fact, PC-stable only addresses a part of the problem of ordering sensitivity – the variant is only insensitive to the ordering of the tests that lead to the discovery of the skeleton but is still sensitive to ordering when finding colliders and orienting edges. Other variants of the PC algorithm have been proposed to address these two problems, but it turns out that, in practice, they might lead to less useful results than simple PC-stable. Check Colombo and Maathuis (2012) for more details.

Another challenge for the PC algorithm is computational. Performing a significant number of conditional independence tests in a very large dataset might be computationally expensive. One way to address this challenge is to parallelize the algorithm (Le et al., 2015). Fortunately, gCastle provides us with a parallelized version out of the box.

To use the parallel version, simply specify the variant:

```
pc_parallel = PC(variant='parallel')
```

The results for the stable and parallel versions of the algorithm are identical for our example so we do not present them here (but you can find them in the notebook).

PC algorithm for categorical data

In our example, we used continuous data, but the PC algorithm can also work for categorical data. Recall that the main principle of how PC works is independence testing. By default, PC uses Fisher's z-test (Fisher, 1921) in order to test independencies between variables. Fisher's z-test works well for continuous and linear-Gaussian data.

For categorical variables, we need another approach.

gCastle provides us with a number of independence tests that can be used in this context. Two of them, χ^2 and G^2 (Tsamardinos et al., 2006), can be used directly in the PC algorithm, by simply passing a string to the `ci_test` parameter.

For the χ^2 test, use the following:

```
pc_cat = PC(ci_test='chi2')
```

For the G^2 test, use the following:

```
pc_cat = PC(ci_test=g2)
```

We can find more tests in the `castle.common.independence_tests.CITest` object. The tests include Neyman's test, the Cressie-Read test (Cressie and Read, 1984), and more.

In order to use them, we need to pass a function (without calling it) to the `ci_test` parameter:

```
from castle.common.independence_tests import CITest
pc_cat_alt = PC(ci_test=CITest.cressie_read)
```

We can also use an arbitrary custom test as long as it returns a three-tuple where the last element represents the p-value of the test – structurally speaking: `(_, _, p_val)`.

This modular design is really powerful. Notice that all causal libraries used in this book so far – DoWhy, EconML, and gCastle – promote an open, modular, and flexible design, which makes them well suited for future developments and facilitates research.

The time has come to conclude this section. We'll get back to the PC algorithm briefly in later sections of this chapter to reveal one more hidden gem that can be really helpful in real-world scenarios.

In this section, we learned about constraint-based causal discovery methods and introduced the PC algorithm. We discussed the five basic steps of the PC algorithm and applied them to our example DAG. Next, we generated data according to the DAG and implemented the PC algorithm using gCastle.

We discussed two limitations of the algorithm and introduced two variants of the PC algorithm aiming to address them. Finally, we discussed how to use alternative conditional independence tests including the ones provided by the library and the custom ones.

In the next section, we'll introduce the second major family of causal discovery methods – score-based methods.

Score-based causal discovery

In this section, we'll introduce **score-based methods** for causal discovery. We'll discuss the mechanics of the **GES** algorithm and implement it using gCastle.

Tabula rasa – starting fresh

The very first step of the PC algorithm was to build a fully-connected graph. GES starts on the other end of the spectrum, but first things first.

GES is a two-stage procedure. First, it generates the edges, then it prunes the graph.

The algorithm starts with a blank slate – an entirely disconnected graph – and iteratively adds new edges. At each step, it computes a score that expresses how well a new graph models the observed distribution, and at each step, the edge that leads to the highest score is added to the graph.

When no more improvement can be achieved, the pruning phase begins. In this phase, the algorithm removes edges iteratively and checks for score improvement. The phase continues until no further improvement can be achieved by removing edges.

The entire first and second phases are executed in a greedy fashion (hence the *greedy* part of the algorithm's name).

GES might return a CPDAG, which corresponds to a Markov equivalence class for a given DAG (hence the *equivalence* part of the name).

GES – scoring

In order to compute the score at each step, Chickering (2003) uses the Bayesian scoring criterion. Huang et al. (2018) proposed a more general method based on regression in **Reproducing Kernel Hilbert Space** (**RHKS**), which allows for mixed data types and multidimensional variables.

gCastle's implementation offers two scoring criteria: **Bayesian Information Criterion** (**BIC** or `bic`) and **Bayesian Dirichlet Equivalent Uniform** (**Bdeu** or `bdeu`). The latter is intended to work with discrete variables exclusively.

GES in gCastle

Implementing the GES algorithm in gCastle is straightforward:

```
ges = GES(criterion='bic')
```

To train the model, use the `.learn()` method (analogously to what we've done for the PC algorithm):

```
ges.learn(pc_dataset)
```

We used the dataset generated according to the graph in *Figure 13.5*. Let's plot the results to see how GES performed:

```
GraphDAG(
    est_dag=ges.causal_matrix,
    true_dag=pc_dag)
plt.show()
```

The resulting plot is presented in *Figure 13.8*:

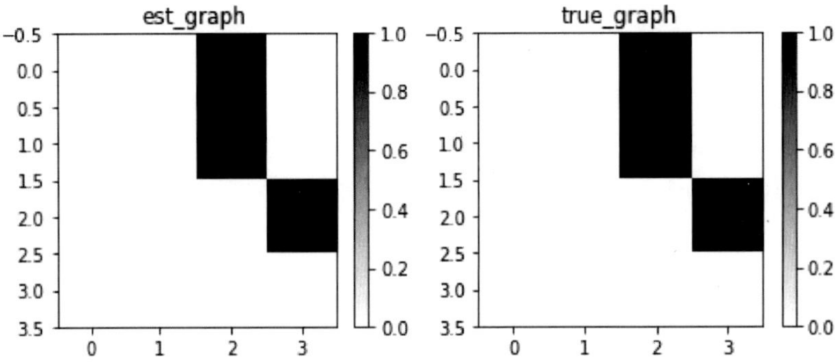

Figure 13.8 – Results of the GES algorithm

As we can see in *Figure 13.8*, the GES algorithm did a very good job and retrieved the perfect graph.

In general, the GES algorithm can be proven to be optimal (based on the so-called **Meek Conjecture**; see Chickering (2003) for details), but the guarantees are only asymptotic.

In the limit of a large sample, GES converges to the same solution as PC. In my personal experience, I found GES repeatedly underperforming compared to other methods (including PC), but please note that my observations do not have a systematic character here.

As a final remark, we need to highlight that GES requires that there's no hidden confounding in our dataset.

In this section, we introduced score-based causal discovery methods, discussed the GES algorithm, and applied it to our PC dataset. In the next section, we'll cover functional causal discovery methods.

Functional causal discovery

Functional causal discovery (also called **function-based causal discovery**) is all about leveraging the information about the *functional forms* and *properties of distributions* governing the relationships between variables in order to uniquely identify causal directions in a dataset. In this section, we'll introduce the logic behind function-based methods, using the **Additive Noise Model** (**ANM**) (Hoyer et al., 2008) and **LiNGAM** (Shimizu et al., 2006) as examples. We'll implement ANM and LiNGAM and discuss the differences between the two. By the end of this section, you will have a good understanding of the general principles of function-based causal discovery and you'll be able to apply the ANM and LiNGAM models to your own problems using Python and gCastle.

The blessings of asymmetry

Tyger Tyger, burning bright,

In the forests of the night;

What immortal hand or eye,

Could frame thy fearful symmetry?

William Blake – Tyger (1794)

(Blake, 2009)

Symmetry plays a special role in human life. We rate symmetric faces as more beautiful (Grammer and Thornhill, 1994), we use symmetry in architecture (*Figure 13.9*) and in everyday design such as cars, planes, and trains, and have a preference for symmetrical objects (Enquist and Arak, 1994).

Figure 13.9 – Three famous structures leveraging symmetry: Taj Mahal in India (top left; image by Maahid Photos), Pyramids in Egypt (bottom left; image by Diego Ferrari), Notre Dame in France (right; image by Max Avans) – all images can be found at Pexels.com

Iain Johnston and colleagues argue that symmetry is fundamentally connected to the process of evolution and its "preference" to compress information (Johnston et al., 2021).

That said, symmetry only tells a part of the story. Perfectly symmetrical faces and objects are perceived as unnatural – *fearfully symmetrical*. It seems that nature likes to be asymmetrical sometimes and a large class of real-world variables is distributed in a non-symmetrical manner.

In *Chapter 3*, we demonstrated that when we have two causally and linearly-related normally distributed variables, we have no way to decide which direction is causal, based solely on the data. The behavior of the regression in both directions is *symmetrical* in the sense that the residuals in both cases are independent, not containing any information that we could leverage to decode the causal direction. In other words, the linear-Gaussian causal mechanism does not leave any *traces* in pair-wise relationships.

Is there anything we can do about it?

It seems that the linear-Gaussian case is hard, but moving into either the non-linear or non-Gaussian realm *breaks the symmetry*.

Let's see how.

ANM model

ANM (Hoyer et al., 2008) is a causal discovery algorithm that leverages the fact that when two variables are related non-linearly, the causal mechanism *does leave traces*.

Let's see it in practice.

We'll start by generating some non-linear data:

```
x = np.random.randn(1000)
y = x**3 + np.random.randn(1000)
```

Let's plot it:

```
plt.figure(figsize=(10, 7))
plt.scatter(x, y, alpha=.5, color=COLORS[0])
plt.xlabel('$X$')
plt.ylabel('$Y$')
plt.show()
```

Figure 13.10 shows the results:

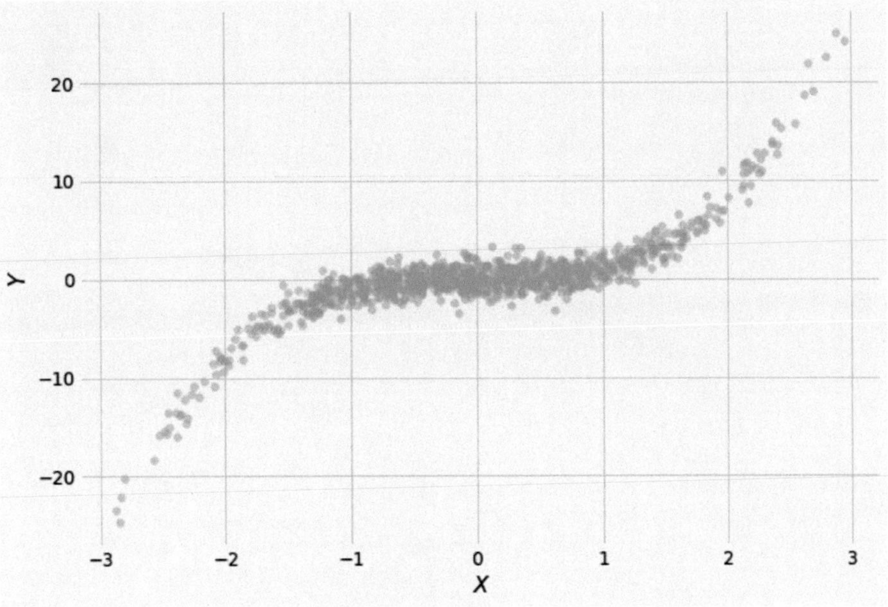

Figure 13.10 – Scatter plot of our non-linear dataset

Now, let's fit two non-linear **spline regressions** to our data – one in the causal (*X* -> *Y*) and one in the anti-causal (*Y* -> *X*) direction.

We'll use 150 splines in each model:

```
n_splines = 150

# Instantiate the models
model_xy = GAM(n_splines=n_splines)
model_yx = GAM(n_splines=n_splines)

# Fit the models
model_xy.fit(x.reshape(-1, 1), y)
model_yx.fit(y.reshape(-1, 1), x)

# Generate predictions
y_pred = model_xy.predict(x.reshape(-1, 1))
x_pred = model_yx.predict(y.reshape(-1, 1))
```

Let's plot the data alongside the fitted regression curves. *Figure 13.11* presents the results:

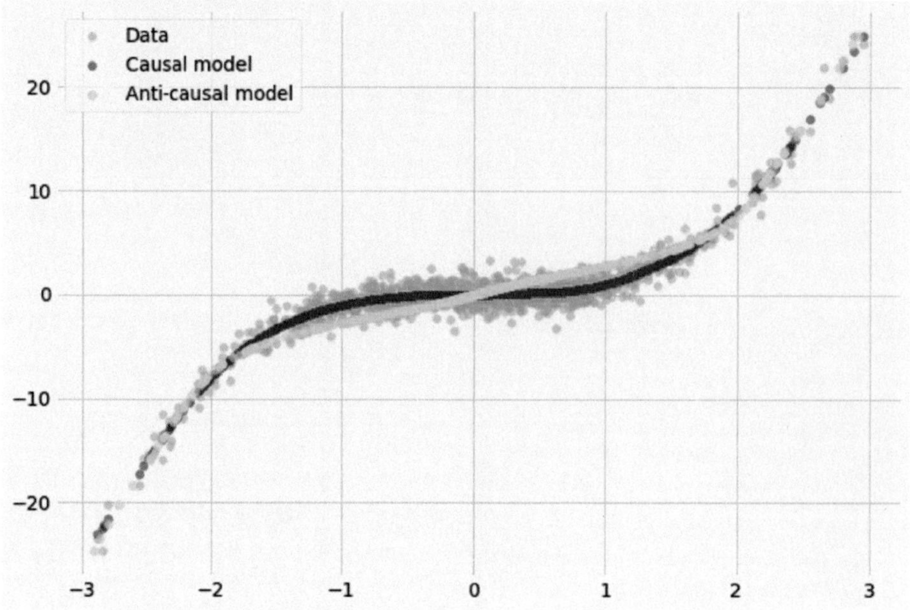

Figure 13.11 – Scatter plot of non-linear data with two fitted regression curves

The two lines representing the causal and the anti-causal models differ significantly.

Let's compute the residuals for both models:

```
residuals_xy = y - y_pred
residuals_yx = x - x_pred
```

Let's now plot them:

```
plt.figure(figsize=(15, 7))

plt.subplot(121)
plt.scatter(x, residuals_xy, alpha=.5, color=COLORS[0])
plt.xlabel('$X$', fontsize=14)
plt.ylabel('$Y-residuals$', fontsize=14)

plt.subplot(122)
plt.scatter(residuals_yx, y, alpha=.5, color=COLORS[0])
plt.xlabel('$X-residuals$', fontsize=14)
plt.ylabel('$Y$', fontsize=14)

plt.show()
```

Figure 13.12 presents the results:

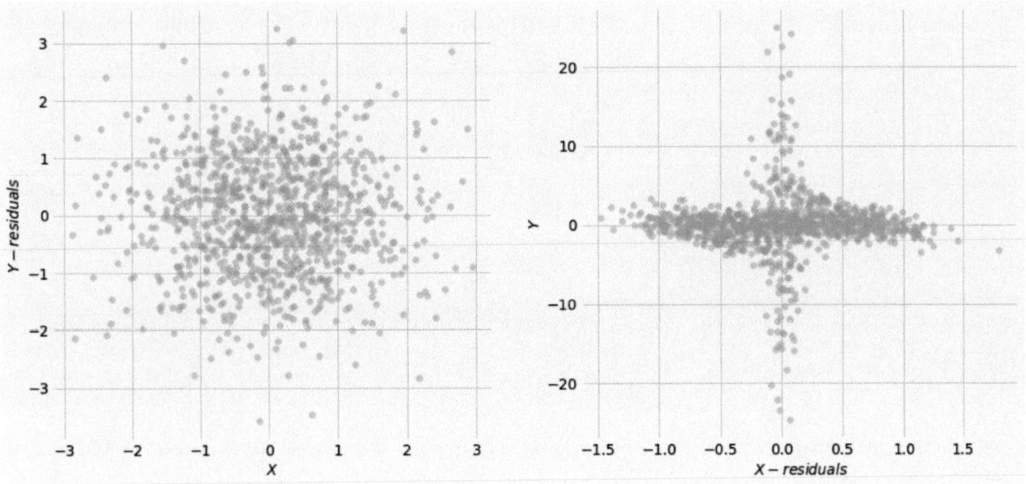

Figure 13.12 – Scatter plots of residuals for the causal and the anti-causal model

As we can see in *Figure 13.12*, the residuals for both models form very different patterns. In particular, the residuals for the anti-causal model (right panel) form a cross-like pattern, indicating a lack of independence between the residuals (x axis) and the predictor (y axis).

This is great news for us!

If we can algorithmically decide which patterns indicate independence, we can retrieve the information about the causal direction.

Assessing independence

It seems clear that none of the traditional correlation metrics such as Pearson's r or Spearman's *rho* will be able to help here. The relationship in the right panel of *Figure 13.12* is non-monotonic, violating the basic assumption of both methods.

Luckily, many methods exist that can help us with this task. One of the methods traditionally used in ANM models is called **Hilbert-Schmidt Independence Criterion** (**HSIC**). HSIC can easily handle patterns like the one that we obtained for the anti-causal model.

Let's compute HSIC for both models. We'll use the implementation of HSIC provided by gCastle.

Let's import the function first:

```
from castle.common.independence_tests import hsic_test
```

Now, let's compute the HSIC statistic:

```
# Compute HSIC
is_indep_xy = hsic_test(
    x = x.reshape(-1, 1),
    y = residuals_xy.reshape(-1, 1),
    alpha=.05
)

is_indep_yx = hsic_test(
    x = y.reshape(-1, 1),
    y = residuals_yx.reshape(-1, 1),
    alpha=.05
)
```

gCastle's implementation of HSIC returns `1` when two variables are independent and `0` when they are dependent, given a specified significance level alpha. We use the `.reshape()` method to reshape our arrays into two-dimensional arrays, as required by the API.

Let's print the results:

```
is_indep_xy, is_indep_yx
```

This gives us the following:

```
(1, 0)
```

The result says that the residuals are independent for the model in the *X* -> *Y* direction, while they are dependent for the model in the *Y* -> *X* direction.

We expect the residuals from the causal model to be independent. Hence, we can conclude that, according to our model, the true causal model is the one in the *X* -> *Y* direction.

This is correct!

Congrats, you just learned how to implement the ANM model from scratch!

There are also other options to implement ANM. You can use another non-linear model instead of spline regression (for instance, gCastle's implementation of ANM uses Gaussian process regression). You can also use other tools to compare the residuals. For instance, an alternative approach to independence testing is based on likelihood. Check this notebook for implementation: `https://bit.ly/ANMNotebook`.

ANM only works when the data has independent additive noise; it also requires no hidden confounding.

To implement ANM using gCastle, use the `ANMNonlinear` class.

LiNGAM time

While ANM relies on non-linearity to break the symmetry between the causal and anti-causal models, LiNGAM relies on non-Gaussianity.

Let's compare residual patterns in two linear datasets: one with Gaussian and one with non-Gaussian noise.

Let's start by generating the data:

```
SAMPLE_SIZE = 1000

x_gauss = np.random.normal(0, 1, SAMPLE_SIZE)
y_gauss = x_gauss + 0.3 * np.random.normal(0, 1,
    SAMPLE_SIZE)

x_ngauss = np.random.uniform(0, 1, SAMPLE_SIZE)
y_ngauss = x_ngauss + 0.3 * np.random.uniform(0, 1,
    SAMPLE_SIZE)
```

We used the uniform distribution in the non-Gaussian case.

Let's take a look at *Figure 13.13*, which presents the Gaussian and non-Gaussian data with fitted regression lines in causal and anti-causal directions:

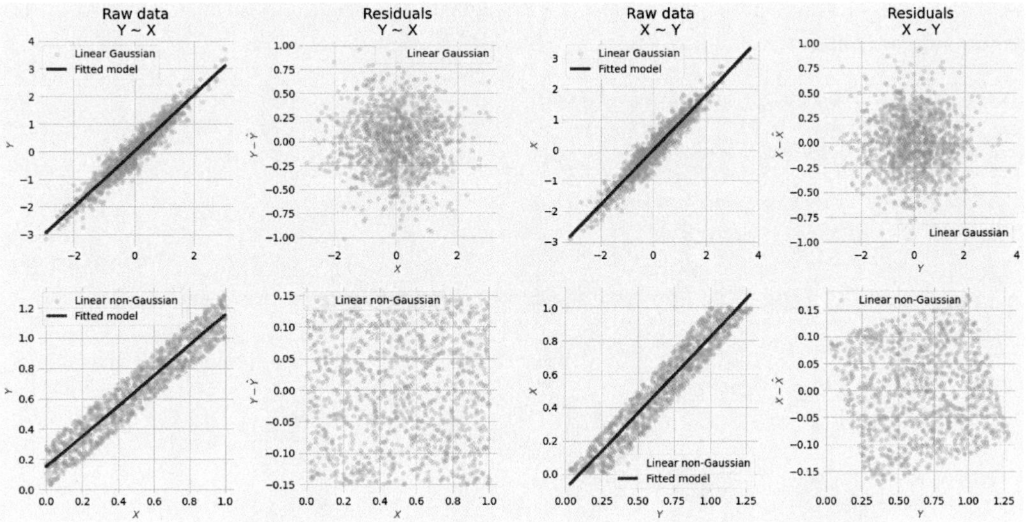

Figure 13.13 – Gaussian and non-Gaussian data with fitted regression lines

In the top panes of *Figure 13.13*, we see two Gaussian models with fitted regression lines (first and third columns) and their respective residuals (second and fourth columns). In the bottom panes, we see two non-Gaussian models (first and third columns) and their residuals (second and fourth columns).

Although both Gaussian and uniform distributions are symmetric themselves, the uniform is asymmetric rotationally. Notice how the residuals form a rotated pattern in the bottom-right corner. The intuition behind this asymmetry is closely related to the **independent component analysis** (**ICA**) model.

ICA is an algorithm frequently used to recover the source signals from noisy overlapping observations. A popular example of ICA usage is the source separation in the so-called **cocktail party problem**, where we have a multi-track recording of multiple speakers speaking simultaneously and we want to separate those speakers' voices into separate tracks.

It turns out that we can achieve it under certain assumptions using ICA. One of the core assumptions here is the non-Gaussianity of the source signals, which allows us to presume that there's a bijective mapping between the noisy recording and the source.

As LiNGAM relies on ICA internally, it also inherits this assumption.

The second assumption is linearity. ICA can only hold linear data and, again, LiNGAM inherits this limitation.

The good news is that LiNGAM does *not* require the faithfulness assumption.

Let's see LiNGAM in action!

LiNGAM in action

We'll start with the data that we generated for the PC algorithm to see what happens when LiNGAM's assumptions are not met.

Recall that `pc_dataset` was linear and Gaussian.

Let's instantiate and fit the model:

```
lingam = ICALiNGAM(random_state=SEED)
lingam.learn(pc_dataset)
```

Let's plot the results. *Figure 13.14* presents the comparison between the predicted and the correct adjacency matrix:

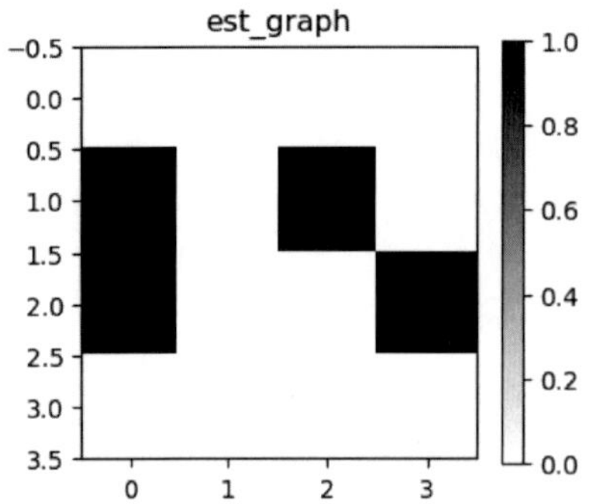

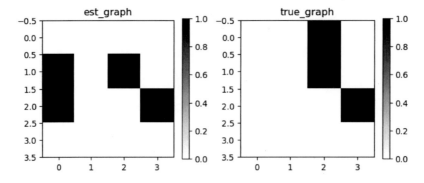

Figure 13.14 – LiNGAM results

We can see that LiNGAM has predicted two edges correctly (1 -> 2 and 2 -> 3) but it has missed the edge 0 -> 2. Additionally, the model hallucinated two edges (1 -> 0 and 2 -> 0). These results are not very impressive, especially for such a simple graph. That said, this is expected as we violated one of the basic assumptions of the method.

Using legal data with LiNGAM

Let's generate the data that LiNGAM can deal with. Let's keep the same causal structure that we used for `pc_dataset`, and only update the functional forms:

```
a = np.random.uniform(0, 1, N)
b = np.random.uniform(3, 6, N)
c = a + b + .1 * np.random.uniform(-2, 0, N)
d = .7 * c + .1 * np.random.uniform(0, 1, N)
lingam_dataset = np.vstack([a, b, c, d]).T
```

Let's re-instantiate and refit the model:

```
lingam = ICALiNGAM(random_state=SEED)
lingam.learn(lingam_dataset)
```

Figure 13.15 demonstrates the model's results on the new dataset:

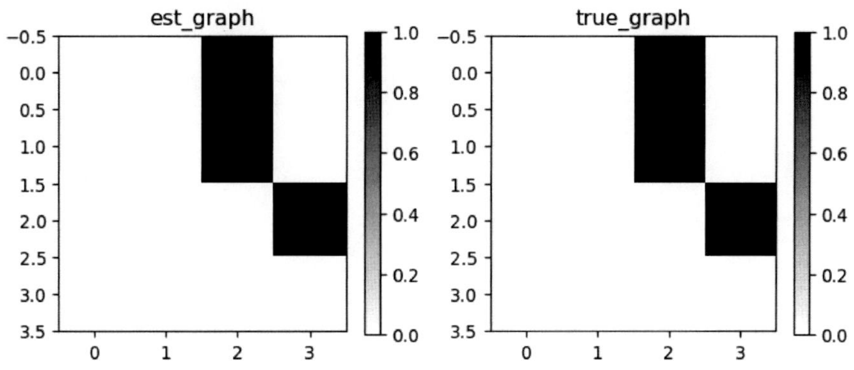

Figure 13.15 – LiNGAM on non-Gaussian data

This time, the model was able to perfectly retrieve the true graph.

A great feature that LiNGAM offers is that it does not only retrieve the causal structure but also the strength of the relationships between variables. In this sense, LiNGAM is an end-to-end method for causal discovery *and* causal inference.

Let's check how well LiNGAM did with retrieving the coefficients. We can access the learned weighted matrix via the `weight_causal_matrix` attribute:

```
lingam.weight_causal_matrix
```

This returns a weighted adjacency matrix as a `castle.common.base.Tensor` object:

```
Tensor([[0.    , 0.    , 1.003, 0.    ],
        [0.    , 0.    , 0.999, 0.    ],
        [0.    , 0.    , 0.   , 0.7   ],
        [0.    , 0.    , 0.   , 0.    ]])
```

Figure 13.16 presents these results in the context of the original structural equations. Let's see how well the algorithm managed to recover the true coefficients.

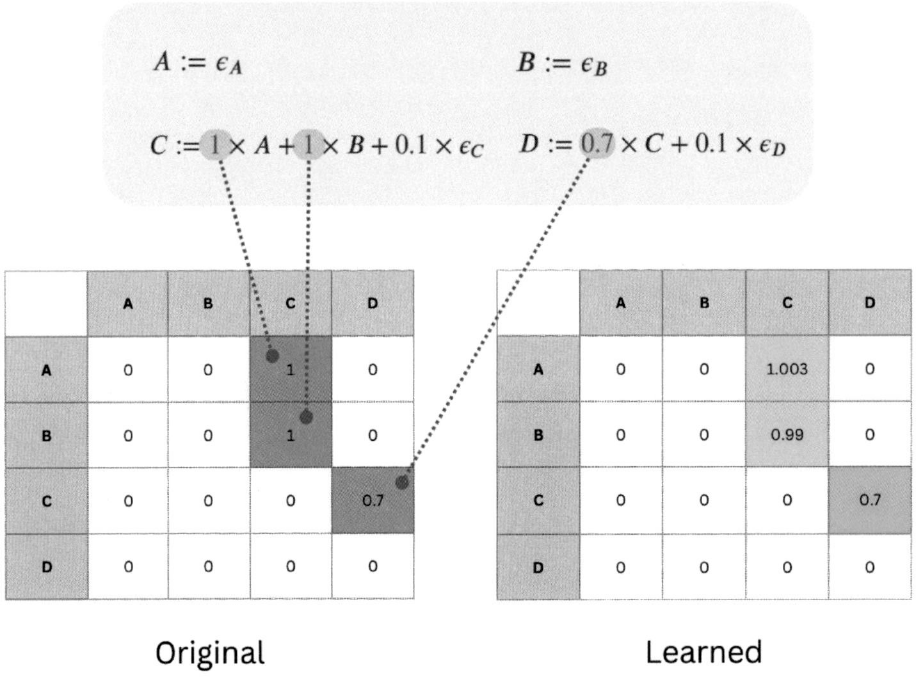

Figure 13.16 – LiNGAM results (right) versus the original DAG (left) and the original structural equations (top)

In *Figure 13.16* (top), we see the set of original structural equations (the ones that we implemented). On the bottom, we see the original DAG (left) and the learned matrix (right). The blue dashed lines map the coefficients from the equations to the respective cells in the original DAG. The green cells on the right contain the coefficients retrieved by LiNGAM. Dark green emphasizes the perfectly retrieved coefficient.

These results are pretty good!

Before we conclude, there are a couple of things that are good to know about LiNGAM. First, LiNGAM uses ICA in the background, and ICA is a stochastic method. Sometimes, it might not converge to a good solution within the default number of steps.

You can modify the number of steps by modifying the `max_iter` parameter:

```
lingam = ICALiNGAM(
    max_iter=2000,
    random_state=SEED
)
```

Second, LiNGAM is not **scale-invariant**, which might result in estimation errors.

Get more direct

DirectLiNGAM (Shimizu et al., 2011) is an ICA-free variation of LiNGAM. The model uses a series of regressions in order to determine the causal order.

It's guaranteed to converge to the true solution in the infinite sample regime when the model assumptions are strictly met. The number of steps required for convergence scales linearly with the number of variables.

Of course, we never have access to an infinite number of samples in the real world. That said, DirectLiNGAM has been shown to outperform its counterpart on simulated finite sample data as well (Shimizu et al., 2011).

DirectLiNGAM also solves the scaling issue. The cost for the improvements is in computational time. The time scales as a power function of the number of variables (nodes).

Using DirectLiNGAM with gCastle is straightforward:

```
d_lingam = DirectLiNGAM()
d_lingam.learn(lingam_dataset)
```

The results are identical to the regular model, so we skip them here. You can see the plots and the learned weighted matrix in the notebook.

More variants of the LiNGAM model exist than the two we discussed here. The LiNGAM framework has been extended to work with time series, cyclical graphs (Lacerda et al., 2008), and latent variables, among others. For implementations and references for some of these variants, check the Python LiNGAM library (`https://bit.ly/LiNGAMDocs`).

It's time to conclude our journey with functional-based causal discovery for now.

In this section, we introduced functional-based causal discovery methods. We've seen how non-linearity and non-Gaussianity can help us break the symmetry and follow the traces left by causal mechanisms in order to gain valuable insights.

We learned how to implement the ANM model from scratch using Python and HSIC independence tests from the gCastle library and how to use the algorithms from the LiNGAM family using gCastle. Finally, we discussed the main limitations of ICA-LiNGAM and discussed how to address them using DirectLiNGAM.

In the next section, we'll introduce the most contemporary family of causal discovery methods – gradient-based methods.

Gradient-based causal discovery

In this section, we'll introduce **gradient-based causal discovery** methods. We'll discuss the main contributions of this family of methods and their main disadvantages. Finally, we'll implement selected methods using gCastle and compare their performance with other families.

What exactly is so gradient about you?

2018 was an exciting year for the causal discovery community. Xun Zheng from CMU and his colleagues presented an interesting paper during the 2018 NeurIPS conference.

The work was titled *DAGs with NO TEARS: Continuous Optimization for Structure Learning* and introduced a novel approach to causal structure learning (though we need to say that the authors did not explicitly state that their method is causal).

The proposed method (called **NOTEARS**) was not based on a set of independence tests or local heuristics but rather treated the task of structure learning as a joint, continuously-optimized task.

One of the main breakthroughs in the paper was the differentiable function encoding the acyclicity constraints. In other words, the authors proposed a function that we could optimize continuously, making sure that the graph we're fitting to the data is acyclic.

Before we continue, it's good to mention that gradient-based methods are essentially score-based – we compute a numerical summary of the quality of graph data fit in the optimization process.

Nevertheless, we've chosen to think about them as a separate family because the fact that they use continuous optimization comes with unique opportunities and challenges.

Let's see how to encode the acyclicity constraint as a differentiable function. It turns out that the formula is very concise:

$$\mathcal{R}(A) = tr(e^{A \odot A}) - d$$

In the preceding formula, the following applies:

1. A is the adjacency matrix of a graph, G
2. e is a matrix exponential
3. $tr_{(.)}$ is a trace of a matrix
4. d is the number of nodes in a graph represented by A
5. $\odot$ is the Hadamard (element-wise) product

For a quick introduction to matrix exponentials, check `https://bit.ly/MatrixExponential`.

It turns out that when $\mathcal{R}(A)$ is equal to zero, a graph represented by the adjacency matrix A is a DAG. Otherwise, it's not. This is a very convenient way to measure what the authors refer to as the *DAG-ness* of a graph.

Let's implement this formula in Python:

```
from scipy import linalg

def check_if_dag(adj_matrix):
    A = adj_matrix
    return np.trace(linalg.expm(A * A)) - A.shape[0] == 0
```

First, we import the `linalg` linear algebra module from SciPy. We'll need it for the matrix exponential operation.

Next, we multiply the adjacency matrix element-wise by itself. Note that this step is only effective for weighted adjacency matrices. For binary matrices, $A \odot A = A$.

Next, we perform matrix exponentiation using the `linalg.expm()` function.

Finally, we compute the trace of the resulting matrix and subtract the number of rows in the adjacency matrix, which is equivalent to the number of nodes in the graph represented by this matrix (or the number of variables in our problem).

If this quantity (note that trace is a scalar value) is equal to zero, we return `True`. Otherwise, we return `False`.

Let's test the function on the `pc_dag` DAG that we created at the beginning of this chapter:

```
check_if_dag(pc_dag)
```

This returns the following:

```
True
```

The result is as expected.

Let's build a simple cyclic graph:

```
dcg = np.array([
    [0, 1, 0],
    [1, 0, 0],
    [0, 1, 0]
])
```

Let's evaluate it using our function:

```
check_if_dag(dcg)
```

This gives us the following:

```
False
```

This result is also as expected.

Gradients for $\mathcal{R}(A)$ are easy to compute and so it's naturally compatible with gradient-based optimization methods.

The overall loss function in NOTEARS consists of the mean squared error component $\|X - XA\|_F^2$ with a number of additional regularization and penalty terms. The function is optimized using the augmented Lagrangian method (Niemirovski, 1999) subject to the constraint that $\mathcal{R}(A) = 0$ (see Zheng et al., 2018, for the full definition).

In the main loss component, X is an $n \times d$ data matrix, where n is the number of observations and d is the number of features, A is the adjacency matrix, and $\|.\|_F^2$ is the squared Frobenius norm (`https://bit.ly/MatrixNorm`; see also *Chapter 14* for definition).

Shed no tears

The authors have tested NOTEARS against a selection of traditional methods including PC, LiNGAM, and **FGES** (**fast GES**). In their experiments, the authors found that NOTEARS either outperformed or performed on par with the best traditional methods (depending on the setting).

These initial results brought a lot of excitement to the community and inspired new lines of research.

The initial excitement cooled down after the publication of two research papers that examined the NOTEARS algorithm. Kaiser and Sipos (2021) have shown that NOTEARS' sensitivity to scaling makes it a risky choice for real-world causal discovery. Reisach et al. (2021) demonstrated similar inconsistencies in the performance of gradient-based methods between standardized and unstandardized data and pointed to a more general problem: synthetic data used to evaluate these methods might contain unintended regularities that can be relatively easily exploited by these models, as the authors expressed in the title of their paper, *Causal Discovery Benchmarks May Be Easy To Game*.

GOLEMs don't cry

GOLEM (Ng et al., 2020) is an algorithm that improves over NOTEARS. The algorithm uses a likelihood-based objective (rather than an MSE-based one like in NOTEARS) and soft DAG-ness constraint (rather than a hard one like in NOTEARS), which leads to facilitated optimization and faster convergence. The authors demonstrate that GOLEM outperforms NOTEARS on synthetic data.

These changes do not seem to address all the issues raised by Reisach et al. (2021) and it seems that GOLEM's performance is affected by the unintended variance patterns introduced by synthetic data-generating processes. In particular, the model's performance tends to degrade in the normalized data scenario, where *unfair* variance patterns are minimized. Note that the same is true for NOTEARS (check Reisach et al., 2021, for the details).

> **NOTEARS, GOLEM, and linearity**
>
> The original version of NOTEARS was designed to work with linear data. It's the same for GOLEM. An extension of NOTEARS exists that works with general non-parametric models (Zheng et al., 2020).

The comparison

Now, let's generate three datasets with different characteristics and compare the performance of the methods representing each of the families.

We'll start by building the dataset:

```
true_dag = DAG.scale_free(n_nodes=11, n_edges=15, seed=SEED)

DATA_PARAMS = {
    'linearity': ['linear', 'nonlinear'],
    'distribution': {
        'linear': ['gauss', 'exp'],
        'nonlinear': ['quadratic']
    }
}

datasets = {}

for linearity in DATA_PARAMS['linearity']:
    for distr in DATA_PARAMS['distribution'][linearity]:
        datasets[f'{linearity}_{distr}'] = IIDSimulation(
            W=true_dag,
            n=2000,
            method=linearity,
            sem_type=distr)
```

First, we generate a graphical structure according to the scale-free model. Our graph will have 10 nodes and 15 edges. *Figure 13.17* presents the graph:

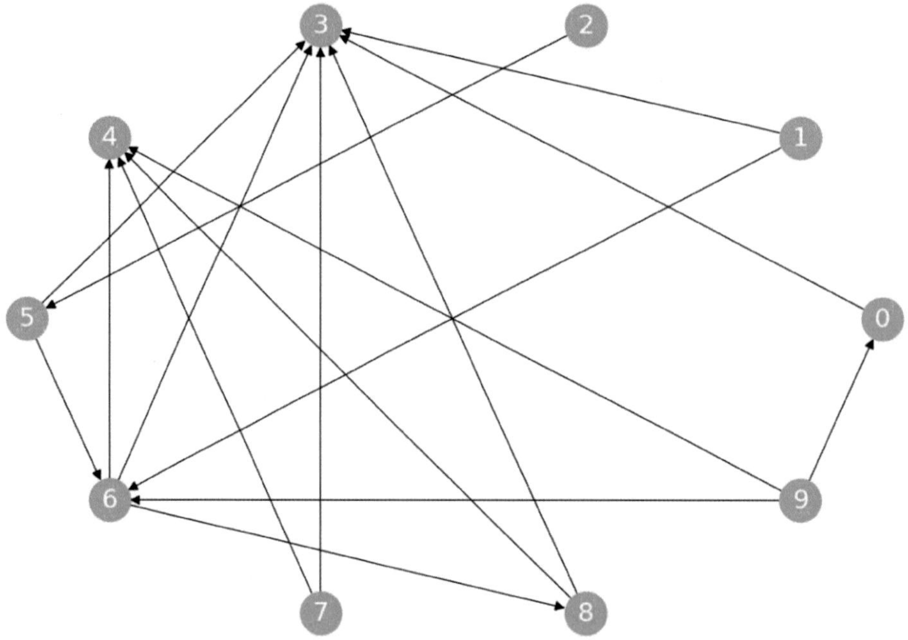

Figure 13.17 – The graph for the comparative experiment

Next, we define what type of functional relationships and/or noise we want to have in our SCM (linear with Gaussian and exponential noises and non-linear quadratic).

Finally, we iterate over the defined settings and generate the observations. We store the observations in the `datasets` dictionary.

Now, let's create an object containing the methods we'll use:

```
methods = OrderedDict({
    'PC': PC,
    'GES': GES,
    'LiNGAM': DirectLiNGAM,
    'Notears': NotearsNonlinear,
    'GOLEM': GOLEM
})
```

We're now ready to start the experiment. You can find the full experimental loop in the notebook for this chapter.

We present the results in *Figure 13.18*. The best-performing models for each dataset are marked in bold.

Dataset	Model	SHD	FDR	F1	No. undir. edges
Linear Gauss.	PC	5	0.2	0.75	1
Linear Gauss.	GES	17	0.5833	0.4762	2
Linear Gauss.	DirectLiNGAM	11	0.3889	0.6471	0
Linear Gauss.	NotearsNonlinear	11	0.4667	0.5161	0
Linear Gauss.	**GOLEM**	**0**	**0**	**1**	**0**
Lineaer Exp.	PC	5	0.1875	0.7647	2
Lineaer Exp.	GES	18	0.625	0.4286	2
Lineaer Exp.	**DirectLiNGAM**	**0**	**0**	**1**	**0**
Lineaer Exp.	NotearsNonlinear	12	0.44	0.5882	0
Lineaer Exp.	**GOLEM**	**0**	**0**	**1**	**0**
Non-lin. Quad	PC	14	0.5714	0.3871	1
Non-lin. Quad	GES	13	0.5714	0.3871	1
Non-lin. Quad	DirectLiNGAM	16	1	NaN	0
Non-lin. Quad	**NotearsNonlinear**	**7**	**0.1818**	**0.6667**	**0**
Non-lin. Quad	GOLEM	18	0.6111	0.4118	0

Figure 13.18 – Results of the model comparison

In this section, we introduced gradient-based methods for causal discovery. We discussed the continuous acyclicity constraint (DAG-ness), and its innovative character. We discussed the main challenges that gradient-based methods face. Finally, we carried out an experiment comparing algorithms from different families on a synthetic dataset.

In the next section, we'll see how to combine causal discovery algorithms with expert knowledge.

Encoding expert knowledge

Combining expert knowledge with automated methods can be incredibly beneficial. It can help algorithms learn while inspiring human stakeholders to deepen their own insights and understanding of their environments and processes.

In this section, we'll demonstrate how to incorporate expert knowledge into the workflow of our causal discovery algorithms.

By the end of this section, you'll be able to translate expert knowledge into the language of graphs and pass it to causal discovery algorithms.

What is expert knowledge?

In this section, we think about *expert knowledge* as an umbrella term for any type of knowledge or insight that we're willing to accept as valid.

From the algorithmic point of view, we can think of expert knowledge as a strong (but usually local) prior. We encode expert knowledge by *freezing* one or more edges in the graph. The model treats these edges as existing and adapts their behavior accordingly.

Expert knowledge in gCastle

Let's see how to encode external knowledge using gCastle.

Currently (gCastle 1.0.3), one algorithm supports adding external knowledge – the PC algorithm – but support for more algorithms is planned.

We'll take the linear Gaussian dataset from the previous section's experiment and we'll try to improve PC's performance by adding some external knowledge to the algorithm.

We start with an additional import. The `PrioriKnowledge` object will allow us to conveniently define and pass the knowledge to the algorithm:

```
from castle.common.priori_knowledge import PrioriKnowledge
```

Next, we instantiate the `PrioriKnowledge` object and pass the number of nodes to the constructor:

```
priori_knowledge = PrioriKnowledge(n_nodes=10)
```

Next, we add the required and forbidden edges:

```
priori_knowledge.add_required_edges([(7, 3)])
priori_knowledge.add_forbidden_edges([(0, 9), (8, 6)])
```

I checked the plots for the experiment in the notebook to find the edges the PC algorithm got wrong in the previous section's experiment. We added some of them here.

Now, we're ready to instantiate the model and train it:

```
pc_priori = PC(priori_knowledge=priori_knowledge)
pc_priori.learn(datasets['linear_gauss'].X)
```

Note that, this time, we pass the `priori_knowledge` object to the constructor.

Let's compare the results before and after sharing our knowledge with the algorithm. *Figure 13.19* summarizes the results for us:

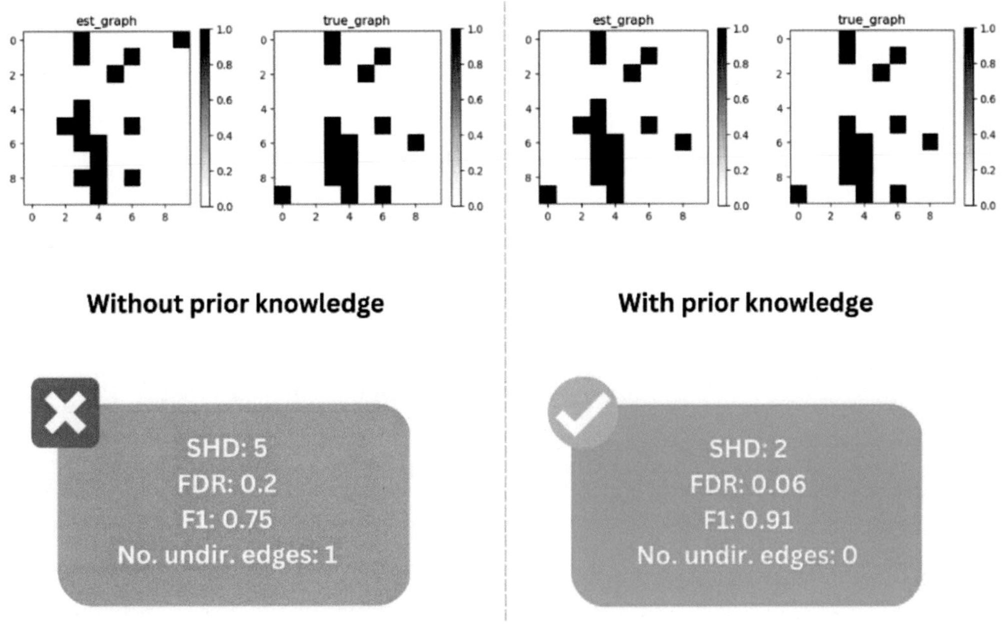

Figure 13.19 – Results for the PC algorithm before and after adding prior knowledge

In *Figure 13.19*, we see that all metrics that we record have been improved after adding external knowledge to the algorithm. We could continue adding and restricting more edges to improve the algorithm further.

In this section, we've learned how to encode and pass expert knowledge to the PC algorithm. Currently, only one algorithm in gCastle supports external knowledge, but as far as I know, the developers are planning to add support for more algorithms in the future.

Wrapping it up

We started this chapter with a refresher on important causal discovery assumptions. We then introduced gCastle. We discussed the library's main modules and trained our first causal discovery algorithm. Next, we discussed the four main families of causal discovery models – constraint-based, score-based, functional, and gradient-based – and implemented at least one model per family using gCastle. Finally, we ran a comparative experiment and learned how to pass expert knowledge to causal models.

In the next chapter, we'll discuss more advanced ideas in causal discovery and take a broader perspective on the applicability of causal discovery methods in real-life use cases.

Ready for one more dive?

References

Barabási, A. L. (2009). *Scale-free networks: a decade and beyond*. Science, 325(5939), 412-413.

Barabási, A. L., and Albert, R. (1999). *Emergence of Scaling in Random Networks*. Science, 286(5439), 509–512.

Blake, W. (2009) *The Tyger*. Songs of Experience. In William Blake: The Complete Illuminated Books.

Cai, R., Wu, S., Qiao, J., Hao, Z., Zhang, K., and Zhang, X. (2021). *THP: Topological Hawkes Processes for Learning Granger Causality on Event Sequences*. ArXiv.

Chickering, D. M. (2003). *Optimal structure identification with greedy search*. J. Mach. Learn. Res., 3, 507–554.

Chickering, M. (2020). *Statistically Efficient Greedy Equivalence Search*. Proceedings of the 36th Conference on Uncertainty in Artificial Intelligence (UAI). In Proceedings of Machine Learning Research, 124, 241-249.

Colombo, D., and Maathuis, M.H. (2012). *Order-independent constraint-based causal structure learning*. J. Mach. Learn. Res., 15, 3741-3782.

Cressie, N., and Read, T.R. (1984). *Multinomial goodness-of-fit tests*. Journal of the Royal Statistical Society: Series B (Methodological), 46(3), 440-464.

Enquist, M., Arak, A. (1994). *Symmetry, beauty and evolution*. Nature, 372, 169–172

Erdös, P. and Rényi, A. (1959). *On Random Graphs I*. Publicationes Mathematicae Debrecen, 6, 290-297.

Fisher, R. A. (1921). *On The "Probable Error" of a Coefficient of Correlation Deduced From a Small Sample*. Metron, 1, 1-32.

Glymour, C., Zhang, K., and Spirtes, P. (2019). *Review of Causal Discovery Methods Based on Graphical Models*. Frontiers in genetics, 10, 524.

Grammer, K., and Thornhill, R. (1994). *Human (Homo sapiens) facial attractiveness and sexual selection: the role of symmetry and averageness*. Journal of comparative psychology, 108(3), 233–242.

Heckerman, D., Geiger, D., and Chickering, D.M. (1995). *Learning Bayesian Networks: The Combination of Knowledge and Statistical Data*. Machine Learning, 20, 197–243.

Hoyer, P., Janzing, D., Mooij, J. M., Peters, J., and Schölkopf, B. (2008). *Nonlinear causal discovery with additive noise models*. In D. Koller, D. Schuurmans, Y. Bengio, & L. Bottou (Eds.), Advances in Neural Information Processing Systems, 21. Curran Associates, Inc.

Huang, B., Zhang, K., Lin, Y., Schölkopf, B., and Glymour, C. (2018). *Generalized score functions for causal discovery*. In Proceedings of the 24th ACM SIGKDD International Conference on Knowledge Discovery & Data Mining, 1551-1560.

Hyvärinen, A., Karhunen, J., and Oja, E. (2001). *Independent Component Analysis*. Wiley.

Johnston, I. G., Dingle, K., Greenbury, S. F., Camargo, C. Q., Doye, J. P. K., Ahnert, S. E., and Ard A. Louis. (2022). *Symmetry and simplicity spontaneously emerge from the algorithmic nature of evolution*. Proceedings of the National Academy of Sciences, 119(11), e2113883119.

Kaiser, M., and Sipos, M. (2021). *Unsuitability of NOTEARS for Causal Graph Discovery*. ArXiv, abs/2104.05441.

Lacerda, G., Spirtes, P. L., Ramsey, J., and Hoyer, P. O. (2008). *Discovering Cyclic Causal Models by Independent Components Analysis*. Conference on Uncertainty in Artificial Intelligence.

Le, T.D., Hoang, T., Li, J., Liu, L., Liu, H., and Hu, S. (2015). *A Fast PC Algorithm for High Dimensional Causal Discovery with Multi-Core PCs*. IEEE/ACM Transactions on Computational Biology and Bioinformatics, 16, 1483-1495.

Ng, I., Ghassami, A., and Zhang, K. (2020). *On the Role of Sparsity and DAG Constraints for Learning Linear DAGs*. ArXiv, abs/2006.10201.

Nemirovski, A. (1999). *Optimization II: Standard Numerical Methods for Nonlinear Continuous Optimization [Lecture notes]*.

Peters, J., and Bühlmann, P. (2015). *Structural intervention distance for evaluating causal graphs*. Neural computation, 27(3), 771-799.

Peters, J., Janzing, D., and Schölkopf, B. (2017). *Elements of Causal Inference: Foundations and Learning Algorithms*. MIT Press.

Rebane, G., and Pearl, J. (1987). *The recovery of causal poly-trees from statistical data*. International Journal of Approximate Reasoning.

Shimizu, S., Hoyer, P.O., Hyvärinen, A., and Kerminen, A.J. (2006). *A Linear Non-Gaussian Acyclic Model for Causal Discovery.* J. Mach. Learn. Res., 7, 2003-2030.

Shimizu, S., Inazumi, T., Sogawa, Y., Hyvärinen, A., Kawahara, Y., Washio, T., Hoyer, P.O., and Bollen, K.A. (2011). DirectLiNGAM: *A Direct Method for Learning a Linear Non-Gaussian Structural Equation Model.* J. Mach. Learn. Res., 12, 1225–1248.

Sprites, P., Glymour, C., and Scheines, R. (2000). *Causation, Prediction, and Search.* MIT Press.

Tsamardinos, I., Brown, L. E., and Aliferis, C. F. (2006). *The max-min hill-climbing Bayesian network structure learning algorithm.* Machine Learning, 65(1), 31-78.

Uhler, C., Raskutti, G., Bühlmann, P., and Yu, B. (2013). *Geometry of the faithfulness assumption in causal inference.* The Annals of Statistics, 436-463.

Verma, T., and Pearl, J. (1990). *Equivalence and synthesis of causal models.* Proceedings of the 6th Conference on Uncertainty and Artificial Intelligence, 222-227.

Zhang, K., Zhu, S., Kalander, M., Ng, I., Ye, J., Chen, Z., and Pan, L. (2021). *gCastle: A Python Toolbox for Causal Discovery.* ArXiv.

Zheng, X., Aragam, B., Ravikumar, P., and Xing, E.P. (2018). *DAGs with NO TEARS: Continuous Optimization for Structure Learning.* Neural Information Processing Systems.

Zheng, X., Dan, C., Aragam, B., Ravikumar, P., and Xing, E.P. (2020). *Learning Sparse Nonparametric DAGs.* International Conference on Artificial Intelligence and Statistics.

14

Causal Discovery and Machine Learning – Advanced Deep Learning and Beyond

Welcome to *Chapter 14*!

We're inevitably moving towards the end of our book, but we still have something to learn!

In the previous chapter, we introduced four families of causal discovery models: constraint-based, score-based, functional, and gradient-based. Each of the families and methods that we discussed came with unique strengths and unique limitations.

In this chapter, we'll introduce methods and ideas that aim to solve some of these limitations. We'll discuss an advanced deep learning causal discovery framework, **Deep End-to-end Causal Inference** (**DECI**), and implement it using the Microsoft open source library Causica and PyTorch.

We'll see how to approach data with hidden confounding using the **fast causal inference** (**FCI**) algorithm and introduce other algorithms that can be used in similar scenarios.

After that, we'll introduce two frameworks that allow us to combine observational and interventional data: ENCO and ABCI.

We'll close this chapter with a discussion of the challenges and open areas for improvement in causal discovery.

By the end of this chapter, you'll understand the basic theory behind DECI and will be able to apply it to your own problems. You will understand when the FCI algorithm might be useful and will be able to use it, including adding expert knowledge.

Finally, you will have a good understanding of how to extend observational causal discovery to interventional data and what challenges we face when applying causal discovery methods to real-world problems.

In this chapter, we cover the following topics:

- Deep End-to-end Causal Inference (DECI)
- Causal discovery under hidden confounding
- The FCI algorithm
- Causal discovery with interventions
- The real-world applicability of causal discovery and open challenges

Advanced causal discovery with deep learning

Xun Zheng and colleagues' *DAGs with NO TEARS* paper (Zheng et al., 2018), which we introduced in the previous chapter, ignited excitement in the causal discovery community and inspired a whole new line of research on gradient-based methods.

The fact that graph search could be carried out using continuous optimization opened up a path for integrating causal discovery with techniques coming from other deep learning areas.

One example of a framework integrating such techniques into the realm of causal discovery is **DECI** – a **deep learning end-to-end causal discovery and inference** framework (Geffner et al., 2022).

DECI is a flexible model that builds on top of the core ideas of the *NO TEARS* paper. It works for non-linear data with additive noise under minimality and no hidden confounding assumptions.

In this section, we'll discuss its architecture and major components and apply it to a synthetic dataset, helping the model to converge by injecting expert knowledge into the graph.

This section will have a slightly more technical character than some of the previous chapters. We'll focus on gaining a deeper understanding of the framework and code.

This focus will help us get a grasp of how advanced methods in causal discovery might be designed and how to implement them using lower-level components.

This is also an opportunity to get a taste of how causal algorithms can be implemented using deep learning frameworks such as PyTorch.

From generative models to causality

In recent years, generative models have made their way to the headlines. Models such as ChatGPT, DALL-E 2, and Midjourney have astonished the general public with their capabilities, sparked broad interest, and inspired a number of debates on the future of AI and even humanity itself; but generative models are far from being new.

The ideas behind generative models can be traced back to the 19th century and the early works of Adolphe Quetelet and – a bit later – Karl Pearson (McLachlan et al., 2019).

Contemporary causal discovery has multiple connections to generative modeling. For instance, DECI uses **causal autoregressive flow** (Khemakhem et al., 2021), while the **Structural Agnostic Model** (**SAM**; Kalainathan et al., 2022) leverages **generative adversarial networks** (**GAN**s; Goodfellow et al., 2020).

Let's briefly review the connection between autoregressive flows and causal models.

Looking back to learn who you are

Autoregressive flows (Kingma et al., 2016) are a subset of the **normalizing flows** framework – a set of techniques traditionally used in variational inference in order to efficiently learn complex distributions by transforming simpler ones.

In particular, autoregressive flows estimate the distribution of variable X_k as a function of the variables *preceding* it.

If we want to express one variable as a function of the variables preceding it, we first need to *order* these variables somehow.

A setting where variables are ordered and their value only depends on the variables that are *preceding* them resembles a **structural causal model** (**SCM**), where nodes' values only depend on the values of their parents.

This insight has been leveraged by Ilyes Khemakhem and colleagues (Khemakhem et al., 2021), who proposed an autoregressive flow framework with causal ordering of variables (**CAREFL**).

DECI further builds on this idea, by modeling the likelihood of data given the graph in an autoregressive fashion.

Moreover, the model learns the posterior distribution over graphs rather than just a single graph. In this sense, DECI is Bayesian. This architectural choice allows for a very natural incorporation of expert knowledge into the graph. We will see this in action later in this section.

DECI's internal building blocks

At the heart of DECI lies the same core idea that enabled NO TEARS' continuous optimization: the DAG-ness score. Although we introduced this in the previous chapter, let's refresh the definition here:

$$\mathcal{R}(A) = tr(e^{A \odot A}) - d$$

In the preceding formula, note the following:

- A is the adjacency matrix of a graph, G
- e is a matrix exponential
- $tr(.)$ is a trace of a matrix
- d is the number of nodes in a graph, represented by A
- $\odot$ is the Hadamard (element-wise) product

The role of $\mathcal{R}(A)$ is to ensure that we focus our search on **directed acyclic graphs** (**DAGs**). $\mathcal{R}(A)$ is equal to 0 *if and only if* a graph represented by the matrix A is a DAG.

In other words, minimizing this component during training helps us make sure that the recovered model will not contain cycles or bi-directional edges.

The DAG-ness score is one of the components that constitute DECI's loss function; but it's not the only one. A second important component is the **sparsity score**.

The sparsity score is defined using the squared **Frobenius norm** of the adjacency matrix. Formally, this is represented as follows:

$$\mathcal{S}(A) = ||A||_F^2$$

The role of the sparsity score is to (heuristically) promote the minimality of the solution. In other words, $\mathcal{S}(A)$ pushes the graph to follow the **minimality assumption** (for a refresher on minimality, refer to *Chapter 5* and/or *Chapter 13*).

Frobenius norm

The Frobenius norm is a matrix norm (`https://bit.ly/MatrixNorm`) defined as the square root of the sum of squares of absolute values of matrix entries:

$$||A||_F = \sqrt{\sum_{i=1}^{m}\sum_{j=1}^{n}|a_{ij}|^2}$$

When A is an unweighted adjacency matrix, the Frobenius norm measures the sparsity of the matrix. The sparser the matrix, the more zero entries it has.

Note that if the matrix A is real-valued, the absolute value function $|.|$ is redundant (squaring will make the result non-negative anyway). This only matters for complex-valued matrices (which we're not using here, but we include the absolute value operator for completeness of the definition).

The DAG-ness score and sparsity score are used to define three terms used in the model's loss function:

- $\alpha\mathcal{R}(A)$
- $\rho\mathcal{R}(A)^2$
- $\lambda\mathcal{S}(A)$

Each term is weighted by a dedicated coefficient: α, ρ, and λ, respectively.

While the latter coefficient is kept constant over the training, the first two are gradually increased.

The idea here is not to overly constrain the search space in the beginning (even if early graphs are not DAGs) in order to allow the algorithm to explore different trajectories. With time, we increase the values of α and ρ, effectively limiting the solutions to DAGs only.

The updates of these parameters are carried out by the scheduler of the **augmented Lagrangian optimizer** (`https://bit.ly/AugmentedLagrangian`).

The initial values of α, ρ, and λ are set by the user (they play the role of hyperparameters) and can influence the trajectory of the algorithm. In some causal discovery algorithms, including DECI, initial hyperparameter settings can make or break the results.

Finding good values of such hyperparameters might be challenging, in particular when we don't have a relevant benchmark dataset. We will discuss this challenge in greater detail in the last section of this chapter.

Keeping this in mind, let's move forward and see how to implement DECI.

We will learn about more hyperparameters on the way.

DECI in code

Let's implement DECI to get a more concrete understanding of how it works. The code for this chapter can be found in the accompanying notebook (`https://bit.ly/causal-ntbk-14`).

Let's start with the imports.

First, we'll import the `dataclass` decorator and NumPy and NetworkX libraries:

```
from dataclasses import dataclass
import numpy as np
import networkx as nx
```

The `dataclass` decorator will help us make sure that the model configuration is immutable and we don't change it by mistake somewhere on the way. We'll use NumPy for general numerical purposes and NetworkX for graph visualizations.

Next, we'll import PyTorch, PyTorch Lightning, and two convenient tools - `DataLoader` and `TensorDict`:

```
import torch
import pytorch_lightning as pl

from torch.utils.data import DataLoader
from tensordict import TensorDict
```

PyTorch is a popular deep learning framework and PyTorch Lightning (`https://bit.ly/IntroToLightning`) is a wrapper around PyTorch that aims at simplifying PyTorch's workflow (somewhat similar to what Keras does for TensorFlow). We won't make too much use of Lightning's capabilities in this chapter, but we'll leverage its convenient `.seed_everything()` method in order to set the random seed over different libraries.

Next, we'll import a familiar set of objects from gCastle:

```
from castle.datasets import DAG, IIDSimulation
from castle.common import GraphDAG
from castle.metrics import MetricsDAG
```

We'll use them to generate the data, plot the results, and compute useful metrics.

Next, we'll import a number of modules and methods from Causica. Causica (`https://bit.ly/MicrosoftCausica`) is a Microsoft-managed open source library focused on causal machine learning. At the time of writing this chapter (Q2 2023), DECI is the only algorithm available in the library, yet the authors have informed us that other algorithms will be added with time.

First, we import the `distributions` module:

```
import causica.distributions as cd
```

The `distributions` module contains a broad range of objects related to model-specific probabilistic operations.

Next, we import the **Input Convex Graph Neural Network** (**ICGNN**) module, three objects related to the computations of the augmented Lagrangian loss, and a method that computes the *DAG-ness score*:

```
from causica.functional_relationships import ICGNN
from causica.training.auglag import AugLagLossCalculator, AugLagLR,
AugLagLRConfig
from causica.graph.dag_constraint import calculate_dagness
```

ICGNN (Park et al., 2022) is a graph neural network architecture that we'll use to recover the functional relationships between variables.

Finally, we import additional utilities:

- `VariableTypeEnum`, which stores variable type information (continuous, binary, or categorical)
- The `tensordict_shapes()` function, which allows us to easily get information about the shapes of variables stored within a `TensorDict` container

We have skipped these imports here to avoid excessive clutter (check the notebook for a full list of imports).

> **TensorDict**
>
> `TensorDict` is a PyTorch-specific dictionary-like class designed as a data-storing container. The class inherits properties from PyTorch tensors, such as indexing, shape operations, and casting to a device. `TensorDict` provides a useful abstraction that helps to achieve greater modularity.

We're done with the imports; let's prepare for experiments!

We'll start with a quick setup.

DECI training can be accelerated using GPU. The following line will check whether a GPU is available in your system and store the relevant information in the `device` variable:

```
device = 'cuda' if torch.cuda.is_available() else 'cpu'
```

Let's set a random seed for reproducibility:

```
SEED = 11
pl.seed_everything(SEED)
```

We're ready to generate the data. We'll generate 5,000 observations from a simple scale-free graph:

```
# Generate a scale-free adjacency matrix
adj_matrix = DAG.scale_free(
    n_nodes=4,
    n_edges=6,
    seed=SEED
)

# Generate the simulation
dataset = IIDSimulation(
    W=adj_matrix,
    n=5000,
    method='nonlinear',
    sem_type='mim'
)
```

Here, we follow the same process that we used in the previous chapter:

- We generate a graph using gCastle's `DAG` object
- We generate the observations using the `IIDSimulation` object

We picked non-linear data generated using the multiple index model (Zheng et al., 2020). *Figure 14.1* presents our generated DAG.

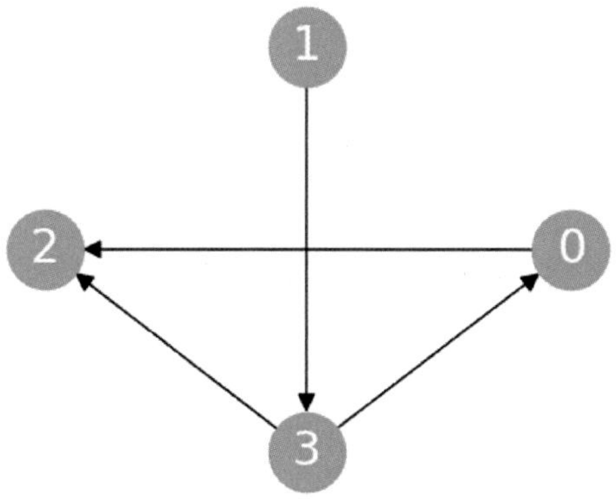

Figure 14.1 – Generated DAG

DECI configuration

As you have probably already noticed, DECI is a pretty complex model. In order to keep the code clean and reproducible, we'll define a set of neat configuration objects:

```
@dataclass(frozen=True)
class TrainingConfig:
    noise_dist=cd.ContinuousNoiseDist.SPLINE
    batch_size=512
    max_epoch=500
    gumbel_temp=0.25
    averaging_period=10
    prior_sparsity_lambda=5.0
    init_rho=1.0
    init_alpha=0.0

training_config = TrainingConfig()
auglag_config = AugLagLRConfig()
```

We use the `@dataclass` decorator with `frozen=True` in order to make sure that we don't alter the configuration object somewhere along the way mistakenly.

We instantiate model configuration (`TrainingConfig()`) and optimizer configuration (`AugLagLRConfig()`) and assign them to variables.

I set the batch size to `512` as I noticed that larger batches work better for small graphs with DECI.

Preparing the data

The dataset that we generated is stored as NumPy arrays. As DECI uses PyTorch, we need to cast it to `torch.tensor` objects.

We'll simultaneously store the tensors in a dictionary and then encapsulate them in a `TensorDict` object:

```
data_tensors = {}

for i in range(dataset.X.shape[1]):
    data_tensors[f'x{i}'] = torch.tensor(dataset.X[:,
        i].reshape(-1, 1))

dataset_train = TensorDict(data_tensors,
    torch.Size([dataset.X.shape[0]]))
```

Let's move the dataset to the device (the device should be cuda if a GPU accelerator had been detected on your system, otherwise cpu):

```
dataset_train = dataset_train.apply(lambda t:
    t.to(dtype=torch.float32, device=device))
```

Finally, let's create a PyTorch data loader, which will take care of batching, shuffling, and smooth data serving during training for us:

```
dataloader_train = DataLoader(
    dataset=dataset_train,
    collate_fn=lambda x: x,
    batch_size=training_config.batch_size,
    shuffle=True,
    drop_last=False,
)
```

DECI and expert knowledge

Thanks to its flexible architecture, DECI allows us to easily inject prior knowledge into the training process.

Let's pick one edge (let's say edge (3, 0)) in our graph and pass a strong belief about its existence to the model's prior.

Figure 14.2 presents a plot of the true adjacency matrix with edge (3, 0) marked in red:

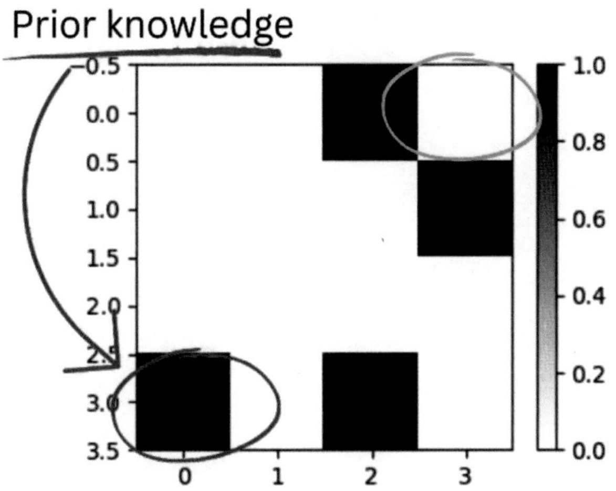

Figure 14.2 – The true adjacency matrix with prior knowledge edges marked

As you can see, there's also another spot marked in blue in *Figure 14.2*. This spot represents the same edge, but pointing in the opposite direction. As we are learning a directed graph (a DAG), the model should automatically understand that if the edge `(3, 0)` exists, the edge `(0, 3)` does not exist. The *DAG-ness penalty* in the cost function pushes the model toward this solution.

Although I haven't tested this systematically, it seems to me that explicitly passing the knowledge about the existence of edge $i \rightarrow j$ *and* the non-existence of edge $j \rightarrow i$ helps the model converge compared to the scenario where we only pass knowledge about the former.

In order to pass the knowledge to DECI, we need to build three matrices:

- An expert knowledge matrix
- A relevance mask that contains ones in the entries that we consider relevant and zeros everywhere else
- A confidence matrix that weights the relevant entries by our confidence, encoded as a float between 0 and 1

The relevance matrix is needed because we sometimes might want to pass our belief about the non-existence of an edge (encoded as 0 in the expert matrix) rather than its existence (encoded as 1 in the expert matrix).

The entries in the relevance matrix inform the model of which entries should be taken into account during the optimization.

Let's put all of this in the code.

First, we generate a zero matrix of the size of our adjacency matrix and assign `1` to the entry `(3, 0)`, where we believe an edge exists:

```
expert_matrix = torch.tensor(np.zeros(adj_matrix.shape))
expert_matrix[3, 0] = 1.
```

Next, in order to get the relevance matrix, we clone the expert matrix (we want the entry `(3, 0)` to be taken into account by the model, so we can just reuse the work we just did) and set the entry `(0, 3)` to `1`:

```
relevance_mask = expert_matrix.clone()
relevance_mask[0, 3] = 1.
```

Now, the `expert_matrix` object contains `1` in position `(3, 0)`, while the `relevance_mask` object contains ones in positions `(3, 0)` *and* `(0, 3)`.

Finally, we clone the relevance matrix to obtain the confidence matrix:

```
confidence_matrix = relevance_mask.clone()
```

We want to tell the model that we're 100% sure that the edge `(3, 0)` exists.

The confidence matrix takes values between 0 and 1, so the ones in the `(3, 0)` and `(0, 3)` entries essentially tell the model that we're completely sure that these entries are correct.

As DECI is a generative model, after the convergence, we can sample from the distribution over the adjacency matrix.

In order to effectively pass the knowledge to the model, we need to pass all three matrices to Causica's `ExpertGraphContainer` object:

```
expert_knowledge = cd.ExpertGraphContainer(
    dag=expert_matrix,
    mask=relevance_mask,
    confidence=confidence_matrix,
    scale=5.
)
```

The last parameter that we pass to the expert knowledge container – `scale` – determines the amount of contribution of the expert term to the loss.

The larger the value of `scale`, the heavier the expert graph will be weighted when computing the loss, making expert knowledge more important and harder to ignore for the model.

The main modules of DECI

DECI is largely a modular system, where particular components could be replaced with other compatible elements. This makes the model even more flexible.

Let's define DECI's main modules.

We'll start with the DAG prior:

```
prior = cd.GibbsDAGPrior(
    num_nodes=len(dataset_train.keys()),
    sparsity_lambda=training_config.prior_sparsity_lambda,
    expert_graph_container=expert_knowledge
)
```

Let's unpack it!

We use the `GibbsDAGPrior` class to define the prior. We pass three parameters to the class constructor: the number of nodes in the graph (which also represents the number of features in our dataset), the sparsity lambda value (this is the λ parameter, which weights the *sparsity score* that we discussed earlier in this chapter), and – last but not least – the expert knowledge object.

The Gibbs prior object will later be used in the training in order to compute the unnormalized log probability of the DAG that we'll use to compute the value of the loss function.

Next, let's build three components representing three elements of a **structural equation model** (**SEM**):

- The adjacency matrix distribution module
- The functional module (which models the functional relationships between variables)
- The noise distribution module (which models the noise term distributions in the SEM)

We'll model the adjacency matrix using the `ENCOAdjacencyDistributionModule` object. ENCO (Lippe et al., 2022) is a causal discovery model that is able to work with observational, mixed, and interventional data. Contrary to many other algorithms, ENCO parametrizes the existence of an edge and its direction separately, and here we *borrow* this parametrization from the ENCO algorithm:

```
adjacency_dist = cd.ENCOAdjacencyDistributionModule(
    num_nodes)
```

`ENCOAdjacencyDistributionModule`'s constructor takes only one argument – the number of nodes in a graph.

Next, we define the functional model. We'll use the ICGNN graph neural network (Park et al., 2022) for this purpose:

```
icgnn = ICGNN(
    variables=tensordict_shapes(dataset_train),
    embedding_size=8,
    out_dim_g=8,
    norm_layer=torch.nn.LayerNorm,
    res_connection=True,
)
```

We pass five parameters here:

- A dictionary of variable shapes (`variables`)
- The embedding size used to represent the variables internally (`embedding_size`)
- The size of the embeddings that represent the *parent* nodes while computing the representations of the *children* nodes internally (`out_dim_g`)
- An optional layer normalization object (`norm_layer`; `https://bit.ly/LayerNorm`)
- A Boolean variable telling the model whether we want residual connections to be used in the internal neural network or not (`res_connection`)

ICGNN will be responsible for parametrizing the functional relationships between the variables in our model.

Finally, let's define the noise module.

We'll start by creating a type dictionary. For each variable, we'll create a key-value pair with the variable name used as a key and its type as a value. We'll use Causica-specific type descriptions stored in the `VariableTypeEnum` object:

```
types_dict = {var_name: VariableTypeEnum.CONTINUOUS for
    var_name in dataset_train.keys()}
```

As all the variables in our dataset are continuous, we use the same type (`VariableTypeEnum.CONTINUOUS`) for all variables.

Finally, let's create a set of noise modules for each of the variables:

```
noise_submodules = cd.create_noise_modules(
    shapes=tensordict_shapes(dataset_train),
    types=types_dict,
    continuous_noise_dist=training_config.noise_dist
)
```

We pass the variable shapes and types to the constructor alongside the intended noise distribution.

The information about the noise distribution type is stored in our training configuration object. At the time of writing, DECI supports two noise distribution types: Gaussian and spline. The latter is generally more flexible and has been demonstrated to work better across a wide range of scenarios (Geffner et al., 2022, p. 7), and so we've picked it here as our default type.

Now, let's combine per-variable submodules into a joint noise module:

```
noise_module = cd.JointNoiseModule(noise_submodules)
```

We now have all three SEM modules (adjacency, functional, and noise) prepared. Let's pass them to a common SEM super-container and send the whole thing to a device:

```
sem_module = cd.SEMDistributionModule(
    adjacency_module=adjacency_dist,
    functional_relationships=icgnn,
    noise_module=noise_module)
sem_module.to(device)
```

The SEM module is now ready for training. The last missing part is the optimizer. DECI can use any PyTorch optimizer. Here, we'll use Adam.

First, we'll create a parameter list for all modules and then pass it to Adam's constructor:

```
modules = {
    'icgnn': sem_module.functional_relationships,
    'vardist': sem_module.adjacency_module,
    'noise_dist': sem_module.noise_module,
}
```

```
parameter_list = [
    {'params': module.parameters(), 'lr':
    auglag_config.lr_init_dict[name], 'name': name}
    for name, module in modules.items()
]
optimizer = torch.optim.Adam(params=parameter_list)
```

As we mentioned at the beginning of this section, DECI uses a constrained optimization scheme of augmented Lagrangian. Let's instantiate a learning rate scheduler and augmented Lagrangian loss calculator:

```
scheduler = AugLagLR(config=auglag_config)

auglag_loss = AugLagLossCalculator(
    init_alpha=training_config.init_alpha,
    init_rho=training_config.init_rho
)
```

We pass initial values of `alpha` and `rho` to the `AugLagLossCalculator` constructor. They represent the coefficients α and ρ, which that we use to weight the *DAG-ness score* that we discussed earlier at the beginning of this section.

We're now ready to train the model!

Training DECI

In order to train DECI, we'll use a double `for` loop.

In the outer `for` loop, we'll iterate over the number of epochs, and in the inner `for` loop, we'll iterate over the batches within each epoch (as a result, we iterate over all batches within each epoch).

Before we start the `for` loops, let's store the total number of samples in our dataset in a `num_samples` variable. We'll use it later to compute our objective:

```
num_samples = len(dataset_train)

for epoch in range(training_config.max_epoch):
    for i, batch in enumerate(dataloader_train):
```

Within the loop, we'll start by zeroing the gradients, so that we can make sure that we compute fresh gradients for each batch:

```
        optimizer.zero_grad()
```

Next, we'll sample from our SEM module and calculate the probability of the data in the batch given the current model:

```
sem_distribution = sem_module()
sem, *_ = sem_distribution.relaxed_sample(
    torch.Size([]),
    temperature=training_config.gumbel_temp
)
batch_log_prob = sem.log_prob(batch).mean()
```

Note that we use the `.relaxed_sample()` method. This method uses the Gumbel-Softmax trick, which approximates sampling from a discrete distribution (which is non-differentiable) with a continuous distribution (which is differentiable).

This is important because we cannot push the gradients through non-differentiable operations, which essentially makes training using gradient descent impossible.

Next, still within the batch loop, we compute the SEM distribution entropy (`https://bit.ly/EntropyDefinition`). We'll need this quantity to compute the overall value of the loss for the model:

```
sem_distribution_entropy =
    sem_distribution.entropy()
```

Next, we compute the log probability of the current graph, given our prior knowledge and the *sparsity score* we defined in the *DECI's internal building blocks* subsection earlier (the score is computed internally):

```
prior_term = prior.log_prob(sem.graph)
```

Next, we compute the objective and *DAG-ness score*, and pass everything to our augmented Lagrangian calculator:

```
# Compute the objective
objective = (-sem_distribution_entropy -
    prior_term) / num_samples - batch_log_prob

# Compute the DAG-ness term
constraint = calculate_dagness(sem.graph)

# Compute the Lagrangian loss
loss = auglag_loss(objective, constraint / num_samples)
```

We compute the gradients for the whole model and propagate them back:

```
loss.backward()
optimizer.step()
```

Finally, we update the augmented Lagrangian scheduler, which performs the augmented Lagrangian optimization procedure:

```
scheduler.step(
    optimizer=optimizer,
    loss=auglag_loss,
    loss_value=loss.item(),
    lagrangian_penalty=constraint.item(),
)
```

This concludes our training loop (in fact, in the notebook, we have a couple more lines that print out and plot the results, but we've skipped them here to avoid stacking too much code in the chapter).

Let's take a look at the results!

DECI's results

Figure 14.3 presents the recovered adjacency matrix (left) and the true matrix (right):

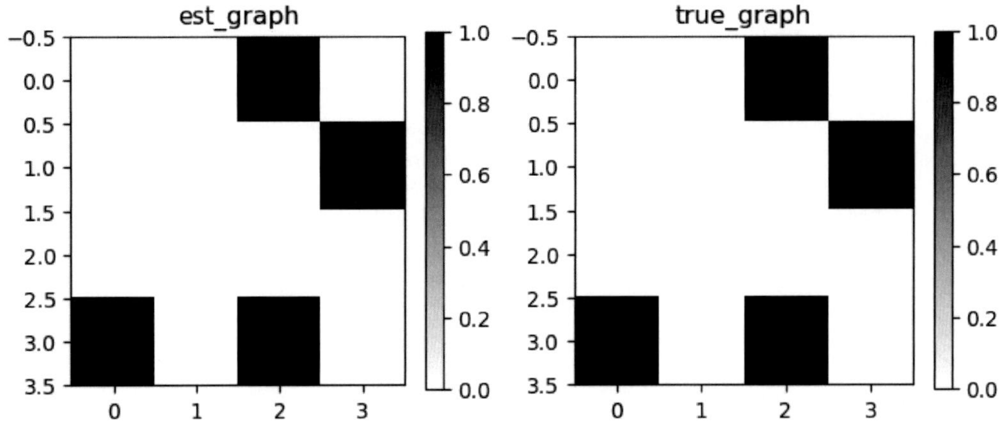

Figure 14.3 – The matrix recovered by DECI and the true matrix

As we can see, DECI did a very good job and recovered the matrix perfectly.

That said, we need to remember that we made the task easier for the model by providing some very strong priors.

I also found out that a number of hyperparameter settings were crucial for making the model results more or less stable for this and similar datasets. I used my knowledge and intuitions from previous experiments to choose the values.

First, I set the embedding sizes for ICGNN to `8`. With larger, 32-dimensional embeddings, the model seemed unstable. Second, I set the batch size to `512`. With a batch size of `128`, the model had difficulties converging to a good solution.

The DECI architecture is powerful and flexible. This comes at the price of higher complexity. If you want to use DECI in practice, it might be a good idea to first work with the model on other datasets with a known structure that are similar to your problem in order to find good hyperparameter settings.

DECI also comes with a number of limitations – it is designed to work with non-linear data with additive noise, and when the data does not follow these assumptions, the model loses its theoretical guarantees (which are asymptotic).

Besides this, DECI requires standard assumptions of no hidden confounding, **minimality**, and general correct model specification.

For details on assumptions, check out Geffner et al. (2022), *Section 3.2*. For theoretical guarantees and their proofs, check out Geffner et al. (2022), *Theorem 1* and *Appendix A*.

Before we conclude this section, let's briefly discuss a capability of DECI that we haven't touched upon so far.

DECI is end-to-end

We used DECI as a causal discovery method, but in fact, it is an end-to-end causal framework, capable of not only causal discovery but also estimating the **average treatment effect** (**ATE**) and (to an extent) the **conditional average treatment effect** (**CATE**).

In this section, we introduced DECI – a deep end-to-end causal inference framework. We discussed the basic theory behind the model and implemented it using Causica's modules and PyTorch. DECI is a flexible and powerful generative model that can perform causal discovery and inference in an end-to-end fashion.

Despite its many strengths, DECI – similar to the models that we discussed in the previous chapter – requires that no hidden confounding is present in the data.

Let's see what to do when the possibility of hidden confounding cannot be excluded.

Causal discovery under hidden confounding

Not all causal discovery methods are helpless in the face of hidden confounding.

In this section, we'll learn about the FCI algorithm, which can operate when some or all confounding variables are unobserved. We'll implement the FCI algorithm using the `causal-learn` package and – finally – discuss two more approaches that can be helpful when our dataset contains potential unobserved confounders.

The FCI algorithm

FCI (Sprites et al., 2000; Sprites et al., 2013) is a constraint-based algorithm. This means that the algorithm uses a set of conditional independence tests in order to decide which edges exist and what their orientations are. The FCI algorithm can be thought of as an extension of the PC algorithm that can work on an extended class of graphs, called **inducing path graphs**. The theory behind inducing path graphs is beyond the scope of our book. If you want to learn more, check out *Chapter 6* of Sprites et al. (2000).

I want more edge types, Mom!

FCI gives asymptotically correct results even under hidden confounding and selection bias.

This is great news!

However, in causality – similar to machine learning – there's no free lunch, and there's a price we need to pay for this otherwise-great feature. FCI (just like PC) might return a **Markov equivalence class** (**MEC**) rather than a fully oriented graph. In other words, some of the edges might not be oriented (even if they are correct). The algorithm also requires the **faithfulness assumption** to be met.

That said, FCI output can be more informative than the standard PC output. The reason for this is that FCI returns more edge types than just simple directed and undirected edges.

To be precise, there are four edge types in FCI (we're following the notation scheme used in the `causal-learn` package):

- When $G_{ij} = -1$ and $G_{ji} = 1$, then i is a cause of j
- When $G_{ij} = 2$ and $G_{ji} = 1$, j *is not* an ancestor of i
- When $G_{ij} = 2$ and $G_{ji} = 2$, then no set d-separates i and j
- When $G_{ij} = 1$ and $G_{ji} = 1$, then there is a hidden common cause of i and j

If this sounds a bit overwhelming to you, you're definitely not alone!

Fortunately, causal-learn also gives a simple visual representation of these types of edges that can be printed out for any found graph (we'll see this in a while).

Implementing FCI

As of the time of writing, FCI is not available in gCastle. We will use the implementation from another library – causal-learn. This library is a Python translation and extension of the famous TETRAD Java library and is maintained by the CLeaR group from Carnegie Mellon University, which includes Peter Sprites and Clark Glymour – the creators of the original PC and FCI algorithms.

Traditionally, we start with the imports:

```
from causallearn.search.ConstraintBased.FCI import fci
from causallearn.utils.PCUtils.BackgroundKnowledge import
BackgroundKnowledge
from causallearn.graph.GraphNode import GraphNode
```

We import the `fci` function, which implements the FCI algorithm and the `BackgroundKnowledge` and `GraphNode` classes, which will allow us to inject prior knowledge into the algorithm.

Now, let's create a confounded dataset:

```
N = 1000

q = np.random.uniform(0, 2, N)
w = np.random.randn(N)
x = np.random.gumbel(0, 1, N) + w
y = 0.6 * q + 0.8 * w + np.random.uniform(0, 1, N)
z = 0.5 * x + np.random.randn(N)

data = np.stack([x, y, w, z, q]).T
confounded_data = np.stack([x, y, z, q]).T
```

We generate a five-dimensional dataset with 1,000 observations and different noise distributions (Gaussian, uniform, and Gumbel).

We create two data matrices: `data`, with all variables, and `counfounded_data`, with the missing variable, `w` (which is a common cause of `x` and `y`).

Figure 14.4 presents the structure of our dataset. The red node, *W*, is an unobserved confounder.

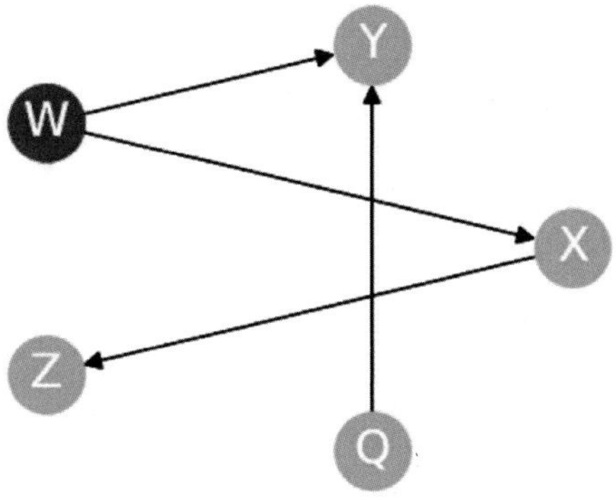

Figure 14.4 – A graph with an unobserved confounder

We're now ready to fit the model.

causal-learn's API is pretty different from the one we know from gCastle. First, the model is represented as a function rather than a class with a dedicated fitting method.

The model function (`fci()`) returns causal-learn's native graph object and a list of edge objects. Let's run the algorithm and store the outputs in variables:

```
g, edges = fci(
    dataset=confounded_data,
    independence_test_method='kci'
)
```

We passed the dataset to the function and, additionally, we specified the conditional independence test that we want to use. **Kernel-based conditional independence** (**KCI**) is a powerful and flexible test that can work with complex distributions. It scales well with the number of variables but can be very slow for large sample sizes.

Let's print the learned graph:

```
g.graph
```

This gives us the following:

```
array([[0, 2, 2, 0],
       [1, 0, 0, 1],
       [2, 0, 0, 0],
       [0, 2, 0, 0]])
```

For most people, this matrix is difficult to read (at least at first), and there's no easy way to meaningfully plot it using `GraphDAG`, which we've used so far.

Fortunately, we can iterate over the `edges` object to obtain a more human-readable representation of the results.

Let's create a mapping between the default variable names used internally by causal-learn and the variable names that we used in our dataset:

```
mapping = {
    'X1': 'X',
    'X2': 'Y',
    'X3': 'Z',
    'X4': 'Q'
}
```

Now, let's iterate over the edges returned by FCI and print them out:

```
for edge in edges:
    mapped = str(edge)\
        .replace(str(edge.node1),
        mapping[str(edge.node1)])\
        .replace(str(edge.node2),
        mapping[str(edge.node2)])
    print(mapped)
```

This gives us the following:

```
X o-> Y
X o-o Z
Q o-> Y
```

Let's decode it.

The meaning of the arrows in the printout is as follows:

- X is not an ancestor of Y – there might be an arrow from X to Y or they might be confounded, but there's no arrow from Y to X
- There's no set that d-separates X and Z – they might be confounded or have some direct causal relationship
- Y is not an ancestor of Q

Looking at the graph, all of this is true. At the same time, the output is not very informative as it leaves us with many unknowns.

FCI and expert knowledge

FCI allows us to easily inject expert knowledge into it. In causal-learn, we can add expert knowledge using the `BackgroundKnowledge` class. Note that we'll need to use the naming convention used by causal-learn internally (`X1`, `X2`, etc.) in order to specify expert knowledge (see the code snippet with the `mapping` dictionary in the preceding section for mapping between causal-learn's variable names and the variable names in our graph).

We instantiate the object and call the `.add_forbidden_by_node()` and `.add_required_by_node()` methods:

```
prior_knowledge = BackgroundKnowledge()
prior_knowledge.add_forbidden_by_node(GraphNode('X2'),
    GraphNode('X4'))
prior_knowledge.add_required_by_node(GraphNode('X1'),
    GraphNode('X3'))
```

In order to identify the nodes, we use `GraphNode` objects and pass node names that causal-learn uses internally (we could reverse our mapping here, but we'll skip it for simplicity).

Now, we're ready to pass our prior knowledge to the `fci()` function:

```
g, edges = fci(
    dataset=confounded_data,
    independence_test_method='fisherz',
    background_knowledge=prior_knowledge
)
```

Note that this time, we also used the Fisher's Z-test instead of KCI. Fisher-Z is a fast but slightly less flexible conditional independence test, compared to KCI. Fisher-Z is recommended for Gaussian linear data, but I've seen it work multiple times for much more complex distributions and relationships as well.

Let's see the results:

```
X o-> Y
X --> Z
Q --> Y
```

As we can see, disambiguating the relationship between *Y* (`X2`) and *Q* (`X4`) and directly enforcing the edge between *X* (`X1`) and *Z* (`X3`) worked well. The `-->` symbol reads *is a cause of*. The retrieved graph combined with expert knowledge is much more informative.

FCI might be a good choice if we're not sure about the existence of edges. The algorithm can give us a number of useful hints. The edges might next be passed in the form of expert knowledge to another algorithm for further disambiguation (e.g., LiNGAM or DECI if the respective assumptions are met). FCI performance can also be improved by using so-called tiers when passing background knowledge to the algorithm (**tiered background knowledge**). For details, check out Andrews et al. (2020).

Other approaches to confounded data

FCI is not the only method out there that can handle hidden confounding.

Another, more recent, solution is called the **confounding cascade nonlinear additive noise model** (**CCANM**; Cai et al., 2021).

CCANM

CCANM is an **additive noise model** (**ANM**-family) model that leverages a **variational autoencoder** (**VAE**) in order to retrieve the causal direction between variables, including mediation and confounding scenarios. The authors have shown that the model outperforms models such as a basic ANM and LiNGAM on a number of benchmarks. CCANM tends to work better with larger sample size (5,000-6,000) observations.

CORTH

CORTH is an algorithm proposed by Ashkan Soleymani from MIT and colleagues (Soleymani et al., 2022). The algorithm uses the **double machine learning** framework to identify the direct causes of a variable of interest. It is framed by the authors as a *causal feature selection algorithm*. The algorithm allows for hidden confounding in the dataset, but *not* between the variable of interest and its direct causes.

CORTH requires that no node in the dataset is a descendant of the variable of interest, but it does not require faithfulness nor acyclicity between covariates and allows for non-linear interactions between them.

In this section, we introduced causal discovery methods that can work under hidden confounding. We discussed the FCI algorithm and implemented it using the causal-learn library. We also learned how to pass prior knowledge to the algorithm and introduced two other methods that can work under different scenarios involving hidden confounding: CCANM and CORTH.

In the next section, we'll discuss methods that can leverage information coming from interventions.

Extra – going beyond observations

In certain cases, we might be able to intervene on some or all variables in order to facilitate or improve the results of a causal discovery process.

In this short section, we'll introduce two methods that can help us make sure that we make good use of such interventions.

ENCO

Efficient Neural Causal Discovery (**ENCO**; Lippe et al., 2022) is a causal discovery method for observational and interventional data. It uses continuous optimization and – as we mentioned earlier in the section on DECI – parametrizes edge existence and its orientation separately. ENCO is guaranteed to converge to a correct DAG if interventions on all variables are available, but it also performs reasonably well on partial intervention sets. Moreover, the model works with discrete, continuous, and mixed variables and can be extended to work with hidden confounding. The model code is available on GitHub (`https://bit.ly/EncoGitHub`).

ABCI

Active Bayesian Casual Inference (**ABCI**; Toth et al., 2022) is a fully Bayesian framework for active causal discovery and reasoning. ABCI requires no hidden confounding or acyclicity and assumes a non-linear additive noise model with homoscedastic noise. A great advantage of ABCI is that it does not necessarily focus on estimating the entire causal graph, but rather on a causal query of interest, and then sequentially designs experiments that most reduce the uncertainty. This makes ABCI highly data-efficient. As a Bayesian method, ABCI makes it easy to encode expert knowledge in the form of a prior(s). Moreover, ABCI allows for different types of causal queries: causal discovery, partial causal discovery, SCM learning, and more.

The model code is available on GitHub (`https://bit.ly/ABCIGitHub`).

In this section, we introduced two methods: ENCO and ABCI. They allow us to combine observational and interventional data. ENCO provides excellent results when interventions for all variables are available (almost error-free on graphs of up to 1,000 nodes), while ABCI provides excellent data efficiency and can help focus efforts where it's most needed. Both frameworks significantly expand the realm of what's possible with causal discovery and can bring benefits even when only minimal interventions are possible.

Causal discovery – real-world applications, challenges, and open problems

Before we wrap up this chapter, let's take a broader perspective and discuss the applicability of causal discovery to real-world problems and challenges that may arise along the way.

In the previous chapter, we mentioned that Alexander Reisach and colleagues have demonstrated that the synthetic data used to evaluate causal discovery methods might contain unintended regularities that can be relatively easily exploited by these models (Reisach et al., 2021). The problem is that these regularities might not be present in real-world data.

Another challenge is that real-world data with a known causal structure is scarce. This makes synthetic datasets a natural benchmarking choice, yet this choice leaves us without a clear understanding of what to expect of causal structure learning algorithms when applied to real-world datasets.

The lack of reliable benchmarks is one of the main challenges in the field as of the time of writing this chapter.

That said, there exists research examining causal discovery methods' performance on real-world data.

We'll now briefly discuss it.

Tu et al. (2019) applied four traditional causal discovery algorithms (FCI, RFCI, PC, and GES) to real-world and (realistically) simulated data for neuropathic pain diagnosis. The dataset contains over 200 binary variables representing various injuries and symptoms.

The results for all causal discovery methods had limited quality in this setting. F1 scores varied roughly between 0.01 and 0.32, depending on the method and setting (top scores required a very large sample size, that is, >16,000 samples).

Huang et al. (2021) applied NO TEARS, DAG-GNN, and **Temporal Causal Discovery Framework (TCDF)** methods to climate data. The dataset consisted of a set of variables representing the interactions of Arctic Sea ice and the atmosphere. The authors concluded that they were able to achieve *reasonable results* (a normalized Hamming distance of around 0.3) compared to the expert graph with NO TEARS and DAG-GNN (but not TCDF).

The authors also report that both methods were sensitive to hyperparameter changes. This is challenging in a real-world setting, where the true graph is unknown and there's no good general benchmark, because we don't know which values of hyperparameters to choose.

Shen et al. (2020) applied FCI and FGES algorithms to Alzheimer's disease data. The FGES algorithm provided promising results with precision varying between 0.46 and 0.76 and recall varying between 0.6 and 0.74, depending on how much expert knowledge was injected into the algorithm.

The latter results show how valuable adding expert knowledge to the graph can be.

Causal discovery algorithms are also used in the industry. Unfortunately, most industrial use cases are protected by non-disclosure agreements and cannot be shared publicly.

I hope that with the rising adoption of causal methods in the industry, this will start gradually changing and we'll start seeing more companies sharing their experiences. This is of paramount importance as industrial use cases provide the research community with a vital injection of motivation. The research community gives back, providing the industry with better and more efficient ideas, which moves the industry forward.

We can observe the effects of such a virtuous circle in traditional machine learning today.

Benchmarking is not the only challenge in contemporary causal discovery.

Many real-world problems might be describable using mixed variable types (discrete and continuous). For most causal discovery methods, this is a major challenge.

ENCO supports mixed types natively, but only when we provide the algorithm with interventional data. The necessity to use interventional data might be a serious limitation in applying this algorithm in certain use cases.

Contemporary causal discovery can be a source of valuable insights and can definitely be helpful, yet it should be used with the awareness of its limitations.

We still haven't reached the stage of a *fully automated scientist*, but I believe that causal discovery research can move us a bit closer toward this milestone.

Understanding which methods can work under which circumstances is crucial and I hope that this book gave you a solid foundation to build such awareness.

Congratulations on reaching the end of *Chapter 14*! Let's summarize what we've learned.

Wrapping it up!

In this chapter, we introduced several methods and ideas that aim to overcome the limitations of traditional causal discovery frameworks. We discussed DECI, an advanced deep learning causal discovery framework, and demonstrated how it can be implemented using Causica, Microsoft's open source library, and PyTorch.

We explored the FCI algorithm, which can be used to handle data with hidden confounding, and introduced other algorithms that can be used in similar scenarios. These methods provide a strong foundation for tackling complex causal inference problems.

After that, we discussed two frameworks, ENCO and ABCI, that allow us to combine observational and interventional data. These frameworks extend our ability to perform causal discovery and provide valuable tools for data analysis.

Finally, we discussed a number of challenges that we face when applying causal discovery methods to real-world problems.

We are inexorably approaching the end of our journey.

In the next chapter, we'll summarize everything we've learned so far, discuss practical ideas of how to effectively apply some of the methods we've discussed, and see how causality is being successfully implemented across industries.

References

Andrews, B., Sprites, P., & Cooper, G. F. (2020). *On the Completeness of Causal Discovery in the Presence of Latent Confounding with Tiered Background Knowledge.* International Conference on Artificial Intelligence and Statistics.

Cai, R., Qiao, J., Zhang, K., Zhang, Z., & Hao, Z. (2021). *Causal discovery with cascade nonlinear additive noise models. ACM Trans.* Intell. Syst. Technol., 6(12).

Geffner, T., Antorán, J., Foster, A., Gong, W., Ma, C., Kıcıman, E., Sharma, A., Lamb, A., Kukla, M., Pawlowski, N., Allamanis, M., & Zhang, C. (2022). *Deep End-to-end Causal Inference.* arXiv.

Goodfellow, I., Pouget-Abadie, J., Mirza, M., Xu, B., Warde-Farley, D., Ozair, S., Courville, A., & Bengio, Y. (2020). *Generative adversarial networks.* Communications of the ACM, 63(11), 139-144.

Goudet, O., Kalainathan, D., Caillou, P., Guyon, I., Lopez-Paz, D., & Sebag, M. (2018). *Causal generative neural networks.* arXiv.

Huang, Y., Kleindessner, M., Munishkin, A., Varshney, D., Guo, P., & Wang, J. (2021). *Benchmarking of Data-Driven Causality Discovery Approaches in the Interactions of Arctic Sea Ice and Atmosphere.* Frontiers in Big Data, 4.

Kalainathan, D., Goudet, O., Guyon, I., Lopez-Paz, D., & Sebag, M. (2022). *Structural agnostic modeling: Adversarial learning of causal graphs.* arXiv.

Kingma, D. P., Salimans, T., Jozefowicz, R., Chen, X., Sutskever, I., & Welling, M. (2016). *Improved Variational Inference with Inverse Autoregressive Flow.* Advances in Neural Information Processing Systems, 29.

McLachlan, G. J., Lee, S. X., & Rathnayake, S. I. (2019). *Finite Mixture Models*. Annual Review of Statistics and Its Application, 6(1), 355-378.

Lippe, P., Cohen, T., & Gavves, E. (2021). *Efficient neural causal discovery without acyclicity constraints*. arXiv.

Park, J., Song, C., & Park, J. (2022). *Input Convex Graph Neural Networks: An Application to Optimal Control and Design Optimization*. Open Review. `https://openreview.net/forum?id=S2pNPZM-w-f`

Reisach, A. G., Seiler, C., & Weichwald, S. (2021). *Beware of the Simulated DAG! Varsortability in Additive Noise Models*. arXiv.

Shen, X., Ma, S., Vemuri, P., & Simon, G. (2020). *Challenges and opportunities with causal discovery algorithms: application to Alzheimer's pathophysiology*. Scientific Reports, 10(1), 2975.

Soleymani, A., Raj, A., Bauer, S., Schölkopf, B., & Besserve, M. (2022). *Causal feature selection via orthogonal search*. Transactions on Machine Learning Research.

Sprites, P., Glymour, C., & Scheines, R. (2000). *Causation, Prediction, and Search*. MIT Press.

Spirtes, P., Meek, C., & Richardson, T. S. (2013). *Causal inference in the presence of latent variables and selection bias*. arXiv.

Toth, C., Lorch, L., Knoll, C., Krause, A., Pernkopf, F., Peharz, R., & Von Kügelgen, J. (2022). *Active Bayesian Causal Inference*. arXiv.

Tu, R., Zhang, K., Bertilson, B., Kjellstrom, H., & Zhang, C. (2019). *Neuropathic pain diagnosis simulator for causal discovery algorithm evaluation*. Advances in Neural Information Processing Systems, 32.

Zhang, K., Peters, J., Janzing, D., & Schölkopf, B. (2012). *Kernel-based conditional independence test and application in causal discovery*. arXiv.

Zheng, X., Aragam, B., Ravikumar, P., & Xing, E. P. (2018). *DAGs with NO TEARS: Continuous Optimization for Structure Learning*. Neural Information Processing Systems.

Zheng, X., Dan, C., Aragam, B., Ravikumar, P., & Xing, E. P. (2020). *Learning Sparse Nonparametric DAGs*. International Conference on Artificial Intelligence and Statistics.

15
Epilogue

Congratulations on reaching *the final chapter!*

This is the last stop in our journey. Before we close, we'll do a number of things:

- Summarize what we've learned in the book
- Discuss five steps to get the best out of your causal projects
- Take a look at the intersection of causality and business and see how organizations implement successful causal projects
- Take a sneak peek into (a potential) future of causality
- Discuss where to find resources and how to learn more about causality

Ready for the last leap?

What we've learned in this book

Back in *Chapter 1*, we started our causal journey by asking about the reasons to use causal modeling rather than traditional machine learning, despite the tremendous success of the latter.

We defined the concept of confounding and showed how it can lead us astray by producing spurious relationships between causally independent variables. Next, we introduced **the Ladder of Causation** and its three rungs – **observations**, **interventions**, and **counterfactuals**. We showed the differences between observational and interventional distributions using linear regression.

After that, we refreshed our knowledge of the basic graph theory and introduced graphs as an important building block for causal models. We discussed three basic conditional independence structures – **forks**, **chains**, and **colliders**, and showed that colliders have a special status among the three, allowing us to infer the direction of causal influence from the data.

Next, we introduced **DoWhy**, and we learned how to implement DoWhy's four-step causal process. This led us to the discussion on assumptions behind causal models and the challenges that we might face when implementing them in practice.

Keeping these ideas in mind, we moved to **(conditional) average treatment effect** ((C)ATE) estimation methods and demonstrated how to implement them using DoWhy and EconML in observational and interventional scenarios.

We closed *Part 2* of the book by implementing meta-learners with tree-based and deep learning methods, and we learned how to implement a Transformer-based `CausalBert` model that allows us to control for confounding coming from natural language.

In *Part 3*, we reviewed various sources of causal knowledge and headed toward a discussion on causal discovery. We started with classic constraint-based algorithms and moved toward modern gradient-based methods, closing with a full implementation of Microsoft's DECI algorithm using PyTorch.

In the next section, we'll discuss five steps to get the best out of your causal project that are based on some of the best practices we discussed in the book.

Five steps to get the best out of your causal project

In this section, we'll discuss five steps that can help you maximize the potential of your causal project.

Starting with a question

Starting with a well-defined question is a necessary step of any scientific or business endeavor, but it has special importance in causality.

A well-defined question can transform an impossible problem into a tractable one. Causal modeling can sometimes be a divide-and-conquer game, and various challenges that might initially seem impossible to tackle can be addressed (sometimes relatively easily) if we're open to refining our questions.

For instance, one mistake that I observe in the industry is starting with very broad questions regarding a *complete causal model* of a process, or even an entire organization/organizational unit. In certain cases, building such a *complete* model might be very difficult, very costly, or both.

Often, answering one or two well-defined causal questions can bring significant benefits at a fraction of the cost of such a big project.

The problem with *over-scoping* the project and asking too broad questions is not unique to causality. It happens in non-causal AI projects as well. That said, under-defined or incorrectly scoped questions can break a causal project much faster than a traditional machine learning project.

One positive is that an organization can understand relatively early on that a project does not bring the expected benefits and shut it down faster, avoiding significant losses. The negative is that such an experience might produce disappointment, leading to reluctance to move toward causal modeling. This can be detrimental because, for many organizations, causal modeling can bring significant benefits, which might often remain unrealized without causal methods.

A well-defined (set of) question(s) is vital to any successful causal project.

Obtaining expert knowledge

Expert knowledge is of paramount importance in causal modeling. Expert insights can help us disambiguate ambiguous edges in a causal graph, narrow down the search space, and evaluate the quality of the output of causal discovery algorithms. Many sources of information can be valuable here – domain knowledge, scientific literature, previous internal experiments, results of simulations, and so on.

Depending on the use case, collecting and validating expert knowledge can be a short and natural process or a long and effortful one, but its value is hard to overestimate.

Note that not all sources of expert knowledge have to come with the same level of confidence. It's a good idea to keep an open mind regarding the (less confident) sources and be prepared to discard them in the process, especially if alternative explanations are more plausible and/or more coherent with other trustworthy sources of information.

It's a good practice to store and manage expert knowledge in a structured and accessible way (e.g., following FAIR (`https://bit.ly/FAIRPrinciples`) or another set of principles that are well suited for your organization and the problem that you're solving).

This is of special importance in the case of larger systems. A lack of good access to collected expert knowledge can lead to frustration and consume a project team's creative energy, which should be directed at solving a problem rather than dealing with avoidable technical issues.

Once collected, information should be stored in a way that enables us to easily access it in the future. This way, we can make sure that we optimally use our resources if this particular knowledge can be reused in future projects.

After collecting expert knowledge, we're ready to encode it as a graph.

In reality, expert knowledge collection and graph generation can be intertwined, and multiple iterations between these two steps can occur.

Generating hypothetical graph(s)

After defining the question and collecting available expert knowledge, we are ready to generate the first hypothetical graph (or a set of hypothetical graphs).

These graphs represent our hypotheses regarding the data-generating process.

They don't have to be perfect or complete at this stage. Hypothetical graphs will allow us to understand what we know and whether we have enough information to answer the question(s) of interest.

Sometimes, even graphs that look non-sufficiently informative at first sight might contain enough information to answer some (or all) of our questions.

Depending on the size of the graph, the size of the project, and your organization characteristics, we might choose different storage options for our graphs – a repository containing (a) file(s) encoding the graph(s) or a graph database (e.g., Neo4j or Amazon Neptune) can all be valid options for you.

Accessibility and the ease of updating the structure are of key importance here.

Check identifiability

It's likely that your first graph will contain some ambiguous edges and/or some unobserved variables. The effect of interest might be possible to estimate even despite this.

To check whether this is the case, you can use one of the advanced identifiability algorithms. You can find some of these algorithms in the Python `grapl-causal` library, developed by Max Little of the University of Birmingham and MIT.

Check the repository and demo notebooks here: `https://bit.ly/GRAPLCausal`.

Even if your effect is not identifiable right away, you might still be able to obtain some actionable information from your model. This is possible for a broad array of models with sensitivity analysis tools (check *Chapter 8* for more details).

For instance, if you work in marketing or sales, you might know from experience that even if there's hidden confounding in your data, the maximum impact of all hidden confounders on sales should not be greater than some particular value.

If this is the case, you can reliably check whether your effect holds under extreme confounding or under the most likely values of confounders.

If your effect turns out to be identifiable right away or you work with experimental data, you can start estimating the effect using one of the methods that we discussed in *Part 2* of our book.

If you have doubts regarding some of the edges or their orientation, you can employ one of the causal discovery methods that we discussed in *Part 3* and confront the output against expert knowledge. If you can afford interventions on all or some variables, methods such as **ENCO** (*Chapter 14*) can lead to very good results.

Falsifying hypotheses

When we obtain an identifiable graph, we treat it as a hypothesis, and we can now learn the functional assignments over the graph (e.g., using the four-step framework from *Chapter 7*). After learning the functional assignments over the graph, we can generate predictions. Testing these predictions over interventional test data is a good way to check whether the model behaves realistically.

Strong discrepancies between predictions and actual effects are a strong indicator that a model has issues (structural, related to estimation or both). A lack of discrepancies does not automatically guarantee that the model is correct (recall the Popperian logic of falsification that we discussed in *Chapter 7* and *Chapter 12*).

The five steps (defining the question(s), collecting expert knowledge, generating a graph, checking identifiability, and falsifying the hypotheses) are usually performed iteratively, and sometimes, their ordering may be altered. They might also involve some advanced techniques that we did not discuss in our book – root cause analysis, causal outlier detection, generating counterfactuals from a functional model, and so on.

Note that the steps we described do not include the actual data collection process. This is because data collection might happen at very different stages, depending on the nature of the question, your organization's data maturity, and the methodology you pick.

In this section, we discussed five steps we can take in order to carry out a reliable causal project:

1. Starting with a question.
2. Obtaining expert knowledge.
3. Generating hypotheses.
4. Checking identifiability.
5. Falsifying the hypotheses.

In the next section, we'll see examples of causal projects carried out in the real world.

Causality and business

In this section, we'll describe a couple of real-world use cases where causal systems have been successfully implemented to address business challenges and discuss how causality intersects with business frameworks.

How causal doers go from vision to implementation

Geminos is a US-based company, with a mission to help businesses across industries solve their challenges using causality. One of Geminos' success stories that I particularly like comes from their engagement with an industrial manufacturer of metal products; let's call them Company M.

I like this story, because it emphasizes the broad applicability of causality that goes way beyond the most popular cases in marketing and econometrics.

Let's see how it worked.

Company M was interested in optimizing the process of production of one of its products. They formulated four main questions:

1. How do we minimize an important characteristic of product *P*?
2. Which variables have the strongest effect on outcome *O*?
3. What has caused a recent change in outcome *O* and how do we revert the change?
4. Why do outliers occur and how do we remove them?

Note that all four questions require at least interventional (rung 2) reasoning, which makes them unanswerable using traditional statistical or machine learning methods.

For instance, question 1 asks what *actions* should be taken to minimize the characteristic of interest of product *P*. This question goes beyond plain understanding of what simply correlates with this characteristic (for context, recall our discussion on confounding from *Chapter 1*). To answer question 1, we need to understand the *mechanism* behind this characteristic and how changes in other variables can affect it.

After defining the questions, Geminos' team consulted the experts and researched relevant scientific literature. Combining information from both sources, the team built their first hypothetical graph.

Company M had recorded a rich set of variables describing their processes for a couple of years before the project started, yet it turned out that some of the variables considered in the graph had not been collected up to this point.

The team addressed this challenge by adjusting the graph in a way that preserved identifiability of the most important relationships, and the client learned which variables should be prioritized for future collection to facilitate further causal analyses.

The knowledge about which variables' collection to prioritize in the future was valuable in itself, as it helped the client understand how to optimally allocate resources. Installing new sensors or altering the existing software architecture can be very expensive, and when it does not lead to insights that bring real business value, it can cause significant losses.

With the updated graph, the team was ready to start validating their hypotheses. They estimated the coefficients in the model described by the hypothetical graph using Geminos' DoWhy-powered platform.

The team compared model outcomes against observational and interventional data and iteratively improved the model. As Owen from Geminos emphasized, "*Interrogating causal models is an important element of the iterative approach taken to causal AI.*"

After a number of iterations, the client was able to answer their questions and optimize the process beyond what they had previously been able to achieve, using traditional machine learning, statistical and optimization tools.

Company M spotted the outliers using causal outlier detection and understood the causal chain behind recent changes, ultimately answering all four key questions they formulated at the beginning of the project. This led to significant improvements in the production process.

The company also learned how to structure and prioritize their new data collection efforts in order to maximize the value, which saved them potential losses related to adapting existing systems to collect data that would not bring clear business value.

Geminos is not the only organization that successfully implements and productionalizes causal solutions. A UK-based company, **causaLens**, offers a causal data science platform that abstracts much of the complexity of building causal models. causaLens has helped numerous customers across industries build more robust solutions by introducing causality. Their use cases include marketing, supply chain, manufacturing optimization and more.

Causal modeling is also used in the digital entertainment industry. **Playtika**, an Israel-based digital entertainment company specializing in mobile gaming uses uplift (CATE) modeling to optimize their user experience. The company has recently open sourced their uplift evaluation library, `uplift-analysis` (check out `https://bit.ly/PlaytikaUplift`).

Causal modeling is also used by Swedish audio streaming giant **Spotify**. The company regularly shares their experience in applied causality through their technical blog and top conference publications (e.g., Jeunen et al., 2022). Spotify's blog covers a wide variety of topics, from sensitivity analysis of a synthetic control estimator (which we learned about in *Chapter 11*; see more at `https://bit.ly/SpotifySynthControl`) to disentangling causal effects from sets of interventions under hidden confounding (`https://bit.ly/SpotifyHiddenBlog`).

Production, sales, marketing and digital entertainment are not the only areas that can benefit from causal modeling. Causal models are researched and implemented across fields, from medicine to the automotive industry.

This is not surprising, as causal models often capture the aspects of problems that we're the most interested in solving. Causal models (in particular **structural causal models** (**SCMs**)) are also compatible with (or easily adaptable to) numerous business and process improvement frameworks.

Let's see an example. **Six Sigma** is a set of process improvement tools and techniques proposed by Bill Smith at Motorola. Within the Six Sigma framework, causality is defined as an impact of some input x on some output y via some mechanism f, formally:

$$y := f(x)$$

Note that this is almost identical to functional assignments in SCMs, which we discussed back in *Chapter 2* (except that we skip the noise variable in the preceding formula).

This makes causal analysis a natural choice whenever decision-making questions are at play.

To learn more about causality from a business point of view, check out *Causal Artificial Intelligence: The Next Step in Effective, Efficient, and Practical AI* by Judith Hurwitz and John K. Thompson (due for release in Q4 2023). Now, let's take a look at the future of causality.

Toward the future of causal ML

In this section, we'll briefly explore some possible future directions for causality from business, application, and research point of views. As always when talking about the future, this is somewhat of a gamble, especially in the second part of this section where we will discuss more advanced ideas.

Let's start our journey into the future from where we're currently standing.

Where are we now and where are we heading?

With an average of 3.2 new papers published on arXiv every day in 2022, causal inference has exploded in popularity, attracting a large amount of talent and interest from top researchers and institutions, including industry giants such as Amazon or Microsoft.

At the same time, for many organizations, causal methods are much less accessible than traditional statistical and machine learning techniques. This state of affairs is likely driven by a strong focus of educational system on associational methods when teaching about data science and machine learning, along with a lack of accessible materials that combine the theoretical and practical aspects of causality (I hope that this book will be a small step in changing the latter).

A number of aspects of causal modeling and causal thinking can be relatively easily adopted by many organizations, bringing them strong benefits.

Here are three skills that offer significant benefits for a wide range of organizations:

- An awareness of the differences between the rungs of the *Ladder of Causation* can help analysts clearly distinguish between problems that can be solved using traditional associational methods and ones that cannot be solved this way. Such awareness empowers organizations to mitigate losses related to investing in machine learning projects that answer ill-posed questions and cannot succeed in the long run.
- The ability to think structurally about a data-generating process and to understand conditional independence structure can help analysts, data scientists, and engineers make better decisions regarding statistical control and understand the challenges to the robustness of their models under distribution shifts. This ability enables teams across an organization to avoid costly surprises caused by misleading predictions generated by mis-specified models.
- The ability to model **conditional average treatment effects** (**CATE**) can help uncover information hidden by traditional A/B testing analysis techniques and bring new opportunities to personalize and revolutionize user experience. Causal personalization might bring better returns than traditional recommender systems. This is true in marketing, churn prevention, and other areas, thanks to CATE models' capability to recognize which units should be treated and which ones should remain untreated.

Despite the relatively low entry barrier, these three ideas seem to be highly underutilized across sectors, industries, and organization types.

Causal benchmarks

From a research perspective, one of the main challenges that we face today in causality is a lack of widely accessible real-world datasets and universal benchmarks – the analogs of ImageNet in computer vision.

Datasets and benchmarks can play a crucial role in advancing the field of causality by fostering reproducibility and transparency and providing researchers with a common point of reference.

Today's synthetic benchmarks have properties that hinder their effective use in causal discovery (Reisach et al., 2021) and causal inference (Curth et al., 2021).

The topic of causal benchmarks is actively researched, and initiatives such as CLeaR 2023's *Call for Causal Datasets* (`https://bit.ly/CLeaRDatasets`) demonstrate the community's rising awareness and readiness to tackle these challenges.

Some useful data simulators that can help to benchmark causal discovery methods have been also proposed recently (see `https://bit.ly/DiagnosisSimulator`).

Now, let's discuss four potential research and application directions where causality can bring value.

Causal data fusion

Causal data fusion (Bareinboim & Pearl, 2016, and Hünermund & Bareinboim, 2023) is an umbrella term for combining data from different sources to perform causal inference. In particular, interventional data might be combined with observational data. Causal data fusion might be particularly useful when combined with uncertainty estimation (e.g., Chau et al., 2021) and active learning paradigms (e.g., Toth et al., 2022).

Causal data fusion's promise is to make causal inference efficient by leveraging information from multiple datasets coming from different sources. This is particularly beneficial in biomedical sciences, where experiments might be expensive, difficult, or risky. Causal data fusion can help make valid and trustworthy conclusions by combining the information from small-sample experiments and large-sample observational datasets.

Although a number of challenges in causal data fusion are effectively solved (Bareinboim & Pearl, 2016), the paradigm seems underutilized in practice, in particular in industry.

This could be perhaps changed by making stakeholders more familiar with the opportunities that causal data fusion offers.

Intervening agents

The 2022/23 generative AI revolution has resulted in a number of new applications, including Auto-GPT or AgentGPT – programs that leverage GPT-class models behind the scenes and allow them to interact with the environment.

Model instances (called *agents*) might have access to the internet or other resources and can solve complex multistep tasks. Equipping these agents with causal reasoning capabilities can make them much more effective and less susceptible to confounding, especially if they are able to interact with the environment in order to falsify their own hypotheses about causal mechanisms.

Agents such as these could perform automated research and are a significant step toward creating the *automated scientist*. Note that allowing these agents to interact with the physical environment rather than only with the virtual one could significantly enhance their efficiency, yet this also comes with a number of important safety and ethical considerations.

Note that these ideas are related to some of the concepts discussed extensively by Elias Bareinboim in his 2020 *Causal Reinforcement Learning* tutorial (`https://bit.ly/CausalRL`).

Causal structure learning

Causal structure learning (Schölkopf et al., 2021) is a broad term encompassing various algorithms aimed at decoding a causal structure from high-dimensional data (e.g., video). Contrary to traditional causal discovery, causal structure learning assumes that some lower-dimensional latent variables exist that describe the causal structure of a system presented in the original high-dimensional representation.

For example, CITIRS (Lippe et al., 2022) learns low-level causal structures from videos containing interventions.

Depending on a model, causal structure models can work in various scenarios (e.g., with known or unknown interventions). This line of research can help us build systems that can intervene in the world and learn causal structures by observing the effects of their interventions (using vision or other modalities).

Note that the term *causal structure learning* is sometimes used interchangeably with the term *causal discovery*, and sometimes *causal structure learning* is understood as a superset of *causal discovery*, which includes the models with and without latent variables.

Imitation learning

When human babies learn basic world models, they often rely on experimentation (e.g., Gopnik, 2009; also vide *Chapter 1* of this book). In parallel, children imitate other people in their environment. At later stages in life, we start learning from others more often than performing our own experiments. This type of learning is efficient but might be susceptible to arbitrary biases or confounding.

Racial or gender stereotypes passed through generations are great examples of learning incorrect world models by imitation. For instance, in modern Western culture, it was widely believed until the late 1960s that women are *physically incapable* of running a marathon. Bobbi Gibb falsified this hypothesis by (illegally) running in the Boston Marathon in 1966. She not only finished the race but also ran faster than roughly 66% of the male participants (`https://bit.ly/BobbiGibbStory`).

Imitation learning is often more sample-efficient than experiments but does not guarantee causal identifiability. We face a similar challenge in modern **natural language processing** (**NLP**). Some **large language models** (**LLMs**) offer powerful causal capabilities learned from language data, but they sometimes fail unpredictably (Kıcıman et al., 2023).

Willig et al. (2023) proposed that LLMs learn a **meta-SCM** from text and that this model is associational in its nature.

Agents learning by imitation and then falsifying learned models by using interventions, or carrying out efficient causal reasoning by leveraging causal data fusion, can be great and efficient learners, capable of fast adaptation to various domains.

For instance, causally aware imitation learning can be very useful to create virtual assistants for business, medicine, or research. These assistants can learn from existing materials or the performance of other (virtual or physical) assistants and then improve by validating the trustworthiness of learned models.

Another broad research direction that intersects with some of the preceding ideas is neuro-symbolic AI – a class of models combining associational representation learning with symbolic reasoning modules.

The causal analysis of LLMs that we mentioned earlier in this section is in itself a promising research path that brings many interesting questions to the table. Thanks to the broad adoption of LLMs, this path has a chance to spark broader interest and attract the funding necessary to achieve significant progress in the near future.

Learning causality

In this section, we'll point to the resources to learn more about causality after finishing this book.

For many people starting with causality, their learning path begins with excitement. The promise of causality is attractive and powerful. After learning about the basics and realizing the challenges that any student of causality has to face, many of us lose hope in the early stages of our journeys.

Some of us regain it, learning that solutions do exist, although not necessarily where we initially expected to find them.

After overcoming the first challenges and going deeper into the topic, many of us realize that there are more difficulties to come. Learning from earlier experiences, it's easier at this stage to realize that (many of) these difficulties can be tackled using a creative and systematic approach.

I like the way the Swiss educator and researcher Quentin Gallea presented the journey into learning causality in a graphical form (*Figure 15.1*).

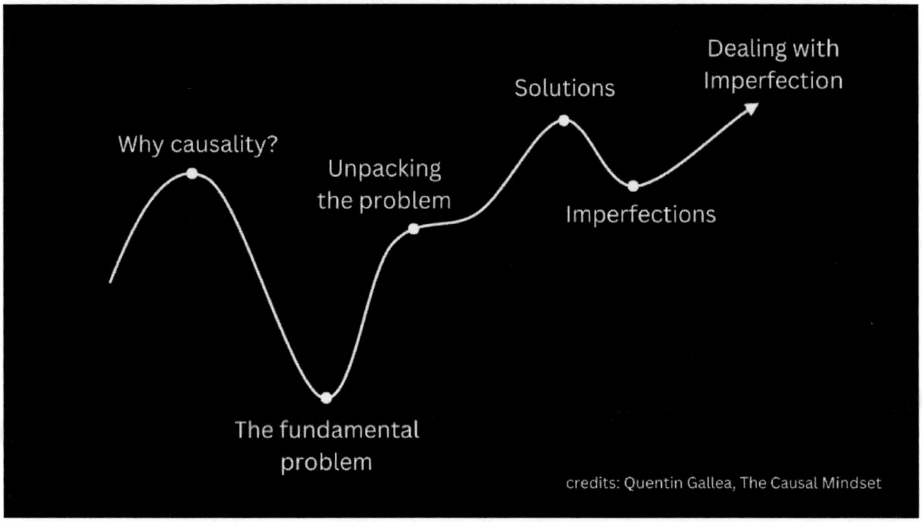

Figure 15.1 – The journey into causality by Quentin Gallea

The figure comes from *The Causal Mindset* (`https://bit.ly/QuentinGallea`), a book that Quentin is working on.

At whichever point of the curve from *Figure 15.1* you find yourself currently, being consistent will inevitably move you to the next stage.

A common problem that many of us face when learning a new topic is the choice of the next resource after finishing a book or a course.

Here are a couple of resources that you might find useful on your journey one day.

First, there are many great books on causality. Starting with Judea Pearl's classics such as *The Book of Why* and finishing with Hernán and Robins' *What If?*, you can learn a lot about different perspectives on causal inference and discovery. I summarized six great books on causality in one of my blog posts here: `https://bit.ly/SixBooksBlog`.

Second, survey papers are a great way to get a grasp of what's going on in the field and what the open challenges are.

Here are three survey papers that can help you understand the current causal landscape:

- *Causal machine learning: A survey and open problems* (Kadour et al., 2022)
- *Deep Causal Learning: Representation, Discovery and Inference* (Deng et al., 2022)
- *D'ya like dags? A survey on structure learning and causal discovery* (Vowels et al., 2022)

Additionally, for a unifying perspective on various causal methods, check out the *Causal Deep Learning* paper by Jeroen Berrevoets and colleagues (Berrevoets et al., 2023).

To stay up to date, get free learning resources, and become a part of a community of like-minded causal learners, subscribe to my free weekly *Causal Python* newsletter: `https://bit.ly/CausalPython`

Let's stay in touch

Community is a catalyst for growth. Let's connect on LinkedIn and Twitter so that we can learn from each other:

- LinkedIn: `https://www.linkedin.com/in/aleksandermolak/`
- Twitter: `@AleksanderMolak`

If you want to consult a project or run a workshop on causality for your team, drop me a line at `alex@causalpython.io`.

For comments and questions regarding this book, email me at `book@causalpython.io`.

Wrapping it up

It's time to conclude our journey.

In this chapter, we summarized what we've learned in this book, discussed five steps to make the best out of our causal projects, took a look at the intersection of causality and business, and sneaked into the (potential) future of causal research and applications. Finally, we listed a number of resources that you mind find useful in the next stages of your causal journey.

I hope finishing this book won't be the end for you, but rather the beginning of a new causal chapter!

I hope to see you again!

References

Bareinboim, E., & Pearl, J. (2016). *Causal inference and the data-fusion problem*. Proceedings of the National Academy of Sciences of the United States of America, 113(27), 7345–7352.

Berrevoets, J., Kacprzyk, K., Qian, Z., & van der Schaar, M. (2023). *Causal Deep Learning*. arXiv.

Chau, S. L., Ton, J.-F., González, J., Teh, Y., & Sejdinovic, D. (2021). BayesIMP: *Uncertainty Quantification for Causal Data Fusion*.

In M. Ranzato, A. Beygelzimer, Y. Dauphin, P. S. Liang, & J. W. Vaughan (Eds.), *Advances in Neural Information Processing Systems, 34, 3466–3477*. Curran Associates, Inc.

Curth, A., Svensson, D., Weatherall, J., & van der Schaar, M. (2021). *Really Doing Great at Estimating CATE? A Critical Look at ML Benchmarking Practices in Treatment Effect Estimation*. Proceedings of the Neural Information Processing Systems Track on Datasets and Benchmarks.

Deng, Z., Zheng, X., Tian, H., & Zeng, D. D. (2022). *Deep Causal Learning: Representation, Discovery and Inference*. arXiv.

Gopnik, A. (2009). *The philosophical baby: What children's minds tell us about truth, love, and the meaning of life*. New York: Farrar, Straus, and Giroux.

Hünermund, P., & Bareinboim, E. (2023). *Causal inference and data fusion in econometrics*. arXiv.

Jeunen, O., Gilligan-Lee, C., Mehrotra, R., & Lalmas, M. (2022). *Disentangling causal effects from sets of interventions in the presence of unobserved confounders*. Advances in Neural Information Processing Systems, 35, 27850–27861

Kaddour, J., Lynch, A., Liu, Q., Kusner, M. J., & Silva, R. (2022). *Causal machine learning: A survey and open problems*. arXiv.

Kıcıman, E., Ness, R., Sharma, A., & Tan, C. (2023). *Causal Reasoning and Large Language Models: Opening a New Frontier for Causality*. arXiv.

Lippe, P., Magliacane, S., Löwe, S., Asano, Y. M., Cohen, T., & Gavves, S. (2022). *CITRIS: Causal identifiability from temporal intervened sequences.* In International Conference on Machine Learning (pp. 13557–13603). PMLR.

Reisach, A.G., Seiler, C., & Weichwald, S. (2021). *Beware of the Simulated DAG! Varsortability in Additive Noise Models.* arXiv.

Schölkopf, B., Locatello, F., Bauer, S., Ke, N. R., Kalchbrenner, N., Goyal, A., & Bengio, Y. (2021). *Toward causal representation learning.* Proceedings of the IEEE, 109(5), 612–634.

Toth, C., Lorch, L., Knoll, C., Krause, A., Pernkopf, F., Peharz, R., & Von Kügelgen, J. (2022). *Active Bayesian Causal Inference.* arXiv.

Vowels, M. J., Camgoz, N. C., & Bowden, R. (2022). *D'ya like dags? A survey on structure learning and causal discovery.* ACM Computing Surveys, 55(4), 1–36.

Willig, M., Zečević, M., Dhami, D. S., Kersting, K. (2023). *Causal Parrots: Large Language Models May Talk Causality But Are Not Causal [ACM preprint].*

Index

A

B

C

D

E

F

G

H

P

Q

R

S

T

U

V

W

X

Y

Other Books You May Enjoy

If you enjoyed this book, you may be interested in these other books by Packt:

Hands-On Graph Neural Networks Using Python

Maxime Labonne

ISBN: 978-1-80461-752-6

- Understand the fundamental concepts of graph neural networks
- Implement graph neural networks using Python and PyTorch Geometric
- Classify nodes, graphs, and edges using millions of samples
- Predict and generate realistic graph topologies
- Combine heterogeneous sources to improve performance
- Forecast future events using topological information
- Apply graph neural networks to solve real-world problems

Applying Math with Python - Second Edition

Sam Morley

ISBN: 978-1-80461-837-0

- Become familiar with basic Python packages, tools, and libraries for solving mathematical problems
- Explore real-world applications of mathematics to reduce a problem in optimization
- Understand the core concepts of applied mathematics and their application in computer science
- Find out how to choose the most suitable package, tool, or technique to solve a problem
- Implement basic mathematical plotting, change plot styles, and add labels to plots using Matplotlib
- Get to grips with probability theory with the Bayesian inference and Markov Chain Monte Carlo (MCMC) methods

Packt is searching for authors like you

If you're interested in becoming an author for Packt, please visit `authors.packtpub.com` and apply today. We have worked with thousands of developers and tech professionals, just like you, to help them share their insight with the global tech community. You can make a general application, apply for a specific hot topic that we are recruiting an author for, or submit your own idea.

Share Your Thoughts

Now you've finished *Causal Inference and Discovery in Python*, we'd love to hear your thoughts! Scan the QR code below to go straight to the Amazon review page for this book and share your feedback or leave a review on the site that you purchased it from.

`https://packt.link/r/1-804-61298-7`

Your review is important to us and the tech community and will help us make sure we're delivering excellent quality content.

Download a free PDF copy of this book

Thanks for purchasing this book!

Do you like to read on the go but are unable to carry your print books everywhere? Is your eBook purchase not compatible with the device of your choice?

Don't worry, now with every Packt book you get a DRM-free PDF version of that book at no cost.

Read anywhere, any place, on any device. Search, copy, and paste code from your favorite technical books directly into your application.

The perks don't stop there, you can get exclusive access to discounts, newsletters, and great free content in your inbox daily

Follow these simple steps to get the benefits:

1. Scan the QR code or visit the link below

`https://packt.link/free-ebook/9781804612989`

1. Submit your proof of purchase
2. That's it! We'll send your free PDF and other benefits to your email directly